D1001086

Villanova University
1842–1992

# 1 8 4 2 — 1 9 9 2

# VILLANOVA

# UNIVERSITY

*American—Catholic—Augustinian*

*For David Burton, with all best wishes, from David R. Contosta 22 September 1997*

## David R. Contosta

Research and Editorial Assistance by
Reverend Dennis J. Gallagher, O.S.A., Ph.D.
Villanova University Archivist

The Pennsylvania State University Press
University Park, Pennsylvania

Library of Congress Cataloging-in-Publication Data

Contosta, David R.
   Villanova University, 1842–1992 : American—Catholic—Augustinian
/ David R. Contosta.
      p.     cm.
   Includes bibliographical references (p.   ) and index.
   ISBN 0-271-01459-8 (alk. paper)
   1. Villanova University—History.  I. Title.
LD5651.V32C668   1995
378.748—dc20                                    94-45427
                                                 CIP

Copyright © 1995 Villanova University in the State of Pennsylvania
All rights reserved
Printed in the United States of America

Published by The Pennsylvania State University Press,
University Park, PA 16802-1003

Second printing, 1996

It is the policy of The Pennsylvania State University Press to use acid-free paper for
the first printing of all clothbound books. Publications on uncoated stock satisfy the
minimum requirements of American National Standard for Information Sciences—
Permanence of Paper for Printed Library Materials, ANSI Z39.48–1992.

# CONTENTS

# FOREWORD

## by Theodore M. Hesburgh, C.S.C.

This history of Villanova is a wonderful contribution not only to our knowledge of the American Catholic past but also to our self-understanding in the 1990s. I take pleasure in hailing its appearance and in recommending it to a much wider audience than old grads of Villanova, although they will, of course, take particular delight in the story as it unfolds.

David Contosta hits just the right note in choosing "American—Catholic—Augustinian" for his subtitle and his unifying theme. The interaction of the first two elements has undoubtedly shaped every aspect of American Catholic life, but nowhere can the process be traced more fruitfully than in the history of America's colleges and universities. From the struggles, trials, and setbacks of the early days, when the faithful were nearly all poor immigrants, to the vast expansion, complexity, and self-searching of more recent times, Catholic institutions of higher education have been continually adjusting to American circumstances, while at the same time maintaining a distinctive presence in the national culture.

But these terms—American, Catholic, and Augustinian—are very broad; they cover a wide variety of forms and experiences. And while all Catholic colleges were affected by the same general influences, the story of each is at the same time unique. For example, Villanova and Notre Dame, both of which were founded in 1842, were affected by the American Civil War quite differently. We learn from this book that the war was one of the factors contributing to the temporary closing of Villanova, while Notre Dame actually gained students during the conflict. In itself, this kind of contrast is merely interesting. But the larger point is that by making it possible to observe such differences, histories like this one raise new questions and suggest further lines of inquiry.

Thus, David Contosta does an expert job of relating the distinctive features of Villanova's story to larger themes in the American and Catholic stories. He also does justice to Villanova's regional context and therein lies the significance of the third element in the subtitle, "Augustinian." From my perspective as a member of a religious community and a longtime university president, I found his treatment of the historical relationship between the Augustinian order and the college particularly interesting. The two were intimately interwoven throughout most of Villanova's history, and especially so until the great expansion of higher education in the twentieth century really took hold. That, of course, demanded a clearer differentiation of religious community and educational institution, a process that began long before formal changes in the charter in 1968.

Among Villanova's presidents, the story of Father Lawrence Delurey, O.S.A., who held office from 1895 to 1910, is particularly poignant. A well-known figure among Catholic educators of the day, Delurey realized that the world of higher education was being transformed and took courageous steps to keep Villanova abreast of the changes. This of course involved him in a continual search for funds, which caused his administration to end in disgrace—despite its successes—when mining stock he had borrowed money to purchase turned out to be utterly worthless.

Another outstanding leader of a later generation was Edward V. Stanford, O.S.A., president of Villanova from 1932 to 1944. Although I was just finishing my theological studies and starting to teach at the time, I remember well how widely respected Father Stanford was among Catholic educators. He won national distinction for his work in coordinating special World War II training programs, such as the Navy's V-12 program, and in 1943 was elected secretary of the prestigious American Council on Education. After the war, Father Stanford served as the first executive director of the Catholic Commission on Intellectual and Cultural Affairs.

I could go on reminiscing about personalities of later times, but, speaking as a university president who lived through the turmoil of the 1960s, I must say that the chapter on Villanova's "counterculture" brought back the most vivid memories. Those were tumultuous times, and David Contosta has performed a real service by re-creating them in such a colorful way.

But while "student unrest" was grabbing the headlines, a great deal more than that was happening on the campuses. Issues of academic freedom, faculty participation in governance, curricular reform, new juridical structures, and the question of "Catholic character"—they are all here, brought up-to-date and discussed in an illuminating way. Besides giving us a fascinating story, this book also furnishes much material for reflection. We need many more like it.

# FOREWORD

## by John Lukacs

Institutional histories are often uninteresting. Their limitations exist not only because of the necessarily circumscribed small circle of expected readers, but also because of the limitations of their sources, which come mostly—and often exclusively—from the bureaucratic archives of an institution, impersonal and largely bereft of personal elements. In the case of Catholic institutions, there is an added difficulty: the inclination to ecclesiastical history, whereby the hierarchies of the church and of its institutions subsume the history of its peoples.

But Villanova University has been fortunate to have secured David Contosta for this commemorative and sesquicentennial history, which happily avoids these restrictions more than often. During the last fifteen years or so, Contosta has demonstrated his ability as a historian of various institutions and people in Philadelphia, and elsewhere, and his knowledge of local history is matched by a clear and honest writing style. The latter has been a result of his understanding that history must not be regarded—or written—as a matter of interest for a restricted circle of people. In a cogent paragraph at the beginning of this volume, Contosta states that this history of Villanova is "written on several levels, with a number of audiences in mind." And an interesting history it is. The author culled many of his materials from sources beyond the archives of the institution itself, including many student and other newspapers. (Excellent reference notes are provided, and a first-rate bibliographical essay concludes the book.)

Villanova, as indeed almost every Catholic institution of higher learning in the United States, has had its ups and downs. It became a university as late as 1953, but by the 1960s it was the largest Catholic institution of higher learning in Pennsylvania. Yet its beginnings were not only necessarily modest but also restricted and difficult. Twice the college had to be closed down (from 1857 to 1865, for example). Internal struggles and personal controversies among its leaders were frequent. An early luminary was Father Middleton, the first real historian of the college, who may deserve at least a scholarly article on his own. The tenures of the college's presidents were, more than often, short. Disagreements and quarrels could lead to veritable institutional and financial crises, as in the case of Father Delurey in 1899. Contosta's extensive description of student activities is telling and illustrative, as are the evolving portraits of the student majority—sociological and political profiles that are largely representative of American Catholic college students in successive periods of the nation's history. (One exceptional and surprising detail is that in 1932 more students preferred Norman Thomas than Herbert Hoover.)

As behooves an experienced historian of Philadelphia, David Contosta makes often interesting and judicious comparisons between contemporary Villanova and the other great Catholic colleges of the Philadelphia area—St. Joseph's and La Salle. The thoughtful leadership of Father Stanford corresponded to the intellectual rise of Villanova. Yet as late as 1952 only 15 percent of the Villanova faculty had doctorates (by 1990 it was 87 percent). Father Stanford was Villanova's Robert Hutchins—to say the least. Aware of the financial loss produced by Villanova football and other factors, he tried to scale down the football program—but in vain. It took half a century to achieve that, and the result was a loud public outcry mostly from alumni, and controversy (1981–83). After several years or so football was reinstated. Whether that story is a melancholy one or an amusing one the reader will decide.

These items are only a few of the nuggets in a volume that can be read—and seen—as a model for similar histories of American Catholic colleges and universities. It is truly composed and written with more than one audience in mind.

# ACKNOWLEDGMENTS

This book would have been impossible without the kindness, help, and encouragement of numerous individuals. I am particularly grateful for the support of Reverend Edmund J. Dobbin, O.S.A., S.T.D., President of Villanova University, and Reverend John J. Hagen, O.S.A., Ph.D., former Augustinian Provincial, Province of St. Thomas of Villanova.

Reverend Dennis J. Gallagher, O.S.A., Ph.D., Villanova University Archivist, guided me through the various archival collections, shared numerous insights into the workings of the Augustinian and university communities, advised on illustrations, read and corrected the manuscript, and assisted in various other ways too numerous to list. Reverend Arthur Smith, O.S.A., M.A., Archivist of the Augustinian Provincial Archives, permitted Father Gallagher and myself generous use of the collections under his jurisdiction. The staff of Villanova University's Falvey Memorial Library were unstinting in their response to numerous queries and requests for materials. Dr. Helen Hayes, Director of Chestnut Hill College's Logue Library, was, as always, helpful in numerous ways. I am grateful to the Urban Archives at the Samuel Paley Library of Temple University for permission to use their newspaper collections.

I also wish to thank Dr. Richard A. Neville, Chairperson of the Sesquicentennial Steering Committee, Dr. Christine A. Lysionek, Managing Director of the Villanova Sesquicentennial, and Dr. Donald B. Kelley, Chairperson of the Sesquicentennial Committee on Historical Exhibits and Projects. They and their committees entertained and approved the concept of this history of Villanova University and have provided much support and encouragement during the months of research and writing.

Several individuals read the manuscript and offered many helpful suggestions: Dr. Philip Gleason of Notre Dame University, Dr. W. Bruce Leslie of the State University of New York at Brockport, Dr. Donald B. Kelley of Villanova, Dr. James M. Bergquist of Villanova, Dr. Fred J. Carrier of Villanova, Dr. Thomas R. Greene of Villanova, Reverend Joseph L. Shannon, O.S.A., former archivist of the Augustinian Provincial Archives, and Dr. John Lukacs.

My editor at the Pennsylvania State University Press, Peter Potter, showed a creative enthusiasm for this project from first to last. In every respect, he was an ideal editor. I am likewise indebted to my excellent copyeditor, Peggy Hoover.

Finally, I must thank my wife, Mary, the holder of a graduate degree from Villanova, who shared my excitement as the saga of her alma mater has unfolded during the past three years. I also want to acknowledge my two small sons, David and Johnnie, for the hours that they spent playing on the floor of Daddy's upstairs study, doubtless enlivening the manuscript in various and mysterious ways.

# INTRODUCTION

## *American—Catholic—Augustinian*

In his inaugural address, given on a sparkling October afternoon in 1988, Villanova's thirty-first president, Reverend Edmund J. Dobbin, O.S.A., referred to the university now under his leadership as American, Catholic, and Augustinian.[1] Speaking of Villanova's American roots, he said: "We cherish our long-standing membership in the community of American higher education. We desire interaction at every level with our sister American institutions of higher learning—locally, regionally and nationally."[2] At the same time, Father Dobbin reminded his audience, "We are deeply conscious of our Catholic heritage and of our responsibility to bear the intellectual and cultural climate of our time. We see no conflict between being Catholic and being [an American] university."[3]

The new president then turned to the Augustinian character of Villanova, reminding his listeners that it was the Augustinian order which had founded Villanova nearly a century and a half before and which had guided it down to the present day. Yet the Augustinian connection at Villanova did not rest upon a rigid or systematic view of learning and life. Instead, Father Dobbin spoke of three "Augustinian essentials."

Referring to the university's seal, in the center of which is a flaming heart, he proposed that the first essential turned on "the relationship between the mind and the heart." This was what the Augustinians' patron saint, Saint Augustine of Hippo, had called the "ardent love of understanding," impelling the scholar to seek truth within the context of the highest religious and human values.[4]

The second Augustinian essential was a devotion to community, born of the Augustinians' own monastic life and of the broader community of believers embraced by Saint Augustine himself. According to Father Dobbin, Augustine's view of monastic life was "a blend of Christian common life with the Greek common pursuit of wisdom."[5] At its best, this larger sense of community had allowed Villanova to embrace all its members: students, faculty, and staff; clergy and laity; religious sisters and brothers; men and women of many races and faiths.

The third Augustinian essential, "the unity of knowledge," was closely related to the themes of community and understanding. This unity of knowledge had long been a goal of Catholic thinkers, and at Villanova it was being reinforced through the university's renewed commitment to the liberal arts.

Although Father Dobbin was not speaking entirely about the past, the terms "American," "Catholic," and "Augustinian" designated the most important forces that have shaped Villanova since its founding 150 years ago. It was through the efforts of the Augustinians that Villanova became a Catholic institution, and it was in American soil that Villanova took root and grew. Through the interaction of the American, Catholic, and Augustinian experiences, Villanova struggled, prospered, struggled, and rose again to become a major university in the nation.

In its earliest years Villanova College (as it was known until becoming a university in 1953) experienced the legal promise of religious liberty in America, combined with periodic outbursts of religious intolerance in a largely Protestant land, including its own area of southeastern Pennsylvania. A constitutional separation between church and state meant that Villanova could not look to governmental authority, as it might have in Europe, for any financial assistance.

The fact that most American Catholics in the 1840s, and for decades thereafter, were often immigrants (or the immediate descendants of immigrants), who possessed little wealth, precluded Villanova from relying on rich donors, as older colleges under non-Catholic auspices did. It was thus the contributed (that is, free) services of the Augustinian priests and brothers, and the meager tuition payments of students, that kept Villanova alive for several generations, and often under sparse conditions.

National and world events also had their impact. An economic depression in the late 1850s, combined with the American Civil War, were contributing factors in the closing of Villanova between 1857 and 1865, and the financial panic of 1893 resulted in serious declines in enrollment. The economic disaster of the 1930s was likewise difficult for Villanova. Both World War I and World War II threatened to deplete the all-male campus. This was particularly so of the second conflict, which involved the United States for a much longer period of time. Yet the sacrifices made by Villanovans in both world wars also allowed them to demonstrate their loyalty as Catholics to the United States.

World War II, and especially the events leading up to it, revealed that the ways Villanovans interpreted both foreign affairs and domestic politics were partly shaped by Catholic concerns. This was true of reactions to Communism—before, during, and after World War II. In addition, Catholic religious and philosophical beliefs, along with the experience of being a minority group in the United States, led Villanovans to criticize what were believed to be excessive individualism and materialism in national life.

Materialism combined with unashamed hedonism was certainly evident in America during the 1920s, as was a revolution in manners and morals among the country's youth. This youth culture was too powerful even for Villanova's Augustinian administrators to avoid altogether. Instead, they sought to institutionalize and thereby contain student social life, including formal dances and a mania for intercollegiate football. At Villanova, as at other American colleges and universities, the extracurriculum now became part of the process of forming "the whole student." It also became a vehicle for integrating students into the Villanova community. The end product was supposed to be a well-rounded "Catholic Gentleman," as several decades of official publications described him.

The Catholic Gentleman survived well into the post–World War II period. He was a well-dressed, generally obedient, and enthusiastic booster of the Villanova Wildcat athletic teams—though there were always some who did not conform to expectations. But the youthful counterculture that swept the United States in the 1960s and early 1970s was too potent for Villanovans to escape. While student demonstrations were generally less frequent and less strident at Villanova than on many campuses, students made serious and partly successful challenges to administrative authority and widened the scope of student rights. At the same time, many of the rebels contended that they were acting within the best traditions of Catholic conscience and social action.

Curricular reforms in American higher education also presented a challenge to Catholic perceptions of truth—at Villanova and elsewhere. This occurred for the first time in the late nineteenth century as more and more colleges and universities adopted the elective system, or modifications thereof. Previously there had been little difference between the studies offered by Catholic institutions and others in the United States, since all educators, regardless of their religious backgrounds, more or less agreed that there was a body of unchanging truth that one generation needed to bestow upon the next. But the rapid pace of industrialization and the proliferation of new knowledge and new specializations, combined with assertions of relative (or pragmatic) truth at the turn of the century, made the old prescribed curriculum seem increasingly irrelevant to the needs of modern American students.

For Villanova and other Catholic schools, neither the elective system nor proclamations of pragmatic truth were acceptable. Both ideas challenged a growing revival of Neo-Scholasticism among Catholics, with its assertions of an unchanging natural law and the unity of truth, as well as the notion that students were not prepared to decide what they needed to know or understand. Even so, Villanova could not ignore the new curriculum ideas and still remain a serious competitor in the field of American higher education. The solution was to find a way of meeting national standards and expectations in a way that would not challenge Villanova's Catholic identity, as conveyed through the Augustinian community that guided it.

The compromise that Villanova's Augustinians and many other Catholic institutions adopted was the creation of new programs in science, engineering, and medicine (or premedicine), while leaving the rest of the curriculum mostly untouched. There was also a largely prescribed curriculum within the new programs themselves. Not until the late 1960s would Villanova adopt something of a real elective system, and even then it continued to contain a heavy core of required courses, with some element of choice among them. But by that time many of the non-Catholic institutions had come back to the idea of core requirements, making Villanova very traditional as well as very much up-to-date as the twentieth century came to an end.

Another American academic custom, at least in the twentieth century, that challenged Villanova's identity as a Catholic institution was academic freedom. Villanova was able to accommodate this expectation quite well except when it came to certain moral teachings of the church. These conflicts grew especially sharp in the 1980s and early 1990s because of the nationwide debate over abortion, and it appeared to have no easy resolution. By then American Catholics were no longer an embattled minority, but part of the mainstream of American life. They shared fully in the nation's prosperity and had held some of the highest public offices in the country. In the aftermath of Vatican II many of the walls separating Catholics from Protestants and Jews came tumbling down. Being a Catholic university in the 1990s even conveyed a positive image to members of other religious groups, who were concerned about the breakdown of traditional values, especially the disintegration of the American family.

The growth and prosperity of Villanova's largely Catholic alumni, combined with the university's rising reputation in the region and beyond, allowed it to obtain impressive sums of money beginning in the 1970s. This success at fund-raising gave Villanova the resources to create a physical setting that was attractive, comfortable, and enjoyable for students and much in line with the highest expectations of student life in the United

States. Such financial developments likewise permitted Villanova to demand higher academic quality from its faculty and student body.

Finally, aggressive fund-raising was necessary at a time when declining religious vocations, at Villanova and throughout the United States, led to far fewer Augustinians on the faculty. The declining numbers of vocations in the province also meant that the Augustinians had no choice but to turn many administrative posts over to lay men and women. Just how and to what degree the Augustinian tradition should be carried on was an important question as Villanova celebrated its sesquicentennial year.

Of course, it is impossible to attribute every facet of Villanova's history to the American, Catholic, and Augustinian experiences. Many forces peculiar to the region or to the institution itself have also fashioned Villanova over the years, including its proximity to Philadelphia, the topography of the campus site, the transportation systems that serve the area, and the prestigious Main Line suburbs that grew up around the institution. Villanova has also felt the imprint of powerful personalities, especially of several visionary leaders.

As an extension of and in addition to these themes, the following account highlights the undergraduate curriculum, student life, faculty development, university governance, financial resources, and the physical development of Villanova's campus. Because of these selections, and because of Villanova's present size with its many divisions, it is impossible to discuss all the programs, groups, organizations, or events that have existed at Villanova College and University. Nor was there any attempt to write a complete history of the Augustinian community, of the seminary and preparatory academy that once existed on campus, or of Villanova's rich tradition of varsity athletics. For similar reasons, readers will not find extensive accounts of the Villanova School of Law, the College of Nursing, or the various graduate programs at an institution that continues to stress undergraduate studies. These subjects deserve a history of their own and are examined here only insofar as they illuminate the larger story of Villanova.

This history of Villanova is also written on several levels, with a number of audiences in mind. Many readers, especially students and graduates, will simply enjoy learning more about a familiar and meaningful place in their lives. Residents of the immediate neighborhood will achieve a better understanding of an important institution in their midst, and men and women of the greater Philadelphia area will find the book another chapter in the long history of their region. Faculty and administration will gain a wider sense of how Villanova came to be what it is today and thereby achieve a keener perspective on how to shape its future. Historians will appreciate the book for what it adds to the story of American higher education, and of the interaction among Catholicism, religious orders, and American culture.

At the risk of sounding immodest, the author would assert that this study of Villanova represents one of the first comprehensive histories of a Catholic university in the United States. While other histories have surely been written, few of them have attempted to explore the complex environment that created a major Catholic university. In this respect the author believes this book is an important contribution to the literature of American higher education, in the tradition established by Laurence R. Veysey in his landmark study *The Emergence of the American University* (1965) and continued more recently in Nicholas Varga's *Baltimore's Loyola* (1990) and W. Bruce Leslie's *Gentlemen and Scholars* (1992). In each of these works the authors have paid particular attention to the various constituencies that gave rise to the American system of higher education. While striving to meet these high standards, this author hopes that he has told a story that will appeal to scholars and popular audiences alike.

# BELLE-AIR TO VILLANOVA

The rolling fields and woodlands of Belle-Air measured just over 197 acres. Located some twelve miles west of Philadelphia on the Lancaster Turnpike, the estate was to be offered at public sale on October 14, 1841.[1] Its purchase by the small Augustinian community in Philadelphia proved a momentous step in expanding the order's mission, for within two years Belle-Air would become Villanova College. A century and a half later, the estate would be home to thousands of students who lived and attended classes in scores of buildings.

Villanova's Augustinian roots reached back to Christian antiquity and to the rule set down by Saint Augustine of Hippo (A.D. 354–430), widely recognized as the greatest thinker of the early Western church. These traditions found their way to the United States some thirteen centuries later, in the early spring of 1796, when Reverend Matthew Carr, O.S.A. (1755–1820), arrived in Philadelphia from Dublin, Ireland. In August of that year Father Carr received permission to create the first Augustinian community in America, with himself as the first Augustinian superior in the United States. That same summer he purchased a lot at Fourth and Vine streets in Philadelphia and shortly thereafter began construction of St. Augustine's Church.

St. Augustine's parish did well enough, but the Augustinian community struggled to remain alive. For a time in the 1820s the order had but one member. Even in 1841 there were just five Augustinians in the entire United States—three in Philadelphia and two in Brooklyn, New York—and all of

Irish birth or ancestry.[2] The three members of the Philadelphia community were Reverend John P. O'Dwyer, O.S.A. (1816–50), who would become the first president of Villanova College; Reverend Patrick E. Moriarty, O.S.A. (1805–75), a famous and sometimes controversial Catholic orator and a major figure in the Augustinian community; and Reverend Thomas A. Kyle, O.S.A. (1797–1867), who later left the Augustinians to become a diocesan priest (that is, a priest who was not connected with a particular religious order).

As experience would show, many of the Augustinians' struggles grew directly out of the American environment in which the order had planted itself. The Catholic population of the United States was relatively small and often faced hostility from the majority Protestants.[3] Even when Catholic ranks began to swell in the 1840s, most of the newcomers were poor Irish immigrants who faced discrimination because of their faith as well as their poverty. With few wealthy Catholics, the Augustinians (and the various ministries that they would establish) had to rely on meager financial support from the faithful—and on their own hard work.

Since the Constitution of the United States specifically forbade any establishment of religion, and by extension any tax support for religious institutions, Catholics (including the tiny Augustinian community in Philadelphia) could not count on the government for financial assistance, as they might have in countries where Catholicism was the official creed. In religion as well as in business, America provided an open market where almost anyone was free to succeed or fail. This would apply to Villanova College and University, as it applied to the Augustinians themselves. The fact that the vast majority of American Augustinians came from Ireland, where they had faced discrimination and hostility from the British government itself, undoubtedly prepared them for facing adversity and adapting to circumstances in a new land.[4]

One of these pioneering Irish Augustinians in Philadelphia, Father Kyle, jumped at the chance to buy the Belle-Air property out on the Lancaster Pike. Its 197 acres included orchards, fields, woodlands, vegetable and flower gardens, a large stone barn, a springhouse, a pigpen, a poultry house, a stable, and a carriage house, along with a two-and-a-half-story dwelling built of stone. In 1841 this well-appointed property belonged to the estate of the late John Rudolph (1760–1838) and was now being sold on his widow Jane's, behalf by trustee John R. Vogdes. A successful Philadelphia merchant and a devout Catholic, Rudolph had bought the property in 1806 from its previous owner, one Jonathan Miller and his wife Sarah. Rudolph named the place Belle-Air after his ancestral home in Maryland and proceeded to complete the house, which Miller had begun but not finished. Because there was no Catholic church in the area, Rudolph imitated early

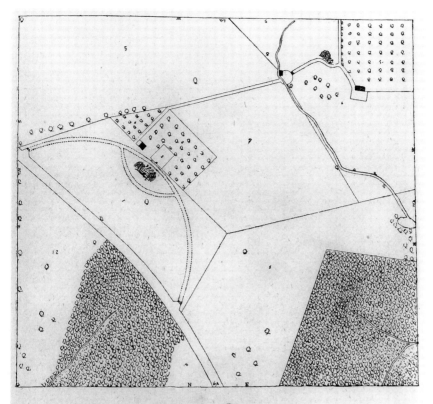

PLATE II —"A PLAN OF BELLE-AIR "—showing (1) the buildings namely, the mansion-house between two willow trees ; a little north-west of it the carriage-house; towards the upper right hand corner, the spring-house, inside a circle ; beyond it, the farm-house shaded by a tree and, near by, a barn ; (2) the carriage drives from the Lancaster Road, and the private ways connecting the buildings and (3) the various divisions of the land in acres, perches and fractions of perches, namely, 1, the lawn (12.61.62) ; 2, garden (0 34.32) ; 3, apple orchard (2.25.50) ; 4, peach orchard (0.96 28) ; 5, field (17 6.70) ; 6, field (16.18.39) ; 7, field (13.5.65) ; 8, field (14 137.93) ; 9, wood-land (11.21.49); 10, field (1.7.60) ; 11, wood-land (8.155.03) ; 12, field (8.18.57) ; then roads (3.18 17) and the total acreage given as 109 acres, 67 perches and 25 hundredths.

Hand-drawn map of Belle-Air during the time of its ownership by the Rudolph family. VUA.

Maryland Catholic families by installing an altar in his dwelling where visiting priests could say Mass during infrequent but much welcomed visits. (This shortage of priests and churches reflected the small Catholic population in early America and the important role of the laity in keeping the faith alive.)

Wishing to preempt other buyers, Father Kyle joined Father Moriarty (or Dr. Moriarty, as he was often known) for a trip to Belle-Air on the morning of October 13, 1841, the day before the public sale was to take place. The two priests might have taken a carriage along the Lancaster Pike, or they could have ridden on the new Philadelphia & Columbia Railroad, which passed through the northern edge of the Belle-Air grounds—a detail of their trip that apparently went unrecorded.

Belle-Air was not unknown to the Philadelphia Augustinians, who had occasionally gone out to the Rudolph farm to say Mass. Moriarty had never seen the place, but Kyle had been there no fewer than nine times during the past eighteen months, had probably become enamored of the estate during his visits, and may have known of plans to sell the farm well in advance of the formal announcement. Moriarty probably accompanied Kyle to the farm on October 13 in his official capacity as commissary general, or head of the Augustinian order in the United States.[5]

Before returning to Philadelphia that day, the two priests agreed to buy Belle-Air for $18,000. According to at least one account, Father Kyle made the purchase on his own, without authority, and contrary to the desire of Dr. Moriarty, as well as against the wishes of the third member of the local Augustinian community, Father O'Dwyer.[6] Whatever O'Dwyer's opinion may have been, it seems doubtful that Moriarty's opposition was intense, for he was present with Kyle on October 13 and later signed two mortgages associated with the sale. However much Moriarty, or O'Dwyer, might have doubted the wisdom of acquiring Belle-Air, they appear to have acquiesced in the transaction.[7]

The Augustinians made a down payment of $2,000 on the Belle-Air property by borrowing the sum from a Mrs. Lennon, a now obscure figure who reportedly belonged to St. Augustine's Church in Philadelphia. They financed the remaining $16,000 through two mortgages from the seller, in this case from trustee John R. Vogdes. One was for $10,000 and the other for $6,000. Several months later the Augustinians spent an additional $3,400 to purchase the farm tools and household furnishings. On January 5, 1842, they received official title to the Belle-Air property. That date would later be used, with some exaggeration, as the founding of Villanova College and University.[8]

Precisely how they obtained more than $20,000 to pay for the property, furnishings, and equipment is unclear. Moriarty launched an immediate drive for funds, and by September 1843 he announced that he had raised some $6,000. The community was able to retire both mortgages on the property by May 1848.[9]

Up to this point Villanova's beginnings were much like those of neighboring Haverford College. Ten years earlier, in 1831, a group of Quakers had purchased an estate of just under 190 acres located about two miles east of Villanova near the same Lancaster Pike. In the fall of 1833 they inaugurated what would become Haverford College.[10] Over the years to come, the two institutions would share certain characteristics but would diverge in many other respects.

Almost exactly a decade after Haverford's opening, members of the Augustinian community moved out to Belle-Air. The exact date was April 17, 1843. During the preceding fifteen months they had rented the property to Mrs. Rudolph, using the interval to make plans for their new home.[11] The first Augustinians to occupy the estate were two lay brothers (men who had taken religious vows of poverty, chastity, and obedience but who were not ordained as priests). They were Brother Dennis Gallagher and Brother Jeremiah Ryan, both born in Ireland. Accompanying them was a Mrs. O'Leary, the housekeeper from St. Augustine's in Philadelphia.[12]

Already living on the Belle-Air property were William Moulden and his wife Julia. The Mouldens were an African American couple who lived in a log house on the site of the future Villanova Law School. (Father Moriarty called the rise on which their modest house stood "Mount Misery" because of the forlorn appearance of the grounds.[13]) William Moulden (1818–93) was the son of a slave couple who had belonged to John Rudolph's father in Maryland and had come to Belle-Air as an indentured servant in 1833 at the age of fifteen. His wife, Julia (1820–88), had been reared by a Quaker woman in the neighborhood but converted to her husband's Catholic faith at the time of their marriage. This couple, who reportedly bore thirteen children, would work for the Augustinians at Villanova for many years and eventually leave their entire estate to the institution.[14]

Meanwhile, the order sent Father O'Dwyer to Europe in search of recruits to bolster their thin ranks. He returned in the summer of 1843 with Reverend Francis Ashe, O.S.A. (1820–48), and Reverend William Harnett, O.S.A. (1820–75). O'Dwyer was then made prior (or superior) of the community at Belle-Air, where he arrived in August almost immediately after returning from overseas. On Saint Augustine's Day, August 28, 1843, he celebrated Mass at the altar that John Rudolph had earlier installed in the southwest parlor of his home. At the same time, O'Dwyer placed the property under the patronage of Saint Thomas of Villanova, a sixteenth-century Spanish Augustinian who was also archbishop of Valencia and well known for his acts of charity. Saint Thomas had been born near the Spanish village of Villanueva, which in Latin became "Villanova."[15] In either Latin or Spanish the word might translate as "new house" or "new town," a fitting name for an academic institution that would become a new home for generations of students.

Belle-Air was now Villanova, but in a physical sense, Belle-Air would disappear only gradually, with the barns, mansion house, woodlands, fields, and various outbuildings remaining for decades. The word "Belle-Air," without the hyphen, would reappear in the twentieth century as the name of the student yearbook (*The Belle Air*) and of an annual student dance (the Belle Air Ball), and as the Belle Air Terrace in the Connelly Center.

Villanova (also spelled Villa Nova, or even Villa-Nova, in the nineteenth and early twentieth centuries) became the name of a college and then a university, but also the designation for the local train station and post office, and ultimately the title of a prestigious suburban enclave on Philadelphia's Main Line. The station, post office, and residential development were named for the college (which came first), rather than the reverse, as some in the Philadelphia area have incorrectly surmised.

Father O'Dwyer had actually launched more than a college in late August of 1843, for the Augustinians intended to create a multipurpose institution, as described in a prospectus published in 1844. The prospectus was signed by Moriarty, who was still commissary general of the order. In it Moriarty proposed that Villanova would "afford a fair opportunity to our brethren to follow the illustrious religious communities [of past ages] which will be forever remembered as the benefactors of society and religion." The Rudolph farm, he added, "affords a religious retreat to persons very often found in this country, who are anxious to retire from the world, and to give their services to religion in the character of the lay brothers of a monastic establishment."[16]

Moriarty also envisioned an orphanage on the property, where boys would be "received at 11 or 12 years of age."[17] In addition to their regular schooling, the orphans would benefit from instruction in various crafts, including bookbinding, shoemaking, and cabinetmaking. This plan became a reality in 1850 when Villanova opened a Manual Labor School for boys from St. John's Orphan Asylum in Philadelphia.[18] It is uncertain just how long this Manual Labor School remained on campus. Because there is no mention of it after the first few years of the college's existence, one is led to conclude that it was not there long.

The farm on which the lay brothers would work was already in operation when the Augustinians purchased Belle-Air. It was maintained by Mrs. Rudolph during the year (1842–43) that she rented the property from the order. The brothers took over the agricultural operations in the spring of 1843 and continued to work the farm in the years ahead. From late May to late August 1843, income from the farm was $210.73, derived from the sale of pigs, calves, lambs, and especially butter, the last item bringing in $170.[19] But the greatest benefit from cultivating the land was the many foodstuffs provided for the dinner table at Villanova.

The college itself, Moriarty explained in his prospectus, was intended for

Reverend John P. O'Dwyer, O.S.A., first President of Villanova College (1843–47; 1848–50). Courtesy of Augustinian Province of St. Thomas of Villanova.

the "good education [of] . . . the children of the less opulent portion of our Catholic people":

> Accordingly, whilst no pains will be spared to give an education equal to that of any other college in the United States, we will reduce our terms to the lowest possible scale. This will be done when the farm is out of debt, the establishment receiving all the produce of our labor: and the teachers being members of a religious order consequently not receiving any salary, the public will have the benefit of our gratuitous labor and talent.[20]

Finally, Moriarty hoped that Villanova would provide an opportunity "to nourish in many youths a vocation for the ecclesiastical state."[21]. Prospects for admitting young men to religious life were opened in December 1843 when Pope Gregory XVI gave the Augustinians permission to establish a "novice-house" at Villanova. The first novice was received in 1848, into what was called the "ecclesiastical" or "scholastic" department in the early decades, and much later the seminary.[22] This department was later described as "distinct and separate from the collegiate, with different books, classes and teachers."[23] For the earliest period, at least, this was an exaggeration, since the shortage of faculty forced some of the priests to teach in both the seminary and the college. Nor would the seminary enjoy a building all its own for more than half a century. In the meantime, the seminary operated out of the Villanova Monastery.

Villanova would thus comprise many elements: a farm, workshops, an orphanage, a monastery, a seminary, and a college. In fact, the decision to open a college was actually not made until 1843. Nevertheless, future generations would use 1842 as the founding date of the college and then the university, perhaps in order to assert that Villanova was a year or two older than several other institutions established about the same time. Villanova's first historian, Reverend Thomas Cooke Middleton, O.S.A. (1842–1923), discussed this matter of foundation dates with much frankness in extensive notes on what he called the Villanova mission:

> In . . . [1843] it was determined to actually start both a monastery and a college. . . . The year "1842" is commonly named as the year of foundation of the College, so it appears in old advertisements of the same College in the newspapers of the day, but the year seems anticipated. . . . If the College is to date its beginning from the time the property was acquired, then 1842 is the correct date, but if the real, actual and formal opening of the College is intended then the [fiftieth anniversary] year is to be postponed.[24]

Despite Middleton's reservations about the founding date, 1842 would become official with the college's Golden Jubilee in 1892–93, leading to centennial and sesquicentennial celebrations in 1942–43 and 1992–93, respectively.

Whatever the correct date, the college would be located in a sylvan retreat far from the dirt, noise, disease, and immoral influences of the city. Perhaps inspired by the romantic spirit of the age, the Augustinian founders of Villanova believed that the more natural surroundings of Villanova could uplift individuals physically, morally, and spiritually.[25] They also seemed to view the rural enclave as a means to revive the medieval monastic tradition. At the same time, they were following an old Philadelphia tradition of moving from the city to a country seat, as John Rudolph had done before them, along the many turnpikes and wagon roads that connected the metropolis with its fertile hinterland.[26] In later years the Augustinians would see themselves as part of a movement to Philadelphia's prestigious Main Line suburbs and would even play a modest role in the development of local real estate.[27]

At the same time, Villanova's proximity to Philadelphia meant that it was close to one of the largest population centers in the United States. Indeed, Philadelphia would remain the second largest city in the nation until 1890, and was the third largest until 1960. At the time the Augustinians acquired Belle-Air, Philadelphia was also a focal point of the American industrial revolution and would soon brag that it was the "workshop of the world." As early as 1850 it led the nation in the production of textiles, machine tools, and railroad locomotives and supported a flourishing ship-building industry. It is not surprising that the combined population of Philadelphia and surrounding Philadelphia County soared between 1840 and 1850—from 285,748 to 408,672. Much of this increase was due to immigration, as men and women from Europe were attracted to the area by its expanding economy and the promise of a better life.[28] Many of these were Roman Catholics from Ireland, who arrived poor and with limited skills. Few if any of them could look forward to attending college, but their descendants would do so in ever-increasing numbers and would one day be in a position to give generous support to a Catholic institution like Villanova.[29] It would be decades, however, before Villanova could begin to tap the wealth of Philadelphia and its environs.

In the meantime, Villanova's Augustinians joined a national movement in the early and mid-nineteenth century to found so-called institutions of higher learning. This was one more instance in which their Catholic and monastic beliefs had to coexist with the competitive realities of American life. For with only a limited tradition of state-sponsored colleges and universities (unlike Europe), private colleges were being founded at a rapid rate in the laissez-faire atmosphere of Jacksonian America. In the words of Frederick Rudolph, one of the best-known historians of American higher education,

> College-founding in the nineteenth century was undertaken in the same spirit as canal-building, cotton-ginning, farming and gold-mining. In none of these activities did completely rational processes prevail. All were touched by the American faith in tomorrow, in the unquestionable capacity of Americans to achieve a better world. In the founding of colleges, reason could not combat the romantic belief in endless progress.[30]

Most of these fledgling colleges were sponsored by religious organizations, which competed energetically for souls in a nation whose laws forbade an established religion and therefore left the door wide open to proselytizing by numerous denominations. Motivated by missionary zeal, as well as by pride and the wish to produce both educated clergy and laymen, each group was determined to have its own college, if only in name.[31] The various denominations also wanted to educate youth in a way that did not threaten their religious beliefs. Thus Villanova's neighbor, Haverford College, spoke of offering a "guarded education" to its Quaker students.[32] Even colleges that were ostensibly secular in governance commonly had clergymen as presidents, including Philadelphia's University of Pennsylvania (with one brief exception) until 1868.[33]

In this sense, there was little difference between Catholics and Protestants. For Protestants it was a rivalry among the denominations (for example, Presbyterians, Methodists, Episcopalians, Lutherans, Baptists, and subdivisions thereof); for Catholics it was a contest among religious communities (for example, Jesuits, Augustinians, Dominicans, Franciscans, Christian Brothers, and later among the various Catholic sisterhoods).[34] The process was wasteful and inefficient, and many of the tiny schools did not survive. Of the forty-two Catholic institutions founded before 1850, only ten would last into the mid-twentieth century as colleges or universities.[35] Villanova was one of the fortunate small colleges which made it, but it would close twice during its first dozen years and would barely stay alive during certain periods thereafter.

Certainly Villanova's debut as a college was small and uncertain. It was also more (and less) than what most would associate with a college in the late twentieth century, for Villanova began by accepting boys as young as age nine or ten. Indeed, for many years Villanova was more of an academy than a true college. (It did not even award its first bachelor of arts degree until 1855.) Eventually the college and the academy would separate into different buildings, but an academy would remain on the Villanova grounds until the 1920s.

This was not an unusual arrangement at a time when most small colleges had to prepare students for advanced work and then had to use their academies as "feeder schools" for the college proper. Georgetown University, for example, began as an academy rather than a true college and maintained a secondary school on its campus for many years, as did La Salle and St. Joseph's colleges in Philadelphia, Loyola in Baltimore, and Notre Dame in Indiana.[36] The University of Pennsylvania and Haverford College, to name two institutions not under Catholic auspices in the Philadelphia area, likewise had their origins as academies. Indeed, as late as 1870 only twenty-six colleges in the entire United States did not maintain secondary schools of some kind.[37] Yet all these schools, including Villanova, were using the word "college" correctly, at least in its European context, where it was traditional for colleges (and especially Jesuit institutions) to offer boys and young men seven or eight years of instruction, comprising what later generations would consider advanced grammar school, high school, and the first two years of college.

Under such circumstances, the initial classes at Villanova College opened on Monday, September 18, 1843, with just seven students in attendance; shortly thereafter three more arrived. The annual cost for boys over age twelve was $125; younger boys paid $100.[38] Despite what the prospectus had said about providing a good education for poorer Catholics, these amounts were beyond the means of working-class families, whose incomes were less than $500 a year in the mid-nineteenth century. Unless offered scholarships by the Augustinians, these early students would have to come from lower-middle-class backgrounds—at the very least.

That Villanova would be an institution for boys only was an automatic and foregone conclusion. (At the time, Oberlin College, founded in 1833, was the only coeducational institution in the entire United States, and it was widely considered to be a dangerous and radical experiment.) Nearly all Americans believed that education was more important for boys and for men, who were expected to be the principal breadwinners in a world where the most rewarding jobs were open to men alone. Expert opinion, as well as religious authorities, also held that men and women thought, felt, and behaved differently, with males demonstrating the greatest capacity for rational thought. Thus, segregation by sex was mandated in education—as in many other aspects of life, from after-dinner conversation in polite society to social clubs and church groups. For this reason it was natural for Catholics to assume that priests (and especially members of monastic orders) would teach boys and that nuns would instruct the girls who did seek a formal education. Besides, one of the purposes for founding Villanova and other church-related colleges and schools (whether Catholic or Protestant) was to recruit members for an all-male clergy.[39]

The first home for Villanova's young charges was the Belle-Air mansion (which stood on the present site of St. Rita's Hall), overlooking the Lancaster Pike. The house had been designed in late Federal style by a local builder named Jesse Horton and begun in 1806. Although unsophisticated in certain ways, particularly if compared with Philadelphia houses of the day, the dwelling was indeed handsome, with neoclassical pilasters on either side of the front door and a triangular pediment above it. Three large dormers illuminated the attic story. Father Middleton, who spent nearly seventy years at Villanova and whose journals, notebooks, histories, and other voluminous records provide a detailed account of life on campus, wrote a vivid description of the house and grounds:

> From the mansion house to the pike ran a straight road, lined by a row of Lombardy poplars (a stately tree at the time much in fash-

ion . . .). At the rear of Mr. Rudolph's house was a large flower garden with lofty box[wood] bushes. . . . The . . . house even as it is at the present day (1887) displays such art and taste as to be an index of culture and refinement of its former owners. . . . Its quaint old fashioned fire-places, some of them now built up, the cupboards even in the parlors, and the hand-carving on the [door] jambs, mantles and balustrades—all go to attest to the somewhat lofty notions of elegance possessed by Mr. Rudolph, and the skill of the craftsmen [who built and decorated the house].[40]

During the first year, 1843–44, this former Rudolph mansion housed everyone and everything: monastery, dormitory, classrooms, and church. Classes took place in the parlors, as did worship services for students, Augustinians, and neighboring Catholics. The students had their meals with the Augustinians on the main floor of the house until the late fall of 1843, when a refectory, or dining room, was created for them in the basement. The priests slept on the second floor of the house, the students in the attic story (with the three dormer windows), and the lay brothers over the kitchen. President O'Dwyer's room occupied the southeast corner of the second floor.[41]

The students' lavatory, or washroom, was in the Rudolph carriage house, which stood just northwest of the mansion. According to Father Middleton's description,

A long wooden trough to hold the [wash] basins was set up along the far side of the shed; . . . [the trough] was open in front, and water was procured from the pumps some 100 feet away; over the trough and against the wall were hung towels, [looking] glasses, etc.[42]

These bathroom accommodations were indeed crude by later standards and must have been bitterly cold on winter mornings. For their most basic needs, students had to use an outdoor privy, known in local parlance as "the chateau"—a bit of Villanova slang that would survive well into the twentieth century as a euphemism for the institution's bathroom facilities. According to a persistent oral tradition, Augustinians who had studied in Belgium or France brought the term to Villanova.

Cramped quarters and inadequate facilities would be a recurrent problem for Villanova over the decades, as there often was not enough money to meet its physical requirements. But the Augustinians did their best at the time and put up a separate building for students as soon as possible. Thus in June 1844 Father O'Dwyer began a multipurpose structure on the site of the lavatory / carriage house. It was designed by a local builder

The "Study Hall Chapel" of 1844, demolished 1902. VUA.

named Thomas O'Rourke and completed, after his unexplained departure, by Brother Thomas O'Donnell. For building materials they dismantled an old stone barn that stood on Mount Misery. When completed, the structure was two and a half stories high and measured 68 by 30 feet. Its plain vernacular lines, with small-paned windows, lunette openings on the attic floor, and neoclassical cupola, harkened back to the Federal—or even rural Colonial—style.

The ground floor of the building formed one large room. In the rear of this room, at each corner, there were two small chambers, with an alcove in between. During the week, the students used the large room as a study hall; on Sundays the larger space became the auditorium of a parish church. The altar and organ were placed in the alcove between the two smaller rooms, one of which served as a sacristy, the other as a small classroom. Sliding doors separated this sanctuary from the study hall on weekdays. Every Saturday night the study-hall desks were pushed against the wall, with the students' benches put in place for Mass the next morning. Until January 1845 the attic accommodated a student dormitory, with the lay brothers residing on the second floor. At that point the brothers moved out and the students occupied their quarters on the second floor. Because of the structure's use for both studies and religious services, the building was later dubbed the "Study Hall Chapel." It stood until 1902, when it was demolished as part of Villanova's great expansion at the beginning of the twentieth century.[43]

Outside this chapel, the college bell hung for years, mounted in the crotch of an old locust tree, calling students to classes and prayers. It was already a historic bell, originally cast in 1753 by the Whitechapel bell foundry in London, England, as a companion to the more famous "Liberty Bell." Both bells hung in the Pennsylvania State House (only later known as Independence Hall). In 1830 the companion bell was sold to St. Augustine's Church at Fourth and Vine streets, where it called the faithful to worship until the church burned in 1844. Three years later, in 1847, fragments of the bell were recast and the refashioned bell was sent out to Villanova. (Appropriately known as the "Sister Liberty Bell" by later generations, it has been on display for many years in the Villanova library. It has been rung to mark important occasions on campus and has been lent for special exhibits in the Philadelphia area.[44])

In 1844 Father O'Dwyer also added two wings to the Rudolph barn, already an impressive stone structure east of the old Belle-Air mansion, on a site later occupied by Austin Hall. The barn's new west wing was for storing corn, the east wing was for farm wagons and carts. The latter also served as a crude gymnasium for the students "in bad weather." Villanova's gymnasium, like so many other facilities on campus, would move from structure to structure during the early decades.[45]

Just as these improvements were under way, the Augustinians suffered a terrible disaster. On May 8, 1844, anti-Catholic rioters set fire to St. Augustine's Church in Philadelphia, which the order had begun back in 1796.[46] The anti-Catholics then vowed to torch Villanova. Although these threats were not carried out, the faculty and students were "in almost continual alarm and panic."[47] As a precaution the community barricaded the doors and windows of the monastery at night, and the lay brothers walked sentry on the grounds. The younger students were sent every evening after supper down the Lancaster Pike to a large stone house (in the present section of Rosemont), where Mrs. Rudolph had moved after leaving Belle-Air. Each morning the boys marched back up the pike to breakfast and classes—until school closed in July for the season.[48]

The anti-Catholic riots were a tragedy for American Catholics, for the Augustinians, and for the reputation of Philadelphia. Most Protestants in the city were appalled by the violence and ashamed of their co-religionists, while Catholics received an ugly confirmation of religious prejudice in America. Horrible though the riots were, they helped lead to the merger (or consolidation, as it was then called) of the City and County of Philadelphia, which in turn allowed the municipality to create a professional police force to fight such mob violence in the future. The riots gave Catholics a greater sense of solidarity and a determination to succeed in spite of all difficulties. At the same time, the riots reinforced their sense of being an embattled minority, and their suspicions of Protestants, as well as the more secular aspects of American life. For the Augustinians and many Villanova students, the riots took on the aura of an heroic, even epic struggle. During difficult times ahead they would look back upon this era and find strength and encouragement by remembering those who had fallen for the faith.[49]

Despite the great financial losses the Augustinians sustained from the riots, the prospects for Villanova appeared good, and classes opened as scheduled in early September 1844. The Study Hall Chapel was nearing completion, and there were two or three dozen students on campus. Yet in February 1845 Father O'Dwyer, the college president, called the boys together after supper one evening and to their complete astonishment told them that Villanova was closed. In an announcement, published in the *Catholic Herald* of Philadelphia, O'Dwyer explained that the losses sustained from the fire at St. Augustine's had forced the closing.[50]

In his fiftieth-anniversary history of Villanova, published in 1893, Father Middleton hinted that this was not the real reason for shutting down the school. Middleton's unpublished notes went further and blamed the closing largely on O'Dwyer's state of mind. Having interviewed Charles J. Kelly, one of the students at the time of the closing, Middleton recorded in his notebook (but not in the published history):

> Fr. O'Dwyer was suspicious, thought the boys were dissatisfied, and his head troubled him. He was worried because some idlers and dolts grumbled at the food—codfish, it was Friday.... [T]he food was [actually] good and wholesome. That same day Fr. O'Dwyer[,] without consulting any body [*sic*], after supper called the boys together and told them the college was closed. This to their great astonishment and regret. Dr. Moriarty and Fr. Kyle were in Europe. Fr. O'Dwyer was almost alone.[51]

O'Dwyer would die just four years later at age thirty-four. The stated cause was "melancholia," a vague but standard diagnosis at the time for a wide variety of mental diseases.[52] In fact, the headaches, suspicious behavior, and the eventual insanity indicate the probability of a brain tumor. If so, it was O'Dwyer's involuntary emotional state in February 1845 that led to Villanova's first closing, not the aftermath of the anti-Catholic riots.[53]

What the other members of the Augustinian community thought of O'Dwyer's precipitous actions apparently was not recorded. Given the sparseness of their numbers, they could not afford to hold it against him in any case, and when they decided to reopen the college in September 1846, O'Dwyer was again at the helm, and almost at once resumed his building projects. In 1847 the college erected a one-story wooden lavatory at the northwest corner of the Study Hall Chapel—complete with a stove, which was no doubt welcome on frosty mornings. A year later O'Dwyer commissioned a small stone railroad station for the college.

It was also in 1848 that Villanova began the first segment of the College Building, which would later form the east wing of Alumni Hall. The plan was to erect this east section first and to expand it westward as enrollment and finances might permit. This three-story structure, built of stone, measured eighty by fifty-five feet and was completed in February 1849. The total cost was $11,958.77. It contained classrooms and a study hall on the first floor and a library chamber on the second level.[54] The dormitories appear to have been on the third floor, to which the students moved from their accommodations in the Study Hall Chapel of 1844. The building as a whole was designed in the Greek Revival mode, a style that had come into vogue in the United States around 1820. Its heavy pilasters on all four sides and triangular roof pediments suggested the lines of an ancient Greek temple, as did the pronounced stone lintels above the windows and doors. Its neoclassical style

Villanova College in 1849. View from the railroad side of the property (*left to right*): east wing of the College Building (Alumni Hall); monastery (former Belle-Air mansion); "Study Hall Chapel." VUA.

Villanova College, 1849. View from Lancaster Pike (*left to right*): "Study Hall Chapel"; monastery (former Belle-Air mansion); east wing of the College Building (Alumni Hall); barn. VUA.

blended well with the Study Hall Chapel and the Belle-Air mansion, which was now functioning exclusively as a monastery and seminary. The three buildings made a handsome row along the ridge facing Lancaster Pike.

Villanova's physical expansion resumed three years later, in 1852. That year the Augustinians enlarged the monastery (former Belle-Air mansion) by extending it to the rear and adding a full third story.[55] The overhanging bracketed eaves on the third floor, and the square cupola on the roof, were attempts to transform the structure into the Italian villa style, which was just beginning to take hold on the east coast. But its clean lines did nothing to disturb the overall classicism of Villanova's buildings. That same year the college erected a two-story stone structure some one hundred yards east of the barn (about where Dougherty Hall stands today) to be used as a laundry and a bakery.[56]

There are no specific records to tell how the college paid for these projects. According to Father Middleton's notes, all improvements "were paid by the [Augustinian] Fathers from ordinary revenues, from donations by the faithful, and never any diocesan subsidy or appeal to the people [that is, the general public]."[57] By "ordinary revenues" he meant by and large the offerings the priests received for masses, sermons, and intentions (or special prayers commissioned by and for particular individuals). It also appears that Villanova resorted to mortgaging its land and buildings to raise money for early improvements and construction, and then retired these debts through

VILLANOVA COLLEGE,
DELAWARE COUNTY PA.

Villanova College, 1872. View from Lancaster Pike (*left to right*): "Gymnasium Chapel"; "Study Hall Chapel"; monastery (former Belle-Air mansion); east wing of the College Building (Alumni Hall). VUA.

the "ordinary revenues" Middleton cited. For example, the college's board of trustees authorized a mortgage of $8,000 in August 1853.[58] In the future Villanova would resort to many such mortgages on its land and buildings as a way of raising immediate funds.

Despite its impressive gains after reopening in 1846, Villanova had to close for a second time a little more than a decade later, in 1857. In this case there were long deliberations within the community over the best use of their limited resources. The Catholic population of Philadelphia and vicinity had grown tremendously over the past dozen years, largely because of the huge Irish immigration following the famine of the 1840s, causing a shortage of both churches and priests. For this reason the Augustinians closed Villanova in June 1857 so they could devote their energies to missionary work and the creation of new parishes. An economic depression, which began in 1857, and then the Civil War, kept the college closed until 1865—still other examples of how the Augustinian mission was shaped by the wider currents of American life.

During this eight-year period Villanova continued to train novices and even to give instruction to a few lay students. And a newspaper account states that Villanova was used as a hospital during the Civil War, but it does not say it was a military hospital, and the story has not been corroborated by any other source.[59] In the meantime it was unclear when and if old Belle-Air would come to life once more as Villanova College. Fortunately, the restoration of peace in the spring of 1865 allowed classes to resume the following September.

In its first two decades of existence, Villanova had thus been shaped by the vicissitudes of being a Catholic institution in a largely Protestant land, and by the open-ended nature of the American economic and political system, which offered great possibilities for both success and failure. The fledgling institution was also closely tied to the resources and ambitions of the Augustinian order that had founded and sustained it.

# THE AUGUSTINIAN COLLEGE

S eventeen years before its reopening in 1865, Villanova had obtained a charter of incorporation from the state legislature in Harrisburg. Dated March 10, 1848, the charter officially designated the young institution as "The Augustinian College of Villanova, in the State of Pennsylvania."[1] Early promotional literature had given the name as "Saint Thomas of Villanova's College" or simply as "Villanova College," but the new title, as it appeared in the 1848 charter, would remain the full and proper designation for the next 105 years—until the college became a university.[2]

The word "Catholic" was not part of the official name, but anyone who read the words "Augustinian College" knew that the institution was Catholic as well as Augustinian. Since its owners were members of a religious order, the college would also reflect certain rhythms of monastic life. And although Villanova College was similar in certain ways to other small, church-related institutions in the latter half of the nineteenth century, its particular character would be molded by the Catholic, Augustinian community that owned the property, set the rules, taught most of the classes, and disciplined the students. "The Augustinian College of Villanova" was indeed an apt and appropriate name.

Yet in obtaining a charter from the State of Pennsylvania, the Catholic, Augustinian College had to apply for this privilege to the state legislature and promise to abide by the provisions set down in public law. In other ways too, Villanova would continue to be shaped by the forces of national and regional life—from financial panics and the realities of the local economy, to the public school movement and prevailing theories of learning. The experience of being American and Catholic would continue to shape Villanova's fortunes.

In order to ensure that Villanova would be operated according to Catholic practices and beliefs, Section 2 of the 1848 Charter required that all seven members of the college's board of trustees must be members "of the Roman Catholic Church . . . and conforming to the rules and discipline of said Church." This requirement would stand until the charter was amended exactly 120 years later.

The board was to be self-perpetuating, in that current trustees had the right to name their successors.[3] The trustees had the authority to raise funds, receive revenues, make investments, buy and sell property, sue or defend themselves in the courts of law, manage institutional properties, appoint a president and faculty, educate "youth and others," and "enjoy and exercise all such powers, authorities and jurisdiction as are held, enjoyed or exercised by any other university or college within this commonwealth."[4] This included wide latitude in the granting of degrees: ". . . Said college shall have the power to grant and confirm such degrees in the arts and science, to such students of the college, and others when by their proficiency in learning, professional eminence, or other meritorious distinction, they shall be entitled thereto, as they may see fit. . . . "[5]

Four of the seven initial trustees were Augustinians: Reverend John P. O'Dwyer, O.S.A., Reverend William Harnett, O.S.A., Reverend James O'Donnell, O.S.A., and Reverend Edward M. Mullen, O.S.A. A fifth clergyman on the board, though not an Augustinian, was Right Reverend Francis Patrick Kenrick, Bishop of Philadelphia. The other two trustees were laymen: Daniel Barr, a merchant; and William A. Stokes, a Philadelphia attorney.[6] This pattern on the board of trustees of having five priests (usually members of the Augustinian community) and two laymen (at least one of whom was a lawyer) would become the norm in future decades and would persist until the board was restructured in the 1960s. This majority of Augustinians, which was not mandated under the charter per se, assured firm Augustinian control over the institution.

Augustinian predominance was reinforced by the governing roles of the provincial councils and local house chapters. The house chapters were meetings held by the members of the Augustinian order who lived at the Villanova Monastery, a habitation that was commonly known to its members simply as "the house"—hence the term "house chapters." These house chapters voted on issues of concern to the local monastic community. But because the Augustinians also owned and staffed the college, they discussed and voted on a wide variety of issues concerning Villanova College. Indeed, because differences of opinion arose from time to time within the monastery over how the college should be conducted, the house chapters provided a vehicle for group discussion and decision.

After 1874, when the Augustinians in the United States received permission from Rome to establish their own province (as opposed to the earlier vice-province that it superseded), the house chapters usually submitted their more important decisions to the provincial authorities. The provincial chapters, held every four years during the early decades, elected the prior-provincial, who headed the American province, and decided other broad questions. Between these quadrennial provincial chapters, policy was determined by the provincial definitories (later called provincial councils). There seemed to be no hard-and-fast rule as to which issues the house chapters of the local monastery would submit to provincial authorities for approval, but any matter involving substantial amounts of money or property usually went to the provincial level for final decision. In the same way, substantial matters taken up by the college's board of trustees often went before the province for ultimate approval.

Although the trustees held formal authority through the charter to choose the college's president, he was in fact designated by the Augustinian community—and in accordance with its personnel needs. Because the community was often involved in far-flung activities, or "missions," the Augustinians changed presidents with amazing frequency. It was not unusual for nineteenth-century Villanova presidents to remain in office for only two or three years and then be transferred to another mission. Consequently, there were twelve presidents of the college between 1843 and 1895. (Actually there were fifteen presidencies altogether, but one man, Harnett, served as president on three separate occasions, and another, O'Dwyer, did so twice.)

A list of Villanova's presidents and their terms during the first half-century illustrates the rapid turnovers in office: Reverend John P. O'Dwyer, O.S.A. (1843–47, 1848–50); Reverend William Harnett, O.S.A. (1847–48, 1850–51, 1855–57); Reverend Patrick E. Moriarty, O.S.A. (1851–55); Reverend Ambrose A. Mullen, O.S.A. (1865–69); Reverend Patrick A. Stanton, O.S.A. (1869–72); Reverend Thomas Galberry, O.S.A. (1872–76); Reverend Thomas C. Middleton, O.S.A. (1876–78); Reverend John J. Fedigan, O.S.A. (1878–80); Reverend Joseph A. Coleman, O.S.A. (1880–86); Reverend Francis M. Sheeran, O.S.A. (1886–90); Reverend Christopher A. McEvoy, O.S.A. (1890–94); and Reverend Francis J. McShane, O.S.A. (1894–95).

The problem of short presidencies was not confined to Villanova, but afflicted virtually all the other colleges run by religious orders in the United States. Georgetown had twenty-two presidents in its first sixty years, Notre Dame listed fifteen chief executives during its first century, and Boston College was headed by no fewer than twenty men from the Civil War to the end of World War II. Philadelphia's La Salle College fit the same pattern, where the Christian Brothers rotated presidents with great rapidity and with consequent hardship for the college. Between 1885 and 1911, for instance, La Salle had six different presidents, two of whom served nonconsecutive terms, and a nearly equal number during the preceding two decades. St. Joseph's College, also in Philadelphia, did only slightly better, with seven presidents during its first half-century (1851–1901).[7]

Adding to the confusion and discontinuities in Villanova's administration was the lack of a definite policy, at least in writing, as to which trustee decisions (regarding the presidency and other important matters) called for concurrence both by the house chapters and by the provincial councils. These vague jurisdictions were not particularly troublesome during the early decades at Villanova, since there was much overlap in membership among the three governing bodies. For example, the college president was commonly a member of the board of trustees, often a member of the provincial council, and a resident of the monastery, where he participated in the house chapters. In addition, the college president and prior of the local monastery were frequently one and the same person. For example, O'Dwyer, Mullen, Galberry, Fedigan, and McEvoy held both posts simultaneously.[8] Three college presidents—Fedigan, McEvoy, and Stanton—rose to the position of prior-provincial, though they did not act in both capacities at the same time. Fedigan and McEvoy occupied all three positions of authority at various times (college president, local prior, and prior-provincial).[9]

Because the president and the members of the three governing bodies were likely to live at the Villanova Monastery, many decisions must have originated in informal conversations. Thus Villanova College was much more like a family enterprise than an impersonal corporation. This familial atmosphere, combined with a lack of formal rules concerning the precise relationships among the governing bodies, worked reasonably well so long as the college was small. But by the early twentieth century the arrangement resulted in near financial disaster for the institution and personal tragedy for one of Villanova's presidents (see Chapter 3). By the 1950s this confusion of authority would create serious disarray in Villanova's administration (see Chapter 6). Like the problem of short terms for college presidents, this confusion in jurisdictions afflicted most other Catholic colleges and universities.[10]

Whatever the vagaries of Villanova's early government, the paramount authority of the religious community made it very much "The Augustinian College," as designated in the 1848 charter. That Villanova was also a Catholic college was just as evident. In an address to the parents of St. Augustine's Parish School in Philadelphia, delivered just a year before he became the first president of Villanova College, Father O'Dwyer contrasted Catholic schools with public schools and left no doubt that Catholic institutions, including those under Augustinian auspices, were very different from their public counterparts:

> In educating the mind a woeful mistake is committed. Too much attention is lavished on the Intellect whilst little or no attention is paid to the Will, the faculty of the Soul, the most closely connected with both the temporal and eternal interests of man. In other words the head is educated[,] the heart is neglected. But my friends, we are bound to cultivate the heart as well as the head, nay even more in as much as the happiness of man is dependent [more] on the former than on the latter. . . . [The public schools] are not Catholic, . . . my' friends[;] they are indifferent and for being such they are indebted to the destitute system of education of which the seeds of religion and morality were parched up and prevented from striking root in their souls.[11]

The main difference between public and Catholic schools, according to O'Dwyer, was that Catholic educators stressed religion and morality along with intellect. Although public schools may not have placed enough emphasis upon these qualities to please Villanova's future president, most colleges at the time, whether Catholic or not, did take great pains to emphasize religion and morality—through their curricula as well as through compulsory attendance at religious services. At Villanova, of course, the instruction in these areas would take on an unmistakable Catholic character. A distinctly Catholic world view would also affect the way Villanovans reacted to social issues, as well as to national and international events, though this would not be greatly pronounced until the middle decades of the twentieth century, when Catholic academic culture reached its fullest development (see Chapter 4).

The actual course of studies offered at Villanova during its first decades was not unlike that at other Catholic institutions, such as Georgetown, Holy Cross, or St. Joseph's, all three of which were Jesuit institutions. This similarity was not limited to Villanova, according to John Cogley, author of *Catholic America*, since "the highly structured Jesuit notion of classical education was soon adopted by practically all Catholic institutions of higher learning."[12] Although Villanova's Augustinians did not have their own unique approach to pedagogy, they were deeply inspired by the humanist traditions of their patron, Saint Augustine, who had been one of the first to blend Christian teachings with Greco-Roman thought.

Villanova was also like most other Catholic colleges in mid-nineteenth-century America in dividing its studies into two levels of instruction. One

Villanova students of varying ages in the nineteenth century. VUA.

was designed for the less mature students, some of whom were as young as nine or ten. The emphasis here was on the classical languages, especially Latin. The upper-division—or true college studies, in the American sense— comprised the various branches of philosophy, including science. For those who intended to enter the priesthood, there were several more years of theology. At Villanova and most other American institutions of higher learning (Catholic or otherwise), the college course was modified from the European tradition to allow for mathematics, English literature, modern languages, and some modern history.[13]

According to the Villanova prospectus for 1849–50, the offerings were "the Greek, Latin, and English languages, History, Geography, the Mathematics, Logic, Rhetoric, Poetry, Natural and Moral Philosophy and Chemistry. . . ." Students could study the modern languages of French, Spanish, German, or Italian for an extra fifteen dollars a year for each language. According to the minutes of the board of trustees, there were also courses in theology, though these might have been intended for young men preparing to enter the priesthood.[14] For the youngest students on campus, there were classes in writing, spelling, and arithmetic. In the 1860s, bookkeeping, music, and drawing were added.[15] Some of these course titles are misleading for those accustomed to the twentieth-century college curriculum. "Natural philosophy" was actually a science course and probably was similar to the modern subject of physics, though not in specific content. "Moral philosophy," instead of being equivalent to an ethics course, was closer to the present-day social sciences and may have included a wide range of topics— from government and economics to a nascent form of psychology.

There were no electives, as they were understood by later generations. Each student had to follow the same prescribed list of courses for a degree. Such a rigid curriculum was not confined to Catholic colleges like Villanova but was standard throughout the nation at the time. One reason for this was the small size of college faculties and the limited financial resources of American colleges. The prescribed curriculum was also rooted in a "faculty psychology," which held that the human mind was like a muscle whose various mental faculties had to be exercised and trained through the study of certain subjects. Among the mental faculties were memory, reason, judgment, conscience, and the will. The most important of these was memory, which educators believed could be perfected only through the rote learning of texts, with the student reciting what he had learned in front of the teacher and his classmates. Students likewise had to memorize and accept certain moral truths without question. In this regard Villanova was little different from Protestant colleges like Harvard (Congregationalist/Unitarian), Princeton (Presbyterian), Franklin and Marshall (German Reformed), Bucknell (Baptist), and Haverford (Quaker). Even the University of Pennsylvania, a

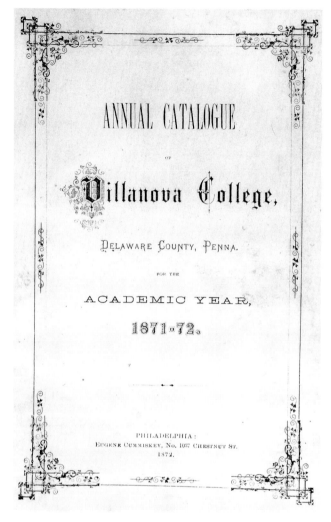

The first Villanova College catalogue, 1871–72, which
replaced the mid-century college prospectus. VUA.

private institution with no official religious ties, offered a curriculum very
similar to Villanova's.[16] However, Villanova and other Catholic colleges
would stand by their prescribed curricula far longer than their Protestant or
nondenominational counterparts.[17]

The faculty that taught this curriculum at Villanova was very small
throughout the nineteenth century. During the first two years (1843–45)

Augustinians posing on the steps of the St. Thomas of Villanova Monastery (former Belle-Air mansion), late 1860s. VUA.

there were just eight men on the teaching staff, including President O'Dwyer, who, like most college presidents of the day, also had classroom duties. Three of the instructors were Augustinians. The other four were laymen, all of whom were Catholics, including a convert from the Episcopal church.[18] By 1892, when Villanova commenced its Golden Jubilee, there were fourteen men on the instructional staff, not counting the president, who did not seem to be teaching at the time. Ten of these were Augustinians, and four were laymen. As before, all were Catholics.[19] With this exclusively Catholic faculty, it is likely that Catholic views of the world were presented throughout the curriculum.

In addition to being Catholic, Villanova's nineteenth-century faculty was overwhelmingly of Irish birth or Irish American ancestry. Of the thirty-seven Augustinians who apparently taught at Villanova between 1843 and 1900, nineteen of them (51 percent) were born in Ireland. Judging by their surnames, another ten (27 percent) appeared to come from Irish American families. Altogether, Irish-born and Irish Americans would seem to account for at least three-quarters of the Augustinians who taught at the college in the nineteenth century. Among the other members of the Augustinian faculty, one was of French Canadian birth and one was from Italy. The remaining six were born in the United States. Several of them may have also been

Irish American, but their surnames indicated a variety of possible origins in the British Isles. Unfortunately, complete lists of the small lay faculty were unavailable for a comparison of ethnic backgrounds.[20] Despite this gap in the evidence, it seems clear that Villanova's early faculty spoke with a strong Irish voice. This is quite understandable, because the founders of the Augustinian order in the United States had been Irish and because the Irish were by far the largest group in the nation's Catholic population after the 1840s.[21] This was not unique to Villanova, since all the early Catholic colleges, with the exception of Georgetown, which was founded in the late eighteenth century, were heavily populated with Irish professors and students.

The one Italian priest at Villanova was Reverend Pacifico Antonio Neno, O.S.A., who arrived in 1865 and remained until 1878 as "prefect of studies," a position equivalent to dean of the college in later years. He then became prior-provincial in 1878, after which he was recalled to Rome by Pope Leo XIII, who made him prior-general of the worldwide Augustinian Order.[22] Unlike Father Neno, who was at Villanova for thirteen years, most of the faculty, clerical as well as lay, spent only a few years at the institution. This was not surprising given the shortage of qualified teachers, the demands on the Augustinians and other religious orders to provide priests for new missions, and the extremely low salaries Villanova had to offer its few lay professors. For the same reasons, frequent changes in the faculty plagued virtually all Catholic colleges at the time.[23]

Besides Father Neno, there were other exceptions to this rule of short faculty tenures at Villanova. Among the longtime professors was Monsieur Pierre M. Arnu, a graduate of the University of Heidelberg in Germany and a teacher of French and German from 1866 to 1903. Then there was Father Middleton, who joined the Villanova faculty in 1865 and remained at the college until his death in 1923. Besides teaching Latin and history, Father Middleton was college president for two years (1876–78), campus librarian for his entire faculty tenure at the institution, and secretary for the province, and college for several decades. He was also a student at Villanova from 1854 to 1858. His life at Villanova thus spanned some eight decades, from the 1850s to the 1920s.

As one would expect, student residence at Villanova was even shorter than for most faculty members. Indeed, it was not unusual at the time for students to stay only a year or two and leave without earning a degree. This phenomenon doubtless reflected the slim financial resources of most Catholic families, a large proportion of whom were immigrants or the descendants of immigrants. Despite earlier plans to lower tuitions once Villanova was clear of debt, tuition ranged from $100 to $150 a year until 1894, when the tuition increased to $200 annually.[24] In fact, no one remained at Villanova long enough to earn an actual college diploma until 1855, when James F.

Monsieur Pierre M. Arnu,
A.M., who taught French
and German at Villanova
College from 1866 to 1903.
VUA.

Dooley and Henry C. Alexander received the first two bachelor of arts degrees awarded by the college.[25]

Like the faculty, the student body was entirely Catholic at first. Villanova's initial prospectus, published in the spring of 1844, even advised that "none but Catholics are received."[26] As late as 1855 an article in the *Pittsburgh Catholic* proposed that Villanova was committed to being an entirely Catholic institution:

> . . . They are determined to make it [Villanova] an *exclusively Catholic College*. . . . Mixed education that was formerly given in our colleges, has produced, no doubt, much evil; and it is a matter of congratulation to find, that those who preside over Catholic institutions, are determined now to remedy this evil.[27] (Emphasis in the original)

However regrettable the author may have found "mixed education," Villanova seems to have abandoned the idea of being exclusively Catholic after reopening in 1865, if not before. As Father Middleton explained it, "In the early years[,] as appears in the advertisements[,] Catholics only were matriculated—afterwards no discrimination was made on the score of difference in belief. *Protestants* and *Jews* were entered" (emphasis in the original).[28] Unfortunately Middleton did not say when the ban was removed, why it was lifted, or just how many Protestants and Jews attended Villanova in the nineteenth century. It may well have been financial stringencies that forced the college to admit those who were not Catholics, for like other small church-related colleges in the United States it could ill afford to turn away anyone who was willing to pay tuition. It also may be that Protestants and Jews were admitted as possible candidates for conversion. Whatever the explanation, it is certain that those outside the Catholic faith represented a tiny minority of the 1,548 students who attended Villanova between 1843 and 1893.

Of these students, 697 of them (38 percent) came from Pennsylvania. Of the Pennsylvanians, 435 (or 21.1 percent of the whole) were from Philadelphia.[29] Most of the remaining students were spread among twenty-four other states. Of these, the three states that sent the most students to Villanova were New York (50), Massachusetts (29), and Maryland (18). One reason for the concentrations from these states was their substantial Catholic populations, while Maryland and New York had the additional advantage of being close to Pennsylvania.

The existence of parishes in New York and Massachusetts that were staffed by Augustinian priests also helped to draw students from these areas. Two Augustinian parishes had been established before 1900 in New York City: St. Paul's in Brooklyn and Our Mother of Good Counsel on Staten Island. In the twentieth century the Augustinians launched two more parishes in the New York area, one in the Bronx and the other at Jamaica, Long Island. Both of these later New York parishes were named for Saint Nicholas of Tolentine, an Augustinian priest who died in 1305. In the Albany diocese, Augustinians were responsible for St. Augustine's, Troy; St. Patrick's, Cambridge; St. Mary's, Waterford; St. James's, Carthage; St. John's, Schaghticoke; St. Paul's, Mechanicville; St. Joseph's, Greenwich; and Immaculate Conception, Hoosick Falls. In Lawrence, Massachusetts, the Augustinians had charge of St. Mary's and Holy Rosary. In the twentieth century they were also at St. Augustine's, Andover.

Back in Pennsylvania there were a number of Augustinian parishes: St. Augustine's, Philadelphia; Our Mother of Consolation, Chestnut Hill (Philadelphia); St. Denis's, Ardmore (later Havertown); Our Mother of Good Counsel, Bryn Mawr; and St. Thomas of Villanova on the campus itself. In the twentieth century the Augustinians founded St. Rita's in South Philadelphia. The lone Augustinian parish in New Jersey was St. Nicholas of Tolentine at Atlantic City.[30] In the latter half of the nineteenth century—as well as later—these churches recruited students for Villanova from among their memberships, provided candidates for the Augustinian order, and also raised generous sums of money for the college (see Chapter 3). Like so much else about Villanova, these vital parish connections made it an "Augustinian College" in fact as well as in name.

In addition to students from the United States, Villanova drew scholars from some sixteen foreign countries during its first half-century. One contingent of foreign students came from the Catholic countries of Central and South America and from the Spanish-speaking islands of the Caribbean. Cuba, with forty-six, was far out in first place among the Spanish-speaking lands, as well as in the first rank among the home countries of all the foreign students at Villanova. It may be that Spanish Augustinians on the island were sending students up to Villanova, but there is no direct evidence of such a connection. Whatever the reasons, the Cuban connection would grow even closer after the Spanish-American War.

Ireland was in second place among the homes of foreign students, with thirty-three going to Villanova during the first fifty years. The many Irish-born Augustinians on campus and the large Irish American population of Philadelphia probably accounted for these numbers. Spain ranked a distant third as a place of origin for the foreign students, with only six coming from the land of Villanova's patron saint. Again, it may have been the substantial Augustinian community in Spain that was responsible for the few Spanish students at Villanova.

Villanova's students who hailed from the United States claimed a variety of ethnic and national backgrounds, but identifiably Irish surnames made up more than 50 percent of the 1,548 individuals who attended between 1843 and 1893. Like the faculty, Villanova's nineteenth-century students also spoke with an unmistakable Irish voice.[31] Yet regardless of their national backgrounds, all the students at Villanova in the nineteenth century appear to have been white, and of course there were no girls or women.[32] If there were a typical student at Villanova during this era, one might say that he was white, Irish-Catholic, and male.

It is difficult to know how Villanova's strong ties to the Emerald Isle manifested themselves on campus during the early decades, since there was no student newspaper to record local reactions to the news from Ireland, to Anglo-American relations, or to Irish American cultural activities in the Philadelphia area. However, it is clear that Villanova's faculty and students held a major program every year for Saint Patrick's Day. On March 18, 1878 (the 17th having fallen on Sunday that year), the college sponsored a debate on the resolution "that moral suasion has been more beneficial to Ireland than physical violence." Following the debate there was a lecture on "The Life and Actions of Daniel O'Connell," and the evening closed with a vocal solo, "Jennie the Flower of Kildare." A newspaper account noted that "the beautiful and spacious hall was festooned with green, intermingled with Irish and American flags in honor of the occasion."[33]

Despite such entertainment, student life was quite restricted at the Augustinian college. Indeed the "College Regulations," drawn up around 1850, seemed to impose something like a monastic regimen on the students: "Boys to rise at 5 1/2; Prayer at 6; Mass at 6 1/2; Breakfast at 7 1/2; Recreation to 8 1/2;

Studies to 12; Examen[ation] at 12; Angelus and Dinner; Recreation to 2; Studies to 4 1/2; Recreation to 5; Studies from 5–6; Spiritual Reading from 6–6 1/2; Angelus and supper at 6 1/2; Recreation to 7; Studies from 7–8; Prayers to 8 1/2; Bed by 9." They had to maintain "Silence" in the refectory, dormitory, study hall, and washroom. The rules specifically prohibited liquor, tobacco, snuff, bad conduct, absence, idleness, negligence, and injustice.[34]

By the early 1890s the rules seem to have been relaxed somewhat, in that periods of silence for students were not mentioned. Even so, the regimentation was very real. Students had to rise in the morning without delay and remain by their beds when dressed, until the signal was given for them to leave the dormitory. They had to be punctual for all meals and pay careful attention to "table etiquette." No one could go off-campus without a prefect (a person in charge of student discipline) or go into any houses or stores without supervision.[35] Remembering his student days at Villanova during the 1880s, poet and humorist Tom Daly wrote:

> Nearly everything delectable was "out of bounds" at Villanova in those days. . . . On the weekly holiday, Thursday [when there were no classes], you could "get up a crowd" to go chestnutting, or walking to Bryn Mawr (where the stores were), or [ice] skating. Ten or more fellows, constituting the "crowd," were entitled to a prefect [to act as a chaperone]; but they had to agree in advance on where they wanted to go—and stick to it.[36]

In addition to abiding by such restrictions, students attended prayers and Mass on a regular basis in the mid-1880s. There were masses for students three times a week (Tuesday, Thursday, and Sunday), and students had to go to confession and take Communion at least once a month.[37] They also had to join the Augustinians in a yearly religious retreat, which lasted for three or four days and in the 1880s and 1890s was held during the second week in December.[38]

Of course, students frequently tested or broke the rules. These infractions and the punishments meted out were recorded in large leather-bound volumes called "Jug Books," a custom at many other Catholic institutions.[39] (According to a local oral tradition, "Jug" was short for "Judgment Under God.") A sampling of misbehavior from the entries for 1856 includes "running away from prayers," "burning fire-crackers in the house," "drawing obscene pictures in studies," "throwing snowballs into [the] basement," "chewing tobacco," "reading novels in study," "stealing eggs," "bringing a tortoise into the study room," "using his book for a tambourine," "throwing Holy Water down another boy's back in chapel," and "smoking behind the pig-pen."[40] A typical punishment for these transgressions in the 1850s was having to translate a number of lines from Greek or Latin. By the 1870s the usual penalty was having "to say from memory a number of lines taken from some of his class books."[41] In both eras serious and repeated infractions could result in expulsion.[42] At no time was there any evidence of corporal punishment.

In the nineteenth century one reason for the rigid discipline was the tender age of most students, the great majority of them being in the early or mid-teens—or even younger. According to Edward Power, "the boys who came to these first colleges ranged in age from six or eight to nineteen or twenty."[43] In addition, their Augustinian teachers and prefects, as well as religious counterparts elsewhere, who were themselves committed to a regimented life, believed that order and discipline were essential to forming good character in their young charges.

During the first fifty years of Villanova College these students spent the better part of ten months on campus each year. In the 1870s the academic year began the first Monday in September and ended the last Wednesday in June, while in the 1840s and 1850s it had extended into mid-July. Christmas recess ran from about December 20 until January 2 or 3, with the Easter break starting on Holy Thursday and lasting until the following Thursday.[44]

Besides the recreational periods built into the daily schedule, students attended a variety of special lectures in the early evenings given by Villanova faculty or outside speakers. During the 1870s, for instance, they attended talks on the "History of India and China" and "The Ballads of Ireland," along with several programs of "magic lantern" slides.[45] In December 1870 there were also lectures and "protests" against the Italian government's recent seizure of Rome and the Papal States, the only recorded instance in the early years of the college in which the Catholic faith of Villanovans provoked a community-wide commentary on international events.[46] There were also regular plays and debates, both activities being stimulated by debating and drama societies founded in 1870. A cornet band, established the same year, contributed to many musical evenings on campus that were frequently attended by the general public as well as by Villanovans.[47]

But the most important public entertainment was the yearly commencement, which featured music, speeches, and recitations in addition to the granting of various honors and degrees. The commencements were thus opportunities for the college to show its achievements to the outside world. In this age before movies, television, and frequent travel absorbed the leisure time of most Americans, college commencements were major sources of entertainment for the general public, and it was not unusual for hundreds of men and women to crowd onto the Villanova campus. Most came out from Philadelphia on the train and remained for the entire day. Because of their great advertising value, Villanova held its first commencement in 1844 and continued to do so (initially in mid-July and then in late June) even before any of its students were eligible to receive degrees. Other Catholic colleges, such as Loyola of Baltimore, also used commencements to draw favorable public attention to themselves, as did institutions not under Catholic direction.[48]

According to Father Middleton, these earliest commencements took place on a "green" just north of the Study Hall Chapel, in an area that in the late twentieth century is bordered by Alumni Hall, St. Rita's Hall, St. Thomas of Villanova Church, and Mendel Field. "A large canvass canopy," Middleton wrote, "was stretched from the trees over the campus and offered to the audience underneath a most delightful place for assembly."[49] By 1855 the commencements had moved indoors to the large study hall in the College Building (now the east wing of Alumni Hall). The 1855 commencement itself attracted a large and illustrious crowd, as attested by the *Pittsburgh Catholic*, which published a colorful account of the exercises. According to its reporter, the hall was

> filled to its utmost capacity by a brilliant attendance of ladies and gentlemen from Philadelphia, who had arrived in a special train provided by the College. Bishop Neumann [later Saint John Neumann], attended by a great number of clergy from different dioceses, presided on the interesting occasion.[50]

Even if one allows for the florid prose about such events in Victorian America, it is evident that Villanova's commencements became more elaborate as the years passed. The exercises on June 28, 1871, were described in great detail by the press:

> Arriving on the campus, the company ... passed under a beautiful arch which had been erected over the entrance, with the word "Welcome" woven in the evergreen. . . . The entrance to the college hall was profusely decorated with flags. . . . The dais upon which the bishop's chair was located was decorated with Pontifical arms, and vases of flowers were judiciously distributed on the platform.[51]

Organized athletics, and especially baseball, were also part of the commencement-day activities by the early 1890s. Baseball made its debut on campus about 1866, with Villanovans playing one another in intramural contests as well as against other teams. The younger Augustinians must have joined some of these local games, since Father Middleton noted in his journal that he received "a *tremendous crack* on the nose while playing third base" on April 30, 1869 (emphasis in the original).[52] Baseball was without rival until the appearance of football in 1894. Both sports seem to have been played on the lawn facing Lancaster Pike, in a space now known as Austin Field.[53]

Each year on July 4 Villanova put on a fireworks display that drew neighboring families as well as students who were still on campus for Independence Day during the earliest period. There were also several fires, which added excitement if not a little terror to student life. In 1852 the monastery (containing the old Belle-Air mansion) nearly went up in flames when an oil lamp hanging from the basement ceiling burned through the southeast parlor floor but was discovered soon enough to be contained. Nineteen years later, in 1871, a barrel of gasoline ignited in the same cellar and was also extinguished in time to save the building. In 1887 the roof of the wash house caught fire, the result of an overheated chimney while the men were rendering lard, and in 1893 the roof of the Study Hall Chapel burned.[54] Several later fires would prove far more devastating.

In the 1880s and 1890s "tramps," the contemporary term for vagrants, enlivened the campus scene from time to time. In September 1886 it was assumed that tramps had stolen fifty pounds of butter from the springhouse. In May 1893, robbers broke into the poultry house and stole one hundred chickens and five turkeys. Then there was the great blizzard of March 12–14, 1888, one of the worst ever to hit the eastern coast of the United States. Father Middleton reported drifts higher than his head, and snow "breast high" over the railroad tracks, blocking trains in both directions. Everyone at Villanova was completely snowed-in for the better part of a week. However, there were no illnesses and plenty of food, doubtless giving students and faculty alike a sense of snug security amid the beauties of a whitened wonderland.[55]

On a more mundane level, the quality of students' lives at nineteenth-century Villanova also depended upon the various comforts and amenities that were available. Until steam heat was introduced in 1874, the college facilities were heated with wood and coal stoves. It was also in that year that gas lights appeared at the college, with gas being manufactured on the premises—reportedly from gasoline. Before the mid-1870s, illumination was provided by oil lamps and tallow candles made by "the help." Water came from wells at first, and later from a dammed-up spring on Mount Misery. The lay brothers and farmhands made ice from a pond that existed for decades on what is now Villanova's South Campus. Once the ice reached a thickness of approximately six inches, an event that commonly occurred in January, the men cut it into blocks with special saws and hauled it up to an ice house near the monastery. There they stored it for the warmer months in a building insulated by double walls, with a space between them filled with sawdust.[56]

Much of the food on both the college and the monastery tables came from the Villanova farm. In 1859 the Augustinians had expanded their lands by purchasing, for $10,000, the Lowry farm of some thirty-eight acres. It adjoined the college property in the present vicinity of Lancaster Pike and Lowry's Lane, southeast of what is now the Villanova Stadium. This brought Villanova's total holdings to about 235 acres.[57]

According to Father Middleton, breakfasts in the 1850s (when he was a student at the college) comprised milk, tea, coffee, bread, molasses, and fried potatoes. At midday the typical fare was bread and molasses, and sometimes a dessert of pie or pudding. The evening meal, then called supper, commonly consisted of mutton, potatoes, and gravy. The molasses, Middleton explained, were provided by the parents of a student from Louisiana. By the late 1870s the molasses had been replaced by fruit jellies and preserves, as well as by a greater variety of meats. Otherwise the meals were similar to those of the 1850s. Middleton said nothing about fresh fruit or green vegetables, which in any case would have been available only during the warmer months.[58]

Student enrollments fluctuated greatly at Villanova during the first fifty years.[59] In the period before the second closing (1857) they reached a high point of 91 during the academic year 1854–55. The low during this era was 24, which came in 1846–47, the year of the first reopening. The post–Civil War high was 136, attained for two consecutive years (1880–81 and 1881–82). The smallest enrollment during this period was 50, which occurred during 1865–66, the year of the second reopening.

There were also spurts of growth in the late 1860s, the early 1870s, and the early 1880s. In both cases these increases appeared to be the main reason for new construction on campus.[60] The first of these was a gymnasium in 1869, which stood just west of today's Alumni Hall. It was a wood structure measuring 81 by 40 feet and contained "ten-pin alleys, horizontal and inclined ladders, trapezes, a vaulting horse, swinging and parallel bars, climbing pole, bouncing board, breast bars, [and] striking bag. . . ."[61] Unfortunately for the students, the growth of the Villanova parish caused the Augustinians to convert the gymnasium into a church in 1872, just three years after its erection. (A century later this decision would have sparked major student demonstrations, but in the 1870s students were conditioned to accept the decisions of their superiors.) Because of its two uses, this structure was later dubbed "The Gymnasium Chapel." Meanwhile, the Study Hall Chapel of 1844 was vacated by the parish and made into a private chapel (or oratory) for the Augustinian community.[62] It was also in 1872 that the Pennsylvania Railroad opened a new stone station with a post office at Villanova.[63] More than a century later the station still stands, although it no longer functions as the local post office.

The next building project was the long-awaited completion of the College Building (now Alumni Hall), the east wing of which had been erected in 1848–49. An increase in the student body from 88 in 1870–71 to 108 in

Right Reverend Thomas Galberry, O.S.A., President of Villanova College, 1872–76. VUA.

1872–73 seemed to provide the rationale for completing the edifice. Under the leadership of the college's president, Reverend Thomas Galberry, O.S.A., the board of trustees voted on September 3, 1872, to enlarge the College Building. The groundbreaking took place without delay on November 28, Thanksgiving Day. The first stone went into the trenches on April 1, 1873, and on April 24 the Pennsylvania Railroad laid a special track (or siding) up to the site for the easy transport of construction materials. On February 5, 1874, the hall was ready for occupancy.

In order to pay for the new center and west wings, the college took out two mortgages. The first, for $16,000, was secured in April 1873 from the Pennsylvanian Company (forerunner of First Pennsylvania and later Core States Bank). The second, for $5,000, came from Philip Lowry, whose parents had sold the Lowry farm to the Augustinians fourteen years earlier. They secured these mortgages with the original 197 acres (the old Belle-Air tract) and buildings already standing on the Villanova campus. Their value in 1873 was $288,000, with the land itself appraised at $198,000—or almost exactly $1,000 an acre.[64]

To design the extension to the College Building, Villanova for the first time hired a professional architect. He was Edwin F. Durang (1829–1911), already well known in Catholic circles as a designer of churches and other ecclesiastical structures.[65] In his rendering of the College Building extension, Durang remained faithful to the Greek Revival style of the 1848 east wing. The new west wing was a duplicate of the east, except that the close proximity of the Study Hall Chapel made it impossible to extend the new west wing back as far as the original structure. The center section, which joined the east and west, had a wide porch along the front with steps leading up from the lawn. On the roof gable there was a large clock, and capping the central portion of the roof there was an octagonal lantern topped by a bronzed dome and cross.

Although the entrance to the original east wing had faced south toward the Lancaster Pike, this was now closed off. The new and enlarged College Building faced north toward the Pennsylvania Railroad tracks, which in those days brought most students and visitors to campus. For practical reasons too the enlarged structure could not face the Lancaster Pike, since the new center and west wings were directly behind the monastery (the former Belle-Air mansion), thus blocking most of the College Building from any view over the pike. Any doubts about this new orientation of the College Building can be laid to rest by a newspaper description of the just-completed structure, published on February 21, 1874:

> The attractive appearance [of the campus] is made manifest at the first view from the [railroad] cars. . . . Instead of the gable end of the

former building [the east wing of 1848], now is to be seen a fine front of one hundred and seventy feet.[66]

The writer then gave an account of the College Building from bottom to top. In the basement there was a new washroom and playroom, each measuring 40 by 50 feet. The basement also contained a boiler for steam heat and hot running water. On the first floor a "wide and winding" staircase gave access to the upper stories. The ground floor included an exhibition room (later known as the Dramatic Hall), a study hall, and the president's office. On the second floor there were laboratories for chemistry and natural philosophy (that is, physics), the college library, classrooms, the music room, the conversation room, and another study hall. The third floor contained two dormitories (presumably one for the college and one for the academy), an infirmary, and a clothes room that could hold 120 "wardrobes." In the attic was a trunk room and a water tank, with a capacity for 6,000 gallons of water pumped from the reservoir on Mount Misery. A dumbwaiter connected the attic, three main floors, and basement.[67] The College Building thus housed the entire school: classrooms, offices, dormitories, library, and auditorium. Students of all ages—from genuine collegians who were pursuing a bachelor's degree, to boys of late-elementary or high-school age—lived and studied in the building.

Dramatic Hall (or Assembly Hall) in the College Building (Alumni Hall), 1894. VUA.

Science laboratory in the College Building (Alumni Hall), 1894. VUA.

There could be no doubt that the Augustinians viewed the new College Building as a triumph for their order and for the Catholic Church in America. In an address on September 4, 1873, on the occasion of raising the thirteen-foot bronze cross atop the building's impressive dome, Villanova's president, Father Galberry, spoke of these dual triumphs before an estimated crowd of one thousand people who had come out from Philadelphia:

> We have all assembled for the purpose of seeing the emblem of our faith and salvation raised on this magnificent structure dedicated to the purpose of education. We [Catholics], in this day numerous, influential, and not destitute of the world's goods, could not forget that forty years ago it would have been a difficult matter to have collected a dozen people together for any Catholic object whatever.[68]

In this spirit of Catholic accomplishment, Galberry convened the first formal meeting of Villanova's alumni on Commencement Eve, June 28, 1875, in the monastery parlor, where Galberry, now bishop-elect of Hartford, Connecticut, addressed them. Following the presentation, they formed themselves into the Villanova Alumni Association and chose their first officers. Minutes of the association list annual meetings (held invariably at commencement time) from 1875 through 1885. After that date there is no trace of the association for a number of years, leading one to assume that it disintegrated

Villanova College Library, located on the second floor of the east wing of the College Building (Alumni Hall), 1894. VUA.

as an organized entity. According to the minutes, their activities were confined to such things as debates, orations, and banquets, and to the awarding of medals to outstanding graduates. There is no record of fund-raising for Villanova, or of any ambitious attempts to publicize the college.[69]

While Villanova's first alumni organization was taking form in the mid-1870s, enrollments began to slump at the college as the American economy fell into another of its periodic depressions.[70] But a return to prosperity in the early 1880s, combined with growth in the local Catholic parish, allowed the Augustinians to resume their momentum at Villanova. Their projects included a fourth floor to the monastery and a new parish and college church on the Villanova grounds.

The monastery's new fourth floor was designed by Durang in the Mansard style, a French motif then quite fashionable in the United States. Sometime before, a front porch with Gothic gingerbread had been built across the front of the structure. Although the old Belle-Air mansion remained encased in the lower front part of the structure, it was no longer recognizable from the outside. Its near disappearance was unfortunate but understandable at a time when institutions as well as individuals in the United States had virtually no interest in architectural preservation and were likely to execute successive additions or remodeling in the fashions of the day. To have left the original mansion intact would also have required the Augustinians to build a completely new monastery at a time when they could not afford to do so.

The initiative for a new church appears to have come from the house chapter in 1882. The provincial definitory, or ruling body of the Augustinians approved the proposal in September and commissioned a church to seat about 800 people at a cost of $35,000. Funds were raised through a series of parish fairs held on the campus, from solicitations among the various Augustinian parishes, and from a mortgage of $15,000. The order once again commissioned Durang as their architect. The foundation was begun in April 1883 and the church was blessed, at its completion, by Philadelphia Archbishop Patrick J. Ryan on July 23, 1887.[71] Rendered in Victorian Gothic style, it was built of Downingtown limestone and trimmed in granite. Its soaring twin spires, reportedly based upon the south tower of Chartres Cathedral, would become a local landmark and powerful symbol of Villanova in the years to come. When the new church was completed, the Gymnasium Chapel reverted to its original use as a college gymnasium.[72]

Seven years after the new Church of St. Thomas of Villanova opened, the college celebrated its first fifty years. Planning for the Golden Jubilee appears to have begun in 1891. As part of these projections, numerous improvements were made around campus. Buildings were painted, fences were repaired, the stone on certain structures was repointed, new gutters were installed on the path leading down to the railroad station, walks and

Early interior view of St. Thomas of Villanova Church, erected 1883–87. VUA.

Reverend Thomas C.
Middleton, O.S.A., President
of Villanova College
(1876–78), College Librarian (1865–1923), and
author of the Golden
Jubilee's *Historical Sketch
of Villanova* (1892). VUA.

roads were resurfaced, shrubs were planted, parts of the grounds were
regraded, the crosses on the church were regilded, and a new organ was
installed in the sanctuary.[73]

In the fall of 1891 Reverend Christopher A. McEvoy, O.S.A., prior of the
Augustinian community at Villanova, asked Father Middleton to write a
history of the institution's first fifty years.[74] Father Middleton's work appeared in June 1893 under the title *Historical Sketch of the Augustinian
Monastery, College and Mission of St. Thomas of Villanova*. The term
*Historical Sketch* was apt, because the volume ran to just ninety-five pages,
including extensive appendices. In fact, it was more of a chronology than a
real history, since Middleton set down the principal dates and events in
order, with very little analysis or explanation. Nevertheless, the book has
been extremely valuable for later historians of Villanova.

The main Jubilee celebration took place on June 21, 1893, Commencement Day. Father Middleton reported in his journal that the weather was
"clear as a bell" with a slight breeze—a perfect June day. The buildings and
grounds were gaily decorated with American flags, papal colors, and flags of
various countries. On a raised pedestal above the porch of the College
Building stood a statue of Saint Thomas of Villanova, and on the outer

columns of the porch were large shields with the years 1843 and 1893. The commencement exercises took place in a tent with seating capacity for four hundred, erected just east of the College Building (Alumni Hall).

Following the ceremonies 240 guests sat down for dinner in the Dramatic Hall, which was fitted for the occasion as a dining room. A long table on the stage was for the various dignitaries, and six more tables running the length of the room were for the rest of the guests. The defunct Alumni Association was also reorganized that afternoon.[75] Father Middleton judged the day a great success, but his habit of blunt honesty compelled him to observe that the food was "barely substantial enough" and that they ran out of Apollinaris water. Unfortunately a south wind had kicked up during the commencement exercises, bringing up foul odors from the "neighboring chateau," or outhouse.

Soon after the festivities, Father Middleton joined several other priests for a trip to Chicago, where they visited the vast Columbian Exposition, held to celebrate the 400th anniversary, one year late, of Columbus's first landing on American soil. What Middleton and his fellow Augustinians thought of the

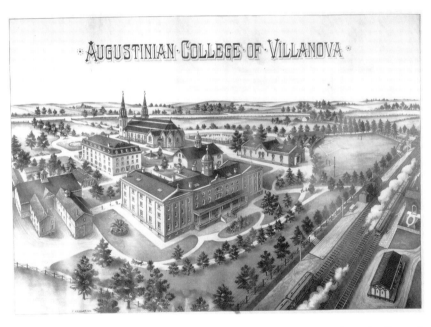

Panoramic view, c. 1890, of the "Augustinian College of Villanova" from the Pennsylvania Railroad side of campus. Buildings in front row (*left to right*): the barn; the College Building (Alumni Hall); the "Study Hall Chapel" (immediately behind the right [west] wing of the College Building); the "Gymnasium Chapel." In back row: St. Thomas of Villanova Monastery and St. Thomas of Villanova Church. VUA.

exhibition has not survived (and there is no evidence that Villanova contributed to any of the exhibits at the fair, as some of the larger colleges and universities in the United States did). But if the priests were like other visitors, they must have marveled at all the new machines and new ideas that were transforming America and the world. Some of these changes found their way back to Villanova and caused the little Augustinian college to make further adaptations to the pace of American life.[76] The three forces that continued to shape Villanova—American, Catholic, and Augustinian—would soon challenge one another in new and ultimately fruitful ways.

# THE NEW COLLEGE

lthough the Golden Jubilee was a colorful success, Villanova College had been experiencing difficulties with enrollment since the mid-1880s. This problem, as well as changes in higher
education and American life, which Villanova could not ignore, led to a bold
but controversial building program around 1900. New academic programs
in the early decades of twentieth century, and a surge in students during the
same period, changed Villanova forever.

The creation of new programs and courses required the college to hire
more lay faculty members than ever before, the beginning of a trend that
would lead to smaller and smaller numbers of Augustinians on the Villanova
faculty. The emergence of what contemporaries called "the new college"
also gave rise to personal tragedies and misunderstandings within the Augustinian order and the wider Villanova community. Yet out of these upheavals
came a larger and better institution. It was also an institution that set itself
up to compete more effectively with other American colleges while trying
to maintain its own strong identity as a Catholic Augustinian institution of
higher learning. As in the past, these tensions played a major role in shaping
Villanova.

Few of these changes, including unprecedented growth, could have been
foreseen at Villanova during the last years of the nineteenth century, when
stagnation and decline were constant worries. From its high point of 136
students during the academic years of 1880–81 and 1881–82, enrollment
slid to only 69 in 1889–90. It then rebounded to 90 in 1891–92, to 120 in
1893–94, and to 152 in 1894–95, but in 1895–96 enrollment fell back to
117, two fewer students than there had been in 1879–80. Even more telling
is that these figures included all three divisions at Villanova: academy, college, and seminary.[1]

The reasons for these low enrollments are not entirely clear. A nationwide recession in 1884, followed by a short recovery and then a devastating depression from 1893 to 1897, doubtless contributed to the college's problems. But a general decline in administration, student amenities, and faculty morale also took its toll. The reality of such problems is attested by the remarkably candid letter that Reverend Francis M. Sheeran, O.S.A., Villanova's president since 1886, wrote to the provincial definitory in the summer of 1890:

> I most respectfully refer for your consideration the following facts respecting the college:
> 1. Enough interest in the College is not manifested on the part of some of the teachers.
> 2. Some [of the teachers] have so far neglected their classes as to cause the students to complain.
> 3. The food served is not what it should have been. The bread was very bad from the beginning of Lent 1889 until the close of the Session. Since September 89 until June 90 meat was never given at supper. Formerly, meat was given at supper two or three times a week. There was no butter for the boys' breakfast on June 20 and 21 last. The bread was also frequently bad.
> 4. Holding [parish] fairs in the College during the scholastic term is prejudicial to the welfare of the College.
> 5. The College has neither philosophical [that is, physics] or Chemical apparatus.
> 6. The College is in need of repairs.... It has not been painted since 1882.
> 7. By examining the Catalogue you will find that more than one half the entries each year are new students, still no increase, why?
> 8. I had more authority under Fr. Coleman [Reverend Joseph A. Coleman, O.S.A., Villanova's president from 1880 to 1886] than I have as Prest. Then there was one chief authority.
> N.B. The Vice-Pres. has kept a record of every class that was not taught.[2]

Father Sheeran strongly hinted that many of the problems stemmed from his own insufficient authority over the institution, the lack of clear lines of administration anywhere in the college, the quality of food served in the student dining room, and disruptive activities on campus. Since he left the college presidency shortly thereafter, one is led to conclude that he resigned in disgust over conditions that he did not have the power to improve. Or it may be that provincial authorities had already decided to replace him and that his blunt letter was something of a final report. In any case, such confusion in authority doubtless stemmed from the overlapping jurisdictions among the various governing bodies (that is, the provincial definitory, the house chapter, and the college's board of trustees) and the resulting confusion over who was actually in charge, problems that would continue to haunt Villanova for many decades to come.

There is no record of a response by the provincial definitory to Father Sheeran, but a rise in enrollment during the early 1890s suggests that the Augustinian community moved to address some of the worst problems. Another plunge in student numbers in the mid-1890s was no doubt due in part to the economic depression that gripped the nation at the time.

Another disturbing fact, which Father Sheeran did not indicate, was that only a fraction of the students were taking real college courses, as demonstrated by the number of bachelor's degrees granted each year. At the commencement of 1890, not one student received such a degree. In 1891 Villanova awarded 2 bachelor of science degrees and no bachelor of arts degrees; in 1892, 1 B.A. and 2 B.S. degrees were awarded; in 1894, 4 B.A.'s and 10 B.S.'s; in 1895, 5 B.A.'s and 13 B.S.'s; and in 1896, 6 B.A.'s and 5 B.S.'s.[3] If one assumes that the degree recipients in 1894 (14 in all) represented one-fourth of the total number of real collegians that year, one can conclude that there were 56 college-grade enrollments among the 152 students at Villanova in 1895 (a rate of 37 percent). Yet even these figures are suspect, since degree candidates were required to spend only one year in residence. Presumably, if they could pass the examinations for either of the two bachelor's degrees, they could walk away with a diploma after spending only one year at Villanova. According to evidence from Father Middleton's journal, the likely figure for collegians in the mid-1890s was around 35, or closer to 25 percent of the total student body. Without a doubt, the majority of students at Villanova were below college grade during the last decade of the nineteenth century, as they had been since the opening of the institution more than five decades before—and as they were at most other Catholic colleges at the time, including La Salle and St. Joseph's.[4]

Such small numbers of real collegians, combined with sluggish or erratic enrollments, finally prompted bold action by the Augustinian leadership. In December 1896 the provincial definitory appointed a committee to "consider measures for improving Villanova and to report thereon."[5] Less than two years later, during the summer of 1898, the provincial chapter unanimously resolved to make a series of physical improvements that might invigorate the college and propel it into the twentieth century.[6]

The driving force behind these reforms was Very Reverend John J. Fedigan, O.S.A. (1842–1908). He was elected vicar-provincial in August 1896 (in the absence of the prior-provincial, Very Reverend Charles M. Driscoll, O.S.A.)

The 1902 portrait, by Thomas Eakins, of Reverend John J. Fedigan, O.S.A., President of Villanova College, 1878–80, and Augustinian Provincial, Province of St. Thomas of Villanova, 1898–1902. VUA.

and was elevated to the post of prior-provincial at the chapter of 1898. Born in County Meath, Ireland, Fedigan became a novice at Ghent, Belgium, where he studied philosophy and theology before taking solemn vows at Villanova in 1868. He served as pastor of several Augustinian parishes, as well as president of Villanova and prior of the Villanova community, holding both these positions in 1878–80.[7] In a full-length portrait by Philadelphia's legendary Thomas Eakins, painted in the spring of 1902, Fedigan comes across as a visionary builder-priest whose hard work in the face of numerous odds has taken its toll. Fedigan's aging but powerful right hand rests on an architect's drawing of one of the two impressive buildings he commissioned for the Villanova campus.[8]

The other important actor in this ambitious undertaking was Reverend Laurence A. Delurey, O.S.A. (1864–1922). Born in Easton, New York, of Irish immigrant parents, Delurey was baptized at St. John's Schaghticoke, one of the Augustinian parishes in the Albany diocese. He entered Villanova College in 1881. Years later a classmate described him as "that red-headed, freckle-faced, hard-fighting Larry Delurey."[9] During his four years at the college, young Larry excelled at sports, drama, and debating, as well as with academics. Graduating valedictorian of his class in 1885, he entered the novitiate that same year and was ordained in 1890. After just one year as a curate at Our Mother of Consolation parish in Chestnut Hill, he was back at Villanova as vice president of the college. In 1895, at the age of thirty-one, he became president of Villanova. He would hold the office for fifteen years, longer than any president in the college's 150–year history. When Fedigan stepped down as prior-provincial, Father Delurey presided over Villanova's many improvements.

That Delurey was able to succeed in invigorating the college was due in part to the support of a powerful prior-provincial like Fedigan (and Fedigan's successors), who gave Delurey the authority he needed to carry out various projects and reforms. Yet much confusion over jurisdiction would remain, with near disastrous consequences at the beginning of the building campaign, and great personal tragedy in its aftermath.

As the expansion began, it was Provincial Fedigan who served as chief spokesman to the public. In January 1899 he told the *Philadelphia Press*, a leading metropolitan newspaper of the day, that he wanted to create "a college worthy of the great archdiocese of Philadelphia, for the Augustinian Order was first founded in Philadelphia toward the close of the eighteenth century and Philadelphia should have the honor of having a college that would rank among the best in the United States."[10] In a letter to the Augustinian province, written in August of the same year, Fedigan was less tactful in his assessment of Villanova's past and future:

Let us remember . . . that the College we have is not what it ought to be, and that walls however extensive, or expensive they may be, do not constitute a College. Nor let us forget that others around us have done what we *must do* if we wish to remain in the race of religious and educational advancement, and if not in this race[,] where will we remain . . . ? Let us build a College we can show to our patrons and train a faculty to rival [any] in the Land.[11] (Emphasis in the original)

Father Fedigan did not specify just how he intended to raise college standards, forcing one to conjecture from what was actually accomplished over the next decade. If his plans could be judged by their results, Fedigan wanted to create entirely separate facilities for the collegians so that their program would not be compromised in the public mind by the younger academy students still on campus. At the same time, he would provide larger and better quarters for the seminarians at Villanova. Finally, he doubtless envisioned new academic programs in order to attract additional students and to bring Villanova more in line with the needs of the scientific and industrial society that had been displayed so vividly just a few years before at Chicago's Columbian Exposition.

The first step was a new monastery and college building. By erecting a new monastery, the Augustinians could turn over the old monastery (the much enlarged and renovated Belle-Air mansion) to the seminarians. A new college building would provide collegians with their own quarters, in addition to more comfortable living conditions and up-to-date instructional facilities. Failure to do so would undoubtedly cause Villanova to lose many students to colleges where dormitories, recreational facilities, and instructional equipment were superior. Villanova could be successful only if it could measure up to certain standards set by the better institutions in the region, and ultimately in the nation at large.

The two new buildings projected by Father Fedigan would be interconnected and stand side by side, extending for nearly 500 feet along the ridge facing south toward Lancaster Pike. The initial estimates held that construction would cost the then staggering sum of $250,000. Not everyone in the province was happy about the commitment to spend such an enormous amount of money—one of the many examples of disarray that continued to threaten the college's administration. Among them was Reverend James T. O'Reilly, O.S.A., a trustee and treasurer of what was called the Provincial Fund. His primary objection was the huge and, he feared, unpayable debt that the Augustinian community would have to take on. In September 1898 he wrote to the provincial definitory setting forth his concerns:

Are we to build to meet the necessities of the community and college, or are we rather to launch out to do something grand and create another debt-burdened institution, under which successive administrations shall sigh for relief from the folly of their predecessors . . . ? I believe in taking chances—I believe in progress—I believe in giving all encouragement to the administration of our Province and of our College; but I also believe that the present course[,] if followed out[,] will only lead to a shameful disaster.[12]

Joining Father O'Reilly in his opposition was Reverend Daniel D. Regan, O.S.A., also a trustee of the Provincial Fund. The third trustee of the fund was Fedigan himself, who was clearly at odds with the other two. However, O'Reilly and Regan found an ally in Father Middleton, who was associate provincial and secretary of the province. For Middleton and his fellow detractors, the project was "Fedigan's Folly."

As provincial secretary and as the chief linguist at Villanova, Middleton took it upon himself to appeal the expansion plans to the Augustinian prior-general in Rome, who then ordered the Villanova province to suspend the contract until his formal consent could be secured. On his own initiative, and with no official authority, Middleton then sent circular letters to all the local priors informing them of the general's order and warning that disobedience "will entail on the parties excommunication [from the order] *ipso facto*."[13] He also wrote to the architect, again without proper authority, ordering him to halt all work on the buildings.

A much exasperated Father Fedigan had to explain himself to the general in Rome, who subsequently granted his permission to proceed with construction in October 1898. By then the cost of the two buildings had risen an additional $35,000, for a total of $285,000. The final bill would actually come to just over $300,000.[14] As events would show, both Father Fedigan and his opponents were right in certain regards. Villanova did have to undertake improvements or face continued stagnation, but the financial strain on the institution was enormous.[15] The inability of the provincial to forge a strong consensus and then to compel obedience to it only exacerbated the matter.

While the argument and dissention continued, Villanova turned once more to the architectural talents of Edwin F. Durang. For the new monastery and college facility, Durang chose a Gothic idiom, which harmonized well with the nearby church. This Collegiate Gothic style was then sweeping campuses in the United States, giving them an ancient respectability through association with seats of learning like Oxford or Cambridge in England. Actual construction commenced in the spring of 1899, with ground broken

A panorama of "Fedigan's Folly," c. 1902. *Left:* New College Hall (1899), later Tolentine Hall. *Right:* The Augustinian Monastery of St. Thomas of Villanova (1899). VUA.

for the new monastery on April 1. That fall, on November 15, workmen started digging the foundations for the college building, to be known officially as New College Hall (later as Mendel Hall and still later as Tolentine Hall). The monastery was finished and occupied in early 1901; New College Hall opened its doors to students in September of the same year.[16]

The completion of New College Hall (sometimes called Main College Hall by contemporaries) and the St. Thomas of Villanova Monastery also meant that the college once more faced the Lancaster Pike (instead of the railroad), even though the vast majority of students and visitors continued to arrive by train. There has never been an official explanation for this realignment, but the shift may have been dictated by the siting of the church, which likewise

overlooked the pike. The road had been upgraded in 1880 by a "Pike Improvement Company" established by two early suburban developers. Indeed Villanova itself had invested $1,000 in the highway enterprise.[17] It may also have been the superior view from the Lancaster Pike side of the campus which dictated the locations for the two new buildings. If the college catalogs of the early twentieth century are any indication, this explanation is possible, since they constantly extolled the "magnificent and unobstructed view of the surrounding country" that students might enjoy from the new hall.[18]

In addition to the view, which doubtless interested the parents of prospective students far more than it did the students themselves, New College Hall provided long-needed facilities. These included a gymnasium, a dining room, and an auditorium, in addition to a new library, lecture halls, and modern laboratories. The building also contained administrative offices for the col-

Gymnasium in New College Hall (later Tolentine Hall), c. 1902. VUA.

Dining room in New College Hall (later Tolentine Hall), c. 1902. VUA.

"Old" St. Rita's Hall (formerly the monastery and thus
containing the Belle-Air mansion), c. 1902. VUA.

lege. The old College Building (Alumni Hall) now became the preserve of the
younger students, receiving the separate designation of St. Nicholas of
Tolentine Academy in 1901. (In 1919 St. Joseph's College would make a
similar move to separate its academy from the college.[19])

The old monastery underwent renovation and reopened for the exclusive
use of seminarians in December 1902. It was briefly known as Belle-Air Hall,
in honor of its original designation, but early in 1903 its name became St.
Rita's Hall.[20] The name came from Saint Rita of Cascia, an Augustinian nun
who died in the mid-fifteenth century and who had recently (1900) been
canonized. Her elevation to sainthood just three years before, in addition to
her Augustinian associations, were probably the reason the new hall was
named for her.[21]

"Old" St. Rita's Hall following the fire of January 10, 1912. VUA.

Ten years after its opening as a seminary facility, St. Rita's caught fire in the early afternoon of January 10, 1912. The fire had been ignited by a defective flue, and a passerby first noticed smoke coming from the fourth floor. Students and faculty rescued valuable manuscripts, documents, and books from the structure before the fire consumed them. Five fire companies converged on the scene and brought the conflagration under control by evening. The walls remained standing, but the fire, water, and smoke damage made an exact reconstruction prohibitive, especially since the college was deeply in debt at the time. In pulling down the structure, the college necessarily destroyed the old Belle-Air mansion, which by then had been altered, at least on the outside, beyond all recognition from the original.[22]

With the seminarians deprived of their home, the prior-provincial, Very Reverend Martin J. Geraghty, O.S.A., sent immediate appeals for funds to the Augustinian parishes and to other "friends" of the order.[23] That spring the community began work on a new St. Rita's Hall. For unexplained reasons, the Augustinians did not choose the Durang firm, and instead gave the commission to George F. Dobbins, a relatively minor Philadelphia architect who had none of the reputation of the Durang establishment. Given the Augustinians' financial difficulties, Durang's services may have been too expensive at the time.

In any case, Dobbins chose a Colonial Revival style for the new St. Rita's, an architectural motif that was popular throughout the eastern United States at the time. Its dome echoed the earlier one atop the old College Building (Alumni Hall), while its stone walls blended with the church, the monastery, and New College Hall. However, a Collegiate Gothic design for the new St. Rita's would have been even more compatible with these older buildings. It was perhaps the lower cost of a plain, Colonial-style edifice that ruled out another massing of pointed towers and archways. Or perhaps the architect concluded that a Colonial design would be truer to the spirit of the older building it replaced.

Whatever the reasons, nothing now remained of the old Belle-Air estate, save for a few farm buildings and the massive old lock and key for the front door (now in the university archives) of the destroyed mansion. In order to erect the new monastery and New College Hall, Villanova also had been forced to demolish several other venerable buildings. These were the Study Hall Chapel of 1844, which came down in August 1902, and the Gymnasium Chapel, which fell to the wreckers in April 1899. Meanwhile, the Augustinians had to move their original cemetery from a lot beside the Study Hall Chapel to its present location between St. Rita's and Austin Hall.[24] In the process, the old neoclassical row of college buildings had essentially disappeared. The east wing of the former College Building (Alumni Hall), rendered in the Greek Revival style and begun in 1848, was all that remained. Even it was obscured from the Lancaster Pike side of campus by a combination of foliage and the new St. Rita's Hall. Physically, Villanova was indeed a new college.

Adding to the new look on campus was yet another seminary building, begun in 1912 and completed two years later. Known variously as St. Mary's Hall or Corr Hall, the facility resulted from the then munificent gift of $100,000 from Bernard Corr (1828–1912). Born in Ireland, Corr rose from humble immigrant origins to become a wealthy entrepreneur who made most of his money in real estate and the stock market, leaving about $2 million at the time of his death. Corr was known for his philanthropy to Catholic institutions, but just why he chose Villanova for the largest of all his gifts is unexplained in the few sources that survive about Corr or the building he endowed.[25]

To design Corr Hall the Augustinians turned to Francis F. Durang (1884–1966), who had succeeded his father as the head of the Durang firm.[26] The younger Durang followed his father's tastes and created a Gothic Revival design for the new seminary building, complete with a medieval chapel and castellated towers. By returning to the Gothic idiom, Durang caused the new St. Rita's, with its Colonial lines, to appear even more out of place on a new campus that was, ironically, attempting to look instantly old and venerable with its expanse of medieval walls and towers.

In addition to these major building projects several smaller improve-

Corr Hall, completed in 1914 and designed by architect Francis F. Durang. VUA.

ments were made, and more modern amenities were introduced. In 1906–7 the college built a small grotto at the point where the walk from the railroad station entered the campus (near the present Falvey Hall). In it were statues of Saint Augustine, Saint Nicholas of Tolentine, and Saint Rita, carved in white Carrara marble.[27] Surrounded by trees and shrubbery, the Grotto (now demolished) would be a landmark for generations of Villanova students.

Certain modern utilities emerged on campus even before the new buildings arose. In 1896 electric lights, which had made such a stunning impression at the Chicago exposition, appeared on campus for the first time, and in 1899 the first telephone was connected to President Delurey's office, then in the old College Building (Alumni Hall). The following year, 1900, the train station received its first public telephone. Other improvements at the station included a tunnel under the tracks (1901) and an elevation of the railroad bridge (1915) by three and a half feet, under Spring Mill Road. As in the past, Father Middleton, who celebrated the fiftieth anniversary of his ordination to the priesthood in 1914, dutifully chronicled all these changes in his journal.[28]

The Grotto, constructed in 1907 and demolished in 1949, with statues of St. Nicholas of Tolentine (left) and St. Rita of Cascia (right), both Augustinian saints. VUA.

Far beyond Villanova, the Augustinians laid the foundations for a school and college in Havana, Cuba. In 1899, a year after the Spanish-American War, the prior-general of the worldwide Augustinian order, in concert with the Spanish Augustinians, began negotiations to turn Augustinian property in Cuba over to the American province (whose headquarters were at Villanova), as a way of safeguarding these possessions in the aftermath of Spain's defeat and expulsion from the island. Prior-Provincial Fedigan sent Reverend William A. Jones, O.S.A. (1865–1921), then master of clerical studies (or director of Villanova's Augustinian seminary) to Cuba to take charge of the Augustinian properties there. In 1903 Father Jones opened a school at the parish church of El Cristo in Havana, purchasing land with $20,000 supplied by the Villanova province.[29] In this way the historic ties between Villanova and Cuba were maintained and strengthened. (Father Jones left Cuba in 1906 to become Bishop of San Juan, Puerto Rico.[30])

Meanwhile, Villanova had turned to another and equally important aspect of forging the new college: reforming the curriculum. Many of these curriculum changes were in answer to national trends. Among the most important of these was the emergence of true American universities, with graduate programs and professional schools, and elective systems of undergraduate studies. Villanova would have to adapt to these realities or face continued stagnation and possible decline.[31]

The greatest champion of the undergraduate elective system was Charles

William Eliot, who became president of Harvard in 1869 and remained in that post for the next forty years. In his inaugural address he attacked the old faculty psychology that had been a main argument for the traditional, prescribed curriculum. According to Eliot,

> The young man of nineteen or twenty ought to know what he likes best and is most fit for. . . . The elective system fosters scholarship, because it gives free play to natural preferences and inborn aptitudes, makes possible enthusiasm for a chosen work.[32]

In Eliot's opinion, students came to college with different interests, and it was these interests that motivated them to study and to prepare themselves for a rewarding career. It was therefore incumbent on the colleges to allow them to pursue these natural inclinations. The elective system would also release professors from the drudgery of teaching unhappy students who were restive with the subject matter and bored by rote learning and classroom recitations. At the same time, professors would be much freer to develop their own specialties and teach subjects that were of interest to them. Finally, the elective system permitted Harvard and other institutions to move toward a more modern curriculum without attacking or dismantling the older subjects right away, thus avoiding some of the more destructive confrontations with faculty and alumni. In Eliot's words, "We would have them all, and at their best."[33] In this liberal atmosphere, the "fittest" would survive ( in Darwinian terms ), and that would decide the curriculum.[34]

Closely related to the elective system was greater specialization in the workplace and ultimately in academia. This was especially true of the new graduate schools, based on German models, with their graduate seminars and doctoral degrees. In theory, the elective system allowed undergraduate students to specialize in certain areas, either as preparation for graduate or professional studies, or for careers requiring only a bachelor's degree.

Of course, the elective system had real drawbacks. For one, it had to depend upon a high level of maturity among undergraduate students—an unlikely scenario, according to the critics—that would lead them to group courses appropriately and not to choose certain offerings merely because they were undemanding. The elective system was also expensive in that it required a great multiplication of courses, new facilities, and an increase in faculty. Because of these and other problems with the elective program, in the early twentieth century many colleges developed a modified elective system that coupled so-called free electives with choices from prescribed categories (often called distributional requirements). In addition, students had to select a "major" (and sometimes a "minor") concentration of subjects. Under these modified plans, students tended to take distributional requirements during their first two years of college, and then concentrated on their major and minor subjects during the junior and senior years.

One consequence of the modified elective system was to transform American colleges into unique institutions that had no parallel anywhere in the world. The first two years of the American college experience thus came to resemble an advanced high school, where students pursued more general subjects at an introductory level. The last two years of college anticipated graduate education in that students took classes in their specialities and often had to research and write an undergraduate thesis.

For some critics, the American college seemed a wasteful duplication at both ends of the curriculum. Better for the college to disappear altogether, they argued, and have American students imitate the German system by moving from excellent preparatory schools directly to the university. Such negativists predicted that the vast majority of colleges in the United States would fold in the near future, particularly the smaller and more traditional institutions, many of which were affiliated with religious organizations.[35] These predictions understandably alarmed small colleges as the twentieth century began, and Villanova was no exception. At the time, no one could know that the American college would adapt and find a permanent niche for itself in the nation's educational scheme. Catholic colleges like Villanova would work out their own unique accommodation with this transformation in higher education.[36] In doing so, Villanovans would again have to accommodate their Catholic world view to certain powerful forces in American life.

For several reasons, even the modified elective system proved unacceptable to Villanova. It was not only too expensive, but it also challenged a religious, philosophical, and hierarchical tradition that held that there were certain truths that Catholic students must learn in a highly disciplined environment. The increasing emphasis on Neo-Thomism as a basis for Catholic higher education in the twentieth century would also make any kind of real elective system unacceptable at most Catholic colleges and universities (see Chapter 5).

What Villanova did undertake was the introduction of new programs. In order to understand these innovations, it is well to look at Villanova's curriculum before the changes introduced at the beginning of the twentieth century. Since the early 1870s at least, Villanova had offered the bachelor of arts and bachelor of science degrees, in addition to a "Commercial Diploma."[37] The commercial course was on a secondary-school level and thus not a genuine college degree. For the actual bachelor's degree, students were to take four years of prescribed courses, which included "Philosophy, both mental and moral, Christian Doctrine, General Literature, Latin and Greek, General Mathematics, History, the Natural Sciences, and at least one of the Modern Languages."[38] In its general outline, these requirements had changed little from the 1850s. Those pursuing the bachelor of science degree took almost the same subjects as those working toward the B.A., but they substituted additional science courses for the classical languages. Instead of four years of study, the B.S. required only two years of coursework and was clearly not as prestigious as the bachelor of arts degree. But the minimum residence requirement for both the B.S. and the B.A. was still just one year on the Villanova campus. The commercial diploma involved a two-year course featuring bookkeeping, banking, shipping, and business correspondence, along with more traditional offerings. In all three programs the courses were prescribed, and there were few if any electives.[39]

Although written examinations were given at the end of each term, the faculty relied on daily classroom recitations both as a principal tool of learning and as a method of evaluating performance. According to the catalogs, "Recitations are oral. All lessons must be thoroughly learned, and their rendering by the student must show that he fully understands them before leaving class."[40] Education was thus a matter of exercising the mental faculties, and especially of memorizing a prescribed body of knowledge. It did not call upon students to analyze, question, or reflect upon the subject matter at hand, or to undertake laboratory investigations to gain experiential knowledge of the subject. Neither did the professors normally give lectures that drew upon a variety of sources, including their own original research.

Instead of replacing its prescribed curriculum with an elective or even modified elective system, Villanova, and most other Catholic colleges in the early twentieth century, added more programs.[41] Each college had a prescribed set of courses. These requirements were listed, as they had been before, according to the student's year in the program. Hence all freshmen in a given curriculum took the same offerings, as did all sophomores, juniors, and seniors. The requirements for the bachelor of arts and the bachelor of science degrees were little different from before. Greek and Latin remained (with science courses substituted for the classics in the B.S. degree). The only new requirements were "Civics, Political Economy, History of Philosophy, and Philosophy of History."[42]

There was an entirely new program in engineering, commencing in 1905 and organized under what was then called the School of Technology. Civil Engineering was the first of the engineering programs, followed shortly by Mechanical, Electrical, Sanitary, and Chemical Engineering. In 1906 Villanova offered preprofessional courses in medicine. The same year Villanova launched a program in prelegal studies and in 1908 a "Preparatory Course for Teaching." A more extensive premedical course came in 1915, organized under a School of Science and doubtless inspired, as at many other institutions, by the harsh criticism of American medical education by Abraham

Engineering students and faculty on the edge of Mendel Field, 1927. The rear of the Grotto is barely visible in the background. VUA.

Electrical Engineering Laboratory in New College Hall (later Tolentine Hall), c. 1910. VUA.

Flexner in 1910.[43] All these programs were prescribed and included heavy doses of the old liberal arts curriculum in addition to the technical and professional classes. With the exception of laboratory sessions, the principal teaching method remained classroom recitation.

These changes in Villanova's curriculum closely paralleled what was happening at many other Catholic institutions. For example, La Salle College introduced programs in civil engineering, chemical engineering, and pre-med during the early twentieth century.[44]

At Villanova the expanded curriculum, new buildings, and general tenor of advancement may have prompted a campaign to introduce greater academic symbolism. In any case, the college began requiring both the lay faculty and upperclassmen to wear academic regalia, a practice that was widespread at universities in the British Isles and beginning to take hold at some American schools. According to the *Catalogue* of 1902–3,

> The Juniors and Seniors are obliged to wear the College undergraduate gown and cap all the year, except when away from the campus or when engaged in athletics. On solemn academic festivities or occasions the Bachelors wear their proper hoods. All lay professors, members of the faculty, wear the College gown and cap in and around the College, and the hood, if they possess a degree, on occasions in which the College is officially interested or represented.[45]

This requirement lasted only a decade, for in the *Catalogue* of 1911–12, seniors alone had to wear the cap and gown—and not everyday to class but only for special academic programs.[46]

Beyond these superficialities, Villanova had managed to expand its curriculum without abandoning its tradition of liberal education and prescribed courses. The new offerings also answered a growing need in the United States for engineers, lawyers, physicians, and scientists at the turn of the century. Villanova's reward for the new buildings and programs was an impressive increase in enrollment. The number of genuine college students went from 38 in the fall of 1898, to 76 in 1905, to 132 in 1914—an increase of nearly three and a half times. A small but rising percentage of these were day students, another innovation of the Delurey presidency. (This phenomenon may have been assisted in part by the completion, in 1907, of the Philadelphia and Western interurban trolley line that passed through the south end of campus and linked Villanova with West Philadelphia, then a flourishing middle-class section of the city.[47]) Just as important for the college's reputation, the ranks of collegians began to surpass those at the academy, and by 1914 the college enrollment was more than twice that of the academy (132 to 56).[48]

The growth of the student body and the expansion of course offerings also meant a larger faculty. The teaching staff increased more than twofold, from 15 in 1902–3 to 34 in 1909–10, remaining at about that level for the next decade. Many of the new faculty members were laymen, and in 1909–10 they actually outnumbered the Augustinian professors 19 to 15. Although all the laymen were Catholic, this was the first time since the very earliest years that the lay faculty had surpassed the number of religious. By sending some of the younger priests off for training in the new disciplines, however, the religious faculty was able to regain its primacy on campus. By 1914–15 the balance was 18 religious to 15 lay, and in the years just ahead the Augustinians would continue to maintain a slight edge over the lay professors.[49] Salaries for full-time lay faculty ranged from $1,300 to $2,200. Since some of the lay faculty also received "board," one can assume that several of them lived at the college.[50]

In order to pay for this expansion in faculty and buildings, Villanova had to attract increasing numbers of students, who in turn made greater and greater demands on the teaching staff and physical plant. Villanova thus found itself trapped in a vicious cycle of having to concentrate on the quantity rather than the quality of its students, and this would remain the case so long as its revenues came almost exclusively from student tuitions and fees. (By contrast, in the early twentieth century nearby Haverford College received several large gifts from wealthy Quaker benefactors, which enabled it to make capital improvements not tied to tuition and fees, as well as to build a respectable endowment and thus become more and more selective in its student body.[51])

As part of the overall expansion, Villanova again reorganized its alumni in 1906 (the alumni association, which was renewed in 1893 at the Golden Jubilee, apparently having collapsed after several years). This latest initiative came once more from the college president—now Father Delurey. The organizational meeting took place in the auditorium of New College Hall on June 13, 1906, with class representatives going as far back as 1868. According to the minutes, the assemblage began with "a prodigious shaking of hands and introducing of Old'Uns to the youngsters, and swapping of wondrous happenings of bygone days—some of which were true."[52] After electing officers, the reborn alumni organization, now renamed the Villanova Alumni Society, resolved to hold yearly meetings in June and to set the annual dues at five dollars. They then retired to a banquet, where they were entertained by the college glee club.

At their annual meeting in 1907, held on June 18, the old grads had another lively reunion, "full of mirth and vigor and college cheer."[53] They also resolved to sponsor "a permanent and lasting memorial to the alumni[,] . . . a building . . . to be called 'Alumni Hall.' "[54] (Thirteen years would elapse before this dream materialized, and it would take the form not of a new hall but of an extensive remodeling of the old College Building.)

At their banquet in May 1914, held at Philadelphia's Bellevue-Stratford Hotel, the Alumni Society voted to establish a permanent endowment fund for the college. The initiative had come from the college's president, who was now Reverend Edward G. Dohan, O.S.A. Leading the list of contributors, with a gift of $500, was Reverend A. J. Plunkett, a priest (but not an Augustinian) from the diocese of Hartford, Connecticut, and president of the Alumni Society. Unfortunately there were few other significant contributions and the endowment fund grew hardly at all in the years immediately ahead.[55]

As if to celebrate all the college's recent successes—growing enrollments, new curricula, a new and handsome physical plant, and a reinvigorated alumni organization—Villanova managed to secure two Presidents of the United States as commencement speakers during the first decade of the century. These were former President Grover Cleveland in 1902 and President William Howard Taft in 1910, both of whom received honorary degrees from Villanova. In his remarks Cleveland proposed that one of the most important goals of higher education "should be the cultivation and maintenance of a high standard of American citizenship." He went on to congratulate Villanova for its devotion to this task, one that a Catholic college shared with all institutions of higher learning regardless of religious affiliation. President Taft, in his address, paid high tribute to Pope Leo XIII, to the Roman Catholic Church, and to its religious orders and their educational activities.[56] Just how President Delurey managed to attract these prominent speakers is unknown.

Despite such celebrations, the costs of Villanova's recent expansions were tremendous. In order to pay for the new monastery and College Hall, which totaled just over $300,000 in the end, the Augustinian Province and Villanova College drew upon several sources. The largest amount, nearly $103,000, came from the various Augustinian parishes. Once again, the Catholic Augustinian connection was central to Villanova's identity, mission, and success.[57]

Besides the money contributed by the Augustinian parishes, an additional $67,000 came from the Augustinian Provincial Fund, made up of savings accumulated over the years by the province. The Augustinian Mission Band, which earned money by giving retreats, sermons, and the like, added $40,000 to the building cause. Another $65,000 came from donations by Villanova alumni and friends. Sales of land belonging to the college brought an additional $47,000. While waiting for some of these funds to arrive, the province took several mortgages on the Villanova property and buildings, but was able to retire all but $20,000 of the various mortgages by the time Father Fedigan ended his term as prior-provincial in 1902.[58]

Throughout the four years from 1898 to 1902, many of the details of executing the new buildings fell to Father Delurey, the college president, as did the responsibility for furnishing them and implementing all the new programs at Villanova. Indeed, Delurey came to personify the college's great strides. Thus in an invitation to the annual meeting of the Alumni Society in 1909, Father Middleton referred to their leader as "the indefatigable President, Dr. Delurey," adding, "Let us make it a 'Delurey Year.' . . . Come and imbibe the Delurey slogan, 'Progress.' "[59]

In order to give Delurey the authority to carry out all the necessary tasks, he was appointed to the college's Building Committee by the province and was appointed prior and procurator (or treasurer) of the Villanova Monastery. In addition he was treasurer of the college, all the while continuing to serve as president of the institution. If this were not enough, he was the headmaster of the academy.[60]

Once funds had been raised for the buildings, it was still necessary to discover ways to pay for landscaping, furnishing, and equipping New College Hall and financing the salaries of additional lay faculty.[61] The college met these demands in the same way as before, by selling land, receiving contributions from the Provincial Fund, and mortgaging its property. Between 1902 and 1906, for example, the province contributed $36,400 to the college. The college raised approximately $184,000 through land sales between 1902 and 1905. The largest parcel was 51.28 acres, which was apparently the land the college owned south of Lancaster Pike and west of Ithan Avenue. It was sold in 1905 for $179,480.[62] By this time Villanova had parted with nearly 117 of the 235 acres it had owned after acquiring the Lowry farm in 1859. Indeed, the sale of the Lowry property in 1888 was the largest such transfer until the 1905 sale of land south of the pike. By December 1905 Villanova would own just over 118 acres, approximately half of what it had possessed at the high point in the late 1850s.[63] At the time no one at Villanova could imagine that the institution would need large amounts of land for expansion only four or five decades later. By then Villanova would have to buy part of it back, and at greatly increased prices.

As with the building projects themselves, it fell to Father Delurey to manage all the details. In addition to arranging for the land sales, he was forced to borrow large amounts of money to meet the college's expenses. The college had no endowment of consequence beyond its dwindling land holdings and the contributed services of the Augustinians. Tuitions also remained modest, averaging $250 a year during the first decade of the century.[64] Raising them appreciably no doubt would have discouraged students from attending at a time when the college was trying to build its enrollment.

Among the loans raised by Father Delurey was a note for $30,000, signed

Panorama of campus buildings, sometime between 1914 and 1920, showing open fields, from the railroad side. *Left to right:* Corr Hall; Alumni Hall; the spires of St. Thomas of Villanova Church; St. Thomas of Villanova Monastery; New College Hall (later Tolentine Hall). VUA.

by him in his capacity as treasurer of the college in 1908 and held by the Union Bank of Brooklyn, New York.[65] On the advice of a lay faculty member, Dr. John M. Reiner, Delurey invested this money in the stock of the Idaho-Maryland Mining Company. Indeed, he had borrowed the money expressly for that purpose, in hopes of raising funds for the college as the stock increased in value. Unfortunately the stock was worthless, and Delurey failed to pay the $30,000 note to the Brooklyn bank. The lender then confronted the provincial authorities and threatened to sue for recovery of the money.[66]

All of this came to a head in June 1910. On Saturday, June 18 Father Delurey hosted President Taft at commencement—without question the high point of his college presidency and one of the greatest moments in Villanova's early history. Just two days later, Father Delurey was summoned before a "private chapter" of the province. After questioning him about the matter, the group passed swift judgment:

> Unanimously resolved that Dr. Delurey be removed from all offices—Presidency and Procuratorship of Villanova; membership with Trustees of [same] and ... Definitories. That he be deprived of both active and passive vote. That under obedience he be forbidden to hold communication in any way with ... Dr. John Reiner. That he be de-

The President of the United States, William Howard Taft (*left*), who gave the commencement address at Villanova on June 18, 1910, and received an honorary doctor of jurisprudence. Taft is accompanied by Reverend Lawrence A. Delurey, O.S.A., president of Villanova College, 1895–1910. VUA.

clared excommunicate[d] [from the order] with reservation to the [Augustinian] general.[67]

The private chapter then demanded that Delurey "hand over all property—books, papers, contracts, money, etc., hitherto appertaining to your several offices and positions at Villanova."[68] If he failed to cooperate, he was informed, he would be turned over to the law as an "embezzler." Two members of the chapter then followed him to his office where he promptly turned over the materials. That evening Delurey wrote a formal letter of resignation.[69]

As it turned out, Father Delurey had borrowed far more than $30,000. In November 1911 an accountant determined that the debts of the college amounted to $233,540 incurred over a ten-year period.[70] Only $30,000 of this had been raised for speculative purposes, the rest having been used to pay the expenses of an expanding college. Even so, it would take the college until January 1919 to defray these obligations.

Meanwhile Villanova became enmeshed in a long legal dispute with Frieda Reiner, wife of the now retired Dr. Reiner, who sued Villanova to recover $4,100 that her husband had lent the college while a member of the faculty. The trial dragged on until March 1914 and was widely reported in the Philadelphia newspapers, along with numerous details of the college's financial dealings under Father Delurey's presidency. The jury held in favor of Villanova, concluding that the loan from Dr. Reiner had not been authorized by the corporation. Having won the case, and its argument that Father Delurey had acted improperly, the college voluntarily paid Mrs. Reiner the $4,100.[71]

Delurey himself was eventually banished to the Augustinian community in Havana, Cuba, and forbidden to return to the United States until after the Reiner trial.[72] In 1919 he was allowed to retire to his native New York State, ending up in his boyhood parish at Schaghticoke, where he lived for some time with his brother and occasionally said Mass at the local church. By then he was suffering from several ailments, and at age fifty-eight, on December 21, 1922, he died.[73]

Delurey had made several attempts to clear his name with provincial authorities, but to no avail. In truth, the college's board of trustees itself had approved a number of the mortgages and other loans taken out during Delurey's presidency, though not the controversial note for $30,000.[74] Then there were the tremendous responsibilities Delurey had carried for fifteen dynamic years. He was often exhausted and doubtless used poor judgment at times, but there has never been any evidence that he himself benefited financially.[75] Delurey was never formally exonerated, either in his lifetime or after, but he did receive a quiet recognition when a small dormitory was named for him on the Villanova campus in 1943. By then, few if any people at the college remembered the life and times of Father Delurey.

In a larger sense, the Delurey tragedy was part of the price Villanova paid for its dramatic expansion. If Father Middleton, who had opposed the building project from the beginning, was tempted to say "I told you so," he apparently held his tongue—or at least his pen. Father Fedigan had died in 1908 and was not there to protect his old friend, Larry Delurey, or to convince provincial authorities to see their president's difficulties in the context of institutional progress.

Yet another reason for the financial fiasco of the Delurey years was the continuing habit of appointing one individual to multiple posts. In Delurey's case this was partly effective, since it gave him the power he needed to accomplish the college's ambitious projects. At the same time, he was over-taxed by all his duties and subject to no internal checks—such as an active and independent board of trustees, sound financial advice, or periodic audits by an outside agency—to keep his own judgment in balance. Perhaps be-cause of the Delurey-Reiner affair, Villanova returned to less-powerful presi-dents with short tenures, but maintained the practice of overlapping jurisdic-tions within the college and Augustinian community. It would be several more decades before both Villanova and the Augustinians were willing to face this critical problem of administration.

But now there were more immediate problems, caused by the outbreak of World War I. In August 1914, just a few months after the Reiner suit was settled, the major European powers had gone to war. What the students or the Augustinian community thought about this, or about the American deci-sion to enter the conflict in April 1917, is unknown. Given the large number of Irish Americans among the faculty and student body, there may indeed have been some misgivings about the United States fighting on the side of Great Britain, but there is no way of knowing the degree to which such sentiments existed.

In any case, it was clear by the end of 1917 that the Villanova community was gearing up for war. *The Villanovan* (a monthly student publication begun in 1916 and later to become a weekly student newspaper) reported in December 1917 that Reverend Monsignor George Waring, chaplain of the 11th U.S. Cavalry, had come to campus to speak to the students. He talked about the ideals of the American war effort and what students could do to help overthrow Prussianism and make the world safe for democracy.[76]

By April 1918 the *Villanovan* was citing the large number of Catholics who had enlisted in the armed forces. Then, countering the old charge by anti-Catholics that members of their faith were unpatriotic because of sup-posedly divided loyalties between Rome and the United States, the writer concluded that these huge Catholic enlistments, including 202 Villanova men, would demonstrate once and for all the patriotism of American Catho-lics.[77] If nothing else, such statements showed that Villanovans still saw themselves as a somewhat persecuted minority in the United States.

As early as the fall of 1917 there were worries at Villanova that the declaration of war by the United States would have a damaging effect on enrollment, but the slowness of American mobilization in 1917 did not have any appreciable impact that September.[78] A year later the threat to student numbers became very real, as millions of young men enlisted or were drafted. Villanova saved itself from a drastic decline in students enrolled by agreeing in August 1918 to accept a unit of the Student Army Training Corps (SATC), established at a number of American colleges and universities to train potential officers.[79] As at other institutions, the government paid full tuition for the SATC students, along with thirty dollars a month for their maintenance.[80] While this helped to keep enrollments at acceptable levels, the *Villanovan* concluded that the SATC program was also one more way their Catholic college could demonstrate its loyalty and patriotism.[81]

Induction day for the SATC at Villanova was October 1, 1918. Three companies stood on the lawn before New College Hall and recited their oath. The American flag was raised as the Corr Hall Band (presumably made up of seminarians) played the National Anthem. The college president, Reverend James J. Dean, O.S.A., then addressed the men. According to one count, 274 recruits joined the program.[82] Even more elaborate induction ceremonies had been planned, but had to be scaled back because a deadly influenza epidemic had broken out on campus at the end of September, infecting 173 students. On October 1 the Army imposed a quarantine on campus, complete with guard posts at all the entrances. Seven nurses from the Bryn Mawr Hospital, aided by six Sisters of Saint Joseph, came to nurse the sick. Before the epidemic was over in November, three Villanova students (all seminarians) died.[83] There was a similar outbreak and quarantine at Philadelphia's St. Joseph's College, but no fatalities among its students.[84]

When news of the Armistice reached campus on November 11, 1918, the three companies of Villanova's SATC paraded down the Lancaster Pike to Bryn Mawr, where Father Dean was one of the speakers at a local ceremony. Afterward the men marched back to campus, lit a huge bonfire, and burned the German Kaiser in effigy.[85] In early 1919 the SATC was replaced at Villanova with an Army ROTC unit, but interest soon waned and it was disbanded after a couple of years.[86]

In the midst of war, Villanova observed its 75th anniversary, or Diamond Jubilee. Because of hostilities the observance was quiet and mostly confined to commencement exercises on June 11, 1918. The speaker was the Vice President of the United States, Thomas R. Marshall, who received an honorary doctor of laws degree. In his sermon for the Diamond Jubilee Mass, Father Dean spoke about the special mission of Catholic education, and in doing so explained why there were limits to curriculum reform at Villanova's new college:

> You have heard ofttimes of the dangers that ensue to the community as well as to the individual from Godless schools. . . . Common sense tells us that, in spite of our boasted liberty of thought and conscience, we have no right to think what is evil, no right to say what is not true, no right to do what is morally wrong. . . . Christ alone can save the world and make men free. Surely there is little to be hoped for from a system in which ethical culture has displaced religion and a suggested hygiene has taken the place of *time-honored moral principles*.

> Upon the great body of Catholic laymen depends in great measure the welfare of both Church and State. We must stand as a unit; an insuperable barrier against the . . . tide of intellectual anarchy and the threatening avalanche of a false economic socialism. . . .
>
> We have a philosophy that is the outgrowth of the noblest efforts of human reason, enlightened by divine revelation and enriched by the experience of centuries. To know that philosophy and to apply it to the questions of the present day is the task for which the educated laity should be fitted, and nowhere can that philosophy be learned to better advantage—if at all—than in our Catholic Colleges and Universities.[87] (Emphasis added)

Such a unity of moral and intellectual truth gave little room for an elective curriculum. For the foreseeable future, the new college would be circumscribed by a Catholic philosophy that already stood in stark contrast to what Father Dean had claimed was the excessive individualism and materialism of modern American life. What Father Dean did not know was that the war still in progress when he made his Diamond Jubilee remarks would change the world forever, helping to unleash major social changes in the decade just ahead. His own world view would be tested as never before, and with these tests there would be even more questions about what it meant to be a Catholic college in America. In the process, the new college the Augustinian community had set out to build became far newer than any of them could have imagined.

# CATHOLIC GENTLEMEN

I n his Diamond Jubilee sermon Father Dean had spoken at length on the crucial importance of a moral and intelligent Catholic laity. His message also found strong support in the *Villanova College Catalogue* for 1922–23. "The aim of the Augustinian Fathers in founding Villanova College," it read, "was to offer young men an opportunity of receiving a thorough liberal education. . . ." Such an education "would develop all the faculties of soul as well as body, and . . . find its expression in a clear-thinking, right-acting [Catholic] Gentleman. . . ."[1]

In many respects this goal of educating the whole man was nothing new for Villanova, or for liberal arts colleges in general. But in the period between the two world wars this mission took on new contours. It appeared more militantly Catholic than ever before, reflecting a growing movement within the church (and within the Philadelphia Archdiocese in particular) to provide every child with a religious education. At the same time, the movement to educate the whole man, with special care for the student's social development, became an integral part of American higher education in the 1920s and 1930s. In many ways Villanova's Augustinian leadership was quite successful in combining this national emphasis upon the well-rounded student with its own ideal of the Catholic Gentleman.

Despite these local parallels with wider trends in American higher education, one should begin an examination of student life at Villanova between the two world wars by seeing it as part of an expanding and impressive system of Catholic schools in the United States, which stood at the center of the church's efforts to pass the faith on to future generations. By 1920 Catholics in the United States supported more than five thousand parish schools, hundreds of academies and high schools, and several dozen colleges. According to Jay Dolan, in his *American Catholic Experience*, this situation was unique "in the world of Roman Catholicism . . . [and] in the United States."[2]

The uniqueness of this vast network of Catholic schools in the United States arose from several factors. One was the tremendous growth of American public education in the nineteenth and early twentieth centuries. Another was an often unmistakable Protestant bias in the public schools, complete with readings from the King James Version of the Bible (that is, a Protestant version), Protestant forms of prayer, and anti-Catholic remarks in textbooks or other instructional materials. Just as dangerous, according to church authorities, was the increased possibility that Catholic youngsters who went to public school would meet and marry persons outside the faith and thereby be lost to the church. Finally, Catholics objected to the insufficient moral and religious training in the public schools. (Ironically, many public school systems had banned such instruction because of the impossibility of satisfying members of all religious groups, including Catholics, whose children attended the public system.) Because many citizens, largely Protestant, had come to believe that public schools were essential for the assimilation of immigrant children, as well as for the preservation of American republican ideals, they concluded that Catholics who opposed public education were being unpatriotic.[3]

In 1884 the American bishops, meeting in the Third Plenary Council of Baltimore, confronted the public school crisis by decreeing that each Roman Catholic parish must provide a school within two years or the pastor could be removed from his position. At the same time, Catholic parents were told that they had an obligation to support their parish school financially and to enroll their children in it.[4] An outspoken and unrelenting champion of this parish school movement was Philadelphia's Cardinal Dennis J. Dougherty (1865–1951), who headed the archdiocese from 1918 until his death thirty-three years later. Even four decades after his passing, Cardinal Dougherty remains an unforgettable figure in the minds of Philadelphia's Catholics—from those who remember his episcopate to those who have heard the many stories about this indomitable man whose ample girth seemed to grow in proportion to his increasing power over the local archdiocese.

Born in the coal country of eastern Pennsylvania to an Irish immigrant family, Dougherty himself had been forced to attend public schools, a fate from which he vowed to save the Catholic children of Philadelphia. He frequently cited the education decrees of the Third Plenary Council and

His Eminence Dennis Cardinal Dougherty, Archbishop of Philadelphia (*center*), and His Excellency, Most Reverend Francis J. Spellman, Archbishop of New York (to the left of Dougherty), during a visit to Villanova College in 1942. VUA.

virtually commanded parents to send their children to Catholic schools. In a letter to one pastor, the cardinal made himself unmistakably clear on this point, asserting: "Theories subversive of our Holy Religion are often taught in non-Catholic schools. Priests and parents *are bound* to provide a religious education for children" (emphasis added).[5] Although this particular letter referred to education at the lower levels, it is evident that the cardinal wanted the young people under his care to attend Catholic high schools and colleges. "If a parish school be necessary in the lower grades," he wrote in 1927, "it is still more necessary in the higher; because it is in the higher grades that history, literature, and the experimental sciences are taught in connection with which theories are advanced in non-Catholic universities, colleges, and high schools . . . that are dangerous to Religion."[6] Accordingly, the cardinal forbade Catholic youths to attend non-Catholic colleges or universities without special permission. Indeed, many who remember these policies will still regale the listener with stories of how Catholic high schools and academies routinely refused to send students' transcripts to non-Catholic institutions, a policy that continued for more than a decade beyond Cardinal Dougherty's own death in 1951.[7]

During the interwar period, Villanova offered its young men the solid Catholic education that Cardinal Dougherty had wished in several ways. Most important, there was a continuing though declining majority of Augustinians on the faculty. At the beginning of the twentieth century Villanova's faculty of 15 members had included 11 Augustinians and 4 lay teachers. Then the new course offerings in science and engineering caused the total number of faculty to reach 22 in the academic year 1906–7. Because the Augustinians had little or no training in these new areas, the college had no choice but to hire additional lay people, bringing their total to 10 during that same academic year of 1906–7 (or 45 percent of the total faculty). Over the next three and a half decades the faculty continued to grow, reaching a total of 73 in 1939–40.[8] Throughout this period the Augustinians represented slightly more than 50 percent of Villanova's teaching staff. This growth in lay faculty was typical of other Catholic colleges during the interwar period, as increased enrollments and new course offerings outpaced the ability of religious orders to provide sufficient teachers trained in the proper disciplines.[9]

While the laity had made gains among the faculty, the Augustinians continued to control the board of trustees, with five of the seven members belonging to the order. All administrative officers likewise continued to be Augustinians, except for the dean of the School of Engineering, who was a layman as well as a Protestant. The rest of the lay faculty appears to have been Catholic. It was also totally male until 1938, when three lay women were hired. By the early 1940s, however, the women had left Villanova for unknown reasons and the faculty reverted to being all men.[10]

In addition to instruction by a Catholic faculty, Villanova students continued to have compulsory religious services and annual retreats. During the 1920s and 1930s the academic year began with a Solemn High Mass. Students were required to attend Mass twice a week, on Thursday and Sunday, and to go to Confession at least once a month. There was a one-day religious retreat in early October, and a three-day retreat at the beginning of the second semester in late January or early February. Students who were not Catholic had to attend all such exercises, except for Mass and Confession, unless they opted to fulfill their religious duties by attending a church of their choice. In addition to religious services per se, lay as well as religious professors commonly began each class with a brief prayer, a practice that would continue well into the post–World War II period.[11]

Despite these accommodations, those outside the faith remained in a distinct minority of the student body throughout the interwar period. In October 1932, for example, the *Villanovan* reported that 89.5 percent of the students that year were Roman Catholic. Two years later the newspaper stated that 88.3 percent of the freshman class had chosen Villanova because

Student members of the Villanova College Sanctuary Society, before the main altar in the St. Thomas of Villanova Church, 1938. VUA.

it was a Catholic college. Surprisingly, the greatest number of non-Catholics on campus during this period were Jewish. In 1929, with a total enrollment at 977, there were 71 Jews at Villanova, compared with only 30 Protestants and 1 Russian Orthodox. There was no explanation for the Jewish enroll-ment, which represented just over 7 percent of the total, but it may have stemmed from the fact that Villanova was within easy commuting distance for Jewish residents in the western part of the city and some of the western suburbs.[12] What impact this religious minority may have had on campus life is also unknown.

Besides an overwhelmingly Catholic student body and faculty, various aspects of the curriculum, combined with the philosophy underlying it, made Villanova a distinctly Catholic college. All students, for instance, still had to take courses in Catholic doctrine. In addition, the curriculum re-mained largely prescribed, reflecting the Catholic belief at the time that there was a body of truth that must be handed down to the next generation. Lending powerful support to this assertion was the philosophy of Neo-Thomism, or Scholasticism, which had been adopted by the Roman Catholic

Church as its official philosophy through the papal encyclical *Aeterni Patris* (*Eternal Father*), issued in 1879.[13]

According to its proponents, Scholastic philosophy could unify all knowledge, as it had at the time of its principal founder, Saint Thomas Aquinas. It was the task of the modern Thomas to forge a new unity of faith and reason. In the words of the Catholic historian Philip Gleason,

> Scholastic philosophy recommended itself as the unifying discipline because it was closely associated with the faith, supporting and elucidating it, and yet was rational rather than fideistic. In philosophy the student learned a great deal of his religion on the basis of reason rather than as straight doctrinal teaching based on authority. Hence philosophy was the most appropriate way for collegians to learn their faith. And since Scholastic philosophy and natural law had applications in politics, social teaching, the family, and ethics generally, it not only presented the fundamental truths in the most cogent form, it also spelled out their implications in other areas of knowledge.[14]

Philadelphia's Cardinal Dougherty was a strong advocate of Scholasticism, and there is every reason to believe that Villanova's clerical faculty subscribed to its major tenets. Indeed, editorials in the *Villanovan* were filled with praise for Thomistic philosophy throughout the 1930s.

Since editorial policy was strictly controlled by the newspaper's faculty moderator (invariably an Augustinian), one can be sure that these accolades for Scholasticism reflected official thinking. Typical of them was a piece published in the spring of 1937, which recommended Scholasticism as the solution for the world's many problems:

> At the root of these problems, are false philosophical principles. When the Protestant Reformation overthrew the Catholic tradition, it also discarded the joy of medieval education: Scholasticism. And until the world returns to the philosophy of Scholasticism, there can never be any hope of real education, of real social reform, or of real social progress.... The greatest of all systems of philosophy is Thomism—the philosophy of St. Thomas Aquinas.[15]

Alternatives to Thomas were the heresies of free thought, secularism, and pragmatic morality. In December 1936 the *Villanovan* condemned "freethinking" in religious doctrine "because it refuses to acknowledge the sufficiency or soundness of clearly defined truths."[16] According to the 1940 *Belle Air*, Americans could not "much longer permit the evil of secularism to gnaw its way into the minds of our youth and there corrode our sense of justice, order, generosity, loyalty, peace, [and] human rights." According to the writer, the only antidote was a return to "Christian principles." Thus it was "the purpose of the *Belle Air* of 1940 to encourage deeper study and broader application of the old ... traditions of twenty centuries of Christianity."[17] With this as its official theme for 1940, each section of the yearbook began with a statement about the benefits of a Catholic education in various aspects of campus life and thought.

A half-dozen years earlier the *Villanovan* had carried a front-page story about a lecture by Reverend James B. Gallagher, O.S.A., a Villanova faculty member who roundly condemned pragmatic ethics as a violation of natural law. According to Father Gallagher,

> Man is subject to the natural law whether he wishes it or not. It would be a perversion of the order of the world to admit that man is without a law.... Since man's nature is always the same, it is wrong to think that ... politics or business may be governed by one code of morality, while in private life he [that is, man] is guided by one altogether different.[18]

True morality was neither relative nor pragmatic, but grounded in universal, unchanging truths.

The details of such a philosophy were doubtless lost on all but the most conscientious students at Villanova, but the majority of graduates probably went away from college with at least a vague belief in certain fixed principles that the Catholic Gentleman should try to apply in later life. But what the great bulk of students undoubtedly remembered best about their four years at Villanova was that other side of shaping the Catholic Gentleman: a loyal and enthusiastic participation in the college's extracurriculum.

Extracurricular activities were nothing new at Villanova in the 1920s and 1930s, but they expanded greatly and became an official part of campus life during this period. The title of an admissions brochure from 1934, "Life Has Many Sides," highlighted the balance that Villanova hoped to achieve between academics and social life. In addition to acquiring "a trained mind and a critical judgement," the young man would discover that "the social life of the student ... [is the] most effective instrument ... in the development of character." Then, making a mild analogy to military training, the brochure indicated to prospective collegians that "the social development of Villanova students begins on the first day of the freshman year and continues until graduation. In that time the raw recruit is transformed into a man of many accomplishments."[19]

Such glowing remarks about the benefits of campus social life also appeared in the *Villanova Bulletin,* as the annual catalogs were now called, under the heading "Extra Curricular Activities":

> The development of the social side of a student's life is an important factor in college training. Initiative and leadership in organized religious and social movements for the common welfare of his fellows, are qualities expected of college men generally. Student organizations and activities furnish splendid opportunities for this development.[20]

The *Villanova Bulletin* from this era also associated Villanova's social life with the culture of the nearby city, as well as the peacefulness of Villanova's suburban setting. Students could thus enjoy the best of both worlds, not unlike the suburban Main Line population that had grown up around the campus over the decades. Throughout the 1920s and 1930s the annual bulletins offered a compelling portrait of these dual opportunities:

> With its setting of nearly one hundred and sixty acres in one of the most beautiful and wealthy residential sections in America, the Campus is among the showplaces in the Philadelphia district. . . . Villanova combines the advantages of city and country. The absence of any large settlement in the immediate vicinity assures the seclusion necessary for student life, while easy access to Philadelphia affords an opportunity for visiting the many industrial plants of a great manufacturing center and of consulting the various libraries of a metropolitan city.[21]

Through such statements Villanova purposely sought to associate itself with the sophistications of city life and the social cachet of living on the Philadelphia Main Line, a suburban area that in many ways reached its apex of beauty and prestige during this period between the two world wars. The Main Line was in fact a succession of suburban enclaves and country houses that radiated out from the various stations along the Pennsylvania Railroad west of Philadelphia with such names as Overbrook, Ardmore, Haverford, Bryn Mawr, Rosemont, Villanova itself, Wayne, Devon, and Paoli. The term "Main Line," as a collective designation for these communities, derived originally from the "main line of public works," a series of railroads and canals owned by the State of Pennsylvania that linked Philadelphia and Pittsburgh. Later the "main line" of the Pennsylvania Railroad followed essentially the same route from Philadelphia.

By the 1920s and 1930s the name "Main Line" had become synonymous in many people's minds with rich living and high social status, making it a favorite setting for novels, plays, and movies about upper-class suburbia. The most famous of these would be *The Philadelphia Story*, a comedy by Philip Barry (1942) that was the basis for a movie of the same name, and later a musical entitled *High Society*. Indeed Barry's play was based upon life at a large estate in Villanova known as "Androssan." It belonged to the Robert L. Montgomery family, whose daughter Hope Montgomery Scott (in her nineties and still living at Androssan at the time of this writing) was the model for the character Tracy Lord, played by Katharine Hepburn, in *The Philadelphia Story*.[22]

Although Villanova College used its location on the Main Line as a selling point in its promotional literature, few if any Villanova students came from elite families in the area, whose Protestant establishment sent its sons to various Ivy League institutions in the northeastern states.[23] By contrast, the bulk of Villanova's students in the region came from Philadelphia's Catholic high schools.

Villanova also shared its Main Line location with several other colleges, namely Haverford (a Quaker men's college), Bryn Mawr (a nonsectarian private college for women), and Rosemont (a Catholic women's college operated by the Sisters of the Holy Child Jesus). Villanova had little if any contact with either Haverford or Bryn Mawr, both of which drew their students from well-to-do Protestant families. However, Rosemont (founded in 1921) was only a mile or so away from Villanova and became a place where Villanova men frequently went to find dates. Later Rosemont would collaborate with Villanova in various social and academic activities.

Meanwhile, the United States was in the grip of powerful social forces that Villanova College could neither dismiss nor ignore. Although these forces had been mounting for some time, they came to a head during the 1920s. Radio, movies, and the automobile all came of age during this roaring decade, as did compulsory education into the high school years in most states, and a full-blown consumer culture fed by slick advertising and easy credit. A revolution in manners and morals also led to scantier clothing for women and a casual system of "dating" between the sexes (as opposed to the more formal courtship patterns of the past). For the first time in American history, a separate youth culture emerged, supported by mass education and the mass media. Young people in their late teens and early twenties had their own music, their own slang, and their own styles of dressing, and delighted in using all three as vehicles of rebellion against the older generation. This youth culture manifested itself most strongly among prosperous young people living in large metropolitan centers on the east coast, but most teens and young adults were affected by the new ways to some extent.[24]

The region's Catholic youth were certainly not immune to the new currents, especially since many of their families now represented second- and third-generation Americans whose occupations and incomes were propelling a good portion of them into the middle class. Such young men were attracted to Villanova's Main Line campus, and their ideas about college life—derived from the movies, newspapers, and popular fiction—could not be denied entirely if the college wanted to succeed.

At the same time, the numbers of young men entering Villanova increased far beyond what anyone could have imagined just a few years before. This surge was part of a nationwide trend during the 1920s, fueled by prosperity and the manifold needs of an urban, industrial society, which required more and more college graduates. Yet student increases in Catholic colleges were even greater than at most other institutions, as Catholics prospered and sought to make the most of the nation's expanding economy. On average, enrollments at Catholic colleges in the United States increased by 19 percent every year during the 1920s.[25] Villanova was well in line with these averages, as enrollment rose from 214 collegians in 1919 to 977 in 1929, for an increase of more than 450 percent in just ten years. Compared with colleges and universities as a whole in the United States, Villanova did extremely well. Between 1927 and 1928, for example, its total enrollment went up by 13 percent, as opposed to a national average of just 2 percent that same year.[26]

Such numbers would have presented disciplinary problems for Villanova even if its young men had not been exposed to the excitements of the jazz age. But their expectations of modern college life made the challenges even greater for Villanova's administration. Villanova coped with these realities much as other colleges and universities of the time did—by encouraging the students to organize a set of activities and to make these a regular and predictable part of each academic year.[27] More than that, Villanova was soon insisting that participation in organized extracurricular activities was almost as important as what went on in the classroom. The proper balance of academics and social life would result in the well-rounded young Catholic who could hold his own with anyone in the world of business and the professions.

One also suspects that a well-organized social life among the students harmonized, in spirit at least, with the ordered monastic lives of their Augustinian administrators and teachers. Whether true or not, a persistent failure to participate in such organized activities might be interpreted as disloyalty to Villanova—and to the high calling of a Catholic Gentleman.

In her penetrating study of college life, Helen Lefkowitz Horowitz referred to students who conformed to the rhythms of official campus society as the "organized." She divides the remaining students into the "outsiders," who steer an independent but largely silent course, and the "rebels," who are outspokenly critical of campus mores—and often of certain practices in American society at large.[28] What characterized Villanova and other Catholic colleges during the interwar period (in contrast to secular or nominally Protestant institutions such as Columbia or the University of Chicago) was their comparative lack of either independents or rebels. Perhaps it was the similarity of their backgrounds as lower-middle and middle-middle class Roman Catholics that made Villanova's students so willing to conform. Or perhaps it was a religious view of the world that placed a premium upon hierarchy, tradition, and conformity of belief, which explained the paucity of rebels or outsiders on the Villanova campus.

The Villanova student's introduction to organized social life started with freshmen hazing, a standard practice on most campuses at the time. It is impossible to say just when hazing began at Villanova, since the earliest mention of it came in the first issue of the *Belle Air*, published in 1922. In it a senior reminisced that in January 1919, after the freshmen had returned to classes without their military uniforms, "the upper-classmen quickly took us in hand and put us through various degrees of the Ancient and Eternal Order of Hobble Gobble."[29] Since the writer assumed that readers were already quite familiar with the Order of Hobble Gobble, one is left to assume that it had existed on campus for some time. Unfortunately, he did not offer any details, for the sake of future generations, on the founding and precise definition of this "ancient order." Although the full story of Hobble Gobble may never be known, reports of its activities turn up in subsequent numbers of the *Belle Air*. In 1923 the Gobbler took out its shears and cut the freshmen bald.[30] In compensation for their lost locks, the frosh received "scull caps" in the college colors of blue and white.[31]

These rites of initiation were calculated to build class spirit and loyalty to the college. In addition to the hazing, solidarity was reinforced throughout the year by contests between the freshmen and the sophomores. One of these was an annual tug-of-war across the old ice pond, by then known to students as the "duck pond," which was located south of the corner of Ithan Avenue and Lancaster Pike. Held in early November as the last event of freshmen initiation, the losers ended up in a frigid and muddy drink. This tug-of-war was apparently part of a freshman-sophomore field day, which featured a variety of other contests. There were also impromptu battles—as in February 1929, when a snowstorm touched off a freshman-sophomore snowball fight and tug-of-war covered by the Philadelphia newspapers. In addition to these class competitions, there were events for first-year students alone, such as the annual "Freshmen Smoker." At one such smoker in March 1924, the program included a magician, a pie-eating contest, and a boxing and wrestling exhibition, ending with a rousing rendition of college songs.[32]

In a rare verbal protest from the period, an editorial writer for the *Villanovan* in October 1929 came out against freshmen hazing, denouncing it as a humiliation and demanding that it be stopped. Apparently the practice had

Student tug-of-war at the "duck pond" (South Campus), 1930s. VUA.

gotten out of hand, with upperclassmen going beyond institutionalized practices and picking on individual freshmen. Villanova's president, Reverend James H. Griffin, O.S.A., agreed with the article and announced in the fall of 1930 that limits would be placed on freshmen initiation. It seems that the Ancient and Eternal Order of Hobble Gobble disappeared, along with the worst episodes of personal hazing. It is revealing, however, that Father Griffin did not banish all the indignities of freshmen harassment, as photographs from the late 1930s and early 1940s attest. These depict freshmen singing songs and making silly gestures while wearing beanies and ill-fitting clothes.[33]

Soon after their arrival students were also introduced to the various "locality clubs," made up of men from their home regions or towns. The purpose of these associations was to strengthen ties among students from the same area while they were in college as well as in the future. During vacations from Villanova, these clubs held dances back home, and it was hoped that in later years these clubs would form the bases for local alumni associations.[34] For the most part these regional clubs corresponded with the Augustinian parishes, which continued to be important vehicles of recruitment. Among them were the Atlantic City Club, the Jersey City Club, the Brooklyn–Long Island Club, the Albany Club, the Connecticut Club, the Lawrence Club, and the Wilkes-Barre Club. There were also clubs for the various Catholic high schools in Philadelphia, in addition to an Italian Club for local Italian American students and a Day Hop Club for commuters.[35]

Freshman initiation, 1939. VUA.

There were no national Greek letter fraternities at Villanova during the interwar period, but there were Greek letter societies within the various disciplines. In 1940 these were Epsilon Phi Theta (liberal arts), Phi Kappa Phi (engineering), and Lambda Kappa Delta (science).[36] Despite their associations with various academic areas, these fraternities were social organizations that held dances and other recreational activities, rather than scholastic honor societies. For example, Phi Kappa Phi, the engineering fraternity, sponsored the annual Owl Hop, held in mid-November following the football game against the Owls of Philadelphia's Temple College (later Temple University).[37] Social fraternities with national associations did not exist at Villanova in the 1920s, or at other Catholic colleges for the most part, because their rituals and symbols had roots in Freemasonry and because the Catholic Church opposed membership in secret societies.[38]

The first student dance on the Villanova campus appears to have been a Thanksgiving dance in November 1918 given by the SATC.[39] Once the precedent was established, dances began to proliferate in the 1920s. By the early 1930s there was the Freshmen Hop, the Sophomore Cotillion, the Farewell Dance, the Junior Prom, and the Belle Air Ball, besides the Owl Hop and a Halloween Dance. The Belle Air Ball, held by the seniors in midwinter, was the social highlight of the season. Minor dances took place in the campus gymnasium, while formal affairs found space in one of Philadelphia's

Belle Air Ball in the Villanova Field House, early 1940s. VUA.

hotel ballrooms, such as the Bellevue Stratford, the Ritz-Carlton, or the Benjamin Franklin.

After the completion of the Field House in 1932, all the dances were held at Villanova. For the major events students typically engaged one of the big name bands of the era, among them Ozzie Nelson (1933), Phil Emerson (1933), the Dorsey Brothers (1935), Isham Jones (1935), Glen Gray (1936), and Jan Garber (1936). There was also a student dance band called the Villanovans, which played on less elaborate occasions. Fierce competitions typically erupted between the juniors and seniors to see who could sign up the most popular performers, even during the depression of the 1930s.[40]

In addition to providing opportunities for class rivalries, the dances introduced young women into Villanova social life for the first time. As on most campuses until the early twentieth century, Villanova men had socialized only among themselves. The advent of the dating system now allowed them to invite young women to college dances and in the process to vie for social prestige among their male classmates, success being measured by the frequency of their dating and the good looks of the women they brought to campus.[41] Dressing up in black tie (or even white tie and tails for the Belle Air Ball) also allowed Villanova men to transform themselves into well-dressed young gentlemen for an evening. With their smart clothes, good manners, and attractive dates, they could ostensibly look forward to fine marriages and successful careers after graduation.

Yet another time to shine socially was Junior Week, a function begun in 1924. It took place during the second week in May, when members of the junior class received their college blazers for the first time. The week's events culminated with the annual Blazer Ball, to which juniors wore their blue blazers and white duck trousers in honor of the college colors of blue and white. In the 1920s they also carried class walking canes, "the mark of a distinguished gentleman."[42] In 1934 another Villanova tradition, Mother's Day, was added to Junior Week, as mothers were invited to campus on the Monday after Mother's Day.[43]

The local hangout during this period was the Pie Shop (also spelled "Pie Shoppe" for several years), located in the basement of the present Tolentine Hall, then known as College Hall (and soon thereafter as Mendel Hall). Presiding over the Pie Shop was Louis Ciamachela, an Italian immigrant from South Philadelphia who originally came to Villanova as a barber in 1922. "Louie" was beloved by generations of students and was something of a campus legend. Following its renovation in 1929, the Pie Shop had a low white ceiling studded with heavy wooden beams, in "the old English tavern

Cover of *Junior Courtier,* 1928, featuring a junior "Catholic Gentleman" in his 1929 class blazer, white ducks, and class walking cane. VUA.

style." It had a marble soda fountain and a lunch counter with steam tables and hot beverage urns.[44]

The Pie Shop was a favorite stop after athletic events, in an era when football dominated the sports scene at Villanova and most other colleges. Villanova often played much larger colleges in football, and the crowds were sometimes so big that the games had to take place in local ballparks or municipal stadiums, as in November 1927 when Villanova faced off against Boston College before 20,000 fans at the Boston Braves field.[45] For such out-of-town games, the college usually chartered several traincars to transport loyal Villanovans en masse. In November 1929, 800 students and alumni went by rail to the game against Bucknell.[46] That same year Villanova began building a new stadium along Lancaster Pike. Completed in 1929, it seated more than 5,500 spectators and cost $70,000.[47] It was in this stadium that fans watched Villanova through two undefeated seasons in 1937 and 1938, coached by the popular Maurice J. "Clipper" Smith.[48]

That the administration took football seriously as a tool for publicity, recruiting, and student solidarity can be inferred from the effort to hire good coaches and from the large salaries they paid them. Head football coach Harry Stuhldreher, who had been one of Notre Dame's famous "Four Horsemen of the Apocalypse," received $7,500 a year in 1927 (two years after coming to Villanova), plus 10 percent of the game receipts.[49] His salary alone was about twice as much as the highest paid lay professor, and nearly four times as much as the lowest paid.[50] In 1939 head football coach "Clipper" Smith, who replaced Stuhldreher in 1935 and who had played at Notre Dame on the same team as the legendary George Gipp, was earning $10,000 a year, still more than twice what any lay faculty member was paid.[51] There is abundant evidence from the house chapter minutes that these salaries, along with the choice of the head football coach and his assistants, were determined largely by the local Augustinians meeting at the monastery, rather than by the college's board of trustees or by the president, another example of confusing jurisdictions that would cause difficulties in the future.

Villanova's alumni, now reorganized as the Alumni Association, had no doubt that sports were a most important tool for publicizing the college. According to the *Villanova Alumnus* for May 1938, "The entire publicity picture at Villanova is predicated upon a proposition that the progress of athletic activities at the college can be advanced and the interests of the institution can be furthered by publicity which will favorably reflect the rise of Villanova in intercollegiate competition."[52] Both before and after this pronouncement, the alumni magazine carried regular features on Villanova athletics, giving special coverage each year to the Homecoming football game.

That Villanova was consciously imitating Notre Dame's tremendous publicity success through its legendary football teams seems evident. Coaches Harry Stuhldreher and "Clipper" Smith both had played football at Notre Dame under the famous Knute Rockne, as did assistant coach Edward Hunsinger (who worked under Stuhldreher at Villanova). When Rockne died in a plane crash in 1931, Villanova held a well-attended memorial Mass for the fallen coach.[53]

At the same time, La Salle College was trying to tap into Notre Dame's football publicity by hiring Marty Brill, who had also played for Rockne, as its head coach in the 1930s. St. Joseph's football program was somewhat more subdued. It fell victim to a shortage of students during World War II and was not revived after the war. Haverford College characteristically refused to use its football program to gain publicity, content to rely on its academic reputation instead of its football team to attract favorable attention.[54]

In stark contrast, Villanova's football games were surrounded by elaborate ritual. In the center of it all was the Villanova Wildcat, the college mascot, which had been suggested by assistant football coach Edward Hunsinger and ratified by a vote of the student body in 1926. (For a number of years the college actually owned a live wildcat, known as "Count Villan," which was taken in a cage to all the games.[55]) It was also in 1926 that Villanova adopted an official march written especially for the band by Edward B. Dingler. The Alma Mater came in 1930 and was written by a well-known songwriter of the day named Joseph Burke, whose son James was a sophomore at Villanova. The college fight song, " 'V' for Villanova," was composed later in the 1930s by Irving R. Leshner, a dance-band musician and professional psychologist.[56]

These musical numbers, mingled with rousing cheers, became the main features of loud pep rallies before football games. The most tumultuous of these was the one held the Thursday evening before the big game with Temple, a grudge match that began about 1927. These rallies formed at St. Thomas of Villanova Church immediately after the semiweekly Mass for students. As the *Villanovan* explained on October 25, 1932, "The freshmen will follow the band, followed by the upper classmen, and march to the new gym [that is, Nevin Field House], where the activities of the rally will commence."[57] A year later the rally included a bonfire, as well as a rousing address by La Salle coach Marty Brill.[58]

In the midst of this football fever, there were only a few weak complaints about the primacy of football on campus. In February 1930, for example, an editorial in the *Villanovan* lamented that the college was known far more for athletic prowess than for intellect.[59] One doubts, however, that the editorial had the slightest effect on football mania. Even the tragic death of a young player failed to dampen the enthusiasm. Instead, it gave Villanovans a student-hero, whose ultimate sacrifice for the college might inspire others.

The young man was Leo Goodreau, who broke his back in a football

Billanova College Mourns Loss of Great Athlete

LEO GOODREAU

Leo Goodreau (1900–
1928), Villanova's hero-
athlete. VUA.

practice in September 1928 and died in the Bryn Mawr hospital several days later. The entire student body attended his funeral at the St. Thomas of Villanova Church and in May of 1930 the newly completed football field was named in Goodreau's honor.[60] For decades both the student newspaper and the yearbook held up the image of Leo Goodreau as the highest type of Catholic manhood, with the *Villanovan* specifically dedicating itself to his memory. As late as September 1959, nearly thirty years after Goodreau's death on the practice field, the *Villanovan* continued this annual tribute. Every few years the newspaper also reprinted the following description of its fallen athlete:

> Villanova . . . has produced many outstanding men throughout its years of Catholic education. Among these men some have been brilliant students, some excellent athletes and others superior gentle-

men. But perhaps one of the finest men ever to enter Villanova, a humble composition of each of those qualities, never graduated. The man today is a shining memory to those of the faculty who have been at Villanova since 1930.... This man, to whom the VILLANOVAN is respectfully dedicated, is Leo Goodreau, a scholar, athlete, and most of all, a gentleman.... The story of Leo Goodreau is in reality [an] inspiration, an inspiration to all Villanovans.... Surely the story of Leo Goodreau lingers in the halls and on the playing fields of Villanova, . . . an ever present inspiration to higher standards of sportsmanship and duty.[61]

Goodreau had become a semimythical character whose loyalty to Villanova had cost him his life.[62]

It is doubtful whether many students in the 1950s, or even the 1930s, gave much thought to emulating the legendary qualities of a Leo Goodreau. As a series of polls in the *Villanovan* indicated, most were intent on having a good time at college. In February 1933 the student newspaper reported that Villanovans spent, on the average, more than twice as much money each year for tobacco products ( $26.00 ) than for books ( $11.46 ). Smokers made up 73 percent of the student body, while 12.5 percent reported that they chewed tobacco. The favorite brands of the cigarette smokers were Camel, Lucky Strike, and Chesterfield; of cigar smokers, Robert Burns and Cremo; and of pipe smokers, Granger, Half and Half, and Sir Walter Raleigh—in that order. (The newspaper did not give any preferences for the chewers.[63]) That smoking was a sign of campus sophistication can also be gathered from the glamorous, full-page tobacco advertisements appearing in virtually every number of the *Villanovan*. Several issues of the *Belle Air* in the 1930s published senior portraits showing many of the men holding lighted pipes or cigarettes.[64]

In addition to smoking, the Villanova gentleman was expected to dress well. Students continued to wear jackets and ties to class on a daily basis, and thus it is not surprising that the average annual expenditure on clothes was $150 per student, according to the 1933 survey. A detailed breakdown revealed that the average Villanova man bought 1.7 suits, 1.2 hats, and 9.4 neckties each year. He acquired a new overcoat every 2.5 years.[65]

Although the newspaper poll did not ask about student drinking habits during this era of prohibition, one suspects that some students did in fact consume alcoholic beverages and looked forward to the end of the "Noble Experiment," when beer and wine might be sold in the campus Pie Shop. A front-page story in the *Villanovan* quickly set them straight: Students had been forbidden to have alcohol at the college well before the Eighteenth Amendment was ratified, and the administration had no intention of lifting the ban following the repeal of prohibition. Students were also forbidden to consume alcohol while off campus, though how this might be enforced was not explained.[66]

Other articles and editorials indicated that students did not always conduct themselves in a way that was becoming to a young Catholic Gentleman. In 1932, for example, editorials in the *Villanovan* admonished students for cutting across the lawn en route to the post office, for damaging pay telephones in the dormitories and stealing money from their coin boxes, and for sloppy dress in the dining room. In 1933 they were chastised for showing up late for Mass and for misbehavior in the Pie Shop, where they had carved their names into the tables and chairs and poured salt into the sugar containers. In nearly all these editorials, students were reminded that such behavior was unbecoming to a "Catholic Gentleman."[67]

In May 1933 the *Villanovan* tried to shame students for using the warm spring weather as an excuse to abandon proper dress:

> Almost traditionally each year the advent of this [warmer] weather is a signal for the students to become lax in their modes of attire. Coats and neckties are discarded at the slightest provocation, and if any unusual amount of energy has to be exerted, shirts are sometimes cast aside likewise. . . . Such unconventionalities are injurious not only to the reputation of the student, but also to that of the college.[68]

This and the other editorials about improper behavior appear to have been inspired by faculty and administrators. Indeed, many of these editorial strictures seemed to come straight out of the student handbooks, published for the first time in 1931.

An introduction to the rules and regulations set down in the student *Handbook* stated that "the standard of correct living set forth as the ideal of Villanova College is that of a Catholic Gentleman."[69] The handbook then went on to forbid students to gamble, drink alcohol, or steal, and added, "Immorality in any form will not be tolerated." Violations of these rules would result in "summary expulsion." Less drastic but still serious penalties awaited "any act of insubordination to anyone in authority." And although the handbook did not say so, students were expected to rise en masse when their professors entered the classroom as a sign of respect.

Students were not allowed to be off campus after 7:30 P.M. without permission, and even then they had to be back before 12:20 A.M., about when the last trains of the day stopped at the campus station. Freshmen "in good standing" could have one such late permission each week, while the upperclassmen were allowed two: Saturday night and one other evening during the week. Students had to receive all visitors in the dormitory parlors. "Lady visitors" were specifically forbidden to enter private rooms.[70]

It was also in the early 1930s that the *Villanovan*, in cooperation with the Holy Name Society on campus, launched a campaign against "unclean speech." In a poll taken during the fall of 1932, some 40 percent of the students said that cursing and swearing were the "greatest danger to morals on the campus." During the annual one-day retreat that year, as well as in the two preceding years, students received personal pledge cards that asked them to promise not to use foul language.[71]

The administration attempted to enforce compliance with the rules by allowing the Student Council, which had been founded in 1925, to function as a student court where offenders against more minor college rules might be tried.[72] But the Student Council did not formulate the rules, enforce the punishments, or have any real power—which the organizers of the council admitted from the very beginning. According to the *Villanovan*, the Student Council would have to conform "to the requirements of a Catholic College in which the administration of discipline must be in the hands of the faculty."[73] Their purpose was strictly advisory, and their advice to the administration commonly concerned the pettier details of college life. In the fall of 1932, for example, they asked that the Thanksgiving vacation be canceled so the Christmas vacation could be extended, and that the swimming pool be opened for several more hours each week. The president of the college granted the request for longer pool hours but declined to cancel the Thanksgiving break.[74]

In order to provide additional facilities for its expanding student body during the 1920s, the college erected several new buildings. In 1920 Villanova completed renovations on the old College Building, which had been constructed in two stages, the east wing in 1848–49 and the center and west wings in 1873–74. The venerable hall received a coat of stucco and a remodeled front entrance, which resulted in the demolition of its spacious front porch. A new gymnasium appeared on the ground floor of the east wing, where the Dramatic Hall—and before that a study hall—had once been. Funds for the project had been raised by the Villanova Alumni Association over a period of years, beginning in 1907 when the organization proposed to erect a building in memory of the college's alumni. Perhaps because they had been able to raise only $12,777 (not enough for a new building, even in those days), they decided to use that fund for renovating the old structure. In honor of their efforts, the building was renamed Alumni Hall at a special banquet held in the building's new gymnasium on October 20, 1920. (The completion of a new gym in Alumni Hall also allowed Villanova to create its first intercollegiate basketball team in the winter of 1920–21.[75])

St. Nicholas of Tolentine Academy remained in Alumni Hall until 1923, when it began its move off-campus and relocated in Malvern, Pennsylvania, under the name "Malvern Preparatory School," owned and operated by the Augustinians. The move was apparently completed by September 1924. By then many had come to believe that the continued existence of an academy on the grounds compromised the reputation of the college, and thus the academy's relocation was greeted with some relief.[76]

It was also in 1923 that Villanova began a new dormitory for upper-classmen known as Austin Hall. The word "Austin" referred to the Augustinian community, and was typically used in the British Isles as a name for the Augustinian order. Austin Hall was rendered in gray stone in a mixture of Colonial Revival and Collegiate Gothic styles. The architects were Wilson Eyre (1858–1944), a well-respected Philadelphia architect, and his partner, Charles J. McIlvain, Jr. (1872–1938).[77] It opened in the fall of 1924 and contained a new college library in its east wing. The following year, 1925, Villanova erected a small radio station, a white wooden building in the

Front entrance to Alumni Hall, after 1920, which once served as the Academy building. VUA.

Austin Hall, completed in 1924 and designed by Wilson Eyre and Charles J. McIlvain, Jr. View from Lancaster Pike, 1950s. VUA.

Colonial Revival mode, now demolished, which stood near the present site of Vasey Hall. In 1928 the college launched yet another dormitory for upperclassmen. Named Fedigan Hall in honor of Reverend John J. Fedigan, O.S.A. (a former president of Villanova College as well as the visionary prior-provincial who had launched Villanova's great building campaign in the late 1890s), the structure was completed in 1929 and resembled a stark Florentine palazzo of the late Middle Ages.[78] The architect, Paul Monaghan (1885–1968), was known primarily as a designer of Catholic churches and other structures commissioned by Catholic institutions in the Archdiocese of Philadelphia.[79]

While Villanova was expanding its campus physically, its chief competitors, La Salle and St. Joseph's, were building entirely new campuses. In 1927 St. Joseph's moved to the Overbrook section of Philadelphia, then an attractive suburban address just inside the westernmost city limits. Two years later, in 1929, La Salle moved to the former Belfield estate near Broad Street and Olney Avenue on the edge of Philadelphia's Germantown section.[80] (Although both of these new campuses were in safe and desirable sections at the time, their neighborhoods deteriorated alarmingly during the last decades of the twentieth century, to the detriment of each institution.)

Meanwhile at Villanova, the administration and board of trustees believed that surging admissions would continue into the foreseeable future and hired the John Price Jones Corporation of New York City, experts in planning and fund-raising, to examine Villanova and to make projections about its needs.[81] In its "Survey and Plan," issued in July 1929, the consulting firm projected about two thousand students at Villanova by 1940 and recom-

Villanova College Library in the east wing of Austin Hall, early 1940s. VUA.

mended an ambitious construction program combined with a campaign to raise more than $2 million (see Chapter 6). In January 1930 Villanova announced its campaign and building plans.

According to the architect's drawings, there would be a cluster of five buildings on the East Campus facing Lancaster Pike. At the head of a new quadrangle was to be a Commerce and Finance Building, to its right a free-standing library building (to replace the already overcrowded library wing in Austin Hall), and to its left a new dining hall. Also included in this complex were two dormitories. On the northeast corner of Ithan Avenue and Lancaster Pike, there would be a new Field House. The college planned to set aside some $800,000 of the fund as a permanent endowment.[82]

Despite the stock market crash in October 1929, no one at Villanova or anywhere else in the nation realized that ten years of depression lay ahead. The college managed to erect the Commerce and Finance Building, completed in 1931 and soon thereafter called Vasey Hall, in honor of Prior-Provincial Nicholas J. Vasey, O.S.A. (1875–1931). The next year, Villanova completed the Field House (renamed Jake Nevin Field House many years later), which featured a combined auditorium-gymnasium and swimming pool. Paul Monaghan, who had rendered the elaborate plans for Villanova's physical expansion, was the architect for both Vasey Hall and the Field House.[83]

Swimming pool in the Villanova Field House, completed 1932. VUA.

By 1932, the year the Field House opened, the tightening grip of the Great Depression made further building impossible. The campaign drive also fell far short of its goal, with the $800,000 endowment remaining only a dream (see Chapter 6).[84] Two disastrous fires also placed great financial hardships on the college.

The first of these fires began in College Hall on January 28, 1928. It was late on a Sunday afternoon as students were returning from the dining room that someone first smelled smoke. Evacuation of the building began and fire companies came from all over the area, but a heavy snow, which had been falling all day, kept several from reaching the scene. Morning revealed a blackened hulk, completely gutted inside. Immediately the college began rebuilding the interior, and by the fall of 1929 the structure was ready for occupancy. The exterior looked much as it had before, except for certain features on the upper story. The building was rechristened Mendel Hall, after the Augustinian abbot and priest Gregor J. Mendel (1822–84) who had discovered the laws of heredity. It would retain this designation until 1960, when it was renamed Tolentine Hall and the name Mendel was transferred to a new science building. Yet college catalogs in the 1930s would give the building's date as 1929, in an effort to show that most of the campus buildings were of recent construction. After several decades of repeating this partly erroneous fact, Villanovans apparently forgot that the outside walls of the building had been started in 1899 and that even its cornerstone (still readable in the early 1990s) bore the date 1900.[85]

Reverend Francis X. Coan, O.S.A., and students in the biology laboratory of "old" Mendel Hall (formerly New College Hall and later Tolentine Hall), late 1930s. VUA.

St. Thomas of Villanova Monastery during the fire of August 2, 1932. VUA.

Villanova College gate on Lancaster Pike, 1920s. VUA.

The other disastrous fire broke out on August 2, 1932, in the St. Thomas of Villanova Monastery. The building was so badly damaged that it had to be demolished, except for its west wing, which remains as St. Thomas Hall.[86] Among the treasures saved from the flames was the portrait of Father Fedigan by Thomas Eakins.[87] Ironically, the portrait, which showed Fedigan standing beside the architect's original rendering of the building, was one of the few items that survived unscathed from the two buildings Fedigan had fought so hard to erect only three decades earlier.

Although the nation was slipping further and further into depression by the time of the second fire, the Augustinian community managed to begin a new monastery in 1933. Completed a year later, it repeated the Gothic lines of the earlier structure and was in many ways more attractive than the building it replaced. Paul Monaghan, who seemed to have settled in as the college's architect, bid on the project, but he lost out in a fierce contest with architect Henry D. Dagit, Jr. (1893–1981), Monaghan's main competitor for Catholic patronage at the time. Dagit and his firm would remain Villanova's architects for the next three decades and place an indelible stamp upon the campus.[88]

As the depression began to make inroads into Villanova's enrollment, its students and their Augustinian mentors tried to carry on the social traditions of the college, and for the most part they succeeded. What they could not know was that national and international events would force them to grapple with an increasingly dangerous world. Villanova's Catholic Gentleman would soon face some of the greatest challenges in modern history. Although campus life would remain similar to that at most other small colleges in the United States, the reactions of Villanovans to national and world events would show that they were very much Catholics, as well as Americans.

# VILLANOVA AND THE WORLD

Villanova had never been immune to the effects of national and international events, including wars and economic disasters. The panic of 1857, and then the American Civil War, had contributed to the closing of the college for eight full years. A depression in the 1890s and then World War I had also made life difficult for the institution. But none of these external events affected Villanova as deeply or as long as the double crises of the Great Depression and World War II, which came one after the other and occupied a decade and a half of world, national, and local history. Besides disrupting life on campus, these upheavals again confronted Villanovans, including its Augustinian leadership, with the question of what it meant to be a Catholic in America.

At the most elemental level, the Depression and World War II threatened Villanova's financial well-being. Enrollments fell drastically as the Depression took hold, then rebounded by the end of the 1930s, only to fall again when Villanova's young men went off to war. The Depression and the war also forced the college to abandon or postpone its plans for physical expansion, thus changing the face of its campus forever. At the same time, the ways in which Villanovans interpreted the cataclysmic events of this period offer valuable insights into the mind of its Catholic faculty and students, and into the forces that shaped their collective consciousness.

Intellectually, Villanova had long dedicated itself to the pursuit of truth, but like all educational institutions, including other American colleges and universities, its view of the world reflected the experiences, current beliefs, and expectations of its various constituencies. For Villanovans these views of past, present, and future were shaped by three principal considerations: being Catholic, being American, and, for a great many Villanovans, being of Irish ancestry.

At Villanova's helm throughout most of the Depression and World War II was Reverend Edward Valentine Stanford, O.S.A. (1897–1966). Born in Boston, Father Stanford owed his middle name to the fact that he had come into the world on February 14, Valentine's Day. He attended Boston College before entering the Augustinian order, and began teaching at Villanova in the fall of 1918 while he was studying for the priesthood. Besides his classes in geometry and mechanical drawing in the Engineering Department, Stanford was college chaplain for several years before becoming president of Villanova in the summer of 1932. He would remain president until July 1944, the second-longest presidential term up to that time—and the third-longest in Villanova's 150-year history. Throughout his presidency, Stanford was active in many organizations of higher education, including the presidency of the Association of American Colleges (the first Catholic ever to hold that position), the National Conference of Church-Related Colleges, and the Association of College Presidents of Pennsylvania. He also sat on the boards of the American Council on Education and the National Catholic Education Association. These positions gave Stanford a keen understanding of American higher education, while giving Villanova wider recognition than it might have otherwise received.[1]

Intelligent, energetic, and firm in his convictions, Stanford was destined to be frustrated by outside forces over which he had no control. Chief among these was the Great Depression. Although many colleges were adversely affected by the economic crisis, several factors made Stanford's Villanova more vulnerable. Many of Villanova's students came from families that had just begun to experience economic success, which perhaps made them more susceptible to the Depression than the sons of economically more substantial families. The relatively small group of alumni and their lack of wealth, compared with graduates of larger and more famous institutions, meant that Villanova had little or no endowment to see it through difficult times. Yet its long experience with meager resources and its ability to rely on the contributed services of its Augustinian faculty and administrators proved to be valuable resources in riding out the economic storm.

The full effects of the Great Depression were not felt at Villanova, or anywhere else in the nation, for several years after the stock market crash of October 1929. The fact that upperclassmen in the early 1930s had entered college during the prosperous years of the late 1920s, and were determined to stay until graduation, also kept enrollments relatively high for a while. Consequently, Villanova reached its pre–World War II peak of 1,022 stu-

Reverend Edward V. Stanford, O.S.A. (*left*), President of Villanova College, 1932–44, and His Eminence Dennis Cardinal Dougherty (*right*) at the Centennial Dinner, September 20, 1942. VUA.

dents in the autumn of 1931, two full years after the Wall Street crash. The next fall, however, enrollment dipped to 823, a decrease of just over 18 percent. In order to help seniors to stay in school during the winter and spring of 1933, which included the worst months of the Depression, the administration allowed needy students to take courses tuition-free. About two dozen seniors took advantage of the offer. That same semester the board of trustees voted to cut professors' salaries by 10 percent in order to offset lost revenues to the college.[2]

Full-time registrations reached their low point in the fall of 1935 with just 701 students, or nearly 40 percent fewer than in September 1931. During this period Villanova's suburban location may have exacerbated enrollment problems, since there were fewer students within easy commuting distance than in the city of Philadelphia, where its chief Catholic competitors were located: La Salle College, which had just built its new campus at Belfield, experienced an actual increase in enrollment during the 1930s. There the student body went from 218 in 1932 to 408 in 1939. St. Joseph's, which had recently moved to its new Overbrook location, likewise experienced an increase—though not as great as La Salle's—from about 200 in the late 1920s to around 300 in 1939.[3] An improvement in the national economy during the mid-1930s led to an increase in student numbers at Villanova to 804 in the fall of 1936. Reacting favorably to the rise, the trustees restored the 10 percent cut from faculty salaries that had taken place three years before. By 1940 enrollment stood at 974, about the same as in the late 1920s.[4]

Since so many of Villanova's students were affected by the Depression, the wide student support on campus for Franklin D. Roosevelt's presidential bid in 1932 is understandable. Besides, most parents of Villanova students were Democrats at the time, as were a majority of Roman Catholics—especially Irish Catholics—who connected the Democratic Party with the interests of the common man and associated the Republican Party with wealthy Protestants and unwarranted attempts to regulate the personal habits of immigrants and their descendants.[5] It is thus not surprising that the *Villanovan* endorsed Franklin Roosevelt in both 1932 and 1936.

Although most students were not yet old enough to cast ballots—the voting age then being twenty-one—the *Villanovan* had begun taking presidential polls in 1928, when Democrat Alfred E. Smith, the first Catholic ever nominated for the office, predictably won the students' support by a large margin. In 1932 Roosevelt handily won the campus poll by 376 votes, compared with 51 who preferred Herbert Hoover. Socialist Party candidate Norman Thomas attracted 135 student supporters, a clear sign of the fear and discontent which Villanovans felt about the nation's economy. Four years later Roosevelt again swept the campus poll with 195 ballots to Alfred Landon's 52. The Socialist Thomas received only one vote that year, an indication that students approved of Roosevelt's programs to cope with the Depression.[6]

That Villanovans benefited directly from Franklin Roosevelt's relief programs could not be disputed. In the spring of 1935, for example, forty-five Villanova students were earning an average of fifteen dollars a week through the Emergency Employment Relief Bureau in Harrisburg, which in turn received funding through the Civil Works Administration (CWA) in Washington. By the fall of 1935 ninety Villanovans were participating in the program. In order to earn their money, students worked as assistants in the library, in laboratories, and in various offices, as well as in the groundskeeping department. The money did not go directly to the students, but was applied to their tuition bills. Villanova students later held similar campus jobs under the National Youth Administration (NYA), another relief agency created under Roosevelt's New Deal.[7]

Campus support for the New Deal was quite strong on the *Villanovan*'s editorial page. The newspaper began by applauding Roosevelt's bank holiday just after his inauguration in 1933 and kept up a steady beat of praise throughout the famous Hundred Days. Later it attacked the Supreme Court for invalidating early New Deal legislation. It also praised such programs as Social Security, the Tennessee Valley Authority, the Wagner Labor Relations Act, and public housing.[8] Often the editorials attacked American businessmen for their greed and immorality, as in November 1934 when an editorialist wrote that "business needs to be again reminded that, economic teachings to the contrary, ethical practices play a definite part in business recovery."[9]

Like many others in the United States, some Villanovans concluded that the American experiment was in great danger during the years of Depression. On the one hand, greed and rampant materialism had plunged the nation into an unprecedented national emergency. On the other hand, radical agitators were trying to take advantage of the misery in order to foment a Marxist revolution among the working classes. Only a return to God could save the United States, according to the *Villanovan*. One editorial went so far as to rejoice that Orson Welles's controversial radio broadcast of *War of the Worlds*, which took place on Halloween night of 1938, had forced many people to recognize their dependence on God.[10]

Such thoughts about the nation's problems and the role that Catholicism might play in saving modern America were in fact local reflections of a much larger phenomenon of the day known as the Catholic Action movement. The ecclesiastical authority for this movement rested in the so-called social encyclicals: *De Rerum Novarum* (*Of New Things*), issued by Pope Leo XIII in 1891, and *Quadragesimo Anno*, proclaimed forty years later (as the title suggests) by Pope Pius XI in 1931.[11] Both documents considered the social and economic upheavals brought about by the industrial revolution, and especially by exploitation of workers and the class hatred that had arisen as a consequence. At the root of this evil, according to *Rerum Novarum*, were a misguided liberalism and materialism. These had produced selfish individualism and greed, along with a disregard for the welfare of society as a whole. Only by practicing true Christian morality could the social order be restored.

In *Quadragesimo Anno* Pius XI repeated the call for social reconstruction according to Catholic principles.[12] The Pope also invited laity to play a major role in this struggle, as "valiant soldiers" who would do battle against atheism, secular materialism, and the newer threat of Communism. In Italy the church commissioned the *Azione Cattolica* to carry out this work among the faithful, and in the United States the National Catholic Welfare Conference (NCWC), forerunner of the American Conference of Catholic Bishops, resolved that individual dioceses were free to sanction Catholic Action groups.[13]

Villanova College's involvement with the Catholic Action movement came mainly through its support for a periodical called *The Christian Front* and its editor, Richard L. G. Deverall (1911– ).[14] Born in Brooklyn, New York, Deverall had come to Villanova in the fall of 1935 under the personal sponsorship of President Stanford, though just how and where Stanford met him is unknown. Yet it is clear that the Villanova president supported his cause. In a letter of recommendation for Deverall to the graduate program at Notre Dame University, Stanford wrote:

> I have taken a personal interest in Mr. Deverall because I believe he has possibilities. This interest dates back a year prior [1934] to his matriculation at Villanova. Since he has not had financial resources of his own, I have secured help for him in every way possible.[15]

Included in this help was a position as assistant in the "chemical laboratory" where he earned $500 a year—$300 of which came from NYA funds. While working on a degree in education, which he received in 1938, Deverall launched *The Christian Front* at Villanova.[16]

Father Stanford was careful to say that the journal was not officially sponsored by the college, but he freely admitted that its editor and all but one of its staff of eight were Villanova students. In addition, the college also provided Deverall with office space in Room 75 of what was then known as Mendel Hall (later Tolentine Hall).[17] Deverall also wrote frequent memoranda to Father Stanford to keep him informed of all his activities.

The first issue of *The Christian Front* appeared in January 1936, and by mid-1937 the magazine claimed a circulation of 3,500 copies an issue. It came out monthly, except for July and August, when a single, mid-summer issue appeared. An annual subscription was one dollar, with single issues selling for ten cents. Deverall built its circulation largely through circular letters to Catholic pastors and to the presidents of Catholic colleges and universities. In addition to the magazine itself, Deverall excerpted certain articles from the magazine and circulated them as leaflets to parishes, Catholic educational institutions, and college newspapers. It also sponsored conferences and study groups. As advertisements for *The Christian Front* indicated, it was more than just a magazine. It was a movement for "PEACE[,] ORDER[,], SOCIAL JUSTICE[,] and against MARXIST COMMUNISM[,] TOTALITARIAN FASCISM[,] INDUSTRIAL CAPITALISM."[18]

In an article by Deverall himself titled "Religion and Economics," the editor denied that economics was a science "in the same sense that chemistry is a science." This was because economics dealt with social behavior, in which the common good was supposed to be "paramount." Economic behav-

# THE CHRISTIAN FRONT

A MONTHLY MAGAZINE OF SOCIAL RECONSTRUCTION

**FOR A STRONGER CATHOLIC PRESS**
An Editorial

**ANOTHER ONSLAUGHT ON MODERN CAPITALISM**

**OUR REPLY TO LOUIS A. J. MERCIER'S ARTICLE**

**LADIES OF THE GRAIL**
By Eva Ross

Cover of an issue of *The Christian Front*, published at Villanova during the mid-1930s. VUA.

**VOL. 2 FEBRUARY, 1937 NO. 2**
**$1.00 A YEAR        10c A COPY**

ior was thus subject to Catholic morality. Neither liberalism nor Communism nor Fascism, none of which was grounded in Christianity, could supply a moral basis. Only the Catholic Church could "restore the science of economics to its proper position." According to Deverall, Catholic Scholasticism, as set down by the philosophers of the High Middle Ages, was the surest guide to economic salvation:

> When we read back in history, we note that during the Catholic Middle Ages—especially from the Eleventh to the Fourteenth centuries—the question of the Church and economics was unchallenged. The great doctors and moralists of the medieval Church ... considered such problems of economics as profits, interest-taking, justice in prices, the living wage, and the money problem. Their decisions were almost universally carried over into economic life and were expressed in the public laws. Many medieval ordinances on the just price found their inspiration in the teachings of St. Thomas Aquinas and the scholastics.[19]

In this regard Deverall was repeating the Pope's own admonition in *Quadragesimo Anno* that modern scholars renew their dedication to Neo-Thomism as a total philosophy of Catholic life, as well as a basis for solving modern problems, including those that afflicted the United States.[20]

Since Marxian Communism also condemned the current economic system, *The Christian Front* took special pains to discredit this philosophy in the process of offering a Christian substitute. In a circular letter to Catholic parishes, Deverall emphasized *The Christian Front*'s battle against Red revolution:

> The CHRISTIAN FRONT is struggling to avert the almost inevitable collapse and revolution in store for American society. THE CHRISTIAN FRONT is attempting not only to attack atheistic Communism, but to realistically endeavor to remove the causes of Communism.[21]

In a *Christian Front* leaflet entitled "The Social Encyclicals," author Norman McKenna insisted that Catholics who ignored the papal calls to combat Communism were in fact guilty of encouraging Communism.[22]

*The Christian Front* also aligned itself with the American peace movement in the late 1930s. In early February 1937 Deverall announced to the national press that his publication supported Senator Gerald Nye's call for a national referendum on war.[23] Two months later he wrote in a circular letter that *The Christian Front* "has dedicated itself to the task of building in America a determined will to peace, that will make impossible our entrance into another aggressive, unjust war."[24] On October 25, 1936 (the Feast of Christ the King), the magazine had sponsored a "Mass for Peace," in which numerous Catholic colleges and universities, including Villanova, participated across the United States.[25] The "Mass for Peace" was organized from *The Christian Front* office on the Villanova campus.

The positions of *The Christian Front* on Communism, peace, and other issues often found an echo in the editorial pages of the *Villanovan*. The connection was by no means a direct one, yet these editorials reveal that there was a general concurrence between the ideas of Deverall's publications and the Villanova community. Like *The Christian Front*, the *Villanovan* argued that Communism was a genuine threat to the United States in the 1930s. In November 1936 an editorial compared Communism to a poison, "a vial of hatred, and irreligion [which] has spread over the face of the earth." Lamentably, the editorialist continued, most Americans did not believe the threat was real. The writer thus felt bound to say, "Let the truth be known by every man: Communism is a potent threat in the United States."[26]

Although this and subsequent editorials railed against the Communists for their many cruelties and vicious attacks on private property, the greatest danger posed by Communism, according to the *Villanovan*, was its hatred of religion and its many depredations against Christianity. According to a piece that appeared late in 1938, "The many fallacies of the entire system of Communism need not be investigated since it is enough to point out the uncompromising proposal of Red Russia: Accept my social and economic program; accept my anti-religious program."[27]

There were suggestions in other editorials about how students might fight the Communist menace. One was support for the Catholic Action movement, in which *The Christian Front* was playing an ambitious part.[28] Another way was through support for Catholic education. On this subject one writer for the *Villanovan* went so far as to charge that the public schools of America, "by keeping Almighty God 'outside,' are in fact friends of Communism." Under the circumstances, "only the schools and college[s] of the Catholic Church in America are the real foes of Communism." This was a great irony, the writer added, because Catholics had often been accused of disloyalty. Now, he proclaimed, "Catholicism is the only force that can save America."[29] He had apparently forgotten the near impossibility of religious instruction in the public schools of a nation where such great pluralism made it impossible to satisfy the beliefs of all parents, in addition to the potential for religious discrimination in the classroom.

The student yearbook, the *Belle Air*, also raised the alarm by choosing anti-Communism as its theme for 1939.[30] The volume opened with dire warnings about the threat Communism posed to the very nature of American life:

> ... At present we are tolerating in the United States a movement instigated by the government of Soviet Russia, which ridicules our whole system as ineffective and is forcing on us the horror of atheistic Communism. This movement is thoroughly opposed to the principles upon which this country was founded.... We cannot betray our God, our country, and ourselves. Communism is treason. Its agents are traitors. It must endure no longer![31]

On the same opening pages of the *Belle Air* there were two large photographs, one of the Pope blessing the multitude in St. Peter's Square, the other of the U.S. Capitol building in Washington, D.C.

For more educated Catholics, Neo-Thomism was supposed to provide a powerful weapon in the battle against Communism. Thus in March 1938 readers of the *Villanovan* were advised:

> The importance of Thomas [Aquinas] to the Catholic college student of today is that he offers a philosophical rock out of the sea of Marxian

dialectical materialism. Against the blind determinism of the Marxian philosophers who see man as an economic animal acting as economic forces predestine him, Thomas raises the exalted position of man by showing what a magnificent creature is this man of reason.[32]

Sixty years later, following the end of the Cold War, such warnings that the United States was about to be overwhelmed by Communism appear shrill, exaggerated, and even quaint. Yet they reflected the fears of a Catholic college, and especially of its Augustinian community, who worried about real attacks on religion in general—and on the Catholic Church in particular—at the hands of revolutionary governments and their agents.

Fears of Communism also had much to do with how Villanovans viewed foreign affairs during the 1930s. One example concerned the anticlerical policies of the Mexican government.[33] In February 1935 an editorial writer for the *Villanovan* exclaimed, "We feel that something should be done, and quickly, to alleviate the suffering of the Christians in Mexico." The United States government, he added, should apply a trade embargo against Mexico until the anticlerical laws were repealed.[34] In April of the same year Villanova's president, Father Stanford, was outraged when some catalogs for a summer school program at the University of Mexico were sent to Villanova's Foreign Language Department. Because of an agreement between the United States and the Mexican government, such items could be sent postage-free. What angered Father Stanford was the fact that Mexico banned religious materials, even if the postage had been paid by the sender. Stanford also charged that the catalogs were propagandistic because they stated that all people were free to practice their religion in Mexico. His response was to protest to Postmaster General James A. Farley and a number of U.S. senators and congressmen, and to alert the Catholic press to what he considered an unfair postal policy between the United States and Mexico. His complaints had no effect, but they demonstrated just how sensitive Stanford was to left-wing anticlericalism.[35]

Given Father Stanford's position on Mexico, it is not surprising that many Villanovans took the side of the Spanish Nationalists under Generalissimo Francisco Franco in the Spanish Civil War (1936–39), as did a great many Catholics in the United States.[36] For Villanovans, Franco was a champion of the church against the Spanish Republicans, who were avowedly anticlerical and who found support among Spanish Communists (although the Republicans were not themselves Communists). This fear for the church in Spain allowed the *Villanovan* to overlook the atrocities committed by Franco, as well as his opposition to Spanish democracy.

As early as October 1936 the *Villanovan* denounced the Republicans in Spain as Communists, anarchists, and terrorists.[37] As the Civil War came to an end, an editorial asserted that American supporters of the Republican (anti-Franco) side were simply a pack of "parlor pinks."[38] Such attitudes contrasted sharply with those at nearby Swarthmore College, a Quaker institution, where the college community raised funds to send an ambulance to anti-Franco forces in Spain.[39] The difference in attitude between the two small colleges, one Quaker and the other Catholic, underlined the Catholic preoccupation with Communism and anticlericalism in Spain. (The absence of any published history of Haverford College since the early 1930s does not allow for any easy comparison with the area's other Quaker college.)

Thus in the wake of Franco's victory in early 1939 the *Villanovan* trumpeted his success:

> We at Villanova rejoice. We tell the world that Franco's victory is our victory and the victory of all right thinking religious and democratic people. Spain will return to her former Catholic glory. Christ will once again reign over all Castile. . . . Franco, we salute you! Long live Spain. Long live Christ, the Prince of Peace.[40]

When it came to Hitler's Germany, the *Villanovan* was entirely condemnatory in the late 1930s. But during the first two years of Hitler's rule, there were some attempts in the campus newspaper to understand his positions in foreign policy, such as Germany's reoccupation of the Rhineland in early 1936. Like many people in the United States and elsewhere in the world, the editorialist believed that Germany had been treated unfairly in the Treaty of Versailles and proposed that allowing Germany to reoccupy the Rhineland was only fair.[41] A year earlier, opinion had been divided over Hitler's decision to rearm. On March 20, 1935, an editorial denounced the Nazi leader as a "Peace Hater" for rearming Germany in defiance of the Versailles Treaty. The following week another writer defended the rearmament as a just reaction to the unfair treaty.[42]

Yet by 1937 and 1938 the *Villanovan* was denouncing Hitler for anti-Semitism: "The darkest ages in civilization do not rival this persecution in horror—it cries out to the heavens for revenge."[43] The newspaper also attacked Hitler and other Fascists for creating a godless nationalism: "Having cast aside God, [they] have set up in His place a new brazen image, the deified State."[44] Editorial opinion also came down against Italy's invasion of Ethiopia in 1935 and against the Italian people for "blindly" following Mussolini.[45] Yet Villanovans seemed oblivious to the Fascist characteristics of the Franco regime and to the fact that both Mussolini and Hitler had aided the Spanish dictator. At the same time, Villanovans agreed with the great majority of Americans that their country should stay out of any European war.[46] This time they were in full accord with most of Swarthmore's students, though Villanovans did not share the traditional pacifism of that Quaker institution.[47]

As Armistice Day (November 11) 1934 approached, the *Villanovan* lamented that Europe was rearming at a furious pace, making a mockery of Woodrow Wilson's crusade to end all wars less than a generation before.[48] Several editorials in early 1935 adopted a strident isolationist tone, opposing U.S. membership in the World Court and demanding "a policy of hands off in regard to foreign questions." Aliens in the United States who agitated for American intervention should be "shipped 'home' on the next boat."[49] Throughout 1935, editorials also agreed with those in Congress who advocated stronger neutrality legislation, including a ban on credit to belligerents.[50] At the same time the United States should try to use "moral persuasion" to keep the peace "without war or bloodshed."[51]

During the second half of 1936 the American press was full of stories about the romance of Britain's Edward VIII with the American divorcée, Wallis Warfield Simpson. Reflecting on the king's impending abdication and plans to marry Mrs. Simpson, the *Villanovan* declared that the woman "does not possess . . . an elementary idea of moral responsibility or decorum."[52] Two years later the campus newspaper was full of support for Britain's efforts to keep the peace over Czechoslovakia, and especially for Prime Minister Neville Chamberlain's meeting with Hitler at Munich.[53]

Yet the overall tone of editorials was decidedly anti-British, no doubt reflecting the large numbers of Irish Americans in Villanova's faculty and student body. This Irish connection was emphasized in 1940 when Joseph McGarrity (1874–1940) left Villanova's library part of his collection of some 10,000 items relating to Irish life. Born in Ireland, McGarrity was a founder of the Clan Na Gael, the American branch of the Fenian brotherhood, and was known throughout his life as a fierce advocate of Irish independence from Great Britain.[54] According to local tradition, McGarrity's friendship with the college librarian, Father Falvey, caused him to choose Villanova as a repository for these materials.

Perhaps in the spirit of Irish-American Anglophobia, in November 1938 the *Villanovan* castigated Britain for winking at German propaganda against the United States being disseminated in South America in hopes, it was alleged, that the British might share in expanded South American trade. Three months later, in January 1939, the *Villanovan* complained that the British were sending their best diplomats and literary figures to the United States as advocates for their point of view in Europe.[55]

The German attack on Poland in September 1939, and the beginning of World War II in Europe, did nothing to change the isolationist tone on campus. In October of that year the *Villanovan* declared that the selfishness of the victors in World War I had created Hitler and that those who were now at war with him had no one to blame but themselves:

> Why should we stop Hitler . . . ? Let them stop Hitler, let the wily and suave diplomats of the old world stop Hitler—they made him. Their greed is responsible for his rise. The national and international selfishness of the Versailles Treaty kindled the fire which has forged and tempered this modern madman [Hitler]. . . .Those who divided the swag in [1919] must now accept the consequences. WE ASKED FOR NOTHING. WE ASK FOR NOTHING NOW.[56]

Such reactions were apparently shared by Villanova's alumni, as reflected in an outspoken article by Aloysius L. Fitzpatrick, class of 1937, that appeared in the February 1939 issue of the *Villanova Alumnus*:

> HURRAH FOR ENGLAND! We'll fight her wars. Hurrah for France! We'll protect her interests. Bravo for Russia. We'll wipe out her enemies. But for the U.S., alas, not even a voice raised in cheer. . . .
>
> War for "insuring democracy" against the dictator nations would be unjust, jeopardizing the lives of citizens; it would be cold, premeditated murder of not only the men on the other side but also those of our own who would make cannon fodder. . . .
>
> Let's take [George] Washington's advice and, following it, we will make America safe for Americans and leave the rest of the world to settle their own quarrels in their own way.[57]

In his customary address at the opening of the academic year on September 22, 1939, Father Stanford conveyed similar though more subdued feelings. He compared the students' situation with their confreres of just twenty-five years before, on a similar September day in 1914, little more than a month after the outbreak of World War I. "Students then," he reminded his young charges, "had no idea what awaited them. But before the freshmen of 1914 had become seniors, the garb of students had changed to khaki uniforms[,] and rough shod boots beat a military tread on these very pavements." He then asked, "Is history to repeat itself . . . ? It is undoubtedly the sincere wish and prayer of every one of us, that in God's Providence, American youth may be spared the repetition of 1917 madness [when the United States entered the war]."[58]

A year later, despite the fall of the Low Countries and France, Father Stanford had not changed his mind about staying out of another world war. In the Fall 1940 issue of the *Villanova Alumnus*, he wrote:

> In days gone by, we were concerned about making the world safe for democracy. Now we know there is no such thing as making the world safe for democracy. Our real problem today is to make democracy function properly in our own country that we may show by our example that democracy is a system that could be safe for the world.[59]

If others wanted to emulate American democracy, so much the better; if not, the United States was not obliged to force it upon them.

A campus poll showed that Villanova students agreed with their president. In October 1939, students said they opposed war by a vote of 538 to 18. A year later, in the fall of 1940, the *Villanovan* came out against the recently enacted conscription law but held that it was the legal and patriotic duty of students to register for the draft.[60] As one might expect, Hitler's attack on the Soviet Union in June 1941 failed to elicit any sympathy for the victim in the pages of the *Villanovan*. In October of that year it criticized the trustees of Philadelphia's Convention Hall for allowing the Communist Party to hold a meeting there, the hall's officials arguing that Soviet Russia was now a victim of Fascism and could thus assist in America's own defense program. In response to the permission thus granted, the *Villanovan* asked:

> Are we to allow Communism, still the most detestable of all forms of un-Americanism, to gain headway under the flimsy disguise of "national defense"?
>
> Has hysteria so poisoned our reason that we are going to plant within ourselves a tape-worm, that we may build up a defense against obesity?[61]

As far as the *Villanovan* was concerned, the war was just another grab for booty by corrupt European powers. This time the American people would not be duped into believing it was some kind of war for democracy—or for any other noble cause.[62] The *Villanovan* did approve of lend-lease, but only because it might help to keep the United States out of the conflict. However, it consistently opposed American naval convoys for such aid throughout the fall of 1941, announcing in October that its unwavering editorial policy would be to oppose any American military involvement in the war. Continuing condemnations of all sides in the conflict led one reader to charge in November that the *Villanovan* was patently anti-British, a charge the editors denied.[63]

In fact, the student newspaper did find fault with all the combatants: Both Germany and the Soviet Union were cruel and dictatorial, as well as devoted to naked materialism and territorial aggrandizement. In addition, the Soviets were outspoken atheists dedicated to destroying Christianity. As for the British, they were out to save an empire that had exploited and persecuted millions of peoples over the centuries, including the Irish. (Even in 1946, after World War II was over, an editorial in the *Villanovan* could say that there were still many in America "whose fires flare and whose souls writhe when the very name of Britain is mentioned."[64])

The debate over whether the United States should enter the war came to a sudden halt with Japan's attack on Pearl Harbor on December 7, 1941. It also meant that the United States now found itself allied with the hated Soviet Union and a suspect British Empire, opinions the *Villanovan* vented in its December 16, 1941, issue. In the weeks and months ahead the newspaper gave its unstinting support to the American war effort, but doubts about America's allies continued to surface. In August 1942 a writer hoped that the Grand Alliance might save the Soviet people from Communism, if only through the superior example of the United States:

> It is our duty as American Christians to set the finest type of example, to show the Russian people the way to God, to common good, to happiness. So far we have not definitely discouraged Communism in our own land. Let us do it today. . . .
>
> Our situation in Russia's trial is unique. We wish her to be victorious. We also wish her reformed. We supply her with the necessities of a military victory. Let us supply her with the necessities of a moral one.[65]

As the war progressed, doubts about Soviet as well as British motives began to mount. In March 1944 the *Villanovan* asserted that the American people were not

> ignorant of the facts that Russia is fighting for Russia and not for democracy, that England is waging war to sustain the Empire, that Eire's [independent Ireland's] neutrality is being violated, . . . that India is truly the victim of aggression, that *imperialistic* tendencies and acts in general are responsible for the present conflict. . . . [66] (Emphasis added)

By June 1945 the student newspaper was crying appeasement over the decision to grant the Soviets a veto in the new United Nations Security Council.[67] Throughout the war, the concerns of Villanovans as Catholics, and often as Irish Catholics, were mingled with their determination to serve as patriotic Americans.

Whatever the doubts about America's allies, Villanovans threw themselves wholeheartedly into the war effort. On December 8, 1941, the day Congress officially declared war on Japan, Father Stanford told students to remain calm and to continue their studies "most diligently" until the time came for them to enter the service. Meanwhile, Stanford urged, they should prepare themselves for whatever might lie ahead: "Neglect of your spiritual and physical welfare, failure to employ your best efforts in your studies, waste of materials of any kind are now offenses against the patriotism which you owe your country."[68]

In actuality Villanova's contributions to the war began in the summer of 1940, when the house chapter voted to allow the college to participate in national defense training programs, the idea being that such preparations would help keep the United States out of war.[69] Pursuant to this vote, the School of Engineering began offering courses to both men and women in the Philadelphia area who wanted to acquire skills for local defense industries. These took place at Cooper Hatch High School in Camden, New Jersey; at Northeast Catholic and West Catholic high schools in Philadelphia; and on the Villanova campus itself. Enrollment for the courses was 355 in February 1941, and just over 500 when the program was repeated in February 1942. Such courses continued to be offered in area high schools as well as on the Villanova campus after the American declaration of war. The college also cooperated with the Civil Aeronautics Board to give classroom work for pilot training. In order to coordinate Villanova's National Defense efforts, Father Stanford appointed three faculty committees in February 1941: one for engineer training, one for civilian pilot training, and one for selective service.[70]

Soon after the United States entered the war, Villanova adopted a special wartime calendar that featured three full terms each year. It remained in place from the spring of 1942 until the spring of 1946. At first the summer term ran from early June to mid-September, the fall term from mid-October to late January, and the spring term from early February to mid-May. Later the starting dates were advanced by a week or two. There were also three commencements annually, following the end of each session. By taking advantage of this accelerated pace a student could theoretically graduate in three years—or at least fit in as much college as possible before being called to military duty.[71]

In addition to a new schedule, there were blackouts, air-raid drills, and compulsory physical-fitness classes three days a week. The college also planted two victory gardens (vegetable gardens), one on the slope between Corr Hall and the Pennsylvania Railroad tracks, the other near the southeast corner of Ithan Avenue and Lancaster Pike (now a parking lot).[72]

At an all-male institution like Villanova there were serious concerns about the effects of military service upon enrollment. During the first year of war there was little decline because the various services were not equipped to accept large numbers of recruits right away.[73] Indeed, by participating in the Army Enlisted Reserve Corps students could receive preliminary officer training while still in college, and also be immune to the draft while in the program. A considerable number of Villanova men enrolled, although exact numbers are not available. The last of them apparently remained on campus until April 5, 1943, when they reported to camp at New Cumberland, Maryland. The men had a special dinner the evening before in the college dining room at old Mendel (later Tolentine) Hall. Early the next morning faculty and friends walked down to the Villanova train station with them to see them off to an unknown fate.[74]

The departure of these students, in addition to those who were drafted or who joined other military programs, would have been disastrous for Villanova's enrollment had it not been for the installation of a Navy officer training unit, known as the V-12 program, in the summer of 1943. Father Stanford began petitioning for such a program at Villanova in the summer of 1940, after hearing that the Navy intended to open new officer training programs on college and university campuses. He was unsuccessful at first, because the Navy decided to award new units to larger institutions, but Stanford's persistence and the American declaration of war in late 1941 eventually resulted in success for Villanova. He not only secured a unit for

At the Villanova train station, faculty and students say good-bye to men of the Army Enlisted Reserve as they depart for active duty on April 5, 1943. VUA.

Navy V-12 men with several civilian students and J. Stanley Morehouse, M.E., Dean of Engineering, 1944. VUA.

the campus in early 1942, but was invited to Washington by the Secretary of the Navy to join six other educators to plan the wartime program, a selection that may have stemmed from his many leadership positions in American higher education.[75]

The first V-12 recruits reported to Villanova on July 1, 1943: 400 apprentice seamen and 200 Marines. Of the group, 250 were former Villanova students; the rest came from all over the United States. The Field House became a "ship's store," where the men were outfitted with uniforms and other equipment. Navy personnel took over offices on the first floor of Mendel Hall (that is, Tolentine), while the 600 V-12 students occupied Fedigan, Austin, and Alumni halls, as well as part of Mendel Hall.[76]

Reveille came for the V-12 men every morning at 6:00, except for Sundays. There was a half-hour of calisthenics and drill on Mendel Field before breakfast at 7:15 in the old Mendel Hall cafeteria. Classes began at 8:30 and continued until 5:45. Lunch was from 1:00 to 1:30, with dinner beginning at

4:45. After that the men had "free time" until 8:00, at which point a compulsory two-hour study period began. There was another hour of free time with "lights out" at 11:00. On Saturday morning there was one hour of drill at 11:15, after which the men were "on liberty" until Sunday at midnight. In addition to this regular schedule, there were special classes in physical training, featuring boxing, judo, swimming, and intramural sports. The V-12 students took their academic classes—with an emphasis on mathematics, physics, and mechanical drawing—along with a dwindling number of civilian students and were taught by Villanova's regular faculty. Only one class, on naval organization, was given by a Navy instructor.[77]

Despite this demanding schedule for the V-12 students, extracurricular activities did not disappear completely from campus. In fact, the Navy wanted the men to participate in activities so long as they did not interfere with training, believing that they would be good for morale. Besides playing intramural sports, the V-12 men helped Villanova to field an intercollegiate football team during the war. Some also worked on the student newspaper and yearbook, both of which shrank in size, partly to conserve paper. As the war went on there were regular stories in the newspaper about Villanovans in the service, including more and more reports of deaths and serious injury to Villanova's sons.[78]

Wartime dances helped to keep spirits high on campus. Formal dances, such as the elaborate Belle Air Ball, were canceled during the height of the war, but there were several casual "hops," and unprecedented summer dances. There were also entertainments like the "musical salute" to the V-12 unit held in the Field House on April 29, 1944. Featuring the Les Brown orchestra, it was sponsored by the Coca-Cola company and broadcast coast-to-coast by the NBC radio network.[79]

Father Stanford described this transformation of the campus scene in the October 1943 issue of the *Villanova Alumnus*:

> At this writing, your Alma Mater has become thoroughly accustomed to the sight of uniformed members of the Navy and Marines. They are everywhere on the campus. They beat a military tattoo on the pavements. They throng the corridors, classrooms and laboratories. They crowd the dining hall. They lend a military touch to the services in the chapel as they kneel at worship. The campus would, undoubtedly, present a novel appearance to you and you would thrill with pride in the knowledge that your college has been privileged to cooperate so intimately in the war effort.[80]

Wartime enrollment figures show that the Army Enlisted Reserve Corps and the V-12 program saved Villanova from real financial disaster. In the fall

Wartime dance at the Field House, Spring 1944. VUA.

of 1942 there were 992 students at Villanova, about the same number as the year before. In early 1943 the count fell to 905, and in the fall of 1943 it stood at 897. Enrollment then slipped to 730 in the spring of 1944, to 537 in the fall of 1944, and to just 493 in the spring of 1945.[81] That enrollments would have been far worse after the summer of 1943, if not for the V-12 program, can be determined by comparing the numbers of civilian and military students on campus. In the fall of 1943 there were 303 civilians and 594 V-12 students, or nearly twice as many military as civilian. By the spring of 1944 the Navy men outnumbered the civilians by 570 to 160—almost four to one. Thereafter the predominance of the V-12 program declined somewhat as the Navy cut back on enlistments and as a few veterans began returning during the last year of the war. Thus in the spring of 1945 there were 318 Navy men and 175 civilians, the latter including some 27 veterans. By then the ratio of military to civilian was slightly less than two to one.[82]

A comparison with La Salle and St. Joseph's colleges is revealing. The relatively small campuses and limited dormitory facilities of those colleges did not allow them to host military training programs, so enrollments plummeted. At La Salle, student numbers declined from 411 in 1940 to 116 in 1944, and at St. Joseph's from just over 300 to only 84 during the same period. Notre Dame, which had considerable residence facilities, followed the path of Villanova with a Navy training program and was saved from the drastic cut in enrollment that affected La Salle and St. Joseph's.[83]

Despite the wartime emergency, Villanova managed to celebrate its 100th anniversary in 1942–43, although many of the events that had been projected had to be canceled or scaled back. (Notre Dame, which also marked its centenary in 1942, likewise had to curtail its celebrations.[84]) Plans for Villanova's centennial observances had begun nearly a decade before, in the spring of 1934, when the college's board of trustees resolved to hold such a celebration. In 1939 the college formed an "executive committee" to oversee the event, and in 1940 Villanova began setting aside funds for the celebration.[85]

The centennial plans included a 100th anniversary history to be written by Reverend Francis E. Tourscher, O.S.A., who had succeeded Father Middleton as librarian and archivist. Besides being familiar with the historical sources, Father Tourscher had just published a history of the American Augustinians under the somewhat misleading title *Old Saint Augustine's in Philadelphia, With Some Records of the Work of the Austin Friars in the United States* (1937). Tourscher had already begun assembling materials for the college history when his unexpected death in 1939 brought the project to an end.[86]

Although there would be no complete centennial history, the *Belle Air* started publishing twenty-five-year segments of the college's history in its 1940 edition. An account of the entire one hundred years, including both pictures and text, appeared in the edition for 1943. Although not as detailed as Father Middleton's *Sketch* a half-century before, it too was more of a chronology than a true history, with very little analysis of decisions and events. It drew heavily on Middleton's work and various internal publications. The college and Augustinian archives were also consulted, but largely, it seems, as a source of photographs and other illustrations.[87]

The centennial observances began on September 20, 1942, with a Solemn Pontifical Mass of Thanksgiving celebrated in the Field House by His Eminence Dennis Cardinal Dougherty, Archbishop of Philadelphia. The ceremony began with a ringing of the old college bell, recently returned to campus and now mounted on a special stand (where it could be struck on the side by its heavy iron clapper, removed temporarily for the ringing). On January 15, 1943, the students held their Centennial Ball in the Field House, using a horse and carriage to transport guests to and from rail and bus stations. In addition to symbolizing Villanova's roots in the preautomobile age, the vehicle was a practical response to gasoline shortages during the war.

The centennial year came to an end with an academic convocation at the Field House on May 3, 1943, which included delegations from dozens of

Centennial Mass, Villanova College Field House, September 20, 1942. VUA.

colleges and universities in the northeastern United States.[88] In his welcoming address Father Stanford remarked that war had disrupted the college's centennial festivities "just as it overshadowed our seventy-fifth anniversary in 1917 and 1918."[89] He might have added, but did not, that the war had disrupted many of his other plans for Villanova, as well as the dreams of hundreds of its young men who had gone to war. Villanovans would have to wait more than two years for peace and for the resumption of the many projects that had been put aside for the duration.

The campus was alerted to the war's end on August 14, 1945, by the ringing of bells. Many students as well as neighboring Catholics converged on St. Thomas of Villanova Church to offer their prayers and thanksgivings. Meanwhile the college band began gathering on Austin Field for an impromptu parade. A fire truck soon arrived from a local company and added its clanging bell to the festivities. According to the *Villanovan*, "Lancaster Pike was alive with more traffic than it has seen since the beginning of the war, and the sound of tooting horns and cheering people became almost deafening as the evening wore on."[90] At least sixty-five Villanovans, including the Navy V-12 men, had given their lives to make this victory possible.

Students and faculty processing from St. Thomas of Villanova Church to the Field House, Commencement 1944. The intersection is Lancaster Pike (U.S. Route 30) and Ithan Avenue. VUA.

Although Villanovans had not welcomed the war, and had expressed serious misgivings about the motives of America's allies, the college and its men had sacrificed much to the nation's cause. In the end Villanova was proud of the patriotic duty that it, as a Catholic institution, had performed for the nation. Of course, no one could realize on that warm August evening of victory celebrations just how the war might affect humanity in the years ahead. Only a later generation could know that the war would remain a major engine of change for the next five decades—at Villanova and in the world beyond. The century-old Augustinian institution would thus face new challenges to its identity as a Catholic college in America.

# COLLEGE TO UNIVERSITY

Ⓞne immediate effect of the war's end was an unparalleled boom in higher education throughout the United States as millions of veterans took advantage of generous educational benefits from the federal government. By the fall of 1946 Villanova's student population was double what it had been just before Pearl Harbor. Within twenty years, with the baby-boom generation in full possession of Villanova, there would be seven times as many students on its Main Line campus (counting all divisions) as before the war. New buildings, new academic programs, a greatly expanded lay faculty, and several administrative reforms would accompany this explosion in numbers. These factors allowed the small liberal arts college Villanova had been throughout its first century of existence to become a university in name as well as in fact.

Although the official change of designation came in 1953, Villanova's transformation from college to university had begun well before that year and continued for many years thereafter. As with earlier changes, the question of how to maintain its Catholic identity within the competitive context of American higher education would present a major challenge. As in the past, these changes at Villanova would be initiated and carried out by the Augustinian leadership.

In certain respects the movement toward university status had begun early in the century with the founding of a School of Engineering in 1905 and a School of Science in 1915. There was also a summer school, beginning in 1918, and a Night School, held at Hallahan High School in Philadelphia, starting in 1928. A School of Commerce and Finance opened in 1921. Ten years later, in 1931, Villanova created a separate Graduate School, although it appears that some form of graduate studies had been offered as early as 1911. The college inaugurated a Department of Nursing in 1933, which offered courses only off-campus.[1]

In the late 1920s Villanova College was subdivided into four separate schools: (1) Arts, (2) Science, (3) Commerce and Finance, and (4) Engineering—each with its own dean. In reality, however, the deans were more like department chairmen and had little or no power to set policy.[2] In the spring of 1940, as part of a comprehensive report on the institution, Father Stanford proposed that these largely symbolic deanships be abolished and replaced by one Dean of the College, a practice at most other small colleges in the United States. The Dean of the College would be in charge of all academic programs, serve as an ex-officio member of all academic committees, and be the director of a merged Arts and Science division. The other divisions (Engineering, and Commerce and Finance) would be headed by directors instead of deans, as they had been before the late 1920s. The faculty would be organized into separate departments, which as of 1940 existed only for Education, Chemistry, Biology, and Engineering.[3]

In many respects Father Stanford was proposing that Villanova should abandon the trappings of a university and affirm its status as a small liberal arts college. Having just passed through the Great Depression, and with no inkling of the great expansion to come only a half-dozen years later, Stanford was in fact looking for ways to make Villanova more cost-efficient. Indeed, he feared that private colleges were facing a large-scale crisis as the 1940s began. Drawing upon insights from his various positions in national and regional organizations of higher education, he began his report on restructuring Villanova College with a warning of the dangers ahead: "There is, in a sense, a handwriting on the wall which, no matter how it may be interpreted, by various educators, reveals difficulties ahead [for private colleges]."[4]

According to Stanford, such difficulties arose from several sources: the decline of private wealth as a result of heavy taxation, increased public funding for municipal and state institutions, the development of junior colleges, and a declining birth rate in the 1930s. "These are facts which admit to little debate," he insisted. Under the circumstances only "the largest and strongest of the independent colleges and universities will survive."[5]

Besides streamlining its administration, Stanford believed that other steps had to be taken if Villanova were to endure as a Catholic college in America, and that quality, far more than quantity, was the proper route for Villanova. Thus the college should strive to improve its laboratories, dining halls, dormitories, and recreational facilities, but the greatest physical need was a new library; the present was still housed in the east wing of Austin Hall, and facilities were so cramped that stacks for some 20,000 books had been built in the basement of Vasey Hall, then the Commerce and Finance Building, to house the overflow.[6]

The emphasis on quality extended to the faculty. Stanford believed that a strong departmental organization would allow chairmen to identify weaker faculty members and make appropriate recommendations to the dean. He also proposed higher salaries for the teaching staff and a procedure, which did not then exist, for establishing rank and tenure.[7]

Finally, Stanford advocated curriculum reforms at Villanova. Central to these reforms was a movement away from the college's still largely pre-scribed curriculum and replacing it with a modified elective system similar to the system many other colleges and universities had adopted around the turn of the century. In Stanford's own words, "Students who are candidates for a particular degree, are, for the most part, forced into a common mold. Majors and minors are largely a fiction, if we have regard to the sense in which these terms are understood in other institutions."[8] In other words, Villanova students did not have the freedom to select genuine majors and minors, as at many other American colleges, especially colleges that were not Catholic.

In particular, Stanford believed that Villanova needed to offer students some genuine choices. As he put it, "The curriculum provides for electives, but this is largely a fiction, as the elective is usually picked for the student and the subject which is offered is largely determined by chance."[9] Of special concern was science and engineering, which gave students few opportunities to take courses in the humanities.

In the last analysis, Villanova had to compete with other colleges and universities in the United States, measuring itself against national standards in higher education. Because it had not adopted such standards, Stanford asserted, Villanova was already experiencing difficulties with "educational accrediting agencies," the nature of which he did not elaborate. But there was no doubt in his mind that the time had come for the college to embrace nationwide standards:

> Some years ago we might have been able to go our own way, without being concerned about what other colleges were doing, but in the present-day educational world we have little choice. We must com-pare ourselves with other colleges.... Such matters, therefore, as accreditation, teacher requirements, rank, tenure, etc. must be gov-erned by standards set up with the general consent of all colleges.[10]

In January 1941 the faculty gave overwhelming approval to Stanford's plans. Four years earlier, in 1937, he had managed to set up a faculty pension program under the Teachers Insurance and Annuity Association (TIAA), making Villanova the first Catholic college to do so. (Villanova's contribution to TIAA was meager, however, and the resulting annuities for faculty were very low, becoming even more inadequate as the years went by.) In May 1941 the college also adopted tenure rules, but under the procedure established at Villanova, decisions about tenure were apparently made by the administration alone, not in collaboration with a rank-and-tenure committee. At some other colleges and universities, by contrast, faculty could exert a strong voice in the matter.[11]

It is also significant that Stanford had apparently worked up his plans for Villanova without any input from the faculty and student body, and that he asked for reactions to his proposals only after he had completed them. While Stanford wanted to move Villanova ahead, he assumed that these changes could come exclusively from the top down, a procedure very much in line with Catholic tradition and the operation of the local Augustinian community. Such hierarchical methods would be seen as serious obstacles to institutional improvement only a decade or two later.

Well before he put his plan together, Father Stanford had realized that improving Villanova would take a great deal of money, far more than the college was able to generate through tuition and other student fees. Throughout his years in office he worked diligently to raise such funds but was often frustrated by the continuing Depression and then by World War II. Yet even if times had been more propitious, Villanova would have faced difficulty in amassing great sums of money, as indicated by the fund-raising survey commissioned under Stanford's immediate predecessor, Reverend James H. Griffin, O.S.A.

The study had been done in 1929 by the John Price Jones Corporation of New York City and was titled "A Survey and Plan of Fund Raising for Villanova College." Besides obtaining money for new buildings, Price Jones pointed to the college's great need for an income-producing endowment, noting that "Villanova is one of the very few institutions of higher learning in the country which is altogether without endowment [of any consequence]."[12] Proposing that the college would have approximately 2,000 students by 1940, the survey estimated that it would need an endowment of nearly $12 million to provide adequately for their needs. More immediately, Villanova had to raise $2,300,000 as a start on this endowment and for the buildings it wanted to erect over the next few years.[13]

One of the most important potential sources of such funds for any institution, according to the Price Jones survey, was its alumni. The survey estimated that there were about 3,000 living graduates of Villanova at the time.

Reverend James H. Griffin, O.S.A.,
President of Villanova College,
1926–32. VUA.

Unfortunately the alumni were not well organized. The college did not have
a complete list of graduates, and it had never engaged a paid alumni secretary to keep track of former students. Since the college's most rapid growth
had come during the last ten years, its alumni were comparatively young.
The great majority of them were under forty and thus not of an age where
they had accumulated significant amounts of money or were making plans
about how to dispose of sizable estates. Even Villanova's older alumni, the
survey concluded, were not particularly wealthy.[14]

To raise substantial sums for endowment, as well as for certain immediate
purposes, Villanova had to go beyond its alumni—and even beyond the
local Catholic community. Since Philadelphia was then the third-largest city
in the United States and one of the nation's most important centers of
manufacturing and trade, there was plenty of wealth to be tapped by colleges and universities in the Quaker City. But as the Price Jones study
pointed out, the wealthiest Philadelphians were likely to be Protestants,
who applied their educational philanthropy to the University of Pennsylvania or to smaller institutions like Haverford, Swarthmore, and Bryn Mawr.[15]
In addition, most Protestants, and even some of the Catholics who were
surveyed, thought that Villanova was mainly a seminary for training priests
and were unaware that it was a genuine four-year college, the great majority
of whose students had no intention of entering the clergy. One reason for
this perception, according to Price Jones, was that the college was not well
publicized in the metropolitan press. In order to be successful at fund-

raising, Villanova would have to mount an aggressive publicity campaign to attract favorable attention from the general public.[16]

Unfortunately, the survey's predictions of how difficult it might be to raise substantial amounts of money proved all too true. The Villanova College Fund, as it was officially called, was launched in January 1930 in the aftermath of the great stock market crash and resultant economic uncertainty. By 1936, the fund had brought in a dismal total of $13,000, well under 1 percent of even the short-range goal of $2,300,000.[17]

Although the Depression was certainly a major factor in the disastrous failure of the fund-raising campaign, Villanova should have been able to do better than it did. The college was determined to remain Catholic and Augustinian, but it would have to make itself known to a wider audience and create a more active alumni organization if it hoped to succeed in future fund drives. Only time would tell if these twin goals could be merged into something that was compatible with the academic world at large as well as with Villanova's own mission.

There is no direct evidence that Father Stanford read the Price Jones survey before or after assuming the presidency in 1932, but his habit of thoroughness in everything he undertook would lead one to suppose that he examined it with great interest. Indeed, many of the steps he took to invigorate Villanova's alumni and to raise the college's endowment followed closely upon the suggestions made by Price Jones.

Realizing that a strong alumni organization was essential to any fund-raising, Stanford tackled this issue shortly after becoming president. Although various associations of Villanova alumni had existed since the nineteenth century, its organization had been weak and its efforts to aid the college had been sporadic. Stanford's first step in reinvigorating the alumni was to hire an alumni secretary in the summer of 1932. Next he encouraged the alumni to establish a magazine that could be used to communicate with former graduates about activities on campus and to raise funds. First appearing in March 1933, the publication was called the *Villanova Alumni News* until 1936, when its name was changed to the *Villanova Alumnus*. It regularly featured a message from the president, as well as reports about what was happening on campus and in the various regional alumni clubs. These clubs were in existence when Stanford took office, but most had become inactive. The magazine also gave extensive coverage to Villanova sports, especially to football.[18]

Besides launching the alumni magazine, Stanford called in 1937 for the reorganization or establishment of local alumni clubs in any area of the nation where there were at least twenty graduates within a radius of fifteen miles. Beginning in 1938, he made annual visits to the various alumni clubs in order to stimulate their interest in the old alma mater, and in December

1940 he could proudly report that there were now twenty-three active alumni clubs, up from just two or three when he began his campaign. Starting in 1936, there was also an annual alumni weekend, usually held in early June. These weekends featured class reunions at five-year intervals. Thus in June 1938, there were gatherings for the classes of 1918, 1923, 1928, and 1933. Supplementing these gatherings were the Homecoming football games in late September or early October, and annual alumni dances. In 1933 the Alumni Ball, as it was called, took place in the newly built Field House, but by the late 1930s the event was being held in a hotel ballroom downtown or in a suburban country club. The National Alumni Association was directed by a board of governors, a president, and other officers, who were elected by the membership.[19]

Father Stanford made constant appeals to the alumni and to any other of Villanova's several constituencies—parents, students, Augustinian parishes, and the college trustees—to build what he liked to call the college's scholarship endowment. His constant emphasis on scholarship funds made a great

Dinner during Alumni Weekend, June 10–12, 1949, in the dining room of St. Thomas of Villanova Monastery. At the head of the table is Reverend Francis X. N. McGuire, O.S.A., President of Villanova College/University, 1944–54. VUA.

deal of sense, given that there were only three "regularly funded scholarships" available in 1932. All the rest offered by the college were unfunded and therefore represented a great loss of potential revenue to the institution, an especially difficult burden during this year of depression. In all, Villanova granted 112 scholarships in 1932 for a loss of revenue just over $100,000. Virtually all such support went to Catholic students, including athletes. In July 1932, for example, the local house chapter directed that "athletic scholarships be awarded to Catholics only." Exceptions to this could be made "only with consent of [the] House Chapter at [the] request of [the] President."[20]

This decision not only confirmed that assistance was reserved for Catholic students, but also showed how powerful the monastery was in running the college in general and the athletic program in particular. Many of the nonathletic scholarships were reserved for high schools under Augustinian auspices, to which the Augustinian parishes were encouraged to contribute. Yet another indication that scholarships were for Catholics only is reflected in a poster sent by Villanova in 1935 to Catholic high schools. It read in part: "Catholic young men who are recent High School Graduates and in need of financial help to assist them through college, are eligible to apply for examination."[21] All this was further confirmation of the tremendous influence the Augustinians continued to have at Villanova, and of the college's strong identification as a Catholic institution.[22]

Ever mindful of Villanova's academic reputation, Father Stanford was by no means elated to find that 88 of 112 scholarships awarded in 1932 went to athletes, and that 44 of those were for football alone, at a time when the football program was losing money. Yet he apparently agreed with the alumni that football was an important source of publicity for the college, and he did nothing to try to scale back the sport at Villanova. The exception was when he had to uphold a short-lived ruling, in 1932, by the Middle States Association of College and Secondary Schools, Villanova's most important accrediting agency, that athletic scholarships were to be discontinued.[23]

In order to raise money for academic scholarships, Father Stanford tried several strategies during the 1930s. One was the establishment of class scholarships. These were formally authorized by the board of trustees in 1934 but had actually started with the class of 1928.[24] The contributions were small even for the 1930s, ranging from a high of $441 for the class of 1935 to $75 for the class of 1933.[25] In addition to these sums, the college was able to obtain several larger donations from individuals. The most impressive of these came from William Simpson, one of the two lay members of the board of trustees, who made three donations of approximately $5,000 each for scholarships.[26] By March 1937 Stanford could announce to the trustees that Villanova's endowment for scholarships was now $72,000, with another $14,000 in general endowment funds. At the end of 1939, scholarship funds had risen to approximately $90,000. The college was still far below several of its competitors among Catholic men's colleges, especially Boston College, which reportedly had an endowment of $385,864 in 1935, and Holy Cross, which claimed one of $170,000 during the same year.[27] It was also a tiny fraction of the $12 million recommended by Price Jones back in 1929. Even so, Stanford's persistence was beginning to pay off, however modestly.

As Villanova's 100th anniversary approached, Stanford announced a Centennial Fund in 1940. The alumni were asked to give $40,000, the money to be used to build a desperately needed library. Although prosperity was returning as the nation began to spend lavishly for armaments, the alumni had managed to raise only $15,000 by October 1941, and as late as the summer of 1944 they were being urged in the *Villanova Alumnus* to fulfill their "Centennial Pledge."[28] Despite all the hard work Stanford and others had put into building up the alumni organization over a decade's time, it still was not a dependable source of fund-raising for the college. Its relatively small size, comparative youth, and lack of substantial wealth remained the major obstacle, a fact that would not change for some time to come.

In any case, Stanford would not be in a position to encourage the alumni further or to carry out his wider plans for the college, for in the summer of 1944 the provincial chapter decided to replace him as president. Stanford had clearly wanted to stay on, as he explained in a memorandum to provincial authorities dated May 14, 1944:

> In view of the critical situation which now confronts the college and the manifest grave disadvantages which will come to the College through a change in administration at this time and because of the experience and contacts which I have gained, I feel it my duty to make it perfectly clear that subject to the will and judgement of my superiors *I am not only willing but also anxious* to continue my present service with the College while the emergency lasts.[29] (Emphasis added)

Although his arguments seem very persuasive from the vantage of half a century ago, Stanford was removed from the presidency and made prior of the Augustinian College, a theological seminary, in Washington, D.C.[30] No rationale for the reassignment has survived, if indeed a written explanation was ever given. Like any reformer, Stanford had undoubtedly made enemies within the Augustinian order, and there is good reason to believe that his detractors prevailed on higher authorities to have him removed.[31] Whatever the reason, Stanford's departure at such an inopportune moment underlined the fact that basic decisions for Villanova College were still being made by the Augustinian hierarchy.

Villanova had been fortunate to have Father Stanford for twelve years. The length of his term, in addition to his considerable abilities, had made for great stability at the college and some progress in fund-raising, despite the Depression and World War II. But long tenures in the presidential office had not been the norm during the two decades before Stanford took the helm, nor would they be—with one exception—in the three decades after he stepped down. Between 1910, when Delurey had been forced to resign, and Stanford's accession in 1932, there were six presidents of Villanova in just twenty-two years. These were Reverend Edward G. Dohan, O.S.A. (1910–17); Reverend James Dean, O.S.A. (1917–20); Reverend Francis A. Driscoll, O.S.A. (1920–24); Reverend Joseph A. Hickey, O.S.A. (1924–25); Reverend Mortimer A. Sullivan, O.S.A. (1925–26); and Reverend James H. Griffin, O.S.A. (1926–32). One of them (Dean) had served for just three years and two of them (Hickey and Sullivan) for only one year each.

Stanford's immediate successor, Reverend Francis X. N. McGuire, O.S.A., would remain at his post for an entire decade (1944–54), only to be followed by five presidents during the next twenty years: Reverend James A. Donnellon, O.S.A. (1954–59); Reverend John A. Klekotka, O.S.A. (1959–65); Reverend Joseph A. Flaherty (1965–67); Reverend Robert J. Welsh, O.S.A. (1967–71); and Reverend Edward J. McCarthy, O.S.A. (1971–75). These terms would average just four years, with Klekotka's six years being the longest and Flaherty's two years the shortest. Such brief presidencies would have made it difficult for anyone to carry out comprehensive reforms, but the press of events that overtook Villanova at war's end would have made serious restructuring very difficult even under the relatively long presidential term of Father McGuire. As a result, many of the reforms advocated by Father Stanford would not become a reality for another two decades.

McGuire was only thirty-four years old when he was called to lead the college in the summer of 1944. Born in the Bronx, New York, long a center of Augustinian influence, McGuire had begun teaching in the Religion Department at Villanova in September 1939. Since 1941 he had served as dean of men, chairman of the Athletic Board, and moderator of the Student Council.[32]

As World War II came to an end, McGuire believed that Villanova's mission was to serve as many men who would want an education at the college, contrary to Stanford's expressed desire to emphasize quality in admissions as soon as the situation warranted. As McGuire explained to the alumni in late 1946, the college would do its best to handle "all the applications coming from the ranks of the Villanova family." Other applicants, "whether returning veterans or seniors being graduated from high school[,] will be admitted as long as there is room."[33] Space, and not academic qualifications, seemed to be the major limiting factor, and even here the facilities would be stretched to the breaking point.

After years of international crises and worry over enrollments, the great postwar expansion at Villanova must have come as a pleasant surprise. The temptation to grow rapidly was hard to resist, and the administration believed that it had a duty to educate as many Catholic young men (and especially the veterans) as it possibly could. As a later Villanova president, Father McCarthy, would put it, "Villanova, like many schools, expanded rapidly after World War II. It was very responsive to the needs of its constituencies."[34]

At the same time, Villanova continued to rely heavily upon tuitions and fees, and thus there was always the lure of raising more money by admitting more students. Consequently, Villanova's great postwar expansion created mutually reinforcing demands for more buildings and equipment, and then additional students to pay for these facilities. Accordingly, the school found itself in a seemingly inescapable cycle of expansion, where the emphasis was on the quantity rather than quality of admissions. Not until Villanova could raise large sums of money not tied to revenue from students could it break this cycle and launch the kind of careful planning that would emphasize quality instead of mere numbers, something that both Father Stanford and Father Griffin had understood in the pre–World War II period.

The great postwar deluge began in September 1946 when 1,946 full-time undergraduate students showed up for classes. This was about twice as many students as had enrolled at Villanova before Pearl Harbor, in the fall of 1941. Some 1,500, or 76 percent of them, were veterans who took advantage of the so-called G.I. Bill of Rights, which offered free tuition and fees to the college or university of one's choice, plus a monthly living allowance.

Many of the men attending Villanova in the fall of 1946—40 percent of them to be exact—had attended Villanova before going into the military, and 15 percent were married. They were overwhelmingly Catholic, in that 88 percent had graduated from Catholic high schools.[35] Most had also grown up nearby: the Middle Atlantic states supplied 85 percent of the student body, with 75 percent of the total enrollment coming from Pennsylvania alone. Although there were no figures on how many came from the immediate Philadelphia area, the fact that a little more than half were commuters (977 versus 969 residents) suggests that most of the students from the Keystone State had grown up fairly close to the college and that many were from Philadelphia proper. There were no figures on the ages of these students, but since three-fourths were veterans one can conclude that most were somewhat older than the typical undergraduate. As legal adults who had been through a war, they would also prove less docile than typical students in the past (see Chapter 7).

In order to accommodate the unprecedented crush, Villanova held classes from 8:00 in the morning to 8:00 in the evening (then an extraordinary schedule). About 200 residents had to sleep in rows of bunk beds set up on

"Temporary housing" on the Field House floor just after World War II. VUA.

the Field House floor until four temporary army barracks, supplied by the U.S. government free of charge, were erected in the early autumn of 1946.[36] In 1947 the Veterans Administration provided three additional wooden structures, two of which were used for classes and faculty offices, and the other of which became a cafeteria and refreshment center. The latter now became Villanova's Pie Shop, still headed by the legendary Louie. The new Pie Shop was located near the present Kennedy Hall. The rest of "Vets Village," as this collection of temporary structures was called, stood east of Vasey Hall on land now occupied by Sullivan, Sheehan, and Bartley halls. (A year later Radnor Township, in which the bulk of Villanova is located, began asking when the structures would be coming down, a forecast of the friction that would erupt between Villanova and the surrounding neighborhood in decades to come.) In order to answer the special needs of former servicemen, many of whom lived or attended classes in Vets Village, the college had established a Veterans Guidance Bureau in the fall of 1945.[37]

Enrollments continued to climb during the late 1940s, reaching 2,650 by September 1949 and then dipping slightly below 2,000 in the Korean War year of 1952. In 1954 the undergraduate student body was back up to

Student residents of the barracks on East Campus, c. 1950. VUA.

around 2,600, and it exceeded 3,000 for the first time in 1956. By September 1964, the first year the baby-boomers arrived on campus, there were 4,500 undergraduates and another 3,000 in Villanova's graduate and professional schools, for a total of 7,500. It was now the biggest Catholic institution of higher learning in the state of Pennsylvania, and one of the largest in the United States.[38]

In addition to this growth on the Main Line campus, Augustinians from the Villanova province, who had been in Havana, Cuba, since the turn of the century, expanded their mission on the island by opening the Universidad de Santo Tomás de Villanueva in 1946. The only private university in Cuba, it was within ten years enrolling thousands of students in liberal arts, law, engineering, business, and architecture. (Its confiscation by Fidel Castro in the early 1960s would prove a great loss to the Augustinians and do much to inflame anti-Communism back on the Pennsylvania campus.[39])

Meanwhile, the size of the faculty at Villanova grew by more than four times in the two decades following World War II—from 78 in the academic year 1944–45, to 331 in 1963–64. This demand for more faculty, in a greater variety of fields, soon outstripped the supply of qualified Augustinians. In 1944–45 Augustinians had represented 65 percent of the total faculty (51 of 78), while in 1963–64 they accounted for just over 14 percent of the whole (47 of 331).[40] This shift to an overwhelmingly lay faculty would have important consequences for Villanova, as did the same phenomenon at most other Catholic colleges and universities in the United States during the same period (see Chapter 8).[41]

In order to accommodate its growing faculty and student body, Villanova had to embark on a vast building campaign. During the two decades after World War II, it put up eleven major buildings, several of which had been postponed for years. The most urgent of these building projects was a new library.[42] Unsettled labor and market conditions made contractors reluctant to bid on a new campus library until the end of 1946, but ground was finally broken on January 22, 1947. Most Reverend Joseph A. Hickey, O.S.A., former provincial of the Villanova Province and now general of the worldwide Augustinian order, turned the first spadefull of earth.[43] The long-awaited library finally opened on April 22, 1949. It provided ample space for 400,000 volumes, in addition to several classrooms, exhibit areas, and an attractive reading room. In 1963 this facility would be rededicated and named in honor of Reverend Daniel P. Falvey, O.S.A. (1906–62), who served as librarian from 1935 to 1962. Four years later, in 1967–68, Villanova built a new four-story library, designed by Albert F. Dagit and Associates, which adjoined the 1947 structure. The newer edifice now became the Falvey Memorial Library, while the older one, turned over for use by the library science program, received the name Falvey Hall.[44]

Although original plans for the library, drawn up around 1930, had placed the structure on the east side of campus near Vasey Hall, the administration

Falvey Memorial Library, completed in 1968 and designed by Albert F. Dagit & Associates.

decided after the war to erect the new library several hundred yards to the west on the edge of what was known as Mendel Field. (The construction of Vets Village on the east side of campus was doubtless one reason for the shift in location.) Also bordering Mendel Field were the Chemical Engineering Building and Navy ROTC Building, likewise begun in 1947 and designed by the Dagit firm. The Navy building was given the name Barry Hall in honor of Commodore John Barry, an early Philadelphia Catholic and long considered to be the "father" of the American Navy. The Chemical Engineering Building, which has never been named for an individual, received a large addition in the so-called international style in 1974 and was designed by architect Howell Lewis Shay, Jr.[45]

Drawings of the library in the 1930s showed an elaborate Gothic Revival structure that complemented both the 1934 monastery and the old Mendel Hall (Tolentine Hall after 1960). By the time the library was begun in 1947, this design had been greatly scaled down, with the Gothic effects confined largely to the two entrances. A full-scale Gothic design would have been prohibitively expensive in the late 1940s, as well as out of character with the plain lines of the international style sweeping the United States during the postwar period. Yet its gray stone walls and subdued Gothic features blended well enough with the construction of its older neighbors, as well as with its contemporaries, the Chemical Engineering Building and the Navy ROTC Building.

The next burst of construction began in the mid-1950s and lasted for about a decade. The first set of these buildings surrounded a quadrangle on the east side of campus, on the site of Vets Village (and where Villanova had projected a cluster of buildings in the late 1920s and early 1930s). This development featured twin residence halls (as dormitories were now called): Sullivan Hall (1954), on the north side of the quadrangle, and Sheehan Hall (1957), on the south side. At the east end of this configuration stood a new Commerce and Finance Building (1956), later named Bartley

Sullivan Hall, built in 1954 and designed by Henry D. Dagit & Sons. VUA.

Hall after Reverend Joseph C. Bartley, O.S.A., dean of the Commerce and Finance School from 1921 to 1962. Faced in the now familiar gray stone, the three new buildings included the same sparse references to the Gothic style as the library and the Navy ROTC facility. The architect for all three buildings was again the Dagit firm.[46]

The mid-1950s building boom also included Villanova's first real student center, begun in 1954 and located in the center of campus. It was named Dougherty Hall, after Reverend Joseph M. Dougherty, O.S.A., Augustinian provincial from 1950 to 1954 and a longtime professor. The facility contained a new Pie Shop (without Louie, who had retired about 1949), a student dining room, pool tables, a barber shop, a radio station, and offices for student organizations. Designed once more by the Dagits, its pointed cupola added an attractive feature to Villanova's already impressive skyline of crosses, domes, and spires.[47]

In 1960 Villanova launched a new science building named Mendel Hall.[48] It was this decision that meant changing the name of the old Mendel Hall (and before that College Hall) to Tolentine Hall, a switch that was confusing at the time and which will doubtless plague future historians of the institution. The new Mendel Hall, yet another Dagit creation, was rendered in the familiar gray stone. It also made a vague gesture to the Collegiate Gothic mode in its main entrance.[49] Like the older building of the same name, the new Mendel Hall was named in honor of Gregor J. Mendel, O.S.A., the founder of genetic theory. At the cornerstone ceremonies Father Donnellon,

Dougherty Hall, built in 1954, Henry D. Dagit & Sons, architects. VUA.

Dougherty Hall dining room during Summer School, 1950s. VUA.

then president of Villanova, spoke of the ongoing link between Mendel and the Augustinians at Villanova:

> It is the intention of the American Augustinians that the spirit and influence of Abbot Mendel will be faithfully reproduced in this new science building. As he has been the lively inspiration for many years on this campus in all the scientific studies undertaken, so he will continue to be indefinitely.[50]

Meanwhile, Villanova's Augustinians had been making plans for a new seminary building. Known as St. Mary's Hall and begun in 1962, the large complex occupied the northwest corner of Spring Mill and County Line roads. Because it was to house a seminary, the Dagits employed more obvious Gothic features on the exterior of the gray stone building than they had on their other recent commissions at Villanova. Its use as a seminary was short-lived, however, for the dwindling numbers of seminarians soon after the building was occupied resulted in its conversion in 1972 to a university residence hall, as well as the site of Villanova's nursing program.[51] Directly across the street from St. Mary's Hall, on the southwest corner of Spring Mill and County Line roads, another major structure of this period went up. This was Garey Hall, started in 1956 as the home of Villanova's law school and named after Eugene Lester Garey (1891–1953), an eminent lawyer, who left a large bequest to the law school.[52]

Besides putting up new buildings, Villanova acquired additional land. In 1968 it paid $3 million for the Foerderer Estate of 249 acres (also known as "La Ronda" and once the property of former U.S. Attorney General Wayne MacVeagh), located approximately two miles east of the campus at the

At the dedication of the Law School, Garey Hall, 1957 (*left to right*): Reverend James A. Donnellon, O.S.A., President of Villanova University, 1954–59; Most Reverend Fulton J. Sheen, Auxiliary Bishop of New York, who hosted a widely viewed television program of the day; Harold G. Reuschlein, Dean of the Law School; and Reverend Henry E. Greenlee, O.S.A., Augustinian Provincial, Province of St. Thomas of Villanova. VUA.

corner of Spring Mill Road and Conshohocken State Road (State Route 23). It appears that there were no plans to expand the university on this site and that the purchase was made mainly as an investment. Whatever the case, Villanova sold the property in 1971 for a reported $5 million.[53] At various times during the 1960s Villanova also made overtures to the Morris family to sell their estate, which abutted the campus northwest of Spring Mill Road and would be essential for physical expansion in the future. Nothing would come of these gestures for more than a decade (see Chapter 9).[54]

It is not surprising that this ambitious building program proved costly to Villanova, and that the college went back to trying to raise funds immediately after the war. In the fall of 1945 Villanova's new president, Father McGuire, explained to alumni that the college would have to expand its physical plant. Villanova's "growth and future status among the foremost colleges in America," he said, "will depend on the steps that will be taken in this present day."[55] In the summer of 1946 McGuire specifically asked the alumni to contribute to a revived library fund. In late 1948 and 1949 he was urging them to participate in what was called the Loyalty Fund, with the funds raised going to help defray the debts Villanova had incurred in erecting new buildings. This Loyalty Fund asked each graduate to send the college one dollar at the beginning of every month. By January 1951 it was clear that the Loyalty Fund was a complete failure, with the *Villanova Alumnus* not even bothering to publish what one must suppose were embarrassingly small amounts.[56]

Despite these meager results, Villanova decided to launch a major fundraising campaign in 1954. In order to prepare for this drive, the college engaged a consulting firm called the American City Bureau, which had offices in Chicago and New York. In their "Evaluation Survey and Case Book," presented on August 10, 1953, the City Bureau listed many of the same problems with fund-raising at Villanova as the Price Jones study had indicated back in 1929, nearly a quarter-century before.

Although the number of living alumni had grown to approximately 13,000 by 1953, they remained relatively young, with half of them graduating within the last ten years and thus unlikely to possess considerable wealth.[57] While not discounting this fact, the City Bureau survey blamed most of Villanova's "poor showing in fund-raising" on the "lack of a well organized and consistent effort."[58] Referring specifically to the alumni, the survey remarked that recent attempts to organize them "have had to face the obstacle of a history of ineffectual alumni cultivation," adding that the alumni were only "lukewarm" toward their alma mater.[59] The survey specifically cited the lack of statistical information on alumni and the again faltering activities of the regional alumni clubs. Of thirty such clubs, only fifteen were now vital concerns.[60]

Beyond its problems with alumni per se, the survey stated that Villanova did not keep either a "card list" of past contributors, showing the amounts they had given and their particular interests, or a list of potential donors. The board of trustees was also an obstacle in raising funds, since only two of its seven members were laymen, and one of them was described as "inactive."[61] Nor had Villanova done enough since the Price Jones study of 1929 to make itself better known to a wider audience. Although most of the public now seemed to realize that Villanova was more than a seminary for training priests, few in the greater Philadelphia area could say anything beyond the bare fact that it offered a college education in a religious atmosphere.[62]

In assessing Villanova's needs, the City Bureau study emphasized the continuing absence of an endowment. While admitting that the college's "living endowment" of Augustinians was probably worth $5 million at the time, its monetary endowment was only $264,000 in 1953, little more (especially when adjusted for inflation) than it had been back in 1939.[63] Thus out of a projected total of just over $20 million to be raised, the survey advised that $6.25 million go toward endowment. The remainder would be applied to new buildings and the improvement of faculty salaries. The total was to be raised in two phases of ten years each: $11,400,000 between 1953 and 1963, and $9,000,000 between 1963 and 1973.[64]

Officially known as the Development Program, the fund-raising campaign was formally launched on December 2, 1954, at a dinner for 350 guests in the Field House. In June of the following year Villanova held an exhibit in Gimbel's department store in downtown Philadelphia, featuring the old college bell, or Sister Liberty Bell, and a scale model of the campus that highlighted the projected new buildings.[65]

In order to get around the problem of having only one active layman on the board of trustees, Villanova created an Alumni Foundation in September 1953. Incorporated under Pennsylvania law, the foundation had a board of nine members, four appointed by the board of governors of the Alumni Association, four elected by the general membership of the Alumni Association, and one appointed by the president of the Alumni Association. Besides coordinating the fund-raising efforts, the Alumni Foundation was to receive the moneys raised and allocate them to the university. Appointed as director of the foundation was Father McGuire, whose stated reason for stepping down from the college presidency in 1954 was to take on this new responsibility. The chairman of the foundation's executive committee was James A. Farley, who had been postmaster general in the Franklin Roosevelt administration. Farley had received an honorary doctorate (L.L.D.) from Villanova in 1942 and seems to have been a friend of Father Stanford.[66]

Although the Development Program was more successful than the campaign of the early 1930s, it fell far short of its goal. As of 1960, when the last report was made, it had raised only $2,800,000—25 percent of its first ten-year goal and 14 percent of the total twenty-year goal of slightly more than $20 million.[67] Villanova would not be able to mount a successful campaign until its alumni had matured further and until it could secure a larger profile in the public mind.

Because the Development Program fell far short of its projections, Villa-nova was forced to borrow large sums of money to finance its physical expansion in the two decades after World War II. The amounts borrowed included $1,500,000 in 1947, another $1,500,000 in 1952, yet another $1,500,000 in 1954, and nearly $1,800,000 in 1957. Just three years later in 1960, Villanova went into debt for an additional $5,000,000. At the end of the 1960s, the institution's capital debt stood at $10,000,000, much of it now raised through relatively low-interest bonds that had been allowed by new state and federal legislation. Because of these debts and because the Development Program failed to reach its goal, Villanova had no choice but to continue relying almost exclusively on student revenues. Until the univer-sity could become more successful at raising funds, it would be impossible to limit enrollment appreciably and thereby improve the quality of students who were admitted. Under the circumstances, there seemed to be no way out of the vicious cycle of accepting more students for the additional reve-nue they provided, and of then having to find even more money to pay for the facilities required by the larger number of students.[68]

At the very time that it was making plans for its Development Program, Villanova opened two new professional schools on campus, one in law and the other in nursing. Like so many other undertakings of the postwar period, projections for a law school at Villanova first arose during the heady expan-sion of the 1920s. The idea had surfaced in 1927 but was abandoned when Villanova failed to secure the blessing of Cardinal Dougherty, who appar-ently feared that a Catholic law school at Villanova would compete with a law school already established at the Catholic University of America in Washington, D.C. Even if permission had been granted, the Depression and then the war may have forced the college to defer the law school until after the war. Indeed, the prosperity of the postwar period and the steady expan-sion of Villanova's student body allowed the idea of a law school to be renewed, and in September 1953 the Villanova University School of Law enrolled its first class.[69]

That same year, Villanova opened a full-time nursing school on campus. Because the great majority of students were women, this decision to open a nursing program would play a crucial role in bringing complete coeduca-tion to Villanova (see Chapter 7). During the past several years, Villanova had also been considering the possibility of launching a medical school, but because of the costs involved decided to postpone the project until the mid-1970s.[70] By then even higher costs and the existence of several excellent medical schools in the Philadelphia area made the idea of a medical school at Villanova impractical.

In opening two more professional schools and projecting a third, the medical school, Villanova was repeating a pattern adopted fifty years earlier at the turn of the century. Instead of allowing for more electives and greater flexibility in existing areas, it expanded the curriculum by offering new programs. As in the earlier period too, it chose new offerings that had an obvious vocational thrust, rather than extending or improving its liberal arts programs. For Catholics in the region, many of whom were still interested in programs that would lead to specific careers, Villanova's School of Law and School of Nursing (like its Engineering and Commerce and Finance schools) were appealing. The renaissance of liberal arts at Villanova would have to wait for another generation.

Meanwhile, the advent of the law and nursing schools, combined with the older programs in engineering, commerce and finance, and the liberal arts, gave Villanova the appearance of a university, as did the increasing size of its student body. Obtaining the legal status of a university would make this official, besides gaining greater notice and prestige with the general public.[71] Actually, the original charter of 1848 had granted Villanova "all such powers, authorities and jurisdiction as are held, enjoyed or exercised by any other *university or college* within this commonwealth" (emphasis added).[72] Since the 1848 charter had designated the institution as "The Augustinian College of Villanova, in the State of Pennsylvania," it was necessary to amend the charter in order to change the name. Yet the board of trustees wanted to alter the charter without having to file a certificate accepting the Pennsylvania Constitution of 1874 and the Pennsylvanian Nonprofit Law of 1933 (both of which had been enacted after Villanova's original charter), as required by law. The trustees accordingly asked the local state representative, M. Joseph Connelly, to introduce a bill in Harrisburg that would allow nonprofit corporations formed before 1874 to change their names without filing such a certificate.

Introduced on March 6, 1953, the bill passed both houses of the legislature and was signed by Governor John S. Fine on August 26, 1953. Villanova then had to enter a petition for university status with the Secretary of the Commonwealth, the Pennsylvania Bureau of Corporations, and the State Council on Education. After receiving their assent, the petition went before the Court of Common Pleas of Delaware County, which signed the final papers on November 18, 1953. As of that date, the institution officially became "Villanova University in the State of Pennsylvania." Other than the change of name, the university charter was identical to the original of

Reverend Francis X. N. McGuire, O.S.A., President of Villanova University (*second row, far left*) and Reverend Edward B. McKee, O.S.A., Vice President of Villanova University (*second row, second from right*) look on during the signing of the court decree granting university status to Villanova, November 18, 1953. VUA.

1848.[73] (Villanova's chief local competitors, St. Joseph's and La Salle, retained the name "college" for another quarter-century. St. Joseph's officially became a university in 1978, while La Salle made the change in 1984. Besides being smaller than Villanova, neither St. Joseph's nor La Salle had opened separate professional schools such as law or nursing.)

Villanova could now call itself a university, but its faculty and administration would soon discover that a change of name was not nearly enough. Other and more far-reaching alterations would be necessary before Villanova could claim to be the equal of other universities in the United States. The need for such changes was highlighted by various studies of the university undertaken by several different agencies. These included the City Bureau survey of 1953 and the report from the Middle States Association of Colleges and Secondary Schools in 1960. Their recommendations covered such areas as admissions, faculty standards, curriculum reform, and administrative structure.[74]

Of the three documents, the City Bureau survey (undertaken in the very year that Villanova changed its name to "University") was the most outspoken in its assessment of the institution's shortcomings and in its recommendations as to how these might be corrected. High on the list of deficiencies was a lack of communication within the institution and the negative atmosphere this created:

> The lack of free flow of information engenders curiosity and suspicion.... Speculation and discussion occurs, too frequently on the basis of inadequate or faulty information.... The net effect of this situation is to create a very wide and serious gap between the administration and the faculty, between the clerical and lay faculties, and between the administration and the student body. Instead of a closely knit team, all striving for the same objectives, we find instead at least three separate groups, each overly concerned with their own objectives and ends, in too many cases, having to function without the sympathy and support of the others, if, indeed, complete apathy and resistance does not intrude.[75]

Closely related to this lack of communication throughout the institution was the absence of clearly defined policies within the administration, with the result that each administrative officer "interprets his conception of what is best for the college into policy for his [own] department."[76] This was especially true for the Dean of the College, a position that had finally been created during the past few years. The City Bureau believed the dean's authority was ill-defined, with the result that he was often circumvented altogether by the various academic departments.[77] The remedy for this problem was an "internal public relations program." This should begin with the Augustinians themselves, who needed to create a consensus on both policy and procedure within the university.[78]

One of the most serious disagreements among the Augustinians, which according to the City Bureau study needed to be settled, was a question of admissions philosophy. One group of Augustinians believed that Villanova needed to adopt higher standards of entry for students, as a way of educating future leaders of the Catholic community. The others, whose philosophy seemed to have the upper hand (if only by default), believed that "any Catholic young man should be accepted and furnished a modicum of training[,] and regardless of individual ability, be provided with a Villanova degree to the end that a greater mass of young people should be furnished some semblance of Catholic education."[79] Because low admissions standards had a direct impact on the quality of Villanova's graduates and hence on the public's judgments about the worth of the institution, admissions policies would have serious ramifications for Villanova when it came to fund-raising and public relations in the years ahead.

Of course, higher standards of entry would be to little avail if Villanova did not provide a quality curriculum and attractive student facilities. In the blunt assessment of the City Bureau, "Unless Villanova wishes to become primarily an institution for the underprivileged[,] it will have to compete, in some measure, with the other first rate institutions, which offer a fine experience in living with a fine educational opportunity."[80] This meant that Villanova would have to offer more electives, as Father Stanford had advocated over a decade earlier, as well as better residence halls and recreational facilities. The students also needed to be given more of a genuine voice in the formation of policy, especially since most of them regarded their Student Council as little more than window dressing.[81]

Even some of Villanova's better facilities had not been designed with the interests of all students in mind. This was particularly true of the Field House, which lacked opportunities for recreation and the so-called minor sports. Consequently, the Field House was not well used and was not an integral part of student activities. Symptomatic of this neglect was Villanova's wasteful and counterproductive emphasis upon big-league football. It simply did not have the resources to compete in this arena, a problem that was exacerbated by the fact that fans in the Philadelphia area already regarded Temple and the University of Pennsylvania as the "home town" teams and were unlikely to shift their allegiances to Villanova. Downgrading football would have many benefits for the university. It would save some $50,000 in annual deficits, it would allow for a wider variety of sports that were better integrated into the total undergraduate program, and it would allay some serious disciplinary problems Villanova had had for a number of years with some of the football players.[82]

Also essential to improving the undergraduate program was a better faculty. The City Bureau's observations and recommendations in this area were extensive:

> The Villanova faculty would benefit materially by the addition of more individuals of wide experience and established reputation. . . . There are too few doctors on the faculty and too many baccalaureates. Too few of the members holding masters are working towards their doctorates. The paucity of published material on the part of the faculty creates a doubt as to whether this group has sufficient time to indulge in research and advanced study.[83]

The figures cited on the degrees held by faculty were especially revealing. From 1942 through 1952 there were more members of the teaching staff who held only bachelor's degrees than those who claimed earned doctorates in their fields. During the academic year 1948–49 the B.A. degrees outnumbered the Ph.D. degrees by more than two to one. Throughout this ten-year period there were also members of the faculty who held no college degree of any sort, the high point coming in 1949–50 when eight faculty did not even hold a bachelor's degree.[84] As late as 1952, the percentage of faculty with doctorates was just 15 percent. In addition to launching a program to achieve a higher number of doctorates on the staff, Villanova needed to raise salaries in order to attract a better qualified faculty, to institute a program of sabbaticals (which did not exist in 1953), and to establish a regular committee system, involving faculty, for determining rank and tenure.[85]

The Middle States evaluation of 1960 reinforced most of the observations made by the City Bureau survey seven years earlier. In order to improve significantly, Villanova would have to raise its standards for faculty and students alike, revise its curriculum to make more room for electives, streamline its administration, and enlarge the board of trustees to include more lay persons. Overall, the Middle States team rated Villanova as "adequate," adding that this was regrettable because the university had the potential to be "Distinguished" or even "Excellent."[86]

The combined observations of the Middle States team and the City Bureau survey resembled in many ways the description of what Andrew Greeley would soon call the "Medium Improvement School." In his controversial study of Catholic colleges and universities, *The Changing Catholic College* (1967), Greeley angered many with his criticisms of Catholic institutions of higher learning. Particularly controversial was his contention that Catholic schools would have to "put aside the old and more parochial forms[,] . . . the traditional familialistic and paternalistic approach to academic organization[,] . . . and chose new norms very similar to those of other American colleges and universities."[87]

After studying nineteen Catholic institutions, Greeley divided them into three categories, what he called Rapid Improvement Schools, Medium Improvement Schools, and Low Improvement Schools. The Middle States had used the word "adequate" to describe Villanova and had gone on to explain why they had used that term in their report. Much of what they said paralleled Greeley's succinct description of the Medium Improvement School:

> The quality of faculty, the level of faculty salary and participation, even the skill of the administration and the intelligence of the student body, is somewhat better in these . . . schools than they were a decade ago, but the improvement that has occurred has occurred almost by accident. The schools have been carried along by the great weight of forward movement in all American academia and Catholic academia in particular.[88]

Applying this insight to Villanova, one might say that the university had benefited greatly from the nationwide growth in college attendance and from the increasing prosperity of American Catholics (as well as the nation at large), but it had not yet made careful plans or taken deliberate steps toward academic excellence. Yet Villanova had made several important initiatives, many of them suggested by the evaluations of 1953 and 1960, to set the stage for genuine academic advancement. Whether it could (or would) adopt all the "new ways" of other American colleges and universities, as Greeley suggested, remained to be seen.

These initiatives affected the administration, the board of trustees, the faculty, and the curriculum. Modest administrative restructuring had actually predated the two campus inspections. In 1949 Villanova had created a Research and Development Office "for the purpose of control and coordination of all research on campus," with headquarters in Galberry Hall. Two years later, in 1951, it established the position of Director of Alumni Affairs. This director was largely concerned with public relations, while the alumni secretary, who reported to the Director of Alumni Affairs, would continue to coordinate the Villanova Alumni Association and the various local alumni clubs.[89] By the early 1950s there was also a Dean of the College, who was theoretically in charge of the entire academic side of the university. He also presided over the Division of Liberal Arts and Sciences. In addition to him, each of the major divisions, such as Engineering, Commerce and Finance, and the Graduate School, were headed by deans, who in reality had very little power, as Father Stanford had indicated. The School of Law had its own dean, who operated more or less autonomously from the rest of the university; the School of Nursing had its own director, who likewise enjoyed considerable independence from the rest of the institution.

At the suggestion of Reverend Joseph I. Boyle, O.S.A., who was himself Dean of the College, the university created a separate office of Academic Vice President in 1956, as well as a separate Dean of Liberal Arts and Sciences. At the same time, Villanova created a Vice President for Financial Affairs and a Vice President for Student Affairs (later called Vice President for Student Life). In 1961 it added a Vice President for Public Relations and Development (later known as Vice President for Institutional Advancement). The following year (1962) the various "Divisions" were renamed "Colleges," and their deans received real responsibility for the programs under them. This included a College of Nursing and a new name for the Part-Time Division, which now became the University College.

There was an Associate Dean in each college, among whose responsibilities was the coordination of graduate offerings with the various departments and with the Dean of Graduate Studies. Finally in 1968, the university authorized an Executive Vice President, who could relieve the president of certain duties and function in his place during absences from campus. These new vice presidencies and restructured deanships had the effect of consolidating and clarifying authority, at the same time that they relieved certain administrators of far too many responsibilities.[90] Such administrative reforms paralleled those undertaken at many other American colleges and universities over the past few decades.[91]

It was also in the late 1960s that Villanova expanded the size of its board of trustees and dropped the requirement, in place since the original Charter of 1848, that board members must be Roman Catholics. The reasons for this decision were twofold. First, the board needed to acquire more members with varied experiences and expertise in order to help handle the complex questions confronting a university of Villanova's size. Second, there were concerns that the religious requirement for board membership might make Villanova ineligible for public aid because of the separation between church and state mandated by the First Amendment of the United States Constitution. Villanova had been alerted to this second consideration by the so-called Maryland College Case, which had recently held that three church-related colleges in Maryland were not eligible for state matching grants because of religious control.[92]

On June 11, 1968, the board of trustees resolved to amend the university's charter to expand its membership from seven to a minimum of eleven and a maximum of twenty-five, and to drop its religious requirement. On September 20, 1968, the Court of Common Pleas of Delaware County approved the charter change. In a new set of By-Laws, adopted by the board on December 17 of that same year, the preamble sought to ensure that the special relationship between the university and the Augustinian order be continued:

> Inasmuch as Villanova University was originally founded by the Priests of the Order of Saint Augustine, Province of Saint Thomas of Villanova, that Province of the Order has had and always shall have a special relationship to the said University. No action in any way diminishing this relationship shall be valid unless it be approved by the unanimous vote of all Trustees present who in turn must constitute at least two-thirds (2/3) of all Trustees in office.[93]

Section 1 of the By-Laws gave additional protection to Augustinian interests by requiring that "one-third plus one shall be members of the Order of Saint Augustine of the Province of Saint Thomas of Villanova."[94] Since at least two-thirds of the trustees would have to be present in order to sever the relationship between the university and the Augustinian community, this "one-third plus one" rule effectively protected the order against losing complete control of Villanova. Equally important for the Augustinians, the By-Laws required that the president of the university be nominated by the "incumbent Provincial of the Province of St. Thomas of Villanova" and then elected by the board. In effect, the provincial would choose the president, with pro forma endorsement by the board of trustees. In order to give the president control over senior members of his administration (a privilege not hitherto enjoyed), he was given the authority to nominate the "Executive Vice-President and the several Vice-Presidents," who were then approved by the board.[95]

Reinforcing the decision to open the board of trustees to a greater variety of individuals, Section 2 of the By-Laws declared that the board "shall, as far as possible, include persons from widely different backgrounds and responsibilities." It added that "no one shall be excluded from serving on the Board solely by reason of religion, race or sex." Following up these provisions with astonishing rapidity, the board appointed its first female and first African-American trustees in 1969: Sister Mary George O'Reilly, S.H.C.J., then President of nearby Rosemont College; and Jesse B. Clark, 3rd, former director of the Cardinal's Economic Opportunity Project and an African-American.[96] It took several more years to expand the board to its maximum number and to achieve a greater measure of diversity. This process somewhat weakened (but by no means ended) the university's close ties to the Augustinian community.

Many other Catholic colleges and universities took similar steps in dropping the religious requirement and expanding board membership, including Notre Dame in 1967 (which was first to undertake the process), Loyola Baltimore in 1970, and St. Joseph's in 1971.[97] They along with Villanova concluded that the times and the American environment demanded such a change. For as Father Fedigan and Father Delurey had realized at the turn of the century, as Father Stanford had observed in the early 1940s, and as Andrew Greeley had declared more recently, Catholic colleges and universities would have to enter more into the mainstream of American higher education or face stagnation and decline. The challenge for an institution like Villanova was to adopt national standards while maintaining its Catholic, Augustinian identity. Only time would tell if it could succeed in striking such a delicate balance.

By the late 1960s the Villanova faculty had also begun to measure up to university standards, as understood on a national level. Between 1955 and 1970 the full-time faculty had grown from 160 to just over 400. Those who held doctorates had reached 46 percent, double the percentage only ten years before. There had also been a sincere effort to raise faculty salaries. In 1966 alone salaries increased 17 percent across the board, with increments of 6 percent in each of the following two years. These placed Villanova in a "competitive" category for the first time, though they were still below many other universities in the region. By 1970 the minimum salary for assistant professors was $9,070 and for full professors, $13,700. The maximums in these two ranks were $10,350 and $18,250.[98]

Meanwhile, slightly better channels of communication between faculty and administration had been created. One of these was the Villanova Faculty Council. The council succeeded an earlier body, known as the Villanova Faculty Assembly, which had been founded during student uprisings in 1969. The assembly was a meeting of any or all faculty who wanted to attend, but as participation began to dwindle after several years, the Faculty Council, representing the various colleges, was created to take its place. Its primary task soon focused on recommendations to the administration about salaries and fringe benefits.[99] The council could make a variety of suggestions to the administration on matters of interest or concern to the faculty. According to a later report, the council enjoyed a mixed pattern of success. In areas where there were no strong opinions on a given proposal by the administration or board of trustees, the council's suggestions were generally implemented. But the council had no way of prevailing in the face of stiff opposition from higher powers.[100]

The local chapter of the American Association of University Professors (AAUP), two decades older than the Faculty Council, had been founded in the spring of 1941.[101] During its first decade on campus the AAUP confined itself largely to making polite suggestions to the administration about such things as parking problems or the difficulties faculty faced in obtaining tickets to athletic events.[102] In the 1950s the AAUP continued along these same lines, requesting a faculty dining room in the projected student center (Dougherty Hall) and faculty permission to use the athletic facilities on campus (both granted). In January 1950 the organization successfully petitioned for tuition remission for the sons of faculty who attended Villanova, and in 1955 it voted to give an annual award for academic excellence to one student in each class. During the 1950s it also held a series of discussions on curriculum and student life. In the 1960s it called for improvements in the university's bookstore and for a rationalization of admissions standards.[103]

In the late 1960s Villanova clarified its rules for promotion and tenure and created a Rank and Tenure Committee, which gave faculty a real voice in decisions. This process apparently began in 1966 when the AAUP chapter began to investigate the whole process of tenure and promotion at Villanova. Among other things, the study revealed that the prevailing Rank and Tenure Committee commonly met only once a year, at which time it automatically confirmed the decisions on promotion and tenure that had already been decided by the administration.[104]

In addition to the fact that faculty played very little part in deciding promotion and tenure, there was no real evaluation of faculty performance when it came to advancing from rank to rank or for achieving tenure. Promotion, for example, was almost automatic once a person served the minimum number of years in a given rank, as set down in the Faculty Handbook: three years for instructors, four years for assistant professors, and five years for associate professors. There were stated criteria for promotion, such as teaching effectiveness, acceptable research, availability to students, and service on committees, but these do not seem to have been applied rigorously.[105]

Tenure was also based in most cases on length of service, since anyone who was promoted to associate or full professor and who had taught at Villanova for at least six years was awarded "permanent tenure." Those who were not promoted to at least the rank of associate professor were eligible for tenure after ten years.[106] As late as 1968, according Reverend John M. Driscoll, O.S.A., who was then Vice President for Academic Affairs, "Assistant professors who have served the minimum number of years in rank are almost certain to be awarded tenure upon their request."[107] An internal administrative history of tenure at Villanova further indicated that many who qualified for tenure did not even bother to apply for it: "Having been at Villanova for years without any indication of dissatisfaction on the part of the administration . . . [,] they already possessed tenure *de facto*."[108]

This internal history of tenure was part of a larger study in the late 1960s on how Villanova might avoid having a faculty that was so heavily tenured that any cost-cutting through faculty retrenchment would prove difficult or impossible. With administrative blessing for a complete restructuring of the tenure process, the recently created Villanova University Senate (see Chapter 8) approved new tenure rules in late 1970, which were accepted the following year by the board of trustees. Those teaching at Villanova full-time in a tenure-track position now had to apply for tenure in their sixth year. Their credentials were examined by the Rank and Tenure Committee, made up of both faculty and administrators, who evaluated candidates according to stated criteria. Anyone not awarded tenure had to leave the university after completing the seventh year.[109]

In 1973 the University Senate and administration approved new guidelines for promotion. The Rank and Tenure Committee now scrutinized applications for advancement according to criteria for each rank. Although effective teaching remained in first place, the new rules placed greater emphasis than ever on scholarly research and publication. In any case, promotion (like tenure) was no longer granted for length of service alone.[110]

It was also in the late 1960s that Villanova finally decided to make its undergraduate curriculum in the Liberal Arts and Sciences more flexible through a series of electives, or distributional choices, in the areas of theology, philosophy, English, foreign languages, history, social sciences, mathematics, and the natural sciences. This new curriculum became effective in the fall of 1970. The other colleges at Villanova also began to provide their students with certain electives in the arts and sciences.[111]

At the same time, student discontent was beginning to mount at Villanova over a number of issues. In this respect too, Villanova was sharing in the experiences of other American colleges and universities. Over the next several years this student discontent would change Villanova as much as its continuing growth in numbers, curriculum reforms, and administrative restructuring. However alarming these disruptions were on the local campus, they would also help in Villanova's continuing transformation from college to university.

# TRADITION AND CHANGE

Like many other Americans in the decades just after World War II, Villanovans were anxious to continue their lives much as before. Although there was no desire to return to the economic sufferings and international crises of the 1930s, they joined most Americans in believing that the familiar patterns of prewar society could be restored with little difficulty.[1] Initially, there were only slight wrinkles in the familiar fabric of campus life, which resumed soon after the war was over. Meanwhile, many of the issues and ideas that had been presented to Villanovans before and during the war were taken up again in the postwar decades, from the advocacy of Neo-Thomist philosophy to warnings against Godless Communism.

Such topics remained part of the continuing dialogue at Villanova over what it meant to be a Catholic college in the United States. In many ways the Cold War made this dialogue easier—for Villanovans, who had been proclaiming the dangers of Communism for years, could join with other Catholics in believing that they were among the most patriotic of Americans. Their traditional emphases upon discipline and eternal truth—also an integral part of Augustinian monastic life—similarly fit the national mood for self-control and intellectual stability during the great Communist scare of the postwar period.[2] The election of John F. Kennedy in 1960 as the first Catholic President of the United States also made Villanovans feel that they and their fellow Catholics were now part of the mainstream of American life.

Yet beneath the surface of self-satisfaction, social consensus, and seeming return to traditional campus life, there were subtle changes at work. Discontent over such matters as dress codes and compulsory religious services pointed the way to more serious dissent only a few years later. The gradual admission of women during the 1950s and 1960s also paved the way for complete coeducation at Villanova, and for future struggles over gender issues and acceptable behavior between the sexes. As the years passed, campus voices on the subject of Communism also became less strident, preparing Villanovans for more serious criticisms of American foreign policy in the years ahead. But in the autumn of 1946 such issues were far from mind as Villanovans made preparations to reclaim the familiar rhythms of campus life. Thus the *Villanovan* urged,

> Let us not forget the war, but let us put World War II into the past where it belongs. Similarly, let us put into the past those things which the war made, of necessity, integral parts of our personal business, social and scholastic lives. . . . Now, let us return things to normal as soon as it is humanly possible.[3]

More-mature minds might have told Villanova students that neither they nor their fellow citizens could discard the recent past—or recapture a vanished age. Yet they were determined to try, and for a time much of the old campus life reappeared and flourished.

The Belle Air Ball, the social highlight of the senior class, had already returned in all its glory on a frigid evening in January 1946. The *Villanovan* gave a glowing description of its rebirth:

> After many years of war and separation, sparkle and gentility . . . returned to the campus. It was evident everywhere that the cruel dragons of fear had been cast down once more and now, with washing of hands, youth was *returning to the business of being young*.
>
>    The crystalline black sky was in sympathy with the merciless cold and the wind was so fierce it seemed to be a live thing grasping and tearing any foolhardy human who challenged its domain. . . . But as the Field House was approached from the hundreds of cars which spotted its hinterland, frigidity lessened in the brilliance of the lobby lights and dissipated entirely with the warmth of good fellowship. . . . The lobby itself so brimmed with fur and top hats that it resembled the ante room of the Metropolitan [Opera's] Diamond Circle. The attendance was so large that the capacity of the wardrobe [the coat room] was exceeded and long queues demonstrated to what peacetime uses war learned skills could be applied.[4] (Emphasis added)

All the elements of the good life, which Villanovans and their fellow Americans were determined to enjoy, appeared on that early postwar evening: lavish clothing, acres of automobiles brimming with gasoline (now available in great abundance), and the warm promise of peace abroad and harmony at home. Though the peace was short-lived, national prosperity would remain a genuine mark of the postwar years, as Villanova's students continued to bask in the glow of glittering balls and famous dance bands.

In May 1946 the Junior Prom featured a large water fountain in the middle of the Field House. Emanating from it were "beams of varicolored lights." The Juniors adopted a Parisian theme in 1951, with a 30-foot model of the Eiffel Tower rising from the Field House floor. The following year they took their motif from the musical movie *On the Town*, starring Frank Sinatra and Gene Kelly, which manifested itself as an 80-foot model of the Brooklyn Bridge. In 1960 the Senior Prom adopted the theme of a "Coronation Ball," with a large crown suspended from the Field House ceiling. Providing the music for these events were name bands like the Glenn Miller orchestra, under his successor Ray McKinley (1949 and 1959), Claude Thornhill (1954), Sammy Kaye (1957), Guy Lombardo (1957), and the Tommy Dorsey band, now directed by Warren Covington (1959).[5]

Some of the postwar dances were elaborate fund-raising events. Beginning in 1953, Villanova held an annual Shamokinaki Dance, held at the Field House to aid Augustinian missionaries in Japan. The exotic name derived from the hometown of Reverend Thomas P. Purcell, O.S.A., a former faculty member at Villanova and one of the missionaries, who hailed from Shamokin, Pennsylvania. The suffix "aki" was intended to give it a Japanese flavor. Pagodas, archways, and lanterns added to the effect. The last of these dances, the "Fifteenth Annual," appears to have been held in 1967.[6]

Whatever the purpose of such dances, both the music and the bands were little different from what Villanova students had known in the 1930s. In some cases the orchestras, though under different leadership, had exactly the same names as they had twenty years before. They were of a type that all but the most conservative mothers and fathers could understand and enjoy. It was as if the rock-and-roll revolution then sweeping the nation did not even exist.

Surviving along with the dance bands were Junior Week and Mother's Day, both held during the second week in May. These events resumed in 1946. In 1948 a new tradition known as the "Diaper Dan Contest" was added to Mother's Day. The mothers submitted baby pictures of their sons, with a prize awarded for the cutest entry.[7]

Juniors as well as other students at Villanova could likewise be assured that when they returned in the fall there would be rousing football games on Saturday afternoons, with all the panoply that surrounded them: pep rallies,

Poster for Shamokinaki Mission Dance, 1957. VUA.

Mothers and sons at Mass in St. Thomas of Villanova Church during Villanova's traditional Mother's Day observances, 1950s. VUA.

bonfires, and residence hall decorations at Homecoming time. The tradition of decorating the halls, invariably based upon the theme of inflicting total defeat on the rival team, had apparently been inaugurated in 1937 by William Connelly, then Director of Athletics, and the prize for the best decorations was still known in 1949 as the William Connelly Award.[8] By 1957 recognition for the best decorations was being called the Nick Basca Award, after a former student described as a "star football player and World War II hero."[9] An article in the *Villanovan* gave a colorful description of the elaborate annual tour of the Homecoming decorations:

> The marching band and the ever-present pep rally fire engine will lead the throng of Wildcat supporters as they march around the campus to observe the dorms dressed elaborately in their [Nick] Basca wardrobes.
>
> At the end of the campus tour, the parade will continue to the rear of Goodreau [Villanova] Stadium, where a gigantic bonfire will feature the rally program.[10]

Student meeting girlfriend
at Villanova train station for
Homecoming Weekend,
1962. VUA.

In 1962 Homecoming festivities included the predictable bonfire, hall decorations, and parade through the campus, followed by a dance at the Field
House, where a Homecoming Queen (one of the students' steady dates)
received her crown.[11]

In order to introduce newcomers to these and other Villanova traditions,
freshmen initiation resumed after a lapse of several years during the war.
Freshmen again had to wear beanies and shortened pants, in addition to
learning college cheers and paying proper respect to upperclassmen (such as
shining their shoes and carrying their books around campus). Freshmen were
also required to attend evening chapel. A special student court composed of
five men from the orientation committee tried infractions of the orientation
rules. If the newcomers cooperated "as a body" the regulations might be lifted

at the end of the fall semester. If not, the frosh would have to endure them "for an indefinite period of time."[12] (This, of course, was an idle threat, since the initiation invariably came to an end in November.) As late as 1963 the student yearbook, *Belle Air*, described freshmen orientation as "sore throats, rolled up trousers, neat bow ties, and snappy dinks [beanies]."[13]

While freshmen initiation and all the activities that followed over the next four years were supposed to take care of the social side of life, compulsory retreats and other services would minister to the students' spiritual needs. There was still a one-day retreat in early October, in addition to a three-day retreat held, beginning in the early 1950s, during Holy Week. Both were compulsory. For these occasions the Field House became a chapel where as many as three thousand students were seated.[14]

This annual round of official student activities, ranging from religious exercises and freshmen initiation, to proms and pep rallies, helped Villanova's administration, as they had during the prewar period, to channel youthful energies into harmless avenues and thereby to maintain student discipline. Allowing upperclassmen to police the freshmen, and the students

A religious retreat for students in the Field House, 1949. VUA.

in general to plan a predictable round of social activities (under the advice of the ever-present faculty moderator) also perpetuated the illusion that the students were in control of themselves—and of campus life in general.

Indeed, not long into the postwar period most middle-class Americans concluded that self-control and self-sacrifice were more essential than ever to the nation's well being.[15] For as soon as the Fascist monster had been slain, the forces of international Communism swept into the power vacuums created by the defeats of Germany and Japan. Like most American Catholics, Villanovans were well prepared to appreciate the Red menace, having been warned for decades about the dangers of atheistic Communism. Indeed, the Cold War, and the nation's mobilization against Communism during the late 1940s and 1950s, allowed many Catholics in the United States to boast that they had anticipated this great danger well before most Americans. Long accused of being un-American because of their religious institutions and status as recent immigrants, Catholics could now feel that they were among the most patriotic of Americans—and above all suspicion of Communist sympathies because of their Catholic faith.

Central to this Catholic crusade against Communism was a belief that the church continued to offer a set of eternal verities that could counteract the excesses of American democracy and capitalism while providing a bulwark of truth against the false doctrines of Marxism. Thus, according to Father McGuire, writing for the *Villanova Alumnus* in 1953 in his capacity as president of Villanova,

> The Catholic College has a most important role and significant place in American life. . . . As a Catholic College, Villanova has made an invaluable contribution to the Church and to the State for one hundred and eleven years. Villanova's existence for so long a period has been assured by the Providence of Almighty God on the one hand and the system of free enterprise[,] which has made America such a thriving nation.[16]

In McGuire's opinion, Villanova had been shaped by its Catholic faith, as well as by the free-market forces of the American economy. The college was thus the result of both Catholic and American values, he seemed to be saying, and in just the proper proportions. Yet on other occasions McGuire worried that the more negative aspects of a market economy were undermining the nation's spiritual foundations. In December 1951 he warned the alumni:

> Here in America our economy is perilously close to destruction and our morality is at the point of decadence. Our concept of spiritual

values has been smothered by the false values placed on our material progress. Our religious sense has been terribly debased by the exaltation of scientific achievement to the pedestal of a national deity. For all this no one else is to blame but us, the American people.[17]

A year later he reiterated these warnings against a corrupt and dangerous materialism:

> A heart confident in God and loyal to His precepts; a resolute will to defend and live by Christian principles; a mind keen to perceive the truth have always been objectives uppermost in the philosophy of education of the Augustinian Fathers.... In our present world the wealth of our material empire stands as a powerful and violent threat to destroy our society unless our spiritual forces are strong enough to keep them in check. Greed for wealth at any cost, lust for power, dishonesty, corruption, cannot be overcome merely by learning.[18]

In appealing for building funds in May 1952, McGuire was almost apologetic about asking for money, and felt obliged to assure alumni that Villanova's spiritual objectives would not be compromised by too great an emphasis upon plant and equipment: "While our spiritual objectives are of primary concern, we cannot overlook the needs for the development of our physical facilities." Spiritual and academic progress, he feared, would be "blocked by grave physical discomfort."[19]

A half-dozen years earlier, in October 1946, McGuire had expressed similar reservations about placing too much emphasis upon the physical growth of the century-old campus, assuring alumni that such changes would not alter Villanova's traditions: "At this moment we are merely enlarging the physical heritage that previous administration[s], earlier faculties, and kindly benefactors have left to us."[20] Like the student writer who had described the first Belle Air Ball after the war, McGuire did not want to think that anything essential had changed at Villanova.

In order to provide students with an opportunity to approach contemporary problems from a Catholic point of view, McGuire established the Villanova Forum in the spring of 1949. Each year the Forum invited well-known scholars and public figures who could speak to current issues. One of the earliest such guests was the world-famous theologian and Neo-Thomist, Jacques Maritain, who addressed an audience of about one thousand in March 1950.[21]

The first dean of Villanova's law school, Harold G. Reuschlein, agreed wholeheartedly with Neo-Thomists like Maritain that there was an unchanging natural and moral law. According to Reuschlein, that law should be the basis for all legal studies at Villanova. "During the last seventy years," he wrote, "no more stupid blunder has been committed than the pseudo-scientific divorce of law from morality in law teaching." At Villanova, however, the law curriculum would be grounded in "the espousal and teaching, without compromise, of a definite philosophy which we refer to as 'the natural law'—by which we mean a brand of legal philosophy coming up through the ages from Aristotle, through Saint Thomas Aquinas—Scholastic Natural Law as distinguished from Rationalist and Rousseauistic Natural Law."[22]

Reverend Charles J. McFadden, O.S.A., of Villanova's Philosophy Department, was even more of a dedicated Neo-Thomist, who wrote and lectured on a variety of subjects, in addition to teaching a popular course on campus called "The Philosophy of Communism."[23] In March 1953 he advised alumni about what was popularly known as the "rhythm method" of birth control. This approach was entirely moral, he concluded, because it was in accordance with both God and nature. "Conception does not take place," he wrote, "simply because the Author of Nature does not deign to cause a new life to come into being from the marital act at this particular time."[24]

McFadden's continuing writings on the subject of Communism also borrowed heavily from Neo-Thomist thought. Communism simply contradicted natural law, according to McFadden. In that sense it was a false philosophy and a false religion, as he proposed in an article for the *Villa-*

Reverend Charles J. McFadden, O.S.A., one of Villanova's Neo-Thomists and a recognized expert in the subjects of Communism and medical ethics. VUA.

*nova Alumnus* in December 1954: "We must be made to understand that Communism is not a mere political, military, and economic movement. Neither is it to be identified solely with Soviet Russia. Communism is basically a philosophy of life—a false religion."[25] Because this was so, military force by itself would not stop Communism. The American people must also be educated as to what was *"false and harmful* about *Communism."* At the same time, they should be informed about "what is *true and beneficial to man in Christianity*" (emphases in the original). McFadden repeated many of these themes in frequent addresses on campus, as well as in the classroom.[26]

In addition to such presentations, Villanovans were frequently called upon to pray for an end to Communism, as they were by the *Villanovan* in the Christmas season of 1954:

> For as [Christ] chose love, truth, and honor as the means of converting men without lifting a sword, so the Communist party chose hate, lies, and deceit along with the sword to win adherents. . . . Accordingly, that centuries old cry of "Peace on Earth," will assume a youthful vigor on this Christmas Day. . . . And if you, the Catholics of the free world, join your voices with those of the angels in echoing this helpful message, then no barrier—not even the Iron Curtain—may keep God-fearing men from hearing it. . . . After all, if men have not been able to conquer this evil of Communism, who can conquer it but God?[27]

Villanovans also resorted to prayer when Soviet tanks rolled into Budapest in November 1956 to put down the Hungarian uprising. On November 8 the Hungarian colors were displayed in the St. Thomas of Villanova Church during a memorial Mass for the "victims of the uprising against Communism." Later that day, classes were suspended for two hours so students could join in prayer for stricken Hungary. In the words of Reverend Joseph A. Kemme, O.S.A., Vice President for Student Affairs at the time, this gesture by Villanova students was especially appropriate: "Since it was students in Budapest who began the freedom move, it is fitting that American students pay tribute to their bravery and patriotism."[28]

Such concerns about Communism understandably affected how Villanovans viewed allegations of widespread Communist infiltration in the government. For example, the activities of Senator Joseph R. McCarthy, the most well-known investigator of supposed Communist subversion in the United States, prompted much comment in the *Villanovan*. Yet contrary to the mistaken notion that American Catholics showed nearly universal support for McCarthy, reaction to him was mixed at Villanova, as it was on most

Catholic campuses.[29] An editorial that appeared in October 1953 expressed such ambivalence:

> [McCarthy] has uncovered evidence of widespread infiltration and has consequently probably reduced the extent of Communist operations at least temporarily. On the debit side, he has caused widespread demoralization . . . by creating an atmosphere of mutual suspicion and fear. . . . The only statement that I could make without fear of serious error is that there is some right on both sides and consequently the McCarthy controversy will continue to rage in American politics.[30]

Nearly seven years later, after McCarthy had been widely discredited, the *Villanovan* praised the university's Belle Masque Society for staging Arthur Miller's *The Crucible* in March 1960:

> Some people regret the passing of the McCarthy-type investigations from the national scene. They mourn that the excitement of clearing the rabid mice out of the barn is gone, and no one has replaced the grand exterminator of evil. . . . Thanks to Belle Masque and the university for having the courage to depict the dubious ethics of barn burning.[31]

A year later the campus newspaper fired a salvo against the John Birch Society for charging that men such as President Dwight D. Eisenhower and Secretary of State John Foster Dulles were tools of the Communists. By launching such character assassinations, the *Villanovan* proposed, the Birch Society was using the same tactics as the Communists themselves.[32]

The question of Communist professors in the United States led the *Villanovan* to take a hard line at first, as in April 1953 when an editorial denied that teachers had the right to exploit their position to poison young and impressionable minds.[33] A decade later, after the worst of the Red scare had passed, the newspaper adopted a more liberal view of academic freedom: "The university that demands intellectual allegiance from either its faculty or student body is not a university at all. It is nothing but an incubator for the nourishment of infantile minds."[34]

In foreign affairs, campus concerns over Communism led the *Villanovan* to resume, at least in the early 1950s, its positive tone toward Franco's Spain, first adopted nearly twenty years earlier during the Spanish Civil War. Thus an editorialist could write in 1954 that the United States should embrace Franco as an ally in the crusade against Communism:

Franco obtained power in Spain largely by opposing the excesses of the extreme Left. His most important support, both inside Spain and abroad, comes from the Catholic Church. Franco, himself, is apparently a very devout Catholic and a very sincere anti-Communist. . . . If again we resurrect the *legends* of the Spanish Civil War and treat Franco like a Fascist monster, we in America will lose by it, for the West will be deprived of a valuable ally.[35] (Emphasis added)

Editorial reaction to Communist North Korea's invasion of South Korea in June 1950 was predictably harsh. In order to contain Communism, the feeling was that the United States would have to use military might against such aggression:

> Three months ago . . . the communist forces of North Korea were slashing down through the countryside of democratic South Korea. . . . The way to peace today is to make the communist forces of the world feel that victory for them would be impossible. . . . As Theodore Roosevelt said, to keep the peace we must speak softly, but carry a big stick.[36]

Yet in 1956, when the Soviet Union decided to crush the Hungarian uprising, the *Villanovan* counseled caution. In answer to those who favored American intervention, an editorialist responded:

> What many of these people fail to realize is the proximity of Hungary to Russia. . . . Russia considers Hungary essential to her own security. Therefore Russia will tolerate no interference in it by any western nation and will fight to maintain it as a satellite. This brings us to the devastating fact that in a war between the United States and Russia, no one would be the victor.[37]

Villanovans might pray for the freedom-fighters in Hungary, but the campus newspaper did not believe that Americans should risk their lives to assist them.

On Communism in Cuba, following Fidel Castro's rise to power, the campus newspaper took a stronger tone. Cuba was far closer to the United States than Hungary, making Communism there much more menacing. Local attitudes toward Cuba were also affected by Castro's seizure of the La Universidad de Santo Tomás de Villanueva in Havana and the expulsion of a dozen Augustinian priests following the Bay of Pigs invasion in April 1961. One of the men expelled was Villanova's Father McCarthy, who was arrested by Castro and forced to seek asylum in the Swiss Embassy in

Havana before being allowed to return to the United States. (McCarthy became president of Villanova University a decade later.) Villanova also accepted forty-one Cuban students, most of them from the Havana campus, when they fled to the United States in 1960 and 1961. They were admitted without having to pay tuition and later secured loans, without interest, from the United States government.[38] Yet two years after the Cuban missile crisis of October 1962, the *Villanovan* was remarking on disagreements between China and the Soviet Union and the doubt that this cast on the theory of monolithic Communism. The same editorial advised that the rift between the two Communist powers might provide an avenue for better relations between the United States and the Soviets.[39]

Even in the darkest days of the Cold War the reaction against Communism among Villanovans did not seem quite as shrill as it had been before World War II. Perhaps this was because much of the rest of the nation had come to share their alarm about Communism, or perhaps the prospect of another world war, this time fought with nuclear weapons, gave many people second thoughts about confronting the Communists directly with armed force, especially the Soviet Union. In this sense Villanovans echoed the sentiments of most other Americans by the late 1950s and early 1960s, in part because they and other Catholics had themselves helped to shape the national debate over Communism.

When it came to partisan politics in the United States Villanovans remained loyal, with only one exception, to the Democratic Party in presidential elections. Although more and more students were members of the nation's growing middle class, loyalty to working-class roots and perceived religious interests caused most to continue voting for Democrats. Thus a poll in the *Villanovan* during the 1948 presidential campaign showed that students favored Harry S. Truman over Republican Thomas E. Dewey. Four years later, 64 percent opted for Democrat Adlai Stevenson over the highly popular Dwight D. Eisenhower, though a majority of students predicted that Eisenhower would win the contest. In 1956 the students reversed themselves and chose Eisenhower by 53.6 percent. Ike's immense popularity, combined with his incumbency, may have tipped the balance for him in the local poll.[40]

Villanovans' tremendous enthusiasm for Democrat John F. Kennedy in his contest with Richard M. Nixon in 1960 was predictable, given Kennedy's Irish background and Catholic faith. As early as September 1957 the *Villanovan* joined many others of the Catholic press in lauding Kennedy as a possible president. "It would be fitting for . . . Senator Kennedy to be the first Catholic president," the writer asserted, "as his whole life has marked him as an admirable representative of his faith." The article went on to paint an ideal picture of Kennedy—"an unbeatable combination of political integrity

The Honorable John F. Kennedy, then U.S. Senator from Massachusetts, received an honorary doctor of laws degree during the convocation at the dedication of the Law School building, Garey Hall, on April 27, 1957. *Left to right:* Reverend James A. Donnellon, President of Villanova University; the future President Kennedy; and the Honorable Richardson Dilworth, Mayor of Philadelphia. VUA.

and boyish charm."[41] This was a Kennedy yet unscathed by scandalous revelations about his personal life or by the political blunders of his truncated presidency. It is not surprising that in the student poll taken in late October 1960 Kennedy swamped Nixon, with 67.3 percent, whereas Kennedy barely won the presidency in the nationwide election in November. In its November 10, 1960, issue the *Villanovan* trumpeted Kennedy's victory in bold headlines.[42]

In retrospect, the fall of 1960 was a golden moment for Villanovans, and for American Catholics in general. Kennedy's election was proof that they were now accepted as loyal Americans. At the same time, there was great satisfaction in knowing that their long-standing horror of Communism was now shared by the nation at large. For educated Villanovans, Neo-Thomism promised absolute and eternal answers to virtually every question—from birth control and the college curriculum, to Communism and a godless legal system. While they now shared the fruits of American prosperity, Villanova's sons could find a spiritual counterbalance in the teachings of their church. Yet beneath the surface there had been certain signs that Villanova students were beginning to question the old ways. By the end of the 1960s these challenges would erupt into a genuine revolt that, when combined with wider doubts about postwar American life, would lead to unforeseen changes on the Main Line campus.

One of the more visible indications of growing discontent concerned the student dress code. As early as February 1946 an editorial in the *Villanovan* lamented that students were not dressing well or behaving like proper young gentlemen:

> It is [not enough] for us to be scholars. . . . We are obliged also to be gentlemen. The plain fact of the matter is that the present men of Villanova have failed incontrovertibly, at least in the outward evidences, to maintain our ancient inheritance of culture. Disorderly and unconventional dress, unshaven faces, and bad grooming in general pervade the halls and campus of our college. But of more moment, the manners and conduct of the men have deteriorated. Propriety and fraternity have yielded to vulgarity and unsympathetic indifference.[43]

Three years later, in March 1949, the problem of proper attire remained, as some students continued to complain about having to wear coats and ties on campus. This time an editorial proposed that proper clothing was an integral part of the student's preparation for adult life:

> Out of the mouths of many Villanovans come growls of dissatisfaction every time an edict concerning coats and ties is sent forth from the

powers that be. . . . A look at the situation from a mature gentleman's point of view can easily dispel any doubt as to the worth and necessity to look like a gentleman. Most of the students at Villanova are not studying to be ditchdiggers. . . . They hope to become doctors, lawyers, teachers, professional men to whom a good appearance will mean solid profit. . . . A tie and a coat may seem to be an overwhelming burden to some, but to a man's employer and colleagues his appearance is an important factor in the man's success. . . . A gentleman has a uniform that suits his work, if he is not dressed for the job he cannot perform his duties to his own best advantage.[44]

Echoing this desire for more casual clothing was a decline in the number of formal dances. In 1949 the seniors voted to have an informal dinner dance, mandating suits and ties instead of tuxedos, the custom before. The following spring the juniors decided to have an "informal" Blazer Ball, meaning that juniors would not be expected to wear their class blazers as in the past.[45]

Meanwhile, campus authorities continued to express unhappiness over violations of the dress code and general student conduct. When three inspectors from the Augustinian community examined Villanova in May 1959 they deplored the "freedom to come and go almost at will." They also complained of the "constant noise and mild disorder in the halls, considerable drinking, [and] failure to fulfill religious obligations,"[46] blaming such conditions on several factors: "The great expansion of the student body and the more mature character of many returning veterans [who had refused to abide by rules that had been formulated for younger students], coupled with an ever decreasing number of priest-prefects [and] larger [residence] halls spread out over a wider area making supervision more difficult."[47]

By the time this Augustinian inspection took place, evidences of student restiveness had found their way into their yearbook, the *Belle Air*. The 1956 edition contained a photograph of students at the compulsory spring retreat. Some looked bored, others fidgety, and several were sound asleep. The caption read: "[S]tudents display mixed reactions to the heavy schedule of the spring retreat."[48] A similar photograph from the 1959 edition carried the sarcastic comment, "SOULS AT REST give varying degrees of attention to retreat sermons."[49]

A decade earlier, in late 1948, students had even gone so far as to organize a demonstration to demand that a traffic light be installed at the corner of Lancaster Pike and Ithan Avenue, where several students had been hit while crossing the street. Some 600 students formed a "human barricade" in the intersection, where they stopped all traffic for over an hour. Afterward the state agreed to put up a light. Six years later, in December 1954, several dozen students again protested after a student and his date were struck by a car while crossing the pike en route to a dance in the Field House. Now they demanded that the speed limit be reduced to 15 miles an hour past the school, this time to no avail.[50]

Ten years later, in May 1964, students complained against the administration's choice of a commencement speaker, Philadelphia Auxiliary Bishop Gerald V. McDevitt. Some 300 seniors marched through campus, neatly dressed in coats and ties, to present a petition to the university president, Father Klekotka. Approximately 700 of the 850 graduates had signed it, protesting that Bishop McDevitt had no national reputation, like many of the commencement speakers that year at other regional colleges and universities, and that he would accordingly do nothing to boost Villanova's reputation.

In fact, the administration had tried to attract some well-known celebrity for commencement but arrangements had fallen through at the last minute. McDevitt was already scheduled to give the baccalaureate sermon and kindly agreed to be reassigned as commencement speaker. Given that graduation was only a month away at the time of the protest, Klekotka politely informed the students that the speaker could not be changed.[51] Although their petition and march were extremely mild by later standards—even at Villanova—such a move would have been unheard of five or six years before. In any case, the protest had the eventual effect of upgrading Villanova commencements, including speakers and honorary degree recipients who were generally of a much higher caliber than before.[52]

Meanwhile certain facets of campus life, so carefully revived just after World War II, were beginning to wane. Among these were the formal balls with their traditional dance bands. Although these lasted into the late 1960s, they were gradually being replaced by concerts starring popular singing groups. The latter included The Four Preps (1964), The Four Seasons (1965), Peter, Paul, and Mary (1965), The Kingston Trio (1966), and The Fifth Dimension (1969).[53] Unlike the formal balls of the past, which virtually required the student to come with an official date, the new concerts allowed the student to attend on a more flexible basis—as an individual, with a date, or as part of a group of friends. Another musical event allowed more talented students themselves to participate. This was the Intercollegiate Jazz Festival, which became an annual weekend event held in late winter. During the mid-1960s it commonly attracted about five thousand people.[54] Attending Villanova at the time was a student named Jim Croce, who graduated in 1965 and went on to become one of the best-known rock singers of the day, only to be killed in a plane crash in 1973.[55]

The adoption of a new academic calendar in 1965, which featured the "short semester system," made such standbys as Mother's Day and Junior Week difficult to schedule, since final examinations were now conducted during the second week in May, the usual date for both events. In 1970 Mother's Day was replaced by Parents Weekend, held in the fall. Junior Week seemed to disappear at about the same time.[56] In place of these dwindling events, Villanovans could attend concerts on campus by top symphony orchestras, most of them sponsored by the Villanova Arts Forum, founded in 1964. Among these were Leopold Stokowski and the American Symphony Orchestra (1963), George Szell and the Cleveland Orchestra (1966), Leonard Bernstein and the New York Philharmonic (1966), Eugene Ormandy and the Philadelphia Orchestra (1967 and 1970), and Wolfgang Sawallisch and the Vienna Symphony (1967). Opera star Anna Moffo also appeared on campus in 1966, and the Pennsylvania Ballet came in 1969.[57]

Complementing these various musical performances were a series of

Eugene Ormandy, Director of the Philadelphia Orchestra (*center*); with Reverend Robert J. Welsh, O.S.A. (*right*), President of Villanova University (1967–71); Most Reverend Augustine Trape, O.S.A. (*left*), Augustinian Prior General; and Reverend Joseph L. Shannon, O.S.A. (*far left*), 1967. VUA.

noted speakers, many of them held under the auspices of the Villanova Forum, which had gone beyond its original mission of providing a platform for Catholic issues and lecturers. The speakers included Reverend Theodore Hesburgh, C.S.C., President of Notre Dame University (1958), U.S. Senator Edmund Muskie (1959), philosopher and educator Mortimer Adler (1964), U.S. Supreme Court Justice Arthur Goldberg (1965), social critic Vance Packard (1966), U.S. Senator Charles Percy (1967), and Ferdinand Lundberg, chronicler of America's wealthiest families (1969).[58]

Such serious fare and the decline of formal dances and other activities associated with an older campus life prompted an editorial writer in the *Villanovan* to announce in September 1967 that traditional college society, as it had been known at Villanova for the past four decades, was all but dead:

> The roaring '20's are over. So are the days of the collegians with raccoon coats who swallowed goldfish. The rah-rah boys of our parents' college days have been demoted to high school, while college students have become more serious minded. Though this campus may not be in the intellectual avant-garde, even at Villanova there has recently been some evidence of improvement.[59]

Yet another indication of such future changes was the growth of coeducation at Villanova in the postwar decades. As at many institutions, coeducation came gradually to Villanova—in this case over a period of fifty years. Beginning in 1918, both nuns and lay women had been attending summer school, and in the early 1930s there had been some talk about admitting women to the Commerce and Finance school. Villanova's evening program, held at first at Hallahan High School and then on campus, had admitted both men and women. According to figures from the alumni office, Villanova had granted its first degree to a lay woman in 1938. At the same time, Villanova was conferring degrees on dozens of nuns each year—seventy-six of them in the summer of 1939.[60] Thus by 1943 some guides to higher education in the United States were listing Villanova as coeducational because of the summer school, evening classes, and other extension programs, all of which admitted women. The 1940s also saw women participating in various student activities at Villanova. In 1940 women from nearby Rosemont College began taking female parts in plays, which had previously been portrayed (often awkwardly) by Villanova men. That same year, Rosemont women joined with Villanova men to create a symphonic band. In the summer of 1942 civilian women enrolled in defense classes at Villanova, and in 1944 a young woman, a Navy WAVE, joined the staff of the V-12 program at Villanova.[61]

The early postwar years saw some discussion of coeducation in the pages

Graduation, Summer School, 1943. In center of front row, left to right, are Reverend Joseph A. Hickey. O.S.A., Augustinian Assistant Prior-General, and Reverend Joseph A. Bartley, O.S.A., Dean of Commerce and Finance and Dean of Part-Time Sessions. VUA.

of the *Villanovan*, most of it negative. Typical of these was a snide piece that appeared in February 1950:

> It is to be understood that some girls do have a place in college. There must be twenty girls in the country who are seriously thinking of getting an education. They usually wind up at MIT or Chicago or some other big school. Then there are girls who want to be teachers. They go to teachers colleges. . . . What then is the status of a girl that goes to a girl's school such as Vassar, Smith, Radcliffe, and others too numerous to mention? These poor creatures are just whiling away the time until they hook an unsuspecting male into matrimony. . . .
>
> College girls do work hard at their studies. Of course, mother could have taught home economics better than any expert who never had to cook and wash and sew, but it would be too easy that way. As for girls taking Chemistry, Calculus, Shakespeare, Accounting and other college subjects, it would be much better if they took a course in furnace tending and window-washing. The latter subjects would be much better suited to their future occupations.[62]

Such sentiments were typical of how many young men, as well as the majority of Americans, viewed women's role in the 1950s. Their proper vocations were as wives and mothers. A college education would therefore be wasted on them according to traditionalists, an assertion that would enrage women a decade later and would help to galvanize the women's movement of the 1960s.

At Villanova, meanwhile, the presence of women on campus became permanent in 1953 with the opening of the School (later College) of Nursing. For a half-dozen years the nursing program was alone in admitting women full-time to Villanova. Then, in 1958, engineering took its first female student.[63] Over the next decade, various other divisions at Villanova were allowed to admit women so long as these female students commuted to campus. The nurses were already living on site, but there were no other residential accommodations for women at the time.[64] Reflecting this increasing presence of women on campus were the rising number of Villanova degrees granted to females (all of them at first from the evening division and various extension programs), from just 6 in 1946 to 88 in 1959. By 1960

Nursing students receive their caps, February 12, 1956. VUA.

Sisters studying science during the Villanova Summer School, c. 1960. VUA.

there were 143 women attending Villanova full-time during the day, the great majority of them in the nursing school.[65]

The nursing program proved to be the opening wedge for genuine coeducation and unleashed several campaigns for greater gender equality on campus, while widening the whole debate over mixed education. In 1954, for instance, the nurses asked to participate in Villanova's cheerleader squad but were refused until the fall of 1964, when the Student Government Association voted to allow them to join the group. When female cheerleaders appeared for the first time at a basketball game against La Salle, played at Philadelphia's Palestra, several La Salle men mocked the Villanova women at halftime by dressing up as female cheerleaders with much padding under their clothes to produce exaggerated breasts and thighs. La Salle men also unfurled a banner that read "Who wears the pants at Villanova?"[66] The fact that the women cheerleaders had been forced to wear baggy culottes, as opposed to skirts that might fly immodestly into the air, may have been partly responsible for the La Salle taunts.[67]

Yet another indication of a somewhat deprecatory atmosphere toward women was the revival of the annual Turf and Tinsel comedies. These had first been held in 1933 and 1934 by a group of football players who made up the Turf and Tinsel Club, the word "turf" referring to the football field, and "tinsel" to the gaudiness of the theater. After a hiatus of fourteen years, the Turf and Tinsel productions were revived in the spring of 1948 and continued to about 1962. In the 1930s, as well as in the 1940s and 1950s, the musical scores for Turf and Tinsel were written by Robert M. Whelan, a skilled musician who since 1932 had been the secretary and business manager of the athletic program. Over the years, Whelan had become something of a campus legend, described by some as "Villanova's Mr. Chips" and by others as "Uncle Bob."[68]

These Turf and Tinsel comedies featured Villanova men dressed up as women, who imitated female song and dance routines. All or most of the male performers continued to be athletes, including Villanova's track star and Olympic gold medal winner, Ron Delaney.[69] Their musical farces played to packed audiences in the Field House and were regularly featured in campus publications as well as in area newspapers.[70] This humorous mockery of women on stage was perhaps a way for Villanova men to assert, in incongruous fashion, their own masculinity, but it resulted in the blatant stereotyping of women, which at the time no one seemed to mind. Among the titles of the Turf and Tinsel productions were "Cleo Was a Lady" (1949); "Jessica James" (1955); "Barbara of Seville" (1956); and "Remember Mimmy" (1960).[71]

Yet by 1966 there was widespread support for complete coeducation at Villanova. In the *Belle Air* that year the growing presence of women on campus was viewed as a positive sign that Villanova was changing for the better:

> One aspect of Villanova tradition has been annihilated in the last fifteen years. We refer to the increasing presence of the feminine creature on our campus. Today we claim to remain stubbornly masculine. But, happily, she is inserting herself into our fabric, and hopefully, she is winning the battle, if indeed, it is not already won.[72]

Once made fun of on stage and ridiculed in student publications, women were now welcomed as a sign of reform. In the fall of 1967 the university announced that all its programs would be open to women beginning in September 1968. By the time of this announcement there were 361 women enrolled in full-time undergraduate programs during the day. The great majority of them (317) were nursing students. Next came the 47 women in

A Turf and Tinsel production, 1950s. VUA.

Arts and Sciences, 35 of them faculty daughters, who were now permitted to attend Villanova tuition-free as faculty sons had been permitted to do for some time. There were 9 women in engineering and none in Commerce and Finance.[73] With the number of women increasing gradually each year, it only made sense to open the entire undergraduate program to them. Admitting women was also a means of attracting a larger pool of well-qualified students. In the years ahead the question of how to regulate the social lives of men and women on campus would become a major bone of contention between students and the administration.[74] Over the next several years both La Salle and St. Joseph's universities, traditionally all-male institutions and Villanova's two local competitors, would adopt coeducation, and for essentially the same reasons as Villanova.[75]

Aerial view of the Villanova University campus, October 1, 1953, looking southeast, with the Lancaster Pike and the Philadelphia & Western tracks toward the right of the photograph, and the "main line" of the Pennsylvania Railroad to the left. VUA.

Although few if any could realize it at the time, cumulative changes on campus, in the nation, and in the world at large would lead to major alterations at Villanova University. By 1968 Villanova was poised to participate in a youthful rebellion known as the counterculture.

# VILLANOVA COUNTERCULTURE

During the 1960s and 1970s, and especially between 1968 and 1974, Villanova University went through what might be called its "counterculture." Although this term continues to embrace a variety of ideas and events, it can be used to designate the widespread criticism of American life mounted by young men and women born in the years just after World War II. These young people, often known as the baby-boom generation, challenged many traditional practices and beliefs.[1]

At the same time, changes in the Roman Catholic Church itself, as manifested by the Vatican II Council, led many to question long-held customs and ideas. Such questioning, combined with a pronounced emphasis upon individual fulfillment, contributed to a decline in the numbers of men and women entering religious orders as well as to an increase in those who chose to leave their religious communities. This phenomenon included the Augustinians themselves, with effects in the long run for the order's relationship to Villanova University. Once again, it was the American, Catholic, and Augustinian experiences that continued to shape Villanova.

Ironically, most of the youthful critics during the 1960s and 1970s had grown up at a time when the United States enjoyed unparalleled wealth at home and extraordinary power in the world at large. Most of them also came from sheltered suburban neighborhoods, whose homes were filled with creature comforts that few could have imagined even a generation before. Yet as they came of age, some of these privileged youths found that not everyone in America shared such benefits and that the country in which they lived was not as perfect as they had been led to believe. Awash with middle-class prosperity and contentment, they were startled to discover poverty, racial and gender discrimination, empty materialism, amoral science, wanton destruction of the environment, stultifying conformity, disregard for honest emotions, illegitimate and often mindless authority, imperialistic foreign policies, adult hypocrisy, and frequent betrayal of the nation's highest ideals. At Catholic colleges and universities, more-sensitive students saw the discrepancies between what they were being taught in religion and philosophy courses and the actions of government in particular and of adults as a whole. Thus it seemed as if parents, teachers, religious leaders, and elected officials had purposely concealed the truth about America by drawing false portraits of contemporary life while omitting all the ugly facts about the past.

A vocal minority of these young people were determined to force the nation to change its ways. Concluding that the middle-class values of the older generation were bankrupt, they attempted to form a culture of their own "to counter" the flawed world into which they had been born. For many, the college or university became a microcosm of the society they wanted to change. At many campuses, in the process, "rebels" completely upstaged "the organized," as Helen Horowitz has called the adherents to traditional student culture.[2]

The question of how extensive Villanova's counterculture became depends to some degree on the point of view of the participants themselves. For some of Villanova's administrators the campus disruptions of this period were frequent as well as trying. For many campus activists the various protests and resistance movements consumed much of their free time at college. Yet Villanova's most extensive demonstrations came later than they did at other campuses and were mild compared with what occurred at places like Berkeley, Columbia, or the University of Wisconsin.[3]

Despite their comparative tameness and, with the exception of protests against the Vietnam War, their tendency to concentrate on local issues, a few of Villanova's protests were large and there were several violent incidents. More significant in the long run, the student upheavals at Villanova (as elsewhere) eventually led the university to move toward a more collaborative style of governance, at the same time that they forced the university to view student needs more seriously. In the long run, Villanova's counterculture would also make students, faculty, and administration more sensitive to social justice and to the rich diversity of the human experience. As in the past, these changes were shaped by the continuing reality of being a Catholic university in America.

The earliest stirring of what might be called a counterculture at Villanova focused on certain campus amenities. Having been reared in comfortable homes, where children were often the center of attention, some Villanova students, at least, assumed that many of the same creature comforts should be found at college. It is thus not surprising that several early demonstrations were over the quality of food served in the student dining room.

The first food riot occurred in February 1967 when a student in the Dougherty Hall cafeteria, the only dining facility for residents at the time, claimed that there was blood caked to the inside of his glass of milk. When he was refused another glass, he and other students began throwing trays of food and overturning tables. Several hundred students then surrounded the monastery and later spilled onto Lancaster Pike, where they blocked traffic for about fifteen minutes. A growing discontent over the quality of the food served in the cafeteria, along with handwritten signs in the residence halls inviting students to join the food riot that particular evening, suggested that the demonstration had been planned. The protest appeared to be somewhat effective in that the food service did upgrade both the quality and quantity of meals, according to the *Villanovan*.

A second such riot took place in December 1970. In addition to protesting the food, students also objected to overcrowding and long lines in the cafeteria, a familiar and frustrating experience for the baby-boom generation. In fact, the Dougherty Hall dining facility was serving more than 1,700 students a day. This time the administration claimed that financial stringencies kept them from making any immediate improvements.[4]

A constant shortage of funds for educational facilities had plagued the baby-boomers since they had entered school, and it became a major complaint when they got to college. Villanovans joined the chorus by criticizing cramped living-quarters. Throughout the 1960s and 1970s they also requested better recreational facilities, and in April 1973 students held a demonstration in front of the Field House when the administration responded citing a lack of money. Numerous other complaints involved rules and student discipline. Spokesmen claimed that the university refused to treat students like adults at the same time that it violated the students' individual liberties. As early as 1959 Villanovans began waging a campaign against compulsory class attendance. In 1966 the administration finally agreed that seniors with a grade-point average of 3.00 or better could have unlimited "cuts." In early 1968 it abolished the "general class attendance requirement" altogether, leaving the question of cuts up to individual departments and professors.[5] (Compulsory class attendance for freshmen would later be reinstated.) A related matter was mounting dissatisfaction with the dress code. In many cases students simply draped their ties across their shoulders, half scorning and half complying with the official requirements. Increasingly, professors refused to enforce the dress code in the classroom, and it became something of a dead letter. In early 1968 the requirement that students wear coats and ties at evening meals was formally abandoned. Although discussions continued from time to time about whether it would be advisable to reinstate coats and ties on campus, the requirement was never resurrected. It was at about this same time that students abandoned the habit of standing when their professors entered the classroom.[6]

Yet another area of local discontent was the compulsory religious retreats, already a source of dissatisfaction for many years. Students had been expected to attend them without question, but in the atmosphere of the 1960s, when many young Americans were refusing to go along with tradition for its own sake—or with programs adults insisted were simply for "their own good"—Villanova's religious retreats prompted scorching criticisms. In February 1967 an article in the *Villanovan* insisted that compulsion was "most often used to shield some kind of incompetence, some kind of rational impotency."[7] In the face of constant complaints and noncompliance, the university dropped the mandatory retreats in the late 1960s. Meanwhile, fewer and fewer professors, and especially the lay teachers, began each class with prayers, a custom that had long prevailed at Villanova.

But the most explosive student issue was the question of parietals. Derived from a Latin word meaning "wall," "parietal" had come to designate administrative authority within "the walls or buildings of a college."[8] By the 1960s the term was used almost exclusively in reference to visitation in student residence halls by members of the opposite sex. For college and university students, the right to have guests in their own rooms, of whatever sex, was an individual right; for Villanova's administration, visitation was a matter of sexual morality and strictly forbidden. The first open challenge to Villanova's parietal policy came in the fall of 1969 when seven Villanova women were put on probation for entering a male dormitory. According to the *Villanovan*, neither the punishment nor the rule made any sense:

> At a time when co-ed dormitories are becoming common place [at other institutions] it should not even be necessary to discuss the issue of visiting hours. The rules simply do not make sense. The students do not want the rules, their rationale is not relevant to today's students: moral paternalism is undesirable; and the rule must be changed.
>
> It is unfortunate that this belaboring of the obvious is necessary—but that's Villanova.[9]

When proposals made through student government and other official channels did not yield results, some students turned to demonstrations. On March 30, 1971, approximately two hundred men entered Good Counsel Hall, a women's residence on South Campus, where they held a sit-in. Some of them remained in the hall for a total of thirty-four hours. Following the board of trustees' refusal to grant parietals on April 13, a group of women held a "girl-in" on April 22 at Sullivan Hall, a male residence near the center of campus. They also burned members of the administration in effigy and then proceeded to the intersection of Lancaster Pike and Ithan Avenue, where they sat down and stopped all traffic. Later in the evening they broke into the university president's office in Tolentine Hall and remained there until early morning. Two years later, in April 1974, about two hundred students occupied Sheehan Hall, a woman's residence opposite Sullivan Hall.[10]

Underlying the administration's long opposition to a liberal visitation policy was the opportunity that it might provide for sexual relations. Since the Catholic Church held that sexual intercourse was permissible only within marriage, the idea of sex in residence halls was unacceptable to the Augustinian priests who administered Villanova and who had grown up in an earlier generation when condemnations of premarital sex were more or less universal. According to Reverend Edward C. Doherty, O.S.A., Director of Housing, the Augustinians would fail in their "purpose if moral guidelines and directives are not provided [for students] as part of our total program." Visitation between men and women in the residence halls, he feared, "would be . . . conducive to pre-marital sexual activity."[11] Reverend James G. Sherman, O.S.A., chairman of the board of trustees, put the matter in language that seemed to reflect a genteel, even Victorian attitude toward relations between the sexes. "We feel parietals [are] a moral issue," he told the *Philadelphia Inquirer*. "A bedroom sounds implicitly that it may not be the best place to meet a lady."[12] In explaining the board's refusal to grant parietals at its meeting on April 13, 1971, the university's president, Father Welsh, also stressed the moral issues:

> All who seriously discussed visitation rights with members of the Board saw clearly that a moral issue is involved. . . . Faced with the obligation which is theirs by reason of their office the trustees judged that the question of morality could neither be ignored nor belittled and judged further that given the state of present dormitory facilities, an affirmative decision [on parietals] would lay them open to the charge of permitting, if not authorizing, activity which is not in accord with generally accepted principles of Christian morality.[13]

Yet Welsh and other members of the administration had to face a strong and growing consensus among colleges and universities in the United States, including a number of Catholic institutions in metropolitan areas, which held that visitation between the sexes was both appropriate and acceptable. It was a classic and seemingly irresolvable clash between the values of a wider American culture and the sincere beliefs of Villanova's Catholic leaders.

It was also on moral grounds that the administration banned a chapter of the Gay Liberation Movement on campus. Father McCarthy, who was president at that time, was quoted as saying that homosexuality was "against Christian philosophy and Augustinian moral principles."[14] On this topic the administration encountered no real opposition, because homosexuality was not an issue for most students. Yet for many young men and women at Villanova, and elsewhere throughout the nation, greater sexual freedom was a matter of individual rights as well as a rejection of adult hypocrisy about sex.

The most serious student challenges to sexual mores, compulsory religious retreats, dress codes, and other campus rules at Villanova took place in the aftermath of the Vatican II Council, which met in Rome's Vatican City between 1962 and 1965. The council's stated purpose was to bring the church up-to-date (*aggiornamento*, as it was called in Italian) with the many changes that had occurred in the twentieth-century world. The council eventually issued some sixteen documents that altered the worship and certain traditions of Roman Catholics and touched off a storm of controversy because they included many challenges to traditional church authority. Reform within the Catholic Church thus coincided with, and in some respects reinforced, the cultural upheaval taking place in the United States.

In order to make the liturgy more understandable and ultimately more familiar, the Vatican Council permitted church services to be done in the various national languages rather than in the traditional Latin. Altars were turned around so that the priest faced the congregation, lay members were allowed to distribute Holy Communion and to form advisory bodies within the parishes. Furthermore, the laity were invited to participate more fully in the singing of hymns during services, much as Protestants had done since the Reformation. Other council directives gave greater voice to the bishops in individual countries, permitted more latitude in biblical scholarship and interpretation, and encouraged an ecumenical dialogue with other Christians. At the same time, the council recognized the legitimacy of other religious beliefs and specifically condemned anti-Semitism. In one of the most far-reaching pronouncements (in its implications for student activism, at least), Vatican II officially embraced the social gospel, encouraging the laity and clergy alike to practice their beliefs in the world at large. In a specific mandate, Catholics were directed to identify with the poor, thus encouraging an empathy with peoples of the Third World.

For many American Catholics, living as they did in a country that extolled open discussion and religious pluralism, Vatican II came as a welcome release from increasingly troubling restraints. More-conservative Catholics often felt betrayed or threatened by changes in their church. Even some of those who did not take extreme positions on the changes were shocked to discover that a system of worship and custom that they had been taught was eternal and unchanging could indeed change—and, in fact, had undergone many permutations over the centuries.[15]

Both the letter and spirit of Vatican II were manifested in various ways at Villanova and played a role in its counterculture. In the summer of 1962, several months before the Vatican meeting began, Villanova hosted a three-day ecumenical conference co-sponsored by the law school's Institute for Church and State and the National Conference of Christians and Jews. Over the next several years Villanova was the site of other ecumenical programs.[16]

Further manifestations of this greater openness about religion involved criticisms of the Catholic Church itself. This was true of the Villanova production, in November 1966, of the play *Luther* by John Osborne. The 1967 issue of the *Belle Air*, which corresponded to the 450th anniversary of Luther's nailing his ninety-five theses on the chapel door at Wittenberg, devoted five pages of photographs to the local production with captions that were unmistakably critical of the Roman Catholic Church in Luther's time. Whether the editors were aware that Luther had also belonged to the Augustinian order before breaking with the church is unclear, but there is no doubt that they saw him as a hero of religious conscience and truth. In the text that accompanied the pictures, the *Belle Air* asserted:

> Few individuals impress that mark of personal force that Martin Luther burned into the conscience of Christian man. He was alone, separated from his Church, his family, his tradition, lonely and brilliant, with a driving impetus for truth and salvation. Faced with the religious and temporal power of civilized man, he dared to say, "Here I stand."[17]

For the campus rebel at a Catholic, Augustinian university, the figure of Martin Luther defying both religious and secular authority over a matter of personal conscience could make an inspiring model.

Some students also complained about what they considered to be the irrelevance of certain religious conventions. At the same time, they were alarmed over the discrepancy between the church's close attention to sexual morality when simultaneously the church seemed to show little concern about the morality of American foreign policy in places like Vietnam. According to a writer for the *Villanovan*,

> One need not waste time on the meaningless trivia of a very traditional Catholicism when the far more meaningful task of being a

Christian is at hand.... Our problem today is not venial sin. Or
mortal sin. Or seven year indulgences or Saint worship or scapular
guarantees. No, an angry God is not about to punish the world.
Rather, a crazy, bitter, war-mongering world is out to destroy itself; to
let its hungry starve, its poor be attacked by rats, its armies kill, its
citizens watch others be killed, robbed, raped and come out with the
universal rationalization[,] I didn't want to become involved.[18]

Such sentiments were in harmony with Vatican II's advocacy of the social
gospel and not far from the call to "Catholic Action" a generation earlier. Yet
such disparagements of traditional Catholic practices would have been un-
thinkable in the campus newspaper just ten years before.

Indeed, the subject of what was suitable for inclusion in student publications touched off one of the major controversies with the administration at
Villanova during the years of counterculture. The first clash came in February 1969 when the Vice President for Student Affairs, Dr. James F. Duffy,
forbade publication of an article entitled "The Student as Nigger," written by
a professor from California State University, which contained several words
judged to be obscene. When Dr. Duffy ordered the article withdrawn, the
*Villanovan*'s editor-in-chief, Irv Anderson, resigned in protest. A second
confrontation came in September 1971 over the *Villanovan*'s publication of
a satire entitled "Strawberries for Eileen." The university president, Father
McCarthy, charged that this article likewise contained obscene language and
threatened to withhold funds from the newspaper if such material continued to be published.[19]

Late in 1972 Father McCarthy followed through on his threat and shut
down publication for two months. This time there had been criticism of the
administration, as well as foul language. The obscenity issue arose from "a
sexually explicit word" uttered by a speaker from the Gay Activist Alliance
and quoted by the *Villanovan* on December 6. Objections to administrative
decisions had appeared in two editorials, both published in the November
15 issue. The first editorial, entitled "Myopia," criticized Reverend Richard
D. Breslin, O.S.A., Dean of Arts and Sciences, for barring a professor from
Villanova's Honors Program because of alleged radical views. The second
editorial, "Endgame," took the administration to task for refusing to get rid of
Villanova's football program, which had run a deficit of $315,000 during the
previous season. In the concluding paragraph, the writer explained why
football should be abolished:

In short, the program is a luxury that Villanova can ill-afford. While
academic departments (this is, remember, a University) yearn for an
extra few hundred dollars, the team eats up potential programs,

courses, innovations. The fate of the team is one thing, the fate of this University is another. Football should be abolished.[20]

Although there was nothing obscene, strident, or particularly disrespectful about this second editorial, such an attack on football at a campus where it once had been the centerpiece of student life (and where it had even produced a student hero in Leo Goodreau) must have sounded like heresy to the older generation. Equally shocking was the fact that the student newspaper, long a dependable support for administrative policies and campus rules, was now playing the role of adversary. In any case, the football program survived for the time being, and the newspaper lost its funding because it did not "adhere to the origins, principles, and purposes of this Catholic institution."[21] Students erected a large banner across the entrance to Dougherty Hall, which housed the newspaper's offices. It read, "R.I.P. The Villanovan 1927–1972 [sic] With Heartfelt Sympathies."[22] Meanwhile, the suspension was picked up by the wire services and carried by many metropolitan newspapers across the nation.[23]

The *Villanovan*'s attack on football was part of a wider criticism mounted by some students and faculty against what they saw as anti-intellectualism at the university. Particularly objectionable was the practice of granting 130 athletic scholarships based not on the financial needs of promising scholars but on athletic prowess.[24] Other complaints about the intellectual tone focused on the Villanova bookstore, which carried only required textbooks rather than an array of other titles too, including "scholarly paperbacks," as was the practice at some other university bookstores in the region. A new bookstore in what became Kennedy Hall was supposed to alleviate this problem, though many students and faculty believed that it fell far short of the goal of making an array of stimulating books available on campus.[25]

Yet other signs of an anti-intellectual atmosphere, the *Villanovan* charged, were the continuing indignities of freshmen orientation. An editorial in September 1969 apologized to the newcomers for the demeaning treatment:

> The VILLANOVAN extends its sincere condolences to the freshmen who were forced to bear the humiliation of the orientation program. The cheering, marching, singing childishness of orientation can only be viewed as an anachronism in the perspective of the "current college mood" which, although not clearly definable, is clearly different from the three day pep rally [the freshmen orientation] that plagued Villanova. . . . It is sufficient for the present that the freshmen remember orientation as the *first insult to their intelligence at Villanova*.[26] (Emphasis added)

Still other editorials attacked the curriculum. Under the heading "Mediocrity," an editorial in January 1972 attempted to set forth the problem:

> At Villanova . . . [the] process of discovery is hindered, in fact almost completely stifled. Why? Because it has become necessary to assume that the student knows very little whenever he comes into the classroom. . . . Villanova has tailored itself to the very worst kind of student and really doesn't offer much to recommend itself to the good one. The huge block of required courses trap the really bright student in a curriculum which is neither new nor challenging.[27]

For the editorialist, the curricular reforms of the late 1960s, with their allowance for far more electives than in the past, had not gone far enough.

The solution, according to some students and faculty, was a "Free School" (later a "Free University"), along the lines of similar programs in operation at other campuses. Beginning in 1966, it offered students topics of contemporary interest that were not covered in the regular curriculum or that were treated insufficiently. The program was both informal and free—"free of tuition, free of tests, free of salaries for instructors, free of censorship."[28] According to the *Villanovan* it represented "an important step toward truly liberal education."[29] Among the offerings were Aspects of Gay Liberation, Propaganda Analysis, Dimensions of Freedom, The Christian Community, Student Rights at Villanova and the World, Yoga, Art for Everyone, and Dynamics of Social Change: Marxism.[30]

A theme that ran through most of these courses, along with the other issues taken up by campus activists, was the matter of a genuine student voice in policy-making at the university. As early as 1960 the *Villanovan* concluded that student government was largely a myth:

> Does student government exist at Villanova? More important, can student government exist at Villanova . . . ? It seems that, the monastic philosophy [of obedience] being righteously observed by members of the Villanova administration, and the philosophy of individualism being almost innately ingrained in the persons of students, no adequate middle ground may be found, whereon students may actually govern themselves in freedom and honor under the approving aegis of the University Administration, without one or the other party involved surrendering its principles.[31]

In this insightful statement, the student writer anticipated the struggle to come between an administration steeped in the hierarchical principles of monastic life and the Roman Catholic Church, on the one hand, and the expectations of individual freedom common among the youth of the baby-boom generation. It was thus another example of how Villanova was struggling to balance the tensions of being a Catholic institution in a country like the United States, with its continuing emphases upon pluralism and individual initiative.

By 1967 the old Student Council had given way to the Student Government Association (SGA). In the spring of that year the entire student body elected the president of the SGA for the first time, instead of having him elected by the delegates to that organization. The *Villanovan* hailed this decision for universal suffrage and direct election as a major step toward real student government:

> The man selected by the students will not be selected merely on the basis of limited power with certain small groups. He must be a man who understands the problems of all the students, not just the people on the second floor of Dougherty Hall [where the student activities offices were located].[32]

One mandate of any student-body president was to bring about a relaxation of campus rules and to obtain more of a voice for students in formulating those rules. Thus in December 1966 the SGA had requested a meeting with the administration to discuss reforming "the existing disciplinary rules and regulations."[33] One result of this initiative was the creation of the Student Court, ratified by a two-thirds vote of the student body in March 1968. The court was composed of two students, two faculty members (one Augustinian and one lay), and the Dean of Men (or Dean of Women, if a female student were charged with a violation). According to the Student Court charter, "No student can be expelled or suspended from Villanova for disciplinary reasons unless the Student Court decides such, and this decision is approved by the Vice-President for Student Affairs."[34]

Later in 1968 the SGA drafted a Student Bill of Rights and submitted it to a referendum of the student body on December 4 of that year. The Bill of Rights was sweeping in the subjects that it covered, as well as in its implications for the university. Students would have the right to be fully informed about the financial policies of the university and to advise in their creation (Article II); the right to "participate in the formulation of curriculum" and to disagree with any opinions or materials presented in the classroom, without the "threat of censure by the teacher" (Article III); the right to examine any areas of interest to them, and in the process to enjoy "free speech, assembly, and petition," to broadcast and publish information and opinions without censorship, and to "establish [a student] government which will best represent their needs" (Article V); the right to the same privacy in residence-hall rooms as anyone else renting property, including protection against illegal search and seizure (Article VIII); and the right to establish the means to enforce all such provisions (Article IX).[35]

Although the Bill of Rights received overwhelming support in the student referendum (869 for and 178 against), the administration declined to accept it.[36] The SGA continued to press the proposal over the next several years and received encouragement from several outside speakers. One was Saul Alinsky, a well-known speaker and professional community organizer, who spoke at Villanova in October 1968 as the Student Bill of Rights was being completed. According to the *Villanovan*, Alinsky had told several hundred students at the Field House that "the guys IN power don't give up power to the guys OUT of power without a struggle."[37] In the winter of 1969, and again in the fall of 1972, new-left advocate Tom Hayden came to campus, partly in response to the growing antiwar movement at Villanova. On his second visit he was accompanied by Hollywood actress Jane Fonda, whom he would soon marry (and later divorce). Fonda's presence was largely responsible for the estimated five thousand people who packed the Field House to hear what she and Hayden had to say. Fonda herself urged the students to "talk to people and spread the word of resistance."[38] Meanwhile, there had been attempts to organize a campus chapter of Students for a Democratic Society (SDS), which Hayden had helped to establish earlier in the decade. The chapter attracted few adherents at Villanova, however, and soon faded from the local scene. While it lasted, however, it helped to draw other members of the student body, who were not themselves members of SDS, into the student rights movement.[39]

Despite the administration's refusal to accept the Student Bill of Rights, students continued to press various principles embodied in the document, such as a say in how university funds were spent. Thus when the administration announced in April 1969, without any consultation or warning, that tuition and room and board would rise from a total of $2,600 annually to $3,000 the following year, many were furious. In fact, Villanova's tuition was among the highest in the region. The University of Pennsylvania and Haverford College, for example, were greater, but Villanova's was higher than La Salle and St. Joseph's, its primary competitors among Catholic institutions in the area.[40]

Protests against the projected increases at Villanova culminated in a thirty-three-hour sit-in on April 21 and 22 by some one thousand students at Tolentine Hall, which continued to house the president's office and the offices of other top administration officials. Father Welsh, then president, agreed (along with the board of trustees) to postpone the increases and to consider some of the students' other demands, which included trustee ap-

proval of the Student Bill of Rights and implementation of a recently proposed University Senate.[41]

The following spring, when a rise in tuition was again announced, the SGA
hired a lawyer to convey their objections to the administration, instead of
resorting to demonstrations. The crux of their argument was that Villanova
was spending its revenues in wasteful and inappropriate ways, including a
$300,000 subsidy for football during the previous season. They also criti-
cized the university for its mediocre record of fund-raising, which forced it
to rely too heavily on tuition and other student fees.[42]

In an attempt to provide a forum where students, faculty, and administration could discuss financial and other sorts of grievances and arrive at a
collaborative solution, Donald B. Kelley, a member of the History Department and Director of the Honors Program, had proposed a University Senate
in 1968.[43] According to Dr. Kelley, in an editorial he wrote for the *Villanovan* in February of that year, Villanova was the only major college or
university in the Philadelphia area that did not have such a body. The growing dissatisfaction on campus now made it imperative for Villanova to follow
the example of other institutions:

> It is time to create a strong and effective University Senate to unite
> administration, faculty, and students in collective discussions which
> concern them all. It is time to create a public forum wherein pro-
> posed university decisions must stand the test of open debate and
> challenge before they are passed into laws. It is time, in short, to
> modernize the decision-making apparatus of this university and make
> it more efficient and democratic.[44]

Petitions for a University Senate began circulating among students and
faculty in the fall of 1968. In November the local chapter of the AAUP
endorsed the concept of such a body by a vote of 23 to 1. But it was the
student demonstrations in April 1969 against increases in tuition, room, and
board, which included demands to establish the University Senate, that
convinced the administration and the board of trustees to endorse the
idea.[45] Father Welsh authorized a "tripartite commission," composed of representatives from the faculty, students, and administration, to explore the
prospects of a University Senate and to make a report in the fall of 1969.
After working for five months, including the summer of 1969, the commission submitted its recommendations in November. In February 1970 the
board of trustees approved the Senate Constitution, which gave the body
power to legislate in academic matters concerning more than one college in
the university and to formulate and pass legislation involving the faculty and

student life. Either the president of the university or the board of trustees could veto measures passed by the Senate.[46]

The Senate Constitution called for 38 senators, 12 from the administration, 12 from the faculty, 12 from the student body, and 2 from the alumni. Of the 12 administrative senators, 5 were ex officio: the Executive Vice President and the Vice Presidents of Academic Affairs, Student Affairs, Financial Affairs, Public Information, and Development. The remaining seven delegates from the administration were appointed by the university president and served at his pleasure. The twelve faculty senators were elected, with representation weighted according to the relative sizes of the various colleges. Student senators, also elected, were required to be at least junior undergraduates, second-year law students, or full-time graduate students with more than one semester at Villanova. Alumni representatives had to be graduates of at least five years and were elected by the general membership of the Alumni Association.[47]

The University Senate held its first meeting in September 1970 amid great optimism. Unfortunately senate deliberations changed few minds in the early years, and confrontations among the three principal groups—students, faculty, and administration—continued. The students sometimes charged that their opinions were ignored in the senate by the faculty and especially by the administration. For example, the senate overwhelmingly passed legislation allowing limited parietals several times beginning in 1970–71, only to have the president and the board of trustees either veto or fail to approve the action.[48] In early 1971 the administration refused to provide the senate with detailed information about the pending university budget. Finally, in April 1973 the board agreed to discuss certain financial matters with the University Senate, but confrontations between the administration and the senate in other areas would continue.

The University Senate by no means replaced other faculty and student-body organizations. The SGA continued to exist, as did the Faculty Council and the Villanova Chapter of the AAUP. Of the two faculty groups, the AAUP became the more militant. As early as 1942, for example, the local AAUP had taken up the question of faculty salaries, becoming increasingly vocal on the subject during the late 1960s—a reflection, perhaps, of the somewhat activist spirit on campus.[49] In September 1966 AAUP president Dr. Bernard F. Reilly, a professor in the History Department, presented the administration with "A Statement on Faculty Compensation." "The simple fact is," he declared, "that current levels of compensation at Villanova are far from competitive even within the relatively restricted area of Catholic University life."[50]

Seven years later, in 1973, the AAUP made a bid to become an official faculty union. A number of issues led to this decision, but a surprise announcement by the administration to increase teaching loads was the principal catalyst in the movement to unionize. However, the AAUP failed to win a vote as the faculty's official bargaining agent in November of that year.[51] Plans for a second vote on union representation in February 1980 were derailed by the U.S. Supreme Court case *NLRB v. Yeshiva University* (1980), which held that under certain circumstances faculty could be considered part of management. In reaction to the decision, the National Labor Relations Board (NLRB) itself canceled the representation vote at Villanova.[52]

Although the AAUP chapter at Villanova was not part of the official governing structure of the university, its activities had a genuine impact on faculty opinion. According to a 1987 Report of the Faculty Council, this was especially true of the AAUP's "information and discussion sessions among faculty."[53]

Confrontations between the faculty and the administration at Villanova were mild compared with what had transpired at New York's St. John's University (operated by the Vincentians) during the late 1960s. There faculty members had been summarily dismissed for insisting on a more collaborative style of governance. Where St. John's administration had been intractable on the question of faculty rights, Villanova's faculty and administration had demonstrated greater cooperation and flexibility.[54]

Despite the creation of a University Senate and assertions that faculty and students should have a larger voice in the formulation of university policy, Villanova students were making no headway on their Bill of Rights. Early in 1974 matters came to a head over a question of due process for sixteen students who were suspended after drugs (mostly marijuana) were allegedly found in their rooms. There were questions about the nature of the evidence against the students as well as the methods of search and seizure used to obtain that evidence. The students were also angry that the administration had not brought the case before the Student Court, thus violating a due process procedure to which the university had formally agreed back in 1968. The resulting frustration led to the largest demonstration in Villanova's history.

An Ad Hoc Committee of Student Leaders responded to these complaints by publishing a list of grievances in the *Villanovan* on February 6. They demanded the immediate implementation of the Student Bill of Rights and the reinstatement of the suspended students, in addition to a Self-Determination Doctrine, which would guarantee students control over their own affairs at the university. The students also wanted a voice in faculty rank and tenure decisions, in part because certain professors sympathetic to their cause had failed to receive tenure or promotion.[55]

In order to press their demands, the ad hoc committee organized a meeting of 1,500 students at the Field House on February 7, 1974, during which

Student-rights demonstration, February 1974. VUA.

they decided to occupy Tolentine Hall. The siege lasted four days. When negotiations broke down, the students occupied Tolentine Hall a second time on February 13 and 14. At that point Father McCarthy agreed to present the Student Bill of Rights to the board of trustees and to implement certain due process procedures regarding student discipline. McCarthy also said that he favored student input on faculty rank and tenure decisions and promised to allow for student discussion of the university budget. However, he denied the requests for student self-determination because of the board's strong opposition to parietals. The students dropped their demand that the suspended individuals be allowed to return to campus when several of them confessed to the charges against them. Most of the other issues were left to future discussion. The two February occupations of Tolentine Hall and the negotiations between students and administration received wide coverage on local radio and television and in the metropolitan press.[56]

The due process question erupted again on April 9, 1974, when fifty-two male students were expelled for refusing to leave a party at Sheehan Hall, a women's residence, when it officially ended at 9:00 P.M. Many of those expelled had been leaders of the Ad Hoc Committee, who contended that the disciplinary action was really in retaliation for their protests earlier in

Students protesting outside administrative offices in Tolentine Hall, February 7, 1974. VUA.

the year. They also charged that their rights to free speech and due process had been violated. Led by former SGA president Richard Brown, twelve of the accused filed suit in July against the university in federal district court, asking for approximately $11 million in damages. The case, known as *Brown v. Villanova*, was eventually settled out of court—that is, in February 1975 the university reinstated the expelled students and they dropped their charges against Villanova.[57]

Besides protests on local matters, Villanova's students expressed concern over national and international issues. These included safety and the environment, civil rights, and the war in Vietnam. For example, students could hear talks in 1966 and again in 1970 from automobile industry critic Ralph Nader, who had recently published his *Unsafe at Any Speed*. In the fall of 1966 Vance Packard, a critic of American advertising and the nation's continuing waste of natural resources, appeared on campus.[58]

By 1970 the Free University was offering a course on ecology. That same year the *Villanovan* carried several articles on the environmental crisis, and in April, as part of Villanova's observances of Earth Week, Paul Erlich, author of *The Population Bomb*, spoke before an audience of 1,200.[59] In April 1971 Villanova hosted a conference called "Fate of the Oceans," a three-day program attended by 150 students from thirty different colleges and universities. Among the speakers was Harris L. Wofford, then President of Bryn Mawr College and who two decades later became a U.S. Senator from Pennsylvania.[60] In this and other forums students questioned an older generation who allegedly believed that unbridled capitalism and exploitation of the earth's resources would ensure prosperity and happiness for all. They also doubted their elders' seemingly blind faith in science and technology.

Beginning in the 1950s, race relations were addressed at Villanova in various ways. In October 1956 the Villanova Law Forum sponsored a lecture by Thurgood Marshall, then special counsel for the NAACP and later an associate justice of the U.S. Supreme Court.[61] And during the late 1950s and early 1960s there were editorials in the *Villanovan* criticizing racism. One of these in October 1961 attacked racism on two grounds, first that it was illogical, because race had nothing inherently to do with intellectual or social ability, and second that it violated a basic Christian obligation to love one's neighbor.[62] It was also in 1961 that U.S. Supreme Court Justice Tom E. Clark addressed the annual Law School dinner on the subject of civil rights.[63]

On the evening of January 20, 1965, Villanovans heard Reverend Doctor Martin Luther King, Jr., speak in a program sponsored by the Villanova Forum. More than four thousand people packed the Field House to hear King, and another thousand were turned away for lack of seating. Three years later, in April 1968, Villanovans mourned King's tragic assassination with a prayer march.[64] Other well-known civil rights spokesmen who visited Villanova were comedian Dick Gregory (1969), author and playwright LeRoy Jones (1971), and Roy Innis of CORE (1970).[65]

Yet on a campus where the number of African American students was negligible, the civil rights movement had little personal relevance, and there were no civil rights demonstrations as such at Villanova. This was certainly not true with regard to the Vietnam War, for thousands of Villanova students faced the draft and the real possibility of being killed or maimed in Southeast Asia. Unlike the environmental or civil rights movements, some Villanovans actively protested against the Vietnam War. Although they were a minority of the student population, it was not unusual to have several hundred students participating in antiwar protests.

For many young Americans the Vietnam War was their first great disillusionment with official power. Brought up to believe that their government

Reverend Dr. Martin Luther King, Jr. (*center*), who spoke at Villanova on January 20, 1965. To the right is Reverend John A. Klekotka, O.S.A., University President, and on the left is Thomas J. Furst, Student Body President. VUA.

was based in the fairest, most moral, and most rational system of politics in the world, they were shocked and angered to discover that the government was waging an unjust war in Vietnam and then lying to the American people in order to conceal its blunders and maintain popular support. Racist attitudes toward the Vietnamese themselves, called "slants" and "gooks," and a policy of military service that fell disproportionately on racial minorities and the white working class, was for many further evidence of the injustice and immorality of the war in Southeast Asia. Finally, many young Americans were appalled by the mounting death toll and atrocities committed by all sides, including the United States. For the generation of baby-boomers, who had been taught that the United States had never started a war and had always fought on the side of justice and right, these revelations were both shocking and infuriating.[66]

Serious reactions to the war in Vietnam began at Villanova in early 1964 as the United States began escalating the conflict. For several years articles and editorials had given both sides of the argument over Vietnam, and by 1966 the antiwar argument had clearly scored a victory in the pages of the *Villa-novan*, though by no means with the majority of students on campus. Nor was the bulk of the faculty won over to the antiwar movement. Many faculty members continued to see the war as a battle against Godless Communism.

Nevertheless, when students returned to campus in September 1966 they could read this on the editorial page of the *Villanovan*:

> The United States, my country and yours, is wrong.... It's nice to have that comforting feeling of always being the Good Guy, the champion of Democracy, the Red, White and Blue knight in shining armor. But delusion dressed up in the fancy duds of patriotism is an expensive convenience for any country.[67]

Some of the most effective pieces were laden with sarcasm:

> So you tell me we are not the aggressors. Yes, I understand; we kill and bomb for peace. You tell me we are there to make the world "safe for democracy." So we are going to kill every last Communist in the whole wide world; and then when we get through with them we'll get every last socialist. Then the "survivors" can all be happy, good, "fellow Americans." How disgustingly homogeneous. What an ideal situation for ruthless, Orwellian type of authoritarian government.[68]

Up to 1967 criticism of the war at Villanova was entirely verbal, but in October of that year about twenty people—a combination of students, Augustinians, and lay faculty—held a silent vigil on the terrace (or "platform," as the students called it) in front of Dougherty Hall, which continued to serve as Villanova's student center. The event was organized by Concerned Citizens, a local contingent that had associated itself with the national Mobilization Group to End the War in Vietnam. A second demonstration took place a month later. This time Concerned Citizens picketed the placement office, then located on the first floor of Sheehan Hall, where recruiters from Dow Chemical were meeting with students. Dow was manufacturing napalm, which was being used with such hideous effects in Vietnam, prompting students at a number of universities to demonstrate against Dow recruiters. The Villanova demonstrators were small in number and confronted several hundred hostile students, who threw water and eggs on them from the second floor of Sheehan Hall and shouted insults. It was also in 1967 that the first "teach-in" occurred at Villanova, a series of lectures and discussions held outside the regular classroom in order to explore the war in Vietnam from a variety of angles. The first of these was led in part by Dr. Fred J. Carrier of the History Department.[69]

In 1969, and again in 1970, Villanova students participated in a nation-wide Moratorium against the war, held on October 15. For the first obser-vance the local Moratorium Committee organized a day of films, lectures, and discussions on the war. The featured speaker was Allard Lowenstein, a freshman congressman from New York who had recently organized Demo-crats against the war and initiated a movement to deprive President Lyndon B. Johnson of the Democratic nomination in 1968.[70] Lowenstein made a dramatic arrival on campus by helicopter and spoke to a crowd on what was called Kennedy Mall (then an open area outside Kennedy Hall that had, ironically, once been part of a secluded seminary garden) about 4:00 in the afternoon. There were also a debate and teach-in on the war in the Vasey Hall auditorium, and antiwar movies at Dougherty Hall.[71] The Moratorium Committee's "Statement of Purpose" for 1969 read in part:

> In pursuing this war the United States has reached the lowest depths of depravity. No single, political act is of greater significance in revers-ing this decline toward the ultimate degeneration of America than ending the war in Vietnam. For the sake of our own country as well as, more obviously, that of Vietnam, and for the sake of all humanity, we must halt the insane slaughter taking place this very minute.[72]

To charge that the United States was depraved and degenerate was a clear and dramatic break with a post–World War II culture that had insisted upon the eternal righteousness of America.

In December 1969 ten individuals from the campus antiwar movement "occupied" a small side chapel in the St. Thomas of Villanova Church for an entire weekend, from 11:00 Friday night until the end of Sunday Masses at 7:00 P.M. Led by students Bob Moser and Joseph Reidy, co-chairs of the Villanova Moratorium Committee, the contingent included Reverend Jo-seph M. Bradley, O.S.A., the university chaplain; Reverend Robert C. Totaro, O.S.A., assistant chaplain; and Dr. Carrier of the History Department. During this time they quietly read the names of all the Americans who had been killed up to that point in Vietnam.[73]

Like other campuses, Villanova saw a series of demonstrations against the local ROTC unit. Led by Concerned Citizens, the first such demonstration at Villanova took place in late March 1968 as the Navy ROTC contingent drilled on Mendel Field. The demonstrators sang antiwar songs and joined in a prayer for peace, led by Reverend George P. Lawless, O.S.A. By 1970 there were persistent calls in the *Villanovan* to abolish the NROTC. Among those making this demand were Dr. Carrier and student Joseph Reidy of the Villa-nova Moratorium Committee. In April 1970 they wrote: "A specter is haunt-ing the American university campus. It is the specter of Death. It haunts in the form of ROTC and Villanova has not escaped its presence."[74] For Reidy, Carrier, and their supporters, Navy ROTC and other involvements with the military were incompatible with Villanova's being a Catholic university. According to *Villanovan* writer Tony Esposito,

> The purpose of a Catholic education should primarily be the teaching of Christian ethics. But how is Villanova different from any other university? Aren't the military and industrial recruiters that come to this campus the same as those of other universities? Although Villanovans receive a more expansive background in Christian teachings than those students at a non-Catholic university, these teachings do not lead to actions that are different from anyone else's. Christians are not even nominally implied by the presence on-campus of the largest NROTC unit in the country.[75]

However sincere, such opposition to Villanova's NROTC program was not shared by most people on campus. In fact, while enrollment in ROTC programs in the greater Philadelphia area dropped by an overall average of 48.1 percent in 1969, Villanova's NROTC unit grew by 6 percent that same year, going from 400 to 425 students.[76]

Although the antiwar movement at Villanova had to contend with a large and flourishing NROTC installation on campus, and although the movement could count on the support of only a minority of the student body, its organizers could usually gather about 500 (approximately one-tenth of the undergraduate population) to turn out for demonstrations in the late 1960s. Villanova could also send the largest number of antiwar protesters to join students from the other colleges on the Main Line (Bryn Mawr, Haverford, Rosemont), in part because it was the largest of these institutions. During the march on Washington in May 1970, held to protest the American invasion of Cambodia, Villanovans filled ten buses with students and provided fifty student marshals trained in crowd control.[77]

Yet in contrast to the protest movement, there was a program at Villanova called "Vietnam Mail Call," instituted by students in the fall of 1965 when they purchased some 20,000 greeting cards to send to the troops for Christmas. In 1969 they began enlisting students from other colleges and universities, and the following year they succeeded in sending nearly 350,000 cards to American military personnel in Southeast Asia. Every year these efforts received wide publicity and were reported in newspapers all over the United States. President Richard M. Nixon was so impressed by the effort that he invited three of the Villanova organizers (Thomas Treachy, Thomas Creagh, and Robert Breslin) to the White House in December 1970 to thank them in person. The three students presented Nixon with a Villanova

Students from Villanova's "Vietnam Mail Call" look on as U.S. President Richard M. Nixon receives them in the White House and signs one of their greeting cards for the troops in Southeast Asia, December 1970. VUA.

warmup suit, and the president signed three of the cards to be sent that year to the troops on the front.[78] Although the students claimed that Mail Call Vietnam was an entirely nonpolitical operation that did not necessarily signal support for the war, their visit to Nixon, a man whom many antiwar activists saw as the very personification of an immoral war, seemed to reflect the somewhat limited opposition to the war on the Villanova campus. Photographs of the White House visitors neatly dressed in suits and ties in some ways looked like a scene out of the 1950s, or even the 1930s.

That these three Villanova students went to the White House only six months after Nixon's invasion of Cambodia in the spring of 1970 had led to massive rioting on campuses and the fatal shooting of students at Kent State and Jackson State universities was also revealing. Unlike many other campuses, which exploded in violence, Villanovans remained remarkably calm, although the university did shut down one day during the Cambodian crisis. A reporter from the *Philadelphia Bulletin* who visited the university on May 6, during a week when many campuses were in upheaval, noted that it was business as usual. Rock music blasted from residence hall windows while students sunbathed or studied for finals on the well-tended Villanova lawns. One student who was interviewed told the reporter, "It's mostly conservative here, . . . though there was some interest in the Moratorium. . . . There isn't much interest in Cambodia or Kent State—some talking, but not much doing." Another student added, "It's the apathy of Villanova and the Main Line."[79]

Instead of rioting, Villanovans who wanted to protest the Cambodian invasion and the slayings at Kent State and Jackson State joined with students from other area colleges and universities in a peaceful march on Independence Square in Philadelphia as well as in Washington.[80] Villanova's student body president, Neil A. Oxman (who later became a famous political media consultant in Philadelphia), took the initiative in drafting a statement signed by twenty student leaders from East Coast institutions and published on May 13, 1970, as a full-page letter in the *New York Times* addressed to President Nixon. It appealed to the President to end the war, accused him of deception and usurpation of the U.S. Constitution, and warned that they would urge every American to help to defeat his policies.[81]

The last major antiwar protest occurred among Villanova students at commencement exercises in May 1971, where Admiral Elmo Zumwalt, Chief of Naval Operations, was the principal speaker. The ceremonies took place at the Philadelphia Civic Center, the site of Villanova commencements from 1965 through 1972.[82] Eight persons were arrested for throwing stink bombs in the lobby, and three hundred members of the faculty (including Augustinian priests) and student body walked out of the hall when Zumwalt began to speak. Many other students stood up and cheered to support the walk out. At that point Joe Morrisey, a political science major and member of Vietnam Veterans Against the War, stood in army fatigues before the stage and chanted, "No more war."[83]

For decades Villanova had called upon its students to become "Catholic Gentlemen." Many would have insisted that the university's demonstrators were anything but gentlemen, but the protesting students and the faculty members who joined them believed that their activities against the war, as well as against other injustices in American life, were grounded in Catholic— and Christian—morality. In that sense they could assert that they stood in the tradition of *Rerum Novarum*, Catholic Action, and Vatican II's call to practice the social gospel. Thus in some ways they were continuing a tradition of "Catholic counterculture" that went back nearly a century.[84]

The administration's view of the more extreme demonstrators, whether against the war or on behalf of student rights, was very different. To Villanova's two presidents who served between 1967 and 1975 they were disruptive agents who often were challenging legitimate authority, moral truth, and the rights of others. The first of these presidents was Reverend Robert J. Welsh, O.S.A. (1921–93). Born in Philadelphia, Welsh taught theology at Villanova between 1955 and 1961, and from 1961 until his elevation to the presidency in 1967 he served as Dean of the College of Arts and Sciences. Like virtually all Villanova's former presidents, the position was assigned to him by his religious superiors, not one for which he had applied. Welsh had been asked by the prior-provincial in late August 1967 to assume the presidency from Reverend Joseph A. Flaherty, O.S.A., who after just two years in office had asked to step down because of poor health.[85]

In August 1969, two years after he himself became president and four months after massive student protests over tuition increases, Welsh warned that he would not tolerate any more serious disruptions. In a letter addressed to the entire university and its friends, he wrote,

> Destructive actions among the few must be defeated by the constructive purposes of the many. Individuals or groups who would wish to bring the university to its knees must recognize the determination of the rest of the community to use every legitimate means to oppose them. . . . However regrettably, such means may include sanctions and disciplinary action, not excluding an appeal to the power of the courts. One can hope that it may not come to this, but criminal activity must be recognized for what it is and dealt with firmly. . . . The university may be a harbor of truth; it cannot be a sanctuary for crime.[86]

That fall, in a talk before the Italian-American Club of nearby Wayne, Welsh commented again on campus disruptions. His remarks were quoted extensively in a local newspaper, the *Suburban and Wayne Times*, and then reprinted in the *Villanovan*:

> I have about had it. I am willing to engage in dialogue, but the students are not interested in dialogue, but only in their own views. . . .
>      We have had the cult of youth too long. We need a recrudescence of values. . . . The problems of the campus are symptomatic of our country. The time has come for us to set our Faith to work, and perhaps our country will not go through a violent revolution.[87]

Welsh believed that he had been misquoted—and quoted out of context—by the notoriously conservative newspaper, and in fact he held that the students did have a right to protest and express their views. But he insisted that students could not be allowed to disrupt the work of the university or to violate the free speech of others.[88]

Yet some students reacted bitterly to Father Welsh's statements. One of the ugliest incidents took place during the last week of April 1971 as part of a protest against an alleged lack of cooperation on student issues from the administration. Early in the morning of April 27, someone threw a Molotov cocktail through the window of Welsh's office in Tolentine Hall. No one was there at the time, and fortunately the device was improperly constructed and did not explode, but the fuse did set fire to a portion of the rug and curtains. The next night another faulty bomb was hurled at a security guard house near Bartley Hall. On April 30 student leaders called a strike, and about five hundred students boycotted classes. According to the *Villanovan*, they also gathered approximately 1,500 signatures calling for Welsh's resignation from the presidency and a restructuring of the board of trustees.

Shortly thereafter Welsh submitted his resignation, although whether he had bowed to student pressure was unclear since the university refused to state any official reason for his departure.[89] The *Villanova Alumnus* for September 1971 observed that student demands may have been a factor but speculated that the most important reason for his stepping down was frustration over not being able "to exercise all the administrative powers and control that he felt appropriate to his office." The article went on to say that Welsh had wanted to make certain changes at the university and had been prevented from doing so. Unfortunately, the article did not explain just who or what had stood in his way. An oral tradition holds that Welsh had wanted to replace certain members of the administration with persons of his own choosing but had been thwarted by provincial authorities. This issue, rather than student pressure, was what probably led to his resignation.[90]

Reverend Edward J. McCarthy, O.S.A., who succeeded Father Welsh in the presidency, was even more adamant about upholding constituted authority. Born in 1912 in Troy, New York, Father McCarthy had taught history at Villanova from 1940 to 1946, when he joined the faculty of La Universidad de Santo Tomás de Villanueva in Havana, Cuba. He returned to the Main Line campus as Dean of Arts and Sciences (1948–50), as Dean of what was then called the Extension and Graduate School (1950–53), and as Vice President for Academic Affairs (1953–57). In 1958 he went back to Cuba, where he served as Executive Vice President of the university until he and twelve other Augustinian priests were arrested and expelled by Fidel Castro following the Bay of Pigs invasion in April 1961. That same year he became the president and principal founder of Biscayne College (later St. Thomas College) in Miami, Florida, a successor to Villanova in Cuba, which opened mainly to serve the thousands of Cuban émigrés who streamed into the Miami area. In 1968 McCarthy became a professor of history at Merrimack College, an Augustinian institution in Andover, Massachusetts.[91]

McCarthy was Villanova's first president to be recommended by a search committee of the board of trustees. The University Senate also considered the candidates through its own search committee and made recommendations to the board. By an overwhelming vote, 17 to 1, the senate designated as its first choice not Father McCarthy but Reverend John M. Driscoll, O.S.A., then Villanova's Vice President for Academic Affairs. Despite the senate's strong support for Driscoll, however, the board selected McCarthy, who took office knowing he was not the first choice of the students, faculty, or administration—all of whom had been represented on the senate's search committee.[92] According to Edward J. Rideout, then Executive Director of the Alumni Association, the board had opted for McCarthy because they believed his absence from campus for several years would allow him to be more open-minded in settling Villanova's troubles than Driscoll, who had been part of the Villanova administration since 1965. Rideout's remarks were published as part of a front-page story from a local newspaper, *Today's Post*, published in nearby King of Prussia.[93]

Gregory Landers, president of the Villanova student body and a member of the University Senate, explained to the same newspaper why the senate had preferred Driscoll to McCarthy. According to Landers, the Senate had been wary of McCarthy's tendency to "advertise his conservatism," adding that McCarthy "made statements about students keeping their noses out of running the school." As for Driscoll, whom Landers clearly preferred, "He listens to everybody, is in tune with the times, objective in his thinking, and makes the right decision at the right time."[94]

McCarthy had in fact made no secret of his conservative attitudes toward university administration and certain social issues. In an interview with the *Philadelphia Bulletin*, which was published in the June 30, 1971, issue, the day before he officially assumed the presidency, McCarthy said, "I look at the problem of Villanova—as at most private colleges—as being one of conserving." Nearly a year later, in a talk before the Wayne-Paoli Branch of the American Red Cross, he outlined an essentially conservative role for higher education:

> Universities have lost their orientation and a clear definition of their objective. They try to be all things to all men.
> We can be concerned about science, ecology, social problems— we can even talk about why those Catholics in Northern Ireland are persecuting my Presbyterian ancestors, but that's not why we're in business.[95]

Soon after taking office he also reportedly told the board of trustees that they "must make certain the ideas of the founders [will] be preserved."[96] "When Villanova ceases to be Catholic," he added on a later occasion, "then Villanova should not exist."[97] In an interview that appeared in the November issue of the *Villanova Alumnus*, the new president reiterated this conservative stance:

> I have certain principles of education that I am very firm about. One is that the people responsible from a corporate point of view is the Board of Trustees and that their authority cannot be eroded or divided in any way. . . . I don't think there should be any question about where the authority lies and how decisions ought to be made.[98]

McCarthy also predicted that he would not be "very tolerant of sit-ins." Remarking to a reporter that "sex still exists," he announced that he was absolutely opposed to residence-hall visitations. At the opening of classes in September 1971 he also made no secret of his belief that student competencies were severely limited. "Students don't know enough to determine what to study," he remarked to the *Philadelphia Inquirer*, adding, "Are they here to learn or run the school?"[99] Consistent with his belief that college students were not mature enough to make important decisions, he opposed lowering the voting age to eighteen, fearing that Villanova undergraduates would elect "Joe Blow a commissioner [of the local Radnor Township] just as a prank."[100]

Father McCarthy now became the target of student criticism, especially for what friends and foes alike described as an unwillingness to compromise his principles. In March 1972 the *Villanovan* charged that, although McCarthy sometimes listened to students, he would never change his mind.[101] A year later the campus newspaper carried another long editorial on McCarthy's attitude toward compromise, accompanied by a cartoon showing McCarthy standing in the center of the Villanova campus, dressed in his black suit and clerical collar, with a well-groomed member of the board of trustees on one side and a long-haired student on the other. All three had dug their heels into the ground and were tugging at "Villanova," represented in the drawing by several familiar buildings. None of them seemed willing to budge.[102] Three years later, in January 1975, the *Philadelphia Inquirer* ran a story about McCarthy's firm stand on administrative prerogatives. It included a statement from a former student who said that McCarthy "bristled whenever his authority was challenged." "He backed down from no one, at least not publicly, and never from a student."[103]

Even the *Villanova Alumnus*, in its issue for June 1974, commented on McCarthy's unwillingness to bend:

> In effect, what it all comes down to is Father McCarthy's concept of how the University is to be governed. It probably would not be unfair to say that the voice of dissent is unwelcome in this administration. . . .

Say what you will for Father McCarthy; he is not a man who changes his mind or backtracks in the face of criticism.[104]

McCarthy's stance may have been part of his basic temperament, but there is a possibility that his unhappy experiences with the Cuban Revolution just a decade or so before made him view any challenge to authority with suspicion. Indeed, shortly after his return from Cuba in 1961 McCarthy had addressed some five thousand high school students attending a publication workshop at Villanova, and made several recommendations about how to stop the growth of Communist dictatorships. Among these were: "Suspect people who are going to save America" and "Defend your own philosophy vigorously."[105]

In fact, McCarthy had agreed to certain compromises following the two occupations of Tolentine Hall in February 1974 and again when *Brown v. Villanova* was settled out of court the following year. But he announced his resignation from the presidency in January 1975, just as an agreement on the Brown case was being reached, and before any of the student demands from the previous winter and spring had been enacted. Although McCarthy, then sixty-three, cited his age as the sole reason for stepping down, his departure from the presidential chair ultimately saved him from having to compromise his views on parietals, which he saw as inconsistent with Catholic morality, and from allowing the students a greater role in university governance, which he deemed contrary to the rational and legitimate powers of the president and board. The *Villanovan*, in any case, interpreted McCarthy's resignation as the only way in which he could maintain his personal beliefs in the face of constant challenges. It also saw his decision as a tragic one, for McCarthy as well as the university:

> Fr. McCarthy will leave Villanova with the courage of his convictions still intact. His impressive self-confidence enabled him to bear the huge responsibility of running a university, yet that same virtue stands out as the tragic flaw which led Villanova into the dark days of controversy and student unrest. . . .
>
> Many voices, once raised in advice and anticipation, went hoarse with frustrated tongues. . . . Fr. McCarthy did not take advantage of the strength around him. He will never know how many friends there might have been.[106]

McCarthy's successor was Father Driscoll, whom the University Senate had strongly recommended for president four years earlier. A native Philadelphian, born in 1923, Driscoll received his doctorate in philosophy from the Catholic University of America. He taught at Archbishop Carroll High School in Washington, D.C., and at Merrimack College in Andover, Massachusetts, before becoming Vice President for Academic Affairs at Villanova in 1965.[107] Chosen as Villanova's president in 1975, he would hold the position until 1988, a thirteen-year tenure surpassed only by Delurey's fifteen-year term at the turn of the century.

Although Driscoll shared essentially the same values as his immediate predecessors, he was not so outspoken in his disagreements with students and felt more comfortable with a collaborative style of leadership. In *Today's Post* Driscoll was described by an old classmate as "a soft-spoken, humble, friendly man." The newspaper itself wrote that "he has distinguished himself as a friend of students and an ally of faculty and administration alike."[108] An article in another local newspaper, the *Main Line Times*, commented on Driscoll's soothing demeanor during a recent interview: "Throughout the interview Driscoll showed a knack for the diplomatic turn of phrase in contrast to the somewhat bluff manner of [his predecessor,] Father McCarthy."[109] The *Catholic Standard and Times* also credited Driscoll with playing a large role in mediating student disputes with the administration in February 1974, as did *Today's Post*.[110] On the subject of student discipline Driscoll himself was quoted by the *Post* as saying, "I would have no intention of being a student baby-sitter. This is not a place for babies."[111] Such comments, coupled with a easygoing personality, somewhat grandfatherly demeanor (at least to the students), and the subsidence of student activism all over the nation, allowed him to preside over a largely peaceful campus.

Soon after taking office Father Driscoll spoke at length with students about their concerns. In January 1976, for instance, he addressed a large audience in the West Lounge of Dougherty Hall. He made no specific promises, but he did say in response to a question about parietals that he would "argue for the best interests of the students." Reactions were mixed, some thinking him "evasive." Others thought that he was behind them but that his "hands are tied" by bureaucratic red tape.[112]

From that point, relations between students and the administration improved remarkably, as Driscoll opened the way for the accommodation of many long-held demands. Although the students did not obtain everything they had wanted, most of their grievances were settled satisfactorily within two years of Driscoll's January 1976 address. Freshmen orientation, long plagued by humiliating dress and deference to older students, was so completely restructured by the fall of 1976 that an editorial writer in the *Villanovan* concluded that it gave hope for even more positive changes on campus.[113] In October of the same year, Reverend John E. Deegan, O.S.A., Vice President for Student Life, said that one of his main responsibilities was to "strengthen the competency, autonomy, and personal integrity of all students."[114] Deegan's comment came on the heels of the recent approval by the board of trustees of what was called a new "Student Life Package," which

Students and parents in the space between Falvey Memorial Library and Alumni Hall during orientation in 1986, a far cry from the freshmen hazing of earlier decades. VUA.

sought to reorganize student affairs so as to give undergraduates more independence and personal responsibility. Editorial comment in the *Villanovan* on the board's action could not have been more positive:

> The passage of the new Student Life Proposal by the Villanova Board of Trustees . . . is quite probably the most important and innovative change since the university first began to admit women. The new Student Life Proposal is a multi-dimensional package, which promises to go a long way in fulfilling Villanova's stated goal of producing graduates who are not only academically but socially prepared for the problems and challenges of the so-called real world.
>
> There are a great many specific issues which the Student Life Proposal touches on. They all however center around the concept of providing the Villanova student with a greater degree of autonomy, in order to facilitate the shaping and strengthening of the individual.[115]

One of the most important aspects of this restructuring of student life was the introduction of limited visitation privileges in September 1976. At first,

members of the opposite sex could visit residence halls from noon to 1:00
A.M. on Fridays and Saturdays, and from noon to 11:00 P.M. on Sundays. In
1979 visitation was extended to weekdays. Hours were 3:00 to 11:00 P.M.,
Monday through Thursday, with the weekend schedule the same as in
1976.[116]

Another aspect of the Student Life Package was a Student Judicial Board
System, approved in the fall of 1977, which provided for due process in
which students were represented. Two judicial agencies were created: a
Residence Hall Judicial Board, which dealt with cases arising in the individual residence halls, and an All Campus Judicial Board, which had jurisdiction
over matters outside the halls. However, neither board could treat cases
involving possible expulsion from the university. In September 1981 the
boards were replaced by one University Judicial Board, composed of three
students, one faculty member, one administrator, and the university's Judicial Affairs Officer. This board could consider all matters of student discipline, and its decisions were final.[117]

The students also secured a voice on the board of trustees in the fall of
1973, when several committees of the board admitted two students each as
voting members. These were the committees on Academic Affairs, Building,
Finance, Investments, Development and Public Relations, and Student Affairs.
Students failed to obtain representation on the university's Rank and Tenure
Committee, largely because faculty feared breaches of confidentiality. But in
1982 faculty entered into an agreement that required them to submit some
kind of student evaluation when applying for tenure or promotion.[118]

A comprehensive Student Bill of Rights was never implemented, though
certain items or ideas contained in it (often modified) were adopted at
varying times as official policy. Thus in place of a Bill of Rights per se, the
university set down a list of student rights and responsibilities as part of a
new and all-inclusive student manual called the *Blue Book*, which first
appeared in 1977.[119]

By granting a number of student wishes, Father Driscoll and his administration were able to bring peace to the university while at the same time
creating new channels of communication. Henceforth university government would be more collaborative, though some students and faculty would
continue to believe that it was not collaborative enough. That the values of
open debate and representative government made such great strides at a
Catholic, Augustinian university like Villanova showed just how far the university (and American Catholics in general) had gone in absorbing the
values of American civic life. With the threat of major student disruptions
behind them, the university could now focus on academic progress and
general excellence.

# ATTAINING EXCELLENCE

By the late 1970s there was little doubt at Villanova about what it took to become a great university. Nearly four decades earlier Father Stanford had begun to point the way with his proposals for improvement, and there had been scores of suggestions from self-studies, accrediting reports, and fund-raising surveys. In order to become a truly excellent university, Villanova would have to improve the quality of its faculty and student body; to provide a challenging curriculum that met the needs and aspirations of its students; to offer academic, residential, and recreational facilities that would make the institution attractive to students, faculty, and staff; to raise the funds to finance such facilities and to increase the university's endowment; to acquire able administrators; and to maintain effective communications among the institution's various constituencies.

In pursuing these goals, Villanova competed with dozens of other universities in the United States, and thus had to measure itself against the standards of American higher education, as well as the expectations of college-bound men and women and their parents. At the same time, Villanova needed to remain true to its own standards and traditions, lest it risk losing its identity and foundering for want of internal direction and consistent public perceptions. As in the past, it would have to balance its mission as a Catholic, Augustinian institution with the demands of the larger American environment. Because of greater diversity within its faculty and student body, coupled with conflicts between issues of academic freedom and the church's teachings in certain areas, this was not always easy to achieve. A continuing decline in the num-

bers of Augustinians on campus also raised concerns about the future relationship between the university and Augustinian community.

In the mission statement Villanova adopted in 1979, the university in fact
pledged itself to the goal of being a Catholic university within the context of
the American system of higher education. Thus one reads in the mission
statement: "Villanova is committed to those same high standards of academic integrity and excellence as well as personal and corporate achievement that characterize all worthy institutions of higher learning." At the
same time, Villanova "emphasizes the values of the Judeo-Christian tradition," and as a Roman Catholic institution "it recognizes its obligations to the
Magisterium [the authoritative teachings] of the Church" in theological matters. That conflicts might arise between the American tradition of academic
freedom and official church doctrine is neither anticipated nor addressed at
this point. The statement then goes on to recognize Villanova's "special
relationship to the Order of St. Augustine by showing appropriate preference to Augustinians in the initial appointment of faculty and staff."

In the area of curriculum, the mission statement declares that Villanova
"emphasizes undergraduate instruction and is committed to a liberal arts
component in each of its undergraduate departments." It encourages "research and scholarly work" by faculty, but only so far as these do not interfere with teaching and "other obligations to the university." Faculty, in cooperation with students and administrators, are invited to participate "in the
development of University policy through appropriate structures of governance." As part of that goal, "Villanova encourages communication among all
the elements of the academic community."

In calling for Villanova to extend its activities to the outside world, the
mission statement specifically urges its faculty, students, and staff to add
their "influence in the search for world peace and justice" and to provide
"public service to the community." Complementing this desire to reach out
to others, the university seeks to "enroll students with diverse social, geo-
graphic, economic, and educational backgrounds" and to use "its financial
aid resources to help achieve this diverse student body."

The term "Catholic Gentleman," employed so often in an earlier generation of publications, had vanished. Instead the university speaks of the "total
person," whom Villanova wishes to develop "intellectually, emotionally, spiritually, culturally, socially, and physically."[1]

Rooted in both tradition and contemporary reality, the mission statement thus set forth goals for present and future development. This interaction between past and present had been highlighted during Villanova's
125th anniversary celebration in 1967–68, the official theme of which was
"Heritage with a Purpose." The university observed its 125th anniversary
with a number of events, including dinners, a concert at Philadelphia's

En route to the Pontifical Mass during Villanova's 125th Anniversary celebration, September 13, 1967. *Left to right:* Methodist Bishop Frederick Pierce Corson; His Eminence John Cardinal Krol, Archbishop of Philadelphia; Reverend Robert J. Welsh, O.S.A., President of Villanova University. VUA.

Academy of Music, and a Pontifical Mass in September 1967 celebrated by John Cardinal Krol, Archbishop of Philadelphia. The climax of the festivities came on April 6, 1968, with an Anniversary Academic Convocation at the Field House attended by representatives from nearly one hundred colleges and universities.[2]

Nearly a decade later, in 1976, Villanova conducted a series of events to observe the 200th anniversary of American independence. The History Department offered a course called "Living History," which included visits to various colonial and revolutionary sites in the area. Donald B. Kelley, in collaboration with the Augustinian Institute on campus, mounted a pictorial exhibit of Villanova's own history in Falvey Memorial Library. The Religious Studies Department sponsored a series of lectures titled "American Religious Values and the Future of America." Villanova's old college bell, the "Sister Liberty Bell," joined the Thomas Eakins portrait of Father Fedigan in a display at the Penn Mutual Life Insurance Building in Philadelphia, where area colleges and universities held a collaborative historical exhibit.[3]

Despite the student discontent on campus between the university's 125th anniversary and the nation's bicentennial, there was great optimism about Villanova's future. When evaluators from the Middle States Association visited in 1970 they concluded their report on a far more positive note than the Middle States team had done ten years before, observing that there was an unmistakable atmosphere of optimism which boded well for Villanova:

> As its final observation the team takes note of the quiet optimism which seems to be the prevailing mood on the Villanova campus this year. There is an air of expectancy; an apparent confidence that something is going to happen which will be good for Villanova.... 
>
> If members of the Villanova community continue to believe as strongly as they do now in the university's future, the next few years may be the best in the institution's history. The potential is there and the mood is certainly right.[4]

Happily, there was more than just a positive mood at Villanova as the 1970s opened, for real progress began to occur on several fronts.

One area of progress was in faculty development. The faculty had continued to grow during the 1960s, reaching 454 full-time members in 1970, up from 241 just ten years earlier. Those who taught at Villanova in 1970 were also better educated; 43 percent held doctorates in 1970, as opposed to only 23 percent a decade before. Salaries had also increased between 1960 and 1970: The maximum for assistant professors went from $7,600 to $10,000, for associate professors from $8,900 to $13,500, and for full professors from $10,800 to $15,400. But according to the president's annual report for 1968–

69, these salaries were only "relatively competitive," and there would have to be continuous efforts to raise them further. That the administration appreciated the connection between faculty salaries and academic quality was also evident in the president's 1965–66 annual report. Noting that Villanova's salaries were still not on a par with other universities in the East, the report held that only serious raises would allow the institution to "attract a faculty which will fulfill to the highest degree the educational aims of Villanova."[5]

The faculty continued to advance in quality during the 1970s, and by 1979 some 64 percent had doctorates.[6] This improvement in faculty credentials caused the Middle States evaluating team to remark in its 1980 report, "The effort to upgrade the educational qualifications of the faculty over the past twenty years is indeed extraordinary."[7] When the accrediting body returned in 1990 they found that 87 percent of the 540 full-time faculty held doctorates. Salaries also rose during the decade. University-wide averages (including the higher-paid law school faculty) went from $29,000 to $53,900 for full professors, from $23,400 to $45,500 for associate professors, and from $19,700 to $34,100 for assistant professors. These figures put Villanova in the 80th to 95th percentile, depending upon rank, with competitive universities in the region, up from an overall 60th percentile ten years before.[8]

The Middle States reports for both 1980 and 1990 commended the strong emphasis upon scholarship among the Villanova faculty. This had been encouraged through tougher standards for promotion and tenure; sabbaticals, which had been adopted around 1970; reductions in teaching loads; and library purchases. Along these lines, one of Middle States' recommendations in 1990 was that the teaching requirement be reduced from 12 to 9 hours a semester for the entire university, and in fact the Middle States' self-study for 1990 demonstrated that the Villanova faculty was now teaching an average of 10.3 hours a semester.[9] In 1990 there were also plans to reduce the average load to nine hours for most full-time faculty, in line with the better colleges and universities throughout the United States.[10]

The results of this greater emphasis upon scholarship, according to the Middle States report of 1980, were "a more vital faculty, and an improved academic climate for the students."[11] But the same report found discrepancies in quality among various departments when it came to hiring, promotion, and tenure. It also discovered that the actual requirements for promotion were often more stringent than those for tenure, when the opposite should have been true. This practice, the report concluded, led to "frustration and disappointment" among faculty who achieved tenure only to be consistently turned down for promotion in the years ahead.[12] In its report for 1990, Middle States cited inconsistencies between the written standards for promotion and tenure, which emphasized teaching, and the fact that faculty scholarship was likely to receive the greatest weight in the actual decisions about tenure and advancement.[13]

Besides commenting on improvements in the faculty and recommending steps to raise its quality even further, the evaluations by Middle States consistently urged Villanova to engage in ambitious fund-raising and long-range planning.[14] Budgetary crises at Villanova during the 1970s and early 1980s only underlined these needs. Such requirements were the result of internal causes as well as outside forces. Among the external factors was the soaring price of energy, arising from the OPEC oil boycott in 1973 and exacerbated by wasteful habits of energy consumption in the United States itself, along with a series of severe winters. Frigid temperatures and record snowfalls in the late 1970s and early 1980s dramatized the situation. Heavy snows in February 1978 and 1979 paralyzed the campus for several days, and in February 1983 Villanova received its largest snowfall ever—21.3 inches. Such weather conditions, combined with an increase in the cost of fuel, placed a severe strain on the university's finances. Rising energy costs had also led to demands for higher wages across the nation as well as locally, and to higher prices for nearly all goods and services. Adding to the inflation had been growing deficit spending by the federal government during the Vietnam War and after.[15] In 1975–76 Villanova faced an increase of $400,000 for heating oil alone.[16]

At Villanova itself, a continuing heavy reliance on student tuitions and fees, and a slight decline in enrollments, only worsened the problem. For example, total undergraduate enrollment declined from 5,486 in the fall of 1973 to 5,284 in 1974. The number rebounded slightly in 1975 but did not exceed the 1973 figure until September 1977, when enrollment reached 5,612.[17] Since 96 percent of the university's income was derived from student-related charges and fees (with only 3 percent from gifts and grants, and a miniscule 1 percent from endowment income), the administration believed it had no choice but to continue increasing student sources of revenue.[18] As of September 1972, for example, the endowment stood at $5,920,000, which provided an annual income of only $150,000—a return of 2.3 percent. Two years later, in September 1974, the endowment had fallen to $5,570,000 because of a declining stock market and rose only gradually during the next four years as the market recovered somewhat and as Villanova added modest sums to the corpus.[19] Thus in February 1974 the board of trustees was forced to approve a tuition increase from $2,250 to $2,400 per year, along with a rise in room and board from the range of $1,300–$1,500 to $1,500–$1,700, depending upon the specific accommodations. Just five years later, in 1979, tuition was up to $3,500, while room and board had risen to approximately $2,200.[20]

With a fixed or relatively shrinking pool of money, there was much contention among the various constituencies within the university over how it should be spent. This contention was exacerbated by a policy of financial retrenchment ordered by the board of trustees in April 1973.[21] In 1975 and 1976, for example, the University Senate rejected the university budget, and only narrowly approved it in 1977 (in part because the university vowed to implement it regardless of the senate vote). The Student Government Association (SGA) also mounted severe criticisms about the budget during those years. For faculty, the main concern was salaries, which they charged had been eroded by inflation. In 1975 faculty asked for an increment of 12 percent (instead of the 4 percent proposed by the administration) in order to keep up with a national inflation rate of 12 percent. Faculty joined students in criticizing the university's failure to allocate funds for recreational facilities requested by the students and enacted as a spending priority by both the University Senate and the SGA. Rejecting the excuse of insufficient revenues, students and faculty alike faulted the administration and board of trustees for their failure to raise the necessary development funds. Some two thousand students assembled peacefully at the Field House in February 1977 to air such grievances.[22]

Throughout the budgetary debate, the question of student recreational facilities continued to surface. Often coupled with this question was criticism of the amount of money spent on varsity sports, and especially on football, which directly benefited only a small portion of the student body. In fact, concern over the amount of money spent on football dated back to the early 1930s, when Father Stanford regretted the large number of athletic scholarships compared with the number awarded on academic grounds. Twenty years later Villanova's continuing emphasis on football scholarships—and on varsity sports in general at the expense of wider opportunities for physical recreation—surfaced in the independent study of Villanova undertaken in 1953 by the American City Bureau. Eight years later, in the fall of 1961, some 94 percent of the students polled by what was then the Student Council agreed that they needed more and better recreational facilities. Still later in the decade this desire reemerged as part of the students' wider criticisms of social and intellectual life at Villanova and their charges that the university was spending money inappropriately. In 1970 a group of unhappy students had specifically complained that Villanova was losing $300,000 a year on football.[23] In July 1973 the Executive Committee of the University Senate went so far as to recommend "the orderly discontinuance of varsity football."[24]

Unhappiness over football in particular, the biggest loser financially, received added support from the final report of the Commission on University Structure and Programs (CUSP), dated February 4, 1977. The commission had been authorized by Father McCarthy, then university president, in May

1973. Its charge was to make recommendations to the president and the board of trustees about what steps might be taken to strengthen the university both academically and financially. In their recommendations, the CUSP cited a 1974 report by the Accounting Department which demonstrated that athletic deficits had gone from $332,000 in 1971–72 to $430,000 in 1972–73. By 1975 football alone was losing $479,000, in part because of extremely poor attendance at games by both students and alumni. The basketball program, in contrast, had a deficit of only $99,300 in 1975. The commission believed that the losses entailed in basketball could be corrected but called for a serious evaluation of whether football was worth the price. According to the commission report, the university could not "sustain a loss of this magnitude [from football] when it is facing a period of declining enrollments and constantly increasing costs."[25]

The CUSP report was reinforced by the findings of an Ad Hoc Committee on the Cost of Athletic Programs at Villanova, created by Father Driscoll in the fall of 1976. The committee's report, delivered three years later in 1979, recommended that money be saved by downgrading varsity football from the NCAA Division 1-A to Division 1-AA. In 1980 the university's self-study for its periodic Middle States review recommended a thorough examination of athletics "in light of educational needs and limited resources." Meanwhile, numerous editorials in the *Villanovan* had decried the high costs of football and demanded that it be downgraded or discontinued altogether.[26]

Continuing criticisms of football deficits at a time of general financial stringencies throughout the university led the board of trustees to vote on April 14, 1981, to discontinue varsity football at Villanova.[27] It was nearly a half-century after Father Stanford had expressed concern over its expense and after repeated recommendations that the sport be dropped. The board's decision had clearly not been made in a vacuum, with no prior suggestions by others in the university that something had to be done about the high cost of the football program.

In his press release concerning the football decision, issued on April 15, Father Driscoll explained that the move had been made primarily so that Villanova could devote its limited resources to academic excellence:

> Villanova's planning for the 1980s calls for intensified rededication to its academic mission as a private, church-related university of the first order. Providing the program facilities and salaries that are absolutely necessary to further that mission demands increasingly careful allocation of limited internal resources.[28]

Driscoll repeated this commitment to academic excellence as the main reason for the football decision in an interview with the *Villanovan* and again in his annual report for 1980–81.[29]

Driscoll received numerous letters of support from academic circles. The well-known author and Harvard sociologist David Reisman wrote him on May 12 to say that he agreed with Villanova's decision to make athletics a greater part of the overall campus experience, rather than an expensive pursuit for the few students who were involved in varsity sports.[30] On May 11 Robert Kirkwood, executive director of the Commission on Higher Education of the Middle States Association, also sent his congratulations to Driscoll: "I wish to express my admiration for the courage and clearsightedness required to make such a decision."[31] Editorial opinion in the Philadelphia newspapers was mixed, with the *Bulletin* praising the decision and the *Inquirer* criticizing it.[32]

From many alumni there was outrage over the vote to drop football, especially from those who had attended Villanova when football was a central feature of college life. Some of their fondest memories of Villanova were the Saturday afternoon football games—and the pep rallies, bonfires, residence-hall decorations, and other hoopla that surrounded them. For these former students, one of the social highlights of each autumn was returning to campus for the Homecoming football game. Others were outraged that there had been no discussion about dropping football in the *Villanova Alumnus*, or through any other channel of alumni opinion.[33]

In defending the lack of public discussion about the fate of football, Driscoll told the *Villanovan* it would have been unfair and demoralizing for the team to have to endure a public debate over its future.[34] The president of Villanova's General Alumni Association, Douglass Murray, refused to accept such an explanation, and in an undated circular letter to the alumni, he complained that the university viewed its graduates merely "as a source of funds with no licence or privilege to offer input on points of major concern to the University. . . . We simply feel that as a group we should be held in higher regard by our Board of Trustees and University Administrators than is currently the case."[35]

Feeling that they had been unfairly ignored during the deliberations over football, the Alumni Association demanded that the university reinstate the program immediately. On May 7, 1981, just three weeks after the announcement that football would be discontinued, an alumni Committee to Restore Football met at the Covered Wagon Inn (later the Main Lion Deli), located in nearby Strafford, Pennsylvania, where they raised a war chest of $100,000 and launched the first of many strategy meetings.[36] The committee also took out a full-page advertisement in the May 18 issue of the *Philadelphia Bulletin*, demanding a return of the game. Villanova's board of trustees agreed to reconsider its decision, but at a meeting on July 14 the trustees came to the same decision as before.[37]

The next major step of the restoration committee was to invite comedian Bob Hope to star in a benefit for Villanova football. The program came off on

December 1, 1981, at Philadelphia's Academy of Music. Hope, now nearing eighty, was in many ways the symbol of an older generation and may have been chosen for his nostalgic associations with traditional campus life (though Hope himself never attended college). With typical humor, Hope told the crowd of two thousand fans at the Academy that they should have their football: "What is a college without a team?" he asked. "It's like Dolly Parton without a tight sweater."[38] During the evening encouraging messages from State Attorney General LeRoy Zimmerman and Penn State football coach Joe Paterno were read.[39]

Several months after the Hope benefit, on April 15, 1982, and exactly one year after the official announcement that football would be dropped, the General Alumni Association demanded Father Driscoll's resignation at a public news conference held at the Presidential Apartments on City Line Avenue in Philadelphia.[40] This outraged the University Senate, which had often called for the demise of football and which now voted to support the president's decision. The Faculty Affairs Committee also passed a resolution in Driscoll's support.[41] Driscoll's own response was "No way!"[42] On April 27 the *Philadelphia Daily News*, with its usual flair for gossip and controversy, ran a front-page story in the sports section about the demand for Driscoll's resignation and all the controversy it had stirred. The headline screamed, "War on the Main Line."[43]

The continuing unhappiness among alumni over football led to concerns that some were withholding financial support from the university, a fear that was justified by analyses of alumni giving.[44] In this atmosphere the University Senate reversed itself in November 1982 and voted to bring back football, as did the SGA in both October and November of the same year.[45] Editorials in the *Villanovan* during the fall of 1982 also began to call for the return of football. At its meeting of December 15, 1982, the board of trustees elected to review its football decision, and almost exactly a year later, on December 13, 1983, the trustees agreed to reinstate varsity football. The board's decision that football would be played at the 1-AA level, rather than the more prestigious but more expensive 1-A level (at which Villanova had competed before 1981) was supposed to save money. Under these new conditions, they played their first varsity football game in five years on September 21, 1985. Villanova played Iona College, beating them 27 to 27.[46]

Cancellation of the football program in 1981 had allowed Villanova to concentrate on its basketball team, which for years had cost far less than football. Although the board of trustees vehemently denied any favoritism toward basketball when making its decision to discontinue football, the CUSP report of 1977 had emphasized the much lower costs of basketball and had recommended keeping the program, at the same time that it proposed football be dropped.[47]

Whatever the compensatory benefits may have been for basketball, Villanova's hoopsters improved rapidly during the early 1980s under the leadership of head coach Roland V. "Rollie" Massimino. The climax came in the spring of 1985, when the Wildcat basketball team took the NCAA Championship at Louisville, Kentucky, on April 1, 1985. The hitherto unranked team won an upset victory over Georgetown by a score of 66 to 64.[48] The triumph was marred, however, when some 7,000 students—and numerous outsiders—went on a rampage through the campus and up and down Lancaster Pike destroying property and smashing dozens of windows. When the Wildcats returned to town the day after their stunning victory, about 75,000 fans met them at Kennedy Plaza in downtown Philadelphia.[49]

Although the NCAA Championship represented the most spectacular athletic achievement in recent Villanova history, its track teams, as well as individual contenders in track and field, continued to excel at a high level. In the spring of 1979 Villanova won the NCAA indoor track championship. In 1988 Villanova's Vicki Huber (class of 1989) finished sixth in the 3,000-meter race at the Summer Olympics, and in 1989 she led the field in the NCAA cross-country championship. In September 1989 the women's cross-country team

Villanova's NCAA basketball championship celebration in downtown Philadelphia, April 2, 1985. VUA.

Nnenna Lynch '93, a Rhodes Scholar (*right*), and Carole Zajac '94
celebrate Villanova's fourth consecutive NCAA national title for the
women's cross-country team. VUA.

captured seven first prizes at New York's Van Courtland Park, completely
shutting out the competition, and in the fall of 1992 the team won its fourth
consecutive NCAA national championship. These achievements in track were
part of a long tradition of excellence that stretched back for decades: Villanova's Paul Drayton (class of 1962) had won a gold medal in the 100-meter
relay at the 1964 Olympics in Tokyo, and in 1956 Villanova's Ron Delaney
(class of 1958) had brought back a gold medal and set a new Olympic record
for the 1,500-meter run at Melbourne, Australia.[50]

Dominating this track program for nearly half a century was coach James
Francis "Jumbo" Elliott (1914–81). At Homecoming 1980, less than a year

Ron Delaney kneels in prayer after winning a gold medal and securing a new Olympic record in the 1,500-meter run at the 1956 Summer Games in Melbourne, Australia. VUA.

before his death, a new outdoor track was dedicated in his honor. During his
years with Villanova he had coached twenty-eight Olympic contenders and
made Villanova's track teams famous all over the nation. Another athletic
legend passed from the scene in 1985 with the death of John "Jake" Nevin
(1910–85). Nevin had been a trainer in the athletic program at Villanova
since 1929 and head trainer since 1946. Shortly before his death the old
Field House was renamed in his honor, to be known as the Jake Nevin Field
House.[51]

While Villanova enjoyed triumphs in basketball and track, its revived
football program continued to lose large sums of money after its resump-

tion, despite competition at a lower level. During the very first year of its return, the football program lost $478,000. By 1991 the shortfall was estimated at more than $1 million, prompting a majority of the faculty to call for a further downgrading of the program to Division III status.[52] The *Villanovan* also observed in the fall of 1990 that student attendance at football games was "pitiful at its best and embarrassing at its worst."[53] Yet as alumni officials pointed out in 1987, Villanova's graduates were contributing more than enough money annually to cover the football deficits and had given more than $5 million to the most recent capital campaign.[54]

Although controversy over football continued, the decision to disband the game and then bring it back had helped build a consensus that Villanova should have more extensive and varied recreational facilities, which would benefit a greater number of students. In the process Villanova satisfied the last major demand made by students during the uprisings of the 1970s.

The question of whether to add a new wing to the existing student center, Dougherty Hall, or to erect a completely separate building, was discussed as early as 1971. In 1976 the administration decided to put up a new, free-standing structure. Dougherty Hall would continue to house student activities offices, such as the newspaper and yearbook, as well as the offices for Student Life, the Pie Shop, and a student dining room / cafeteria. The new center, intended for use by the entire university (rather than students alone), would provide game rooms, small meeting and seminar rooms, a large space for banquets and lectures, a cafeteria, and a cinema. Designed by Vincent G. Kling and partners, the complex was begun in May 1978 and completed in March 1980. Its location was across the walkway and slightly to the east of Dougherty Hall. Because of a gift of $4.8 million from John F. Connelly, a member of the Villanova board of trustees and president of Crown Cork and Seal of Philadelphia, the facility was officially named the Connelly Center at its dedication on September 21, 1980. His Eminence John Cardinal Krol, Archbishop of Philadelphia, presided at the ceremonies. Resembling a ski lodge on the interior, the Connelly Center's peaked roofs blended well with the older Gothic shapes on campus. The Philadelphia Chapter of the American Institute of Architects awarded the building a gold medal upon its completion.[55]

As the Connelly Center was rising in 1979, plans were begun for a new athletic complex, with facilities for many types of physical recreation. Calls for such a complex had been made as early as 1969, and in 1973 the university had gone so far as to choose an architect for the project. At that time Villanova proposed, but never executed, a huge "multi-purpose air-dome stadium" to be constructed at the corner of Ithan Avenue and Lancaster Pike, to replace both the Field House and the Villanova Stadium. By early 1974 somewhat scaled-down plans called for this complex to be built be-

Connelly Center, 1980, designed by Vincent G. Kling & Partners. VUA.

yond the Penn-Central (formerly Pennsylvania and later Conrail) Railroad tracks, near the heating plant. Budgetary stringencies during the mid-1970s made any such construction impossible, despite often angry student demands that the building be put up immediately.

A better financial climate in the early 1980s allowed the university to raise the necessary funds, and ground was broken for a sports complex in the fall of 1983, in a far different and less ambitious design than what had been proposed in the 1970s. Opening ceremonies for the new complex took place on February 1, 1986. Due to a substantial pledge from John Eleuthere duPont, of the well-known duPont corporate family, who was a member of the university's Development Council, the facility was called the John Eleuthère duPont Pavilion. Designed by Daniel F. Tully and Associates, it provided Villanova with the most modern athletic facilities available at the time, including an Olympic-size swimming pool and exercise rooms. The duPont Pavilion's pointed tentlike projections also complemented the campus's older Gothic buildings.[56]

Between 1969 and 1989, in order to provide better residence and dining facilities, which students in the 1960s and 1970s had also complained about,

Stanford Hall on the South Campus. VUA.

the university erected a cluster of seven buildings located beyond Lancaster Pike on what was called the South Campus. These buildings were faced in red brick and rendered in a functional but attractive style, interspersed with trees from a small woods on the site as well as new plantings. Located at the bottom of a small rise and partly obscured by the trees, this red-brick South Campus seemed partly detached from the older campus area, with its stone buildings in the Collegiate Gothic style.

Making much of this physical expansion possible were the first truly successful fund-raising campaigns in Villanova's modern history. These were known as Covenant I, launched in 1977, and Covenant II, begun in 1981. According to Father Driscoll, the word "covenant" referred to Villanova's promise to maintain and improve its special heritage for future generations. As he put it in announcing the campaign, "The Covenant of Villanova University is a promise for the future—a promise to maintain Villanova's tradition of academic excellence and spiritual values so that its rich heritage in the humanities, the sciences and the professions will be available to future generations of scholars and educators."[57]

Although Driscoll spoke of academic and spiritual values at the university, the main thrust of the Covenant Campaigns were improvements in student life so that Villanova could bring itself into line with the better colleges and universities in the United States and thereby compete more effectively for top students. Thus the prospectus for the initial fund drive (the name Covenant I not being adopted until its successor, Covenant II, was launched) explained this thrust. It was "a program designed to improve the quality of student life on campus, to bring student life standards into line with the highest academic standards which the University has maintained, and to enable Villanova to continue in a role of excellence as it has in the past."[58] In student life, as in all other aspects of the university, Villanova had to meet the best expectations of American higher education if it wanted to achieve excellence, and in order to do that it had to raise the necessary funds.

Covenant I, launched in 1977, focused exclusively on providing money for what became the Connelly Center. By 1980 it had raised $9 million— $1 million more than its stated goal. Taking advantage of this momentum, Villanova launched Covenant II in 1981, with a target of $20 million. Instead of focusing on one project, the second drive was multifaceted, yet like its immediate predecessor it emphasized the quality of student life and included such projects as the duPont Pavilion and new residence halls. Covenant II was even more successful than Covenant I, raising some $24 million by the end of 1986.[59]

The reasons for these successes, in contrast to the failures of past campaigns, were due in part to the increasing size and prosperity of Villanova's alumni. In 1977 living alumni totaled 32,500. Although 56 percent of them had graduated within the past fifteen years, there were enough successful alumni to contribute $5 million for the two Covenant campaigns. At the same time the larger number of successful graduates had helped to raise Villanova's profile among the general public.

Villanova was also extremely fortunate, according to Father Driscoll, in securing the large gift from John Connelly for its projected university center. This decision by Connelly was in fact a dramatic breakthrough in the university's fund-raising efforts. Since Connelly was widely considered to be one of the most sagacious businessmen in the United States, his faith in Villanova was taken as a sign by many other potential donors that the university was worthy of support. With the Connelly pledge in hand, other large gifts began to come to Villanova from a variety of sources, many of them from beyond Catholic circles or from individuals and corporations never before associated with the university.[60]

The Augustinian Province of St. Thomas of Villanova also made an impressive contribution of $500,000 to the Covenant campaign, especially when weighed against its own financial stringencies.[61] Yet unlike past fund-raising campaigns, the various Augustinian parishes were no longer a source of money, for a variety of reasons. Because of declining numbers, the Augustinians had withdrawn from several parishes. Some of those that remained under Augustinian auspices were now in poor urban neighborhoods that were in need of outside funding themselves. Even more-prosperous parishes preferred to use their resources for local projects.

In any event, the success of the Covenant campaigns, the construction of a new residential complex, the improved athletic and recreational facilities, a better national economy during the 1980s, and the NCAA Basketball Championship of 1985 all helped to attract positive attention among potential students. During the early and mid-1970s, for example, the number of applications to Villanova had continued to fall. In 1971 the university received approximately 6,000 applications, but in 1975 this number had declined to around 5,000. The rebound came in 1979 with 6,600 applications, rising to 8,300 in 1983, and to 9,677 in 1988.[62]

This increase allowed Villanova to admit more and better students. Full-time, undergraduate freshman enrollment went from just over 1,450 in 1981 to about 1,800 in 1988, while the total undergraduate enrollment rose from 5,924 to 6,716. Totals for the entire university, including the graduate and professional programs, increased from 10,906 to 12,188. Combined SAT scores in the undergraduate division rose from 1,007 to 1,162 during the same period.[63] The greatest beneficiary in this surge was the College of Liberal Arts and Sciences, where both applications and enrollments registered constant gains, the latter rising from 2,521 in 1981 to 3,184 in 1988. The reasons for this were varied, but chief among them was the realization by better-educated and more-prosperous Americans that it was the ability to think, process information, and express oneself well that held the key to success in the so-called "information age" of the late twentieth century.[64]

Throughout the 1980s and early 1990s Villanova students remained overwhelmingly Catholic.[65] The great majority continued to come from Pennsylvania, New Jersey, and New York, though the university was trying harder than ever to attract students from other areas, and with some success. (In 1993, applications from the western United States, where Villanova had recently placed a full-time admissions officer, increased by 25 percent over the year before.[66]) Villanova students were also overwhelmingly white and from upper-middle-class households. In 1988, for example, 90 percent of the undergraduate students listed themselves as being from white, European backgrounds. Approximately 75 percent of their parents earned more than $50,000 annually, and about 25 percent of these had incomes over $100,000. At the same time, average annual family income in the United States was $32,191, while only one-fourth of American families earned more than $50,000 on an annual basis. This meant that the vast majority of Villanova students came from upper-middle-class backgrounds, at least as far as income was concerned.[67]

The prosperity of Villanova families and their suburban life-styles was a major factor in the switch of student party allegiance from the Democratic Party to the Republican Party.[68] In 1964 the student presidential poll gave Lyndon B. Johnson 63 percent to Republican challenger Barry Goldwater's 37 percent.[69] There were apparently no student polls in 1968 or 1972, but a poll just before the presidential election of 1976, conducted by the SGA, gave Republican Gerald R. Ford 48.5 percent and Democrat Jimmy Carter 22.4 percent, with 5.8 percent going to other candidates and 23.3 percent undecided.[70] Four years later, in 1980, Republican Ronald Reagan was the overwhelming choice in a contest conducted by the *Villanovan*: Reagan received 41.7 percent to Carter's 20.5 percent and Independent John Anderson's 15.9 percent. Those who were undecided made up 20.7 percent of the total, with the other 1 percent going to minor candidates.[71] Although there is no record of a poll in 1984, there is no reason to doubt that the great majority of Villanova students continued to prefer Reagan in his successful bid for reelection that year.

In 1988 the student newspaper showed a huge preference for Republican George Bush (55 percent) over Democrat Michael Dukakis (21 percent), with the remainder (24 percent) being undecided or preferring other candidates.[72] The same poll also asked about party registration and ideological preferences. Of those taking part in the survey, 39 percent were registered Republicans, 18 percent were Democrats, 25 percent were independents, and 18 percent were not registered to vote at all. As for political ideology, 60 percent said they were conservatives, and 40 percent responded that they were liberals.[73] In 1992 Villanova students again chose Bush, but by a smaller margin than in 1988. Bush received 38 percent to Democrat Bill Clinton's 33 percent. The remaining 29 percent voted for other candidates or were undecided.[74]

In addition to such polls there were other indications that Villanova students were generally Republican and conservative during the 1980s and 1990s. One was the preponderance of Republican candidates who visited campus. For example, Gerald Ford campaigned at Villanova on October 27, 1976, before a huge crowd of five thousand people at the Field House. Although Jimmy Carter had initially accepted an invitation from Father Driscoll to appear on campus, Carter changed his mind and decided not to come, in part because he feared that antiabortion demonstrators, including Villanova's own prolife organization, would show up to protest his official neutrality on the subject of abortion. On April 25, 1980, George Bush, then vying with Ronald Reagan for the Republican nomination, spoke before a crowd of five hundred at the Connelly Center. In the fall of 1983, former President Ford spent two days on campus, visiting classes, speaking before an audience in the Connelly Center, and attending a black-tie dinner given by the board of trustees. Ford came a third time in 1986 when he spoke at

U.S. President Gerald R. Ford (*right*), shakes hands with Reverend John M. Driscoll, O.S.A., University President, during the presidential campaign, October 27, 1976. VUA.

the first Jumbo Elliott Awards Dinner.[75] It was also in 1986 that Driscoll invited then President Reagan to speak at the 1987 commencement, but two dissident students wrote letters to Reagan asking him not to come, much to the annoyance of the great majority of students on campus. Reagan did not accept Villanova's invitation to speak, though whether the students' dissenting letters played any role in his decision not to appear is unclear.[76]

Several prominent Democrats visited Villanova, but not while campaigning for office. These included Senator George McGovern (October 25, 1988), the Democratic presidential candidate back in 1972; Senator Albert Gore (November 2, 1988), who would be elected Vice President of the United States in 1992; and Kitty Dukakis (March 15, 1989), wife of the recently defeated Democratic presidential candidate Michael Dukakis.[77]

Another indication of student conservatism was praise for Villanova's Navy ROTC program. For instance, on October 21, 1977, the *Villanovan* devoted its entire front page to photographs and positive commentary on the local NROTC unit. Subsequent issues, including that of February 2,

1990, continued to heap praise on the NROTC. Still another example of the students' conservative orientation was widespread support for Republican foreign policy under Presidents Reagan and Bush, climaxing in massive enthusiasm for the Persian Gulf War of February 1991. Although a handful of Villanova students protested the war with a sit-in on campus and by joining in an antiwar march in Washington, D.C., the overwhelming majority supported the war and the American men and women who took part in it. The campus was festooned with yellow ribbons, a sign of solidarity with the troops, as well as American flags. Villanova students also organized a huge rally in support of the war, held at the duPont Pavilion on February 4, 1991. It included the Villanova band, baton twirlers, cheerleaders, and the NROTC color guard, as well as a slam-dunk contest. Sportscaster Don Tollefson of the local ABC affiliate, Channel 6, was master of ceremonies, and there were speeches by Robert Capone, Director of Alumni, and head basketball coach Rollie Massimino. A letter from President George Bush expressing his thanks for the rally was read during the proceedings. In fact, Villanova was the first college or university in the nation to hold such a rally. After it was over the organizers sent videotapes of the event to the troops in the Persian Gulf.[78]

Villanova's president, who was now Reverend Edmund J. Dobbin, O.S.A., did not attend the event and publicly regretted that it had taken the form of an athletic pep rally, as if war were some kind of "game." He also criticized the program for not having more of "an intellectual undertone."[79] These comments provoked several bitter letters in the *Villanovan* from students who thought that Father Dobbin should have been present.[80]

Some believed that another sign of conservatism at Villanova, and on many other campuses in the United States, was the growth and resurgence of fraternities and sororities. These had declined greatly across the nation during the years of the counterculture, when they were viewed as remnants of the social snobbery and inequality that, critics claimed, had characterized student life in the past.[81] In fact, no nationally affiliated social fraternity successfully planted itself at Villanova until the arrival of Tau Kappa Epsilon in 1967. Fraternities remained few in number on the local campus until a great expansion in the late 1970s. The first national sorority came to Villanova in 1981.

By 1989 there were fifteen fraternities and six sororities at Villanova, although none of them had their own houses on campus. That year 35 percent of Villanova's student body belonged to the Greek system, as compared to a nationwide figure of around 20 percent. Perhaps more telling is that Villanova had more students in fraternities and sororities than any other Catholic college or university in the United States, and one of the highest concentrations of any campus in the nation, Catholic or otherwise.[82]

The Delta Kappa Epsilon fraternity at Villanova, 1979. VUA.

Not all students were pleased with this growth among the Greek letter societies. An editorial in the *Villanovan* for January 26, 1989, admitted that the fraternities and sororities did engage in some socially helpful projects, but the writer believed that they generally reinforced "Villanova's reputation as an exclusive white country club."[83] Indeed, the upper-middle-class backgrounds of many Villanova students, as well as their own social aspirations, were certainly factors in making the Greek system so popular on campus.

Despite this proliferation of fraternities and sororities at Villanova, there was no full-scale return to the old campus culture, with its formal balls, football mania, and pep rallies. In some ways, Villanova's students were more serious than in the past, and especially about good grades, at a time when the American economy had slowed and when there was much doubt about whether the present generation would be able to do as well as their parents financially. In this sense, Helen Horowitz has compared such students to the old "outsiders" who had rejected organized campus life in order to pursue their studies and prepare for future careers. Only in the 1980s and 1990s did these "new outsiders" seem to be in the majority on most college and university campuses, including Villanova. Many of the new outsiders, Horowitz suspects, are attracted to the Greek system in a calculated attempt to improve their social skills or to forge important business contacts for the future.[84]

Such apparent conservatism did not mean that student activism had died entirely at Villanova, or that all aspects of the counterculture had disappeared without a trace. Indeed, at Villanova, as on many other campuses, the rebels that remained continued to find a niche with the student newspaper.[85] At the same time, student activism was enlisted in causes that were somewhat different from those during the counterculture of the 1960s and 1970s. Some activists concentrated on such practical issues as safety on campus or on conservative causes like the antiabortion movement. There was also a mild revival of the debate over residence-hall visitation. Still other causes involved social justice and cultural diversity, both intriguing legacies of the earlier counterculture.

Because Villanova was located on several heavily traveled transportation routes, there was much concern over traffic safety. One of these dangerous routes was the Lancaster Pike (U.S. Route 30), which passed through the southern portion of the campus. The other two routes cut across the north side of campus: the former Pennsylvania Railroad (now part of Conrail/SEPTA) and Spring Mill Road (State Route 320). Accidents along these corridors had sparked student protests as early as 1948 and 1954 (see Chapter 7). Several deaths and serious injuries in the 1970s and early 1980s provoked new concerns over pedestrian safety and led to several student demonstrations. These actions resulted in the 1983 installation of a traffic light at the point where students crossed Spring Mill Road from St. Mary's Hall, and to the construction on Spring Mill Road of a new bridge (with pedestrian walkway) over the railroad, the latter completed in late 1993. There were plans to build a walkway under Lancaster Pike at Ithan Avenue, but at the time of this writing it had not yet been undertaken.[86]

There were also protests against increases in tuition, room, and board in 1977 and 1980, but these were mild compared with those that had erupted several years earlier.[87] Just as subdued was the campaign, launched in early 1984, for coeducational residence halls at Villanova. These were by then commonplace at other institutions, including many Catholic universities, as the *Villanovan* indicated more than once.[88] As with parietals, the argument the newspaper gave for mixed residence halls was the opportunities they would afford for a more normal and relaxed relationship between the sexes, thereby helping to prepare students to enter the real world:

> By fostering a more natural, true-to-life living situation for students, coeducational residence halls would easily stimulate interpersonal growth. A more comfortable, relaxed atmosphere would develop, allowing men and women to communicate at levels other than the strictly social. And, as a result, the graduating senior would face the working world with the ability to maintain productive, healthy relationships with members of the opposite sex.[89]

After five years of discussion, the board of trustees approved coeducational residence halls in February 1989.

Ironically the first such arrangement, with men and women living on different floors of the building, took place at St. Mary's Hall, the former Augustinian seminary. Other residence halls would be added to the coeducational list in the years ahead. Still other halls remained single-sex, allowing students to choose between the two types.[90] With coeducational residence halls now in place, arguments were pressed for twenty-four-hour visitation in the halls. A poll in March 1993 showed that 60 percent of the students surveyed wanted twenty-four-hour visitation, but there were no signs that the administration or the board was about to change the rules.[91]

Only vaguely related to the matter of coeducational living arrangements was the issue of cultural diversity, which included issues of race, ethnicity, and gender. In its more radical aspects, cultural diversity was also grounded in the new-left assertion that non-Western traditions were superior to white, male, Eurocentric culture, including the dominant culture of the United States, which had its roots in western Europe.

Whatever the theoretical underpinnings of the cultural diversity movement, figures demonstrate that Villanova's faculty and student body became more diverse during the 1980s and early 1990s. One of these areas was gender diversity. The percentage of women on the faculty rose from 7 percent in the late 1960s to 19 percent in 1980 and 26 percent in 1990.[92] The proportions of female students also continued to rise. By 1973 about one-third of the undergraduate enrollment was made up of women; in 1978 it was 40 percent, in 1985 it was 45 percent, and in the early 1990s it was about 50 percent. The freshman class that entered in the fall of 1993 actually had more women than men: 51.4 percent to 48.6 percent.[93] Villanova's NROTC unit admitted its first woman in 1973 and by 1984, there were seventeen women in the program.[94] Reflecting these larger female enrollments and a rising interest in women's issues, Villanova introduced a Women's Studies program in 1980, and in 1989 a major in Women's Studies was approved.[95]

When it came to racial and ethnic diversity, Villanova had a more difficult time than it did with gender diversity. In 1973, for example, only 2.6 percent of Villanova's students were defined as minorities, and by 1978 this figure had slipped to 2.2 percent. It rose slightly to 2.5 percent by 1980 and was still at 2.5 percent in 1985, the lowest of any university of its size in the state of Pennsylvania.[96] The main reason given for such low enrollments of minority students was the relatively high tuition charged at Villanova, which made it affordable largely to the white upper-middle class. (By 1989 tuition was about $9,500 a year, depending upon the particular program, while room and board averaged $4,500 on an annual basis.[97]) It also may be that many minority students did not feel comfortable going to college in the overwhelmingly white and affluent Main Line suburbs of Philadelphia where Villanova was located.[98] This was a plausible argument, given the fact that other expensive private schools in the area, such as the University of Pennsylvania in Philadelphia proper, had been far more successful than Villanova in obtaining minority students. At the same time, Penn had a much larger endowment than Villanova, which could be used to support minority students.

Grants from the state of Pennsylvania through the Act 101 program, which began at Villanova in 1974, helped to attract some minority students, but they were clearly not enough to make the university affordable to most minorities.[99] By hiring a minority recruiter in 1985 and by setting aside more money for scholarships, the university succeeded in raising its proportions of undergraduate minority students to 3.2 percent in 1986 and to 8.2 percent in 1990. In that same year the university set a goal of admitting approximately 20 percent minority students to the freshman class by 1994. Success would depend on aggressive recruiting as well as on raising more endowment for scholarships. Beginning in the fall of 1989, Villanova awarded twenty full-tuition scholarships to minority students from the "inner city," and there were plans to increase the number as funds became available.[100] Much of this work to attract more minority students was undertaken by the Office of Multicultural Affairs, which had originated in 1969 under the name "Office for Social Action Programs." Since its inception this office had been under the direction of Dr. Edward L. Collymore, himself an African American.[101]

Meanwhile efforts were being made to hire more minority faculty members. In 1990, minorities represented about 5 percent of the full-time teaching staff.[102] In order to increase the number of minorities (as well as women) on the faculty, Villanova had adopted an affirmative-action program for hiring in 1975.[103]

Efforts to increase minorities among the faculty and student body were generally well received, but there was unhappiness over what some students and faculty considered to be an antagonism toward Western civilization among some proponents of cultural diversity, and with it an outspokenly liberal agenda in certain classrooms. At a meeting on November 21, 1991, for example, the student Republican club charged that Villanova's new core curriculum, which required students to take two courses with a multicultural focus, was really an attempt to preach such things as "gay rights and abortion."[104] This assertion, which was in fact groundless, angered proponents of the new core curriculum, including Dr. Michael E. Burke, director of the honors program, who asserted that multiculturalism was a moral and Christian imperative, adding that "the essence of a liberal education is to liberate students from the parochialism inherent in the limited experiences of a single individual life."[105]

In addition to multiculturalism, another legacy of the counterculture at

Villanova, and elsewhere, was an emphasis on service to others, and particularly to those who were disadvantaged in some way. This idea was by no means new at Villanova. Throughout the 1950s Villanova athletes had held an annual Christmas party for the boys of St. John's Orphanage, then located at 40th Street and Woodland Avenue in Philadelphia and with whom Villanova had had a relationship as far back as the 1840s. In the late 1960s Villanova played host to a summer camp for sixth-graders from poor neighborhoods in the city.[106]

Beginning in the 1970s such outreach programs became far more numerous and ambitious. In 1976 Villanova allowed senior citizens to take courses tuition-free, and within several years it was a fairly common sight to see older men and women receiving their diplomas along with students who were fifty or sixty years their junior.[107] One Villanova fraternity inducted a seventy-two-year-old undergraduate, and in 1983 the senior-class valedictorian was a man of sixty-nine.[108] At the other end of the age spectrum, Villanova started playing host to the Pennsylvania Special Olympics in 1979, an event sponsored by Villanovans for Life.[109] In order to help rehabilitate those who had been convicted of crimes, Villanova began offering college-level courses in 1972 at Philadelphia's Graterford Prison.[110]

Several events concentrated on assisting the poor. Chief among these was the annual Balloon Day at Villanova, sponsored by Campus Ministry. Held in mid-April, the event made its debut in 1973. The day featured hundreds of brightly colored balloons along the walkways in the center of campus, interspersed with food and game booths. At approximately 3:00 in the afternoon students released hundreds of gas-filled balloons (a practice later forbidden because of environmental concerns). There was also a rock band and entertainment by magicians, comedians, and others, who helped to give the whole event a carnival flavor. By 1982 Balloon Day raised $3,000 for Campus Ministry projects, and in 1990 the figure was $6,000.[111] Also associated with the theme of poverty was Hunger Awareness Week, sponsored by Campus Ministry and begun about 1978. Resident students were asked to give up their lunch for one day, its cost being donated to food for the hungry.[112]

In some cases Villanovans went far afield in their efforts to help others. As early as 1980 students spent their spring breaks in impoverished mountainous areas of the eastern United States known as Appalachia where they assisted with a variety of projects, including the construction of houses through Habitat for Humanity. Sometimes these spring-break projects took students out of the country, as in 1985 when they went to Mexico and Haiti. The Haitian visits continued on an annual basis and resulted in the opening of the Villanova University School in Port-au-Prince.[113]

Concern over the policy of apartheid in South Africa led to several editori-

Balloon Day, April 22, 1982. VUA.

als in the *Villanovan* that denounced the practice, and to resolutions in 1985 by the local AAUP and University Senate that Villanova should remove all its investments in companies that did business in South Africa. In October of that year the board of trustees announced its intention to adhere to the "Sullivan principles" (widely used guidelines for divesting in South Africa drawn up by the Reverend Leon Sullivan of Philadelphia). Following these guidelines, Villanova would withdraw from all economic activity in South Africa, a decision many colleges, universities, and other institutions in the

United States were making at that time. This process took approximately three years to accomplish and was completed by the fall of 1988.[114]

In late 1989, in addition to the groups already mentioned, Villanova listed several other organizations that were involved in social action of one kind or another. Among these were the Villanova Chapter of Amnesty International, the Villanova Environmental Group, Villanovans Concerned About Central America, the Student Coalition Against Apartheid, the Villanova University Committee for the Homeless, Students Against Sexual Stereotyping, and Villanovans for Life. Many of these groups were coordinated by the Center for Peace and Justice, launched in 1977 by Reverend Ray Jackson, O.S.A., director of Campus Ministry.[115]

Villanovans for Life had been founded in 1973 soon after the U.S. Supreme Court legalized abortion in its *Roe v. Wade* decision. More than any other issue on campus, the question of abortion forced Villanovans to confront the question of what it meant to be a Catholic university in America in the late twentieth century.

Although abortion was often at the center of this debate, the question of Villanova's Catholic identity was also connected to demographic changes within the university itself. The undergraduate student body remained largely Catholic, yet declined somewhat from about 90 percent Catholic in the 1970s to around 80 percent in the early 1990s. As for the total student body in the 1990s, including the law school and various graduate programs, Catholics were closer to 60 percent of the whole.[116]

In its Self-Study for the Middle States evaluation in 1990, the committee on admissions recommended that "the University continue to monitor the religious composition of its student body to insure the continuance of its Catholic character, but that it remain open to students affiliated with other religious denominations."[117] The recommendation established no quotas, however, and did not address the question of what might happen to the Catholic identity of the institution if the proportion of Catholics in the student body fell drastically, for unanticipated reasons, in the years ahead.

The faculty was also far less homogeneous in religious affiliation than it had been in the past, as the academic departments looked more at scholarly credentials than at religious beliefs in their emphasis upon quality among the teaching staff. Although at present the university apparently does not keep figures on the religious affiliations of faculty, Father Driscoll reported as early as 1977 that approximately 35 percent of the faculty were not Catholics, leading one to assume that this figure was even higher in the early 1990s. Meanwhile, the number of Augustinians on the faculty reached the lowest level in the institution's history, as the order continued to decline in numerical strength. In 1990 only 2.8 percent of the full-time faculty (15 of 540) were Augustinians.[118] In order to try to maintain even these slim proportions, Augustinians who had the necessary academic qualifications were still given preference in hiring, but when it came to promotion and tenure they were held to the same criteria as lay professors.[119]

Augustinian influence was somewhat greater in administrative posts, where they were likewise given preference over lay people in the selection process. Yet even here their thinning ranks forced the university to fill more and more administrative positions with lay men and women. In 1968 Villanova hired its first lay vice president in Dr. James F. Duffy, who became Vice President for Student Affairs. By 1992 only three of the thirteen top administrators of the university, including the president, were Augustinians. Of the ten top lay administrators, two were women.[120] It was also in 1968 that Villanova had opened its board of trustees to more lay persons as well as to those who were not Catholic. By 1993, sixteen of its twenty-five members were lay persons, four of them women. One of them was not Catholic and nine were Augustinians.[121]

Father Driscoll and others at Villanova soon realized some of the implica-

His Eminence Josef Cardinal Glemp of Poland (*left*), who received an honorary degree from Villanova on September 19, 1985; John Cardinal Krol of Philadelphia (*center*); and Reverend John M. Driscoll, O.S.A., University President (*right*). The three are seated in the university president's office in Tolentine Hall. VUA.

tions of these demographic changes for Catholic identity and Catholic doctrine at Villanova. Nowhere was this more evident than in issues involving the church's teachings on human sexuality and reproduction, issues that also threatened to compromise Villanova's commitment to academic freedom.

The question of birth control, which the church opposed except for the natural (or rhythm) method, came up in a public forum as early as 1959 when U.S. Senator Edmund J. Muskie spoke on campus in opposition to governmental dissemination of birth control aid to other nations, a subject that was very much in the news because of John F. Kennedy's impending run for the presidency. Muskie agreed with Kennedy in opposing such aid.[122] By the mid-1960s concerns for world ecology had led to discussions about the need to limit population, which inevitably touched on the question of birth control. In 1964 Reverend Arthur McCormick, a Roman Catholic priest, spoke on campus and endorsed the use of birth-control pills as a partial solution to overpopulation in poor countries.[123] Four years later, in 1968, Villanova hosted a conference of the Population Council, where speakers once again advocated birth control.[124]

Thus when Pope Paul VI issued his encyclical *Humanae Vitae* (*Human Life*) in the summer of 1968, a number of faculty at Villanova were greatly disappointed. Seventy faculty members (not all of whom were Catholic) signed a protest, made public in a press release on August 10. In justifying their protest, the professors asserted (quoting from a 1967 study on "The Idea of a Catholic University") that Catholic institutions of higher learning had a duty to examine continuously "all aspects and all activities of the Church and should objectively evaluate them."[125]

An important part of this faculty protest involved the question of academic freedom in a Catholic university. Since the great majority of Catholic Americans (including a growing body of clergy) believed in birth control, the conflict between the church's official teachings on the subject and the right to challenge this position in an academic setting did not create a crisis at Villanova or anywhere else in the American church. However, the far more explosive issue of abortion led to a serious clash between Catholic doctrine and academic freedom at Villanova—and on other Catholic campuses.[126]

Given the intense antiabortion feeling that would develop among many Villanovans, it is interesting that both sides of the issue were presented in relatively dispassionate editorials in the *Villanovan* during the early 1970s.[127] In March 1971 Villanova even held a conference on the subject, cosponsored by the Law School's Institute for Church and State and the College Theology Society of Eastern Pennsylvania, titled "The Abortion Dilemma: Is a Viable Consensus Possible?" At least two of the speakers concluded that abortion should be legal under certain circumstances.[128]

Once the U.S. Supreme Court legalized abortion in *Roe v. Wade*, a case handed down in early 1973, the antiabortion forces seized the initiative on campus. In early 1974, just as tensions over student rights were reaching a peak at Villanova, a group of antiabortion students formed Villanovans for Life under the guidance of Campus Ministry. On January 22, 1974, the first anniversary of the Supreme Court decision, this pro-life group participated in a noon rally at the Federal Court House in Philadelphia led by John Cardinal Krol, then president of the National Conference of Catholic Bishops and a severe critic of the *Roe* decision. On January 22, 1975, and on subsequent anniversaries of the abortion decision, Villanovans for Life joined protest marches in Washington, D.C.[129]

Although the pro-life forces clearly enjoyed the moral support of the Catholic Church, as well as most of their fellow students, there were voices of dissent in the pages of the *Villanovan*, a typical haven, like other campus newspapers in the 1980s and 1990s, for the small group of "rebels" who remained on campus. In January 1982 an editorial charged that pro-life groups were "trying to impose their particular religious beliefs on the entire female population, thus limiting other's freedom of choice. . . ."[130] Ten years later, in March 1992, the newspaper carried pro-life and pro-choice arguments side by side.[131]

By 1992 Villanova had been embroiled in fifteen years of contention between the church's firm and outspoken opposition to abortion and the university's commitment to academic freedom. This was an extremely difficult issue since Villanova's mission statement supported both academic freedom and official church teachings. Resolving this conflict was rendered more difficult by increasingly militant antiabortion groups in the region and by the conservative stance of the local Catholic archdiocese, led throughout this period by John Cardinal Krol.

The first eruption in this ongoing debate occurred at commencement exercises on May 19, 1977, where Reverend Robert Drinan, S.J., a professor at Georgetown University and then a member of the U.S. Congress, received an honorary degree. Although Father Drinan said nothing that day about abortion, antiabortion activists were angry at Drinan for what they considered to be his proabortion votes on several bills in Congress. Protestors gathered outside the Field House, the site of Villanova's commencement that year. One of them carried a sign with a picture of a crucified baby. Others stood beside a coffin with a caption that read "1,000,000 unborn killed per year."[132] The protest came as a complete surprise to Father Driscoll and other administrators at Villanova, who were unaware of Drinan's voting record on issues related to abortion, a fact that Driscoll was careful to explain to both Cardinal Krol and Augustinian provincial authorities.[133]

The next significant event came eight years later, on March 26, 1985, when Father Drinan again spoke at Villanova. His topic was "Liberation

Theology and the Future of Human Rights in Latin America." Although his talk, delivered in the Villanova Room of the Connelly Center, had nothing to do with abortion (or with any of the church's other teachings on sexuality), pro-life demonstrators besieged the site. They carried signs, banged on the glass doors of the lecture room, and shouted "Drinan is a baby killer."[134]

With this incident in mind, Father Driscoll decided to block the appearance of an even more controversial speaker who was slated to address Villanova's annual Theology Institute, to be held on campus that summer.[135] The upcoming lecturer was Dr. Daniel Maguire, a leader in the Catholics For Free Choice movement, which had recently taken out a full-page advertisement in the October 7, 1984, *New York Times.* Signed by ninety-seven people, including Maguire, it proclaimed that not all Catholics agreed with the church's stand on abortion.[136]

In a letter from the Augustinian prior-provincial in March 1985, Father Driscoll first learned that an appearance by Maguire at the Theology Institute would be highly controversial.[137] He therefore asked the institute to cancel Maguire's invitation. But its organizers refused, so in early May, Driscoll himself wrote to Maguire and withdrew the invitation to appear on campus.[138] This action was widely reported in the Philadelphia and suburban newspapers and provoked a strong verbal protest from the Villanova Chapter of the AAUP.[139] The latter concluded that Driscoll's withdrawal of the invitation violated the principles of academic freedom, and it reported the incident to the national office of the AAUP, which proceeded to investigate. Because three other Catholic institutions (Boston College, St. Martin's College, and the College of St. Scholastica) had also canceled invitations to Maguire, the national AAUP decided to conduct a joint inquiry of all four.[140]

Driscoll explained to the investigators from the AAUP that his primary intent had not been to deny academic freedom, but to avoid a demonstration on campus that might lead to misunderstanding and disaffection among the university's largely Catholic constituencies.[141] In its conclusion, however, the AAUP report took polite exception to this reasoning while criticizing Driscoll's decision to withdraw the invitation from Maguire:

> Academic freedom cannot flourish if it is to fall victim to those—even to a university's constituents—who will misconstrue an institution's purpose in providing a platform for controversial figures or views. A university has an obligation to defend academic freedom against intimidation, and threats should be met, not with the suppression of controversy, but with reasoned argument and a firm stand on principle.[142]

Some critics saw this bow to constituent pressures as part of an overall tendency in Driscoll to accommodate powerful opposition. First there had been his reversal on dropping varsity football, and now there was his withdrawal of the Maguire invitation, both decisions having been made in the face of intense criticism (or threatened protest). Yet Driscoll had been praised in the mid-1970s for acceding to a variety of student demands. Thus one might observe that Driscoll himself had been consistent in his efforts to keep peace among various university constituencies, but there were many on the faculty who believed that there could be no compromise on the question of academic freedom.[143]

Continuing questions about academic freedom would have to be confronted by Driscoll's successor, for in the summer of 1988 he stepped down from the second longest presidency in the institution's history.[144] Taking his place at the helm was Reverend Edmund J. Dobbin, O.S.A., then fifty-two years old and a native of Staten Island, New York. Father Dobbin had spent

Former presidents of Villanova stand with Reverend Edmund J. Dobbin, O.S.A., S.T.D., after his Inaugural Mass on October 5, 1988. Together they spanned forty-four years of campus history. *Left to right:* Reverend Francis X. N. McGuire, O.S.A., D.D. (1944–54); Reverend John M. Driscoll, O.S.A., Ph.D. (1975–88); Father Dobbin (1988–present); Reverend Robert J. Welsh, O.S.A., S.T.D. (1967–71); Reverend Edward J. McCarthy, O.S.A., Ph.D. (1971–75). Not pictured but still living at the time was Reverend Joseph A. Flaherty, O.S.A. (1965–1967). VUA.

seventeen years teaching theology at the Washington Theological Union before returning to Villanova in 1987 as assistant to the Vice President for Academic Affairs. His inauguration on October 5, 1988, with more than 150 representatives of various academic institutions, was the first such formal event in Villanova's history. Four of Villanova's former presidents—McGuire, Welsh, McCarthy, and Driscoll—were also there.[145]

Father Dobbin was in office only a few months before he too was faced with a conflict between academic freedom and official church doctrine. The issue arose over a lecture on November 13, 1988, by Reverend Charles E. Curran under the sponsorship of Villanova's Religious Studies Department. Speaking to a packed audience in the Connelly Center's Villanova Room, Curran's topic was "Academic Freedom and Higher Education." There were pro-life demonstrators in the room as well as outside.[146] Curran was controversial because he had recently been dismissed from the theology faculty at The Catholic University of America, in Washington, D.C. Among other things, Curran had advocated birth control as essential for responsible parenthood, had declared that abortion could be justified in order to save the life of the mother, and that homosexual acts, if performed as part of a committed relationship, might be considered moral.[147] News of Curran's dismissal provoked considerable anger at other Catholic institutions, including Villanova.[148] According to Dr. Rodger Van Allen of Villanova's AAUP chapter, Curran's dismissal was "a clear violation of academic freedom."[149]

Although academic freedom now seemed secure, an incident in April 1992 beclouded the issue once again. In this case, posters announcing a pro-choice march to take place on April 5 were taken down from university buildings at the request of Dr. Richard A. Neville, Vice President for Student Life, "because they opposed the university's stance on abortion."[150] Unlike the Maguire case, this decision had not been made by the university president. Nevertheless, Father Dobbin felt obliged to issue an official statement about debate at the university. In it he endeavored to balance Villanova's commitment to the teachings of the Roman Catholic Church with its dedication to academic freedom:

> Villanova has been committed to the moral tradition of teaching of the Catholic Church since the University's founding by the Augustinian Order almost 150 years ago. As a Catholic institution, Villanova embraces the Church's teaching regarding the moral tragedy that is abortion. Villanova affirms its religious, institutional commitment to the principle that all directly intended abortion is morally wrong. To be faithful to this teaching and to its own Catholic identity and mission, the University cannot provide institutional support for a message or activity which promotes or advocates abortion. . . .

At the same time, Villanova as a university endorses unfettered discussion and the exchange of ideas in the search for truth and knowledge. . . . Villanova is open to the many voices of its community in fashioning a means whereby full and frank discussion of controversial moral and social issues is fostered without compromising the institution's obligation to bear witness to the Church's moral teaching. This task will not be simple. It requires time, reflection and the climate of a caring community tolerant of one another's sincerely held beliefs. The participation of the whole community is essential in doing the hard work necessary to preserve the principles of openness to ideas and fidelity to religious beliefs, both being central to Villanova's identity.[151]

Two years earlier *Ex Corde Ecclesiae* (*From the Heart of the Church*), an Apostolic Constitution on Catholic Universities issued by the Vatican in 1990, took up this question of academic freedom and the magisterium of the church. It embraced the concept of academic freedom, but only so long as it was exercised "with a concern for the ethical and moral implications both of its methods and discoveries."[152] In order to reconcile potential conflicts between discoveries based upon reason and the requirements of faith, the document fell back on the old Scholastic idea that there could never be a real conflict between the two, "for the things of the earth and the concerns of faith derive from the same God."[153]

Such a formula would not be an easy one to interpret or enforce, as Villanova found itself torn between two equally valued goals: academic freedom and the moral teachings of Roman Catholicism. Once again Villanova found itself enmeshed in a dialogue over what it meant to be a Catholic university in America, where openness and pluralism had long been a goal of the wider academic community.[154]

Indeed, there were serious concerns that the conflicts over academic freedom would compromise Villanova's drive for academic excellence, but these fears did not materialize. Villanova began to receive national notice for its academic program. Two of these recognitions came in November 1985, when Villanova obtained a long-coveted Phi Beta Kappa chapter, and *U.S. News and World Report* named Villanova the number-one comprehensive university in the East.[155] Coming just seven months after Villanova's NCAA championship, these honors combined with the basketball victory to make 1985 a true *annus mirabilis* for Villanova.

In addition to the improving quality of its students, Villanova's reputation benefited from continuing curricular innovations and reforms. Among these were a series of academic institutes and special studies: the Institute for Church and State (1956), the Honors Program (1965), the Theology Institute (1967), the Criminal Justice Program (1968), the Augustinian Historical Institute (1973), the American Institute of Pakistani Studies (1973), Black Studies (1976), Ethnic Studies (1977), Peace and Justice Studies (1977), the Common Heritage Institute (1979), Women's Studies (1980), the Connelly Law and Morality Institute (1982), Irish Studies (1982), Contemporary Arab and Islamic Studies (1983), the Human Organizational Science Institute (1984), International Studies (1986), Latin American Studies (1988).[156]

In the early 1990s Villanova also revamped its core curriculum for the College of Arts and Sciences. It featured a yearlong humanities seminar for freshmen, two writing-intensive courses and eight writing-enriched courses, a fine arts requirement (for the first time), and two courses that emphasized cultural diversity. Implementation of the new core curriculum, which affected only students in the College of Arts and Sciences, began in the fall of 1992. However, it was hoped that the other undergraduate colleges would develop similar core curricula in the future, with Arts and Sciences leading the way by example.[157]

In order to strengthen its academic programs still further, Villanova undertook a new cycle of planning and fund-raising in the early 1990s. This broader initiative began in early 1984 when Father Driscoll appointed a Program Evaluation Committee (PEC) charged with "the preparation of planning parameters."[158] The PEC study took four years to complete and resulted in a massive six-volume report in the spring of 1988. Among other things, it recommended the discontinuation of several graduate and undergraduate programs that were not academically strong, and the use of resultant funds for programs that were doing well. Agreeing with Villanova's mission statement, the report also stressed the need to concentrate on undergraduate studies at Villanova rather than to add many new graduate programs. At the time, there were approximately thirty master's degree programs in operation, and one doctorate (in chemistry), which was discontinued in 1992, largely because of its high costs. Several of the undergraduate and master's degree programs were also abolished in the aftermath of the report, including studies in library science. At the time of this writing, assessment of graduate programs continues, with the goal of disbanding the weaker master's programs and creating a few select doctoral programs with the clear potential for national recognition.[159]

Just before the PEC report appeared, Driscoll unveiled a "Master Plan" for physical improvements during his State of the University address on February 19, 1988. This included the construction of new housing for 1,200 students (later reduced to 600) on a new West Campus, to be built on the thirty-eight-acre Morris Estate just across Spring Mill Road. Villanova had purchased thirty-three acres of this property in 1978 for $750,000 and another five acres of contiguous property in 1985 for $300,000. However, it took the university a dozen years to convince Radnor Township officials to grant the necessary zoning to build on it. Permission from the township came in early 1990, and construction of the residence halls began in the spring of 1993. These West Campus residences were to be faced in gray stone and designed by the Hillier Group in a simplified Tudor-Jacobean style, which blended well with the Gothic revival edifices nearby, such as St. Mary's Hall and the Law School's Garey Hall. Upon completion of these new halls, Villanova would be able to house approximately 70 percent of its students on campus, thus strengthening its sense of community. By providing more housing on campus, the university also hoped to ease tensions with surrounding neighborhoods, where some residents had long complained of troublesome students who were renting houses or apartments.[160]

The old Morris mansion, it was later decided, would be restored and renovated for use by the university's Development Office. Designed by Philadelphia architect Addison Hutton (1834–1916) and originally known as Dundale, the three-story Morris house contained thirty-five rooms. Built in 1890 in a late-Victorian, eclectic style, its simple but richly appointed interior provided excellent spaces for offices, meeting rooms, and various social activities. For the time being, the university planned to name the restored and renovated mansion Dundale Hall, in recognition of its historical designation.[161] On the main campus the Master Plan proposed a new faculty office building, new student health-care facilities, a new theater, the renovation and expansion of the university's science building (Mendel Hall), and additional parking facilities.[162]

Driscoll's successor, Father Dobbin, reiterated the main points of this scheme, which by the fall of 1988 had developed into what was being called the "Strategic Plan." In addition to physical expansion and improvements, Dobbin emphasized the need to increase Villanova's still-small endowment, one of the university's greatest challenges in the years just ahead, according to the president. At the time it was only $24 million, making it the smallest per capita undergraduate endowment of all Villanova's main competitors. (It was also only twice as large, in absolute terms, as what had been advocated back in 1929. Adjusted for inflation over the intervening sixty years, it was still a fraction of what planners had called for in the late 1920s, when the undergraduate enrollment had been about one-seventh of the 1988 figure.) In the spring of 1991 Dobbin accordingly initiated planning for a new capital drive, called simply "The Villanova Campaign," with a goal of $100 million— $60 million of which was slated for endowment.[163]

Increasing Villanova's endowment would allow for endowed chairs, the expansion of scholarships, and what Father Dobbin called his plan for "right-sizing" the university. A central goal of right-sizing was a reduction of the

Groundbreaking ceremony for the future St. Augustine Center for the Liberal Arts, December 11, 1990. *Left to right:* Reverend Kail C. Ellis, O.S.A., Dean of Liberal Arts and Sciences; Reverend Edmund J. Dobbin, O.S.A., University President; Mr. James A. Drobile, Esq., Chairperson of the Villanova Board of Trustees; and Reverend John J. Hagen, O.S.A., Augustinian Provincial, Province of St. Thomas of Villanova. VUA.

full-time undergraduate enrollment from 6,500 in 1991 to 5,700 by 1996. His reasons for right-sizing were several. After increasing for a number of years, undergraduate applications began to drop as the numbers of eighteen-year-olds declined among the smaller generation of Americans who followed the baby boom. In 1989 freshman applications at Villanova were down by 1.6 percent from the year before, and in 1991 they were down by 14.7 percent from 1990. Only by admitting fewer students, it was reasoned, could Villanova continue to be increasingly selective.

More important, right-sizing would allow the university to concentrate on a higher quality of facilities and student life, instead of constantly running just to catch up with increasing enrollments. Improved facilities, in turn, would help to attract more applicants who valued Villanova for both its academic offerings and student life. In the process of right-sizing, faculty and staff would have to be reduced, though mainly through attrition and slightly larger classes. In many ways this was the realization of a goal that had been

St. Thomas of Villanova Church, 1986, with St. Thomas of Villanova Monastery on the left. VUA.

proposed as early as the 1920s and that had been reiterated many times since.[164]

As Father Dobbin announced these plans, Villanova was preparing for its 150th anniversary. This sesquicentennial celebration afforded Villanova an excellent platform for promoting the new capital campaign. It also gave the Catholic, Augustinian university a superb opportunity to examine where it had been—and where it might be headed in the years to come.

# CONCLUSION

## *PAST AND FUTURE*

**P**reliminary planning for Villanova's sesquicentennial observances began in 1987 when Father Driscoll appointed a
special committee for the purpose.[1] This was later superseded by a Sesquicentennial Steering Committee, chaired by Dr. Richard A. Neville, Vice President for Student Life. The various activities of the sesquicentennial year
were coordinated by a managing director, Dr. Christine A. Lysionek of the
Student Life office.

The celebration began with a cluster of events in September 1992. Among
the first of these was the opening of an archival exhibit, "Villanova, College
to University," in the President's Lounge of Connelly Center.[2] It was created
by the university archivist, Reverend Dennis J. Gallagher, O.S.A., Ph.D., in
conjunction with this author. On the day of its official opening (September
17) Father Dobbin rang the old college bell, long known as the "Sister
Liberty Bell," which stood at the entrance to the exhibit. Father Gallagher
and this author also collaborated in writing both a catalog for the exhibit, as
well as a pictorial history of the university entitled *Ever Ancient, Ever New*
and a series of historical articles for the *Villanovan* entitled "Sesquicentennial Minutes."[3]

September also saw the dedication of a new garden overlooking Lancaster
Pike, with the word VILLANOVA spelled out in flowers. The garden, with its
prominent floral lettering, actually revived a similar garden and familiar
landmark on the Villanova campus that had once occupied a site several
hundred yards west of the new plantings.

Official opening of the Sesquicentennial Exhibit, "Villanova, College to University: 150 Years of Augustinian Tradition and Promise, 1842–1992," September 17, 1992. *Left to right:* Reverend Edmund J. Dobbin, O.S.A., S.T.D.; Dr. David R. Contosta; Dr. Christine A. Lysionek; and Reverend Dennis J. Gallagher, O.S.A., Ph.D. VUA.

It was in September too that a special exhibit, organized by Brother Richard G. Cannuli, O.S.A., opened in the Connelly Center Art Gallery. It featured a variety of art objects associated with the first seventy-five years of Villanova history, to be followed in the spring by a similar exhibit on the last seventy-five years. In the lobby of Connelly Center, one could find a scale model of the Villanova campus constructed under the direction of Mr. Robert J. Casey of the Engineering Department. By September a series of historical plaques giving the date and brief history of Villanova's older buildings and carrying the sesquicentennial logo had been mounted on each of the designated structures. The plaques were researched and written by Father Dennis J. Gallagher and this author, in cooperation with a plaque committee chaired by Mrs. Louise Green of the Falvey Memorial Library. These and other projects of a historical nature were coordinated by the Sesquicentennial Committee on Historical Exhibits and Projects, chaired by Dr. Donald B. Kelley of the History Department.

On September 21, a renovated St. Thomas of Villanova Church was blessed at a special Mass. The next day, September 22, there was the dedication of the

Dedication of the St. Augustine Center for the Liberal Arts, September 22, 1992. Designed by Ueland, Junker & McCauley. VUA.

new St. Augustine Center for the Liberal Arts, a four-story building that for the first time in many years brought all the Liberal Arts departments together and also housed seminar rooms and faculty offices (officially designated as "faculty studies"). The new building, erected at a cost of $17 million, also symbolized the university's rededication to its tradition of the liberal arts, which reached all the way back to the founding of Villanova College 150 years before and which had been central to the Augustinian teaching mission for many centuries. That evening there was an academic convocation, with an address by Archbishop Rembert G. Weakland, O.S.B., of Milwaukee.[4]

Parents' Weekend, September 18–20, which coincided with the inauguration of the Sesquicentennial, included an opening pageant that featured music from fifteen decades, antique cars, and changing styles in dress. Afterward guests could enjoy horse-drawn carriage rides, tours of the campus on buses transformed to resemble antique trolleys, a parade of old cars, a Philadelphia Mummers string band, a football game, and a dance "under the stars" on Mendel Field. On Sunday there was a Mass at duPont Pavilion.

Throughout the rest of the year there were series of lectures, symposiums, and other occasions in honor of the 150th anniversary. One of these was the designation of Villanova as an official arboretum by the International

Parade of antique cars during Sesquicentennial Weekend, September 19, 1992. VUA.

Society of Arbiculture on April 28, 1993, an event coordinated by Kevin O'Donnell, Villanova's superintendent of grounds. It was a recognition of the university's commitment during the sesquicentennial year to preserve and renew its arboreal heritage. Since the earliest days Villanova's campus had been famous for its beautiful trees, which framed buildings, lined walkways, and swept the eye across well-manicured playing fields to bordering woodlands. The university was determined that such vistas would remain for future generations.[5]

The Sesquicentennial's official end, entitled "Supernova," came during Parents' Weekend, September 17–19, 1993. Activities included a cookout and another dance under the stars on Mendel Field, where there was a huge birthday cake (15 by 15 feet) made of blue and white balloons. There were also tours of the campus, a football game, and a kickoff dinner at duPont Pavilion for the public phase of the Villanova Campaign. The latter event took place on September 18, exactly 150 years to the day from when the first classes had opened at Villanova College back in 1843.[6]

Throughout the sesquicentennial year the three formative influences at Villanova—American, Catholic, and Augustinian—were much in evidence. The bands, parades, pageants, and football games were all a familiar part of the American landscape, while the written histories and exhibits showed that Villanova had been shaped by the main currents of American life. The special liturgies, as well as many speeches and symposia, underlined Villanova's Catholic identity. There were also numerous reminders during the sesquicentennial year, and especially in the archival exhibit at the Connelly Center, of the essential role played by the Augustinian community in the founding and growth of Villanova.

For those who participated in Villanova's sesquicentennial observances, these events had many meanings. But for the historian and the archivist such an anniversary provided an opportunity to see how the present had been shaped by the past, and how the past and present might point to certain possibilities in the future.

During its first fifty years Villanova had often struggled just to stay alive, and it was really more of a high school than a college during its first decades. Not until the early twentieth century did the number of college students surpass those in the academy, and only in 1923 did the academy begin its move off campus. Despite Villanova's precarious finances, leaders like Father Fedigan and Father Delurey were willing to take risks for the sake of a better future. Yet until recent years Villanova often had a difficult time meeting the needs of its student body. The increasing numbers and successes of its graduates, and Villanova's own growing reputation in the region (and beyond), finally allowed it to catch up with most of these requirements. At the same time, the university broke with the cycle of admitting greater numbers of students in order to pay for ever more extensive facilities and could now concentrate on seeking higher quality in every area.

These breakthroughs were in part fired by a fierce determination to succeed combined with a belief that the sacrifices of those who had gone before would be dishonored by the failure of later generations. This sense of an obligation to the past has echoed again and again in presidential addresses and student publications, including the *Belle Air*, which for years opened with a historical account of the many Villanovans who had toiled to make the present possible. Such was the thrust of Father Dobbin's many reflections on the sesquicentennial year:

> We stand at a significant point in Villanova's history. The sesquicentennial celebration affords us the opportunity to examine the heritage of this vital institution of ours. History may be a catalogue of dates and events, of successes and failures, but it is more than that. The history of an institution evokes vibrant images of people, of those who have shared their lives, their hopes and their dreams to bring about what we see today. Villanova's memory conjures up the faces and forms of Augustinians and of the many men and women, faculty, students, and staff who have given life to the Villanova personality. . . . In them was our beginning, a kind of leap of faith, which has evolved into the Villanova we know today.[7]

To some extent, as Father Dobbin alluded, Villanova's success was also a matter of maturity. Although 150 years may seem an incredibly long period to an eighteen-year-old student or even to a young adult, it is only two human lifetimes of seventy-five years each. Compared with Harvard and other universities established in colonial times, Villanova was just entering middle age; and next to the ancient seats of learning in Europe, it was a toddler just beginning to walk. In certain respects it simply took Villanova fifteen decades to win a wide reputation for excellence, to produce large numbers of successful and prosperous graduates, and to find its own particular niche in American higher education.

There has also been an element of good fortune in Villanova's rise, as with any successful enterprise. One especially good piece of luck flowed from the decision back in 1842 to purchase the Rudolph farm on the Lancaster Pike. While distance from the city may have discouraged some students in the early decades, Villanova has escaped the fate of many urban colleges and universities that in the late twentieth century have found themselves surrounded by decaying neighborhoods. Villanova's location among Philadelphia's prestigious Main Line suburbs is without doubt an extremely important factor in recruiting high-quality students, who can enjoy the best of its

Reverend Edmund J. Dobbin, O.S.A., S.T.D., Thirty-First President of Villanova University, inaugurated October 5, 1988. VUA.

suburban surroundings in addition to the nearby city during their four years at Villanova. (Of course, it is this same Main Line location that shelters students, mostly the sons and daughters of prosperous suburban families, from the harsh realities of urban life and that has probably hindered Villanova's recruitment of minority students.)

Perhaps more than anything else, Villanova's ability to maintain its Catholic, Augustinian identity while adopting most of the standards and expecta-

Students walking up from the "east quad." Bartley Hall is in the distance, with a portion of Connelly Center in the left foreground, c. 1990. VUA.

tions of American higher education has saved it from becoming just another mediocre private school. This was not always easy, especially in the beginning when anti-Catholicism threatened to destroy the fledgling Villanova College. The challenge posed by elective curricula and pragmatic philosophy in the late nineteenth and early twentieth centuries also made for a prolonged and difficult adjustment, until much of the rest of the academic world came back to the idea of a required core curriculum and met the Catholic colleges and universities at a happy middle ground.

Villanova and other Catholic institutions of higher learning likewise had a difficult time conceding a greater voice to students and faculty, a powerful trend in American higher education during the past few decades. The reforms of Vatican II, certain egalitarian themes from the counterculture of the 1960s, and the growth of a more diverse faculty and administration all assisted in this movement toward a more collaborative style of university governance. Success in fund-raising and the ability to provide a high quality of academic and student life were also promising. Thus, both present and past suggest a good future for the Catholic, Augustinian university in America.

# PRESIDENTS OF VILLANOVA COLLEGE AND UNIVERSITY

|  |  | Birth–Death | Term |
|---|---|---|---|
| 1. | Reverend John P. O'Dwyer, O.S.A. | (1816–1850) | 1843–1847 |
| 2. | Reverend William Harnett, O.S.A. | (1820–1875) | 1847–1848 |
| 3. | Reverend John P. O'Dwyer, O.S.A. | (1816–1850) | 1848–1850 |
| 4. | Reverend William Harnett, O.S.A. | (1820–1875) | 1850–1851 |
| 5. | Reverend Patrick E. Moriarty, O.S.A. | (1805–1875) | 1851–1855 |
| 6. | Reverend William Harnett, O.S.A. | (1820–1875) | 1855–1857 |
| 7. | Reverend Ambrose A. Mullen, O.S.A. | (1827–1876) | 1865–1869 |
| 8. | Reverend Patrick A. Stanton, O.S.A. | (1826–1891) | 1869–1872 |
| 9. | Reverend Thomas Galberry, O.S.A. | (1833–1878) | 1872–1876 |
| 10. | Reverend Thomas C. Middleton, O.S.A. | (1842–1923) | 1876–1878 |
| 11. | Reverend John J. Fedigan, O.S.A. | (1842–1908) | 1878–1880 |
| 12. | Reverend Joseph A. Coleman, O.S.A. | (1842–1902) | 1880–1886 |
| 13. | Reverend Francis M. Sheeran, O.S.A. | (1840–1912) | 1886–1890 |
| 14. | Reverend Christopher A. McEvoy, O.S.A. | (1840–1914) | 1890–1894 |
| 15. | Reverend Francis J. McShane, O.S.A. | (1845–1932) | 1894–1895 |
| 16. | Reverend Lawrence A. Delurey, O.S.A. | (1864–1922) | 1895–1910 |
| 17. | Reverend Edward G. Dohan, O.S.A. | (1870–1936) | 1910–1917 |
| 18. | Reverend James A. Dean, O.S.A. | (1879–1964) | 1917–1920 |
| 19. | Reverend Francis A. Driscoll, O.S.A. | (1889–1945) | 1920–1924 |
| 20. | Reverend Joseph A. Hickey, O.S.A. | (1883–1955) | 1924–1925 |
| 21. | Reverend Mortimer A. Sullivan, O.S.A. | (1887–1949) | 1925–1926 |
| 22. | Reverend James H. Griffin, O.S.A. | (1891–1972) | 1926–1932 |
| 23. | Reverend Edward V. Stanford, O.S.A. | (1897–1966) | 1932–1944 |
| 24. | Reverend Francis X. N. McGuire, O.S.A. | (1909–    ) | 1944–1954 |
| 25. | Reverend James A. Donnellon, O.S.A. | (1906–1971) | 1954–1959 |
| 26. | Reverend John A. Klekotka, O.S.A. | (1915–1978) | 1959–1965 |
| 27. | Reverend Joseph A. Flaherty, O.S.A. | (1916–1993) | 1965–1967 |
| 28. | Reverend Robert J. Welsh, O.S.A. | (1921–1992) | 1967–1971 |
| 29. | Reverend Edward J. McCarthy | (1912–    ) | 1971–1975 |
| 30. | Reverend John M. Driscoll, O.S.A. | (1923–    ) | 1975–1988 |
| 31. | Reverend Edmund J. Dobbin, O.S.A. | (1935–    ) | 1988– |

# ABBREVIATIONS

These abbreviations are used in the captions for the illustrations and in the Notes and Bibliographical Essay.

| | |
|---|---|
| AAUP | American Association of University Professors |
| APA | Augustinian Provincial Archives, Villanova, Pennsylvania |
| *CHR* | *Catholic Historical Review* |
| CUSP | Commission on University Structure and Programs |
| PEC | Program Evaluation Committee |
| *PMHB* | *Pennsylvania Magazine of History and Biography* |
| *RACHSP* | *Records of the American Catholic Historical Society of Philadelphia* |
| VUA | Villanova University Archives, Falvey Memorial Library, Villanova, Pennsylvania |

# NOTES

## Introduction: American—Catholic—Augustinian

1. For the complete text of Father Dobbin's inaugural address, see *Villanova Magazine,* Fall 1988, pp. 4–7.

2. Ibid., p. 4.

3. Ibid.

4. Ibid., p. 5.

5. Ibid., p. 6.

## Chapter 1: Belle-Air to Villanova

1. Thomas Cooke Middleton, O.S.A., *Historical Sketch of the Augustinian Monastery, College, and Mission of St. Thomas of Villanova, Delaware County, Pa.; During the first half century of their existence, 1842–1892* (Villanova, Pa., 1893), p. 13 (hereafter Middleton, *Sketch*).

2. On the early Augustinian community in Philadelphia and elsewhere in America, see Arthur J. Ennis, *No Easy Road: The Early Years of the Augustinians in the United States, 1796–1874* (New York, 1993); Francis E. Tourscher, O.S.A., *Old Saint Augustine's in Philadelphia, With Some Records of the Work of the Austin Friars in the United States* (Philadelphia, 1937); John J. Gavigan, O.S.A., *The Augustinians from the French Revolution to Modern Times*, vol. 4 of *History of the Order of St. Augustine* (Villanova, Pa., 1989), and "Michael Hurley, O.S.A.," in *Men of Heart, vol. 1: Pioneering Augustinians, Province of Saint Thomas of Villanova*, ed. Joseph L. Shannon, O.S.A. (Villanova, Pa., 1983), 1:9–44; Thomas F. Roland, O.S.A., *The Order of Saint Augustine in the United States of America, 1796–1946* (Villanova, Pa., 1947).

3. For an overview of the experiences of Catholics in eighteenth- and nineteenth-century America, see Jay P. Dolan, *The American Catholic Experience: A History from Colonial Times to the Present* (Notre Dame, Ind., 1992), pp. 69–157; James Hennesey, S.J., "Square Peg in a Round Hole: On Being Roman Catholic in America," *Records of the American Catholic Historical Society of Philadelphia (RACHSP)*, December 1973, pp. 167–82.

4. On the Irish clergy in the United States, see Thomas T. McAvoy, C.S.C., "The Irish Clergyman in the United States," *RACHSP,* March 1964, pp. 6–38.

5. Middleton, *Sketch*, p. 12; Joseph L. Shannon, O.S.A., "Thomas Augustine Kyle,

O.S.A.," in *Men of Heart, vol. 2: Noteworthy Augustinians, Province of Saint Thomas of Villanova*, ed. John E. Rotelle, O.S.A. (Villanova, Pa., 1983), 2:64–67.

6. Shannon, "Kyle," pp. 64–67.

7. Mortgage, "Brothers of the Order of Hermits of Saint Augustine to John R. Vogdes, Trustee, For $10,000," January 5, 1842; and Mortgage, "Brothers of the Order of Hermits of Saint Augustine to John R. Vogdes, Trustee, For $6,000," January 5, 1842, in Villanova University: Finances: First Mortgages, Augustinian Provincial Archives (hereafter APA).

8. Middleton, *Sketch*, p. 14; Tourscher, *Old Saint Augustine's*, p. 67; First Mortgages, Villanova University, APA.

9. First Mortgages, Villanova University. The *Catholic Standard and Times*, June 28, 1902, reprinted Moriarty's 1842 appeal for funds. See also "Brief Title to all those two contiguous tracts of land containing together 236 acres 6 perches Situate[d] in Radnor Township Delaware Co. belonging to the Augustinian College of Villanova," APA.

10. Rufus M. Jones, *Haverford College: A History and an Interpretation* (New York, 1933), p. 7.

11. Thomas Cooke Middleton, O.S.A., "Notes on All the Missions in the O.S.A." (manuscript, APA), p. 33 (hereafter Middleton Notes).

12. William C. Harkin, O.S.A., "The Augustinian Lay Brothers," in *Men of Heart*, 1:118.

13. Middleton, *Sketch*, p. 15.

14. Ibid., p. 16; Thomas Cooke Middleton, O.S.A., Journal (bound manuscript volume, APA), 1:213 (hereafter Middleton Journal).

15. Reverend John E. Rotelle, O.S.A, "John Possidius O'Dwyer, O.S.A.," in *Men of Heart*, 1:91; Tourscher, *Old Saint Augustine's*, p. 175.

16. Patrick E. Moriarty, O.S.A., "Prospectus" (n.d.) (on page 2 of a newspaper scrapbook kept by Thomas Cooke Middleton, O.S.A. [hereafter Middleton Scrapbook], APA).

17. Ibid.

18. Middleton, *Sketch*, p. 35.

19. Tourscher, *Old Saint Augustine's*, p. 92.

20. Moriarty, "Prospectus."

21. Ibid.

22. Middleton, *Sketch*, pp. 17–18, 32.

23. Ibid., p. 32.

24. Middleton Notes, p. 37.

25. One of the best works on romanticism, which explains the differences between the Romantic movement and the principal movements before and after, remains Jacques Barzun, *Classic, Romantic, and Modern* (Chicago, 1961). For insight into the belief by Catholics and Protestants alike that the city was not an appropriate place to rear Christian children, see Colleen McDannell, *The Christian Home in Victorian America* (Bloomington, Ind., 1986).

26. Some of the old-fashioned flavor of these rural estates is found in John T. Faris, *Old Roads Out of Philadelphia* (Philadelphia, 1917). The book contains a section on the Lancaster Pike (pp. 110–46). The country house tradition around Philadelphia is also explored in E. Digby Baltzell, *Philadelphia Gentlemen: The Making of a National Upper Class* (1958; reprint, Philadelphia, 1979), pp. 197–222, and in Nathaniel Burt, *The Perennial Philadelphians: The Anatomy of an American Aristocracy* (Boston, 1963), pp. 517–23.

27. For Catholic attitudes toward the city, see Robert D. Cross, "The Changing Image of the City Among American Catholics," *Catholic Historical Review* (*CHR*), April 1962, pp. 33–52.

28. Thomas C. Cochran, "Philadelphia: The American Industrial Center, 1750–1850,"

*Pennsylvania Magazine of History and Biography* (*PMHB*), July 1981, pp. 323–40; Elizabeth Geffen, "Industrial Development and Social Crisis," in Russell F. Weigley, ed., *Philadelphia: A 300-Year History* (New York, 1982), pp. 309, 326–27.

29. On the Irish population of the region, see Dennis Clark, *The Irish in Philadelphia: Ten Generations of Urban Experience* (Philadelphia, 1973).

30. Frederick Rudolph, *The American College and University: A History* (New York, 1962), pp. 48–49.

31. Robert Emmett Curran, S.J., *The Bicentennial History of Georgetown University: From Academy to University, 1789–1889* (Washington, D.C., 1993), 1:11–13; John M. Daley, S.J., *Georgetown University: Origin and Early Years* (Washington, D.C., 1957), p. xvii.

32. Jones, *Haverford College*, p. 3.

33. Edward Potts Cheney, *History of the University of Pennsylvania* (Philadelphia, 1940), p. 257.

34. Rudolph, *American College and University*, pp. 54–58.

35. Edward J. Power, *A History of Catholic Higher Education in the United States* (Milwaukee, 1958), pp. 46–47.

36. Rudolph, *American College and University*, pp. 281–82; Curran, *Georgetown*, pp. 12–13; Daley, *Georgetown*, p. 69; Thomas J. Donaghy, F.S.C., *Conceived in Crisis: A History of La Salle College* (Philadelphia, 1966), p. 73 (hereafter *La Salle*); Francis X. Talbot, S.J., *Jesuit Education in Philadelphia: Saint Joseph's College, 1851–1926* (Philadelphia, 1927), p. 39 (hereafter *St. Joseph's*); Nicholas Varga, *Baltimore's Loyola, Loyola's Baltimore, 1851–1986* (Baltimore, 1990), pp. 31–32; Francis Wallace, *Notre Dame: Its People and Its Legends* (New York, 1969), p. 28.

37. Jones, *Haverford College*, p. 13; Cheyney, *University of Pennsylvania*, pp. 27–40; Frederick Rudolph, *Curriculum: A History of the American Undergraduate Course of Study Since 1636* (San Francisco, 1977), p. 160.

38. Middleton, *Sketch*, p. 22.

39. Helen Lefkowitz Horowitz, *Campus Life: Undergraduate Cultures from the End of the Eighteenth Century to the Present* (New York, 1987), pp. 123–27; Power, *Catholic Higher Education*, pp. 19, 141–43; John S. Brubacher and Willis Rudy, *Higher Education in Transition: A History of American Colleges and Universities, 1636–1976* (New York, 1976), pp. 55, 66–69; Rudolph, *American College and University*, pp. 307, 311, 314–16.

40. Middleton Notes, pp. 32–33, 53.

41. Middleton, *Sketch*, p. 21. In his Notes, Middleton gives a slightly different account of the various accommodations in the mansion. In this other version he has the students on the second story with the priests, the lay brothers and farm hands in the attics. It may be that the arrangements were shifted several times during the year, thereby explaining the discrepancy in the two accounts. See Middleton Notes, p. 53.

42. Middleton, *Sketch*, p. 21.

43. Ibid., pp. 23–25.

44. Middleton Journal, 1:18; *The Villanovan*, October 17, 1950 (hereafter *Villanovan*).

45. Middleton, *Sketch*, p. 23.

46. On the anti-Catholic riots and related violence in Philadelphia, see Elizabeth Geffen, "Industrial Development and Social Crisis," in *Philadelphia: A 300-Year History*, pp. 309, 325–36, and "Violence in Philadelphia in the Late 1840s and 1850s," *Pennsylvania History*, October 1969, pp. 381–410. For background on anti-Catholic nativism, see Colman J. Barry, "Some Roots of American Nativism," *CHR*, July 1958, pp. 137–46; John Higham, "Another Look at Nativism," *CHR*, July 1958, pp. 147–58.

47. Middleton, *Sketch*, p. 22.

48. Ibid., pp. 22–23.

49. For discussions of the riots and the relationship to the consolidation of Philadelphia City and County, see Michael McCarthy, "The Philadelphia Consolidation Act of 1854: A Reappraisal," *PMHB*, October 1986, pp. 531–84; Eli K. Price, *The History of the Consolidation of the City of Philadelphia* (Philadelphia, 1873); and Russell Weigley, "The Border City in the Civil War, 1854–1865," in *Philadelphia: A 300-Year History*, p. 361.

50. *Catholic Herald*, February 20, 1845.

51. Middleton Notes, p. 39. This should be compared with Middleton, *Sketch*, p. 27.

52. Photocopy of Record of Admissions and Discharges, . . . Mt. Hope [Hospital], May 24, 1850, Records of 1840–78. Copy in APA.

53. Rotelle, "O'Dwyer," in *Men of Heart*, 1:97.

54. Middleton, *Sketch*, p. 33.

55. Ibid., p. 38.

56. Ibid.

57. Middleton Notes, p. 33.

58. Minutes, Board of Trustees of Villanova College (hereafter Trustee Minutes), 1:10, August 8, 1853, VUA.

59. Middleton, *Sketch*, p. 41; Middleton Scrapbook. The fact that Middleton, who was a master of details about campus history, does not mention any use of Villanova as a hospital during the Civil War also makes this claim suspect.

# Chapter 2: The Augustinian College

1. An Act to Incorporate the Augustinian College of Villanova, in the County of Delaware and State of Pennsylvania, section 1 (hereafter Charter of 1848), VUA; Acts and Proceedings of Corporation of 1804, 1 (1846–1922), 4, APA.

2. See, for example, *The Metropolitan Catholic Almanac and Laity's Directory for 1845* (Baltimore, 1845), p. 79; ibid., *1847*, p. 87; *Catholic Instructor*, March 19, 1852.

3. Charter of 1848, section 3.

4. Ibid.

5. Ibid., section 6.

6. Ibid., section 10.

7. Power, *Catholic Higher Education*, p. 154; Donaghy, *La Salle*, p. 46: Talbot, *Saint Joseph's*, passim.

8. Tourscher, *Old Saint Augustine's*, pp. 175, 182, 183, 200, 204.

9. Ibid., pp. 191, 200, 204.

10. Power, *Catholic Higher Education*, pp. 148–49.

11. John P. O'Dwyer, O.S.A., Lecture to Parents of St. Augustine's Parish School, August 4, 1842, APA.

12. John Cogley, *Catholic America*, expanded and updated by Rodger Van Allen (Kansas City, Mo., 1986), pp. 197–98. See also Curran, *Georgetown*, pp. 42–44; Daley, *Georgetown*, p. 239; Wallace, *Notre Dame*, p. 28; Varga, *Baltimore's Loyola*, p. 23; David Dunigan, S.J., *A History of Boston College* (Milwaukee, 1947), pp. 55–58.

13. For a further discussion of the curriculum at mid-nineteenth-century Catholic colleges, see Philip Gleason, "The Curriculum of the Old-Time Catholic College: A Student's View," *RACHSP*, March–December 1977, pp. 101–22.

14. Middleton, *Sketch*, p. 34. See also Trustee Minutes, September 18, 1850.

15. Middleton, *Sketch*, p. 42; Middleton Journal, 1:3.

16. Cheyney, *University of Pennsylvania*, p. 259.

17. Rudolph, *American College and University*, pp. 298–99; W. Bruce Leslie, *Gentlemen and Scholars: College and Community in the "Age of the University," 1865–1917* (University Park, Pa., 1992), pp. 11–28.

18. Middleton, *Sketch*, p. 20.

19. Ibid., p. 53.

20. Tourscher, *Old Saint Augustine's,* pp. 171–231.

21. Dolan, *American Catholic Experience*, pp. 127–57.

22. Tourscher, *Old Saint Augustine's,* p. 191.

23. Power, *Catholic Higher Education*, pp. 88–95.

24. Middleton Scrapbook, p. 3; Villanova University, Miscellaneous, APA.

25. Middleton, *Sketch*, p. 40.

26. Quoted in ibid., p. 22.

27. *Pittsburgh Catholic*, June 28, 1855.

28. Middleton Notes, p. 43.

29. In counting the number of Philadelphia students, the author included every student with an address within the metropolitan boundaries established by the consolidation of Philadelphia City and Philadelphia County in 1854.

30. For a list of Augustinian parishes, see Tourscher, *Old Saint Augustine's*, pp. 25–251, passim.

31. This count is based upon the list of Villanova students from 1843 to 1893, which appears in Appendix IV of Middleton, *Sketch*, pp. 59–95.

32. In his journal, 2:168, Middleton wrote that the first "student of color" was admitted to Villanova in September 1901. It is unknown whether any students from Latin America or the Caribbean were of mixed Spanish and Indian background.

33. Unidentified newspaper clipping, Middleton Scrapbook, p. 142.

34. Middleton, *Sketch*, p. 36.

35. College Rules, October 6, 1894, APA.

36. Tom Daly, "Memories of the Mauve Eighties," *Villanova Alumnus,* December 1938, p. 5.

37. *Catalogue 1883–84,* p. 8.

38. Middleton Journal, 1:25, 202; Villanova House Register, 1874–92, p. 104 (hereafter House Register), APA.

39. Power, *Catholic Higher Education*, p. 128.

40. "Jug Book," 1856. VUA.

41. *Catalogue 1873–74,* p. 6.

42. Ibid.

43. Power, *Catholic Higher Education*, p. 113.

44. Villanova College Prospectus, 1872, VUA; College Rules, c. 1890, APA; Middleton Journal, 1:15, 25.

45. Middleton Journal, 1:17, 25, 26, 35.

46. Ibid., p. 12.

47. Ibid., p. 11; Middleton, *Sketch*, p. 44.

48. Varga, *Baltimore's Loyola*, pp. 38–39.

49. Middleton Notes, p. 45.

50. *Pittsburgh Catholic*, June 28, 1855.

51. Unidentified newspaper clipping, Middleton Scrapbook, p. 21.

52. Middleton Journal, 1:9.

53. Ibid., p. 24; Dorie McDougal and James H. DeLorenzo, "150 Years of Villanova Athletics," p. 1.

54. Middleton Notes, pp. 43, 53.

55. Middleton Journal, 1:86, 115, 216.

56. Middleton Notes, pp. 53–54; Middleton Journal, 2:22.

57. Napoleon B. Lowry and Mary Lowry to Augustinian College of Villanova, April 1, 1859, Deeds, APA.

58. Middleton Journal, 2:105.

59. Enrollment figures for the period 1843–93 are from Middleton, *Sketch*, p. 53.

60. See *Catholic Standard*, February 21, 1874.

61. Middleton, *Sketch*, p. 43.

62. Ibid., p. 45.

63. Ibid., p. 46.

64. Trustees, 1:23, September 3, 1872; 1:25, April 16, 1873; House Register, 1874–92, p. 39, January 31, 1879; Middleton Journal, 1:18, 19; Villanova University Finances: Galberry Expansion, APA.

65. On Durang and his work, see Sandra L. Tatman and Roger W. Moss, *Biographical Dictionary of Philadelphia Architects* (Boston, 1985), pp. 229–33.

66. *Catholic Standard*, February 21, 1874.

67. Ibid.

68. Unidentified newspaper clipping, Middleton Scrapbook, p. 32.

69. Minutes of the Villanova Alumni Association, 1875–85, VUA.

70. Middleton, *Sketch*, p. 58.

71. Provincial Register, 1796–1896, p. 169, September 28, 1882; House Register, 1874–92, p. 85, December 26, 1882; Trustee Minutes, August 28, 1886; Middleton Journal, 1:66; Middleton, *Sketch*, pp. 50–51.

72. Marie Teehan, "An Historical Sketch of the Parish of St. Thomas of Villanova, 1843–1989" (typescript, VUA).

73. Middleton Journal, 1:179, 199, 217.

74. Ibid., 112.

75. Reverend Christopher A. McEvoy, O.S.A., to alumni, May 19, 1893, VUA.

76. Middleton Journal, 1:221–24, 228; House Register, 1892–1916, April 20, 1893; *Philadelphia Public Ledger*, June 19, 1893.

# Chapter 3: The New College

1. *Catalogue 1893–94*, pp. 17–20; *1894–95*, pp. 18–21; *1895–96*, pp. 18–20; Middleton, *Sketch*, p. 58.

2. Rev. F. M. Sheeran, O.S.A., to V. Rev. Provincial and V.R. Definitors, July 16, 1890, APA.

3. *Catalogue 1889–90*, p. 25; *1890–91*, p. 24; *1891–92*, p. 24; *1893–94*, p. 31; *1894–95*, p. 30; *1895–96*, p. 29.

4. Donaghy, *La Salle*, p. 48; Talbot, *St. Joseph's*, p. 97; Power, *Catholic Higher Education*, pp. 119–20.

5. Provincial Register, 1796–1896, p. 308, December 31, 1896.

6. Provincial Register, 1896–1914, p. 26.

7. Harry A. Cassel, O.S.A., "John Joseph Fedigan, O.S.A.," in *Men of Heart*, 1:169–85; Tourscher, *Old Saint Augustine's*, p. 200.

8. For a good color reproduction of this Eakins portrait of Father Fedigan, see David

R. Contosta and Dennis J. Gallagher, O.S.A., *Ever Ancient, Ever New: Villanova University, 1842–1992* (Virginia Beach, Va., 1992), p. 30. On the portrait itself, see Lloyd Goodrich, *Thomas Eakins* (Cambridge, Mass., 1982), 2:191, 299.

9. Quoted in Edwin T. Grimes, O.S.A., "Laurence Augustine Delurey, O.S.A.," in *Men of Heart*, 2:132.

10. *Philadelphia Press*, January 13, 1899.

11. Reverend John J. Fedigan, O.S.A., to Very Reverend and Reverend Fathers of the Province of Villanova, Delaware County, August 2, 1899, APA.

12. Reverend James T. O'Reilly, O.S.A., Provincial Trustee to Reverend Father Definitor, September 16, 1898, APA. Copies of this letter were sent to each definitor.

13. Thomas Middleton, O.S.A., Circular to the Trustees of the Several Corporations in the United States in charge of property belonging to the Augustinian Order, April 13, 1899, APA.

14. New Buildings Ledger, Provincial Records by Reverend John J. Fedigan, 1898–1902, pp. 12–16, 24, 28–29, APA; Report of Reverend John J. Fedigan, O.S.A., Provincial, 1898–1902, APA.

15. Fedigan's successor as prior-provincial, Reverend Martin J. Geraghty, O.S.A., told the provincial chapter in the summer of 1902: "It was quite manifest that we would have to go forward or stagnation would be our lot" (Address to Capitularies, July 15, 1902, APA).

16. Provincial Register, 1896–1914, p. 36; Middleton Journal, 2:95, 124.

17. Trustee Minutes, 1:77, May 3, 1880.

18. *Catalogue 1902–3*, p. 13.

19. Talbot, *St. Joseph's*, pp. 122–23.

20. Trustee Minutes, 1896–1914, December 6, 1902, p. 183.

21. *New Catholic Encyclopedia* (Washington, D.C., 1967), 12:514.

22. *Press*, January 11, 1912; Middleton Memorandum, in Miscellaneous History, APA.

23. Very Reverend Martin J. Geraghty, O.S.A., to the Priors, January 17, 1912; Geraghty to Friends, January 1912, APA.

24. Middleton Journal, 2:95, 177.

25. On Bernard Corr, see *Encyclopedia of Pennsylvania Biography* (New York, 1916), 6:2126–27; and *Philadelphia Bulletin*, February 23, 1914; May 4, 1914.

26. Tatman and Moss, *Philadelphia Architects*, pp. 234–36.

27. Daprato Statuary Co., Chicago, Illinois, to Reverend John J. Fedigan, O.S.A., November 17, 1906; Receipt from Daprato Statuary Co., September 10, 1907, in Legal Contracts—Building, APA. The total cost of the three statues was $900.

28. Middleton Journal, 2:45, 48, 107, 147, 155, 261, 262.

29. Trustee Minutes, 1:115, March 9, 1903.

30. Tourscher, *Old Saint Augustine's*, pp. 156–57, 211.

31. The best overall history of the American university system remains Laurence R. Veysey's *Emergence of the American University* (Chicago, 1965). See also Richard Hofstadter and C. DeWitt Hardy, *The Development and Scope of Higher Education in America* (New York, 1952), pp. 29–100; Brubacher and Rudy, *Higher Education*, pp. 143–218; Lawrence A. Cremin, *American Education: The Metropolitan Experience, 1876–1980* (New York, 1988), pp. 19–69.

32. Charles William Eliot, "Address at the Inauguration of Charles William Eliot as President of Harvard College," Cambridge, Mass., 1869.

33. Ibid.

34. For the elective system in general, see Brubacher and Rudy, *Higher Education*, pp.

100–119. On Eliot and the elective system at Harvard, see Charles William Eliot, *Educational Reform* (New York, 1898), and Hugh Hawkins, *Between Harvard and America: The Educational Leadership of Charles William Eliot* (New York, 1972).

35. For a good summary of this debate over the future of the American college, see Veysey, *The American University*, pp. 252–59.

36. Power, *Catholic Higher Education*, pp. 86–87.

37. *Catalogue 1873–74*, p. 11.

38. Ibid., *1898–99*, p. 12.

39. Ibid., *1883–84*, p. 13; see also *1898–99*, p. 12.

40. Ibid., *1898–99*, p. 10.

41. Power, *Catholic Higher Education*, pp. 85–87.

42. *Catalogue 1906–7*, p. 30.

43. Ibid., pp. 93–97; *1908–9*, pp. 136–47; *1909–10*, pp. 109–17; Abraham Flexner, *Medical Education in the United States and Canada* (New York, 1910).

44. Donaghy, *La Salle*, pp. 60–62.

45. *Catalogue 1902–3, p.* 30.

46. Ibid., *1911–12*, p. 30.

47. For an interesting article on this route, see *Suburban and Wayne Times*, February 3, 1994.

48. Middleton Journal, 2:99, 212, 260.

49. *Catalogue 1909–10*, n.p.; *1914–15*, n.p.

50. House Register, 1892–1916, June 3, 1914.

51. Jones, *Haverford College*, p. viii.

52. Alumni Association Minutes, June 13, 1906, VUA.

53. Ibid., June 18, 1907.

54. Ibid. See also John J. Whelan, President, Villanova Alumni Association to Brother Alumnus, May 13, 1907, Alumni file, VUA.

55. *Public Ledger*, May 5, 1914; *Philadelphia Record*, May 5, 1914; *Philadelphia North American*, May 5, 1914.

56. Provincial Register, 1896–1914, p. 71; *Philadelphia Bulletin*, June 18, 1910; *Public Ledger*, June 16, 1902; *North American*, June 15, 1902.

57. One might compare Villanova's success in the various Augustinian parishes with the less successful showing of Wesleyan University in Connecticut in its fund-raising attempts among Methodist congregations. See David B. Potts, *Wesleyan University, 1831–1910: Collegiate Enterprise in New England* (New Haven, 1992), pp. 83–117.

58. Vote for Monastery and College Building, Provincial Register, 1896–1914, p. 26; Very Reverend John J. Fedigan to Very Reverend and Reverend Fathers of the Province of Villanova, August 2, 1899, Fedigan Papers, VUA; Personal Appeal of Reverend J. J. Fedigan, O.S.A., to his many friends wherever found, Fedigan Papers, VUA; New Buildings Ledger, Provincial Records by Reverend John J. Fedigan, O.S.A., 1898–1902, APA; Financing of Monastery and College Building, 1898–1902, APA; Deeds and Real Estate Transactions, APA; Trustee Minutes, 1:107, October 17, 1899; 1:108, November 29, 1899; 1:111, May 7, 1901.

59. Reverend Thomas C. Middleton to Brother Alumnus, June 3, 1909, Alumni file, VUA.

60. Grimes, "Delurey," pp. 135–36.

61. See, for example, Very Reverend Nicholas J. Murphy, O.S.A., Address to Provincial Chapter, June 19, 1906, Provincial Register, 1896–1914.

62. Trustee Minutes, 1:113, July 28, 1902; 1:117, April 7, 1904; Provincial Register, 1796–1896, p. 188, n.d.; 1896–1914, p. 136, April 28, 1905.

63. Trustee Minutes, 1:81, May 2, 1881; 1:190, October 23, 1888; Middleton Journal, 1:119; Blue Print Map of Villanova Property, Blue Print Plan of Real Estate in Radnor Township, Delaware County, Pennsylvania, Deeds, APA.

64. *Catalogue 1904–5,* p. 19.

65. Reverend Lawrence A. Delurey, O.S.A., to Dr. John M. Reiner, December 14, 1908, Delurey-Reiner file, APA.

66. Grimes, "Delurey," p. 145.

67. Private Chapter, June 20, 1910, 1:30 P.M., Provincial Register, 1896–1914, p. 211.

68. Ibid.

69. Reverend Lawrence A. Delurey, O.S.A., to Very Reverend Martin J. Geraghty, O.S.A., June 20, 1910, Delurey-Reiner file, APA; Grimes, "Delurey," p. 146.

70. Grimes, "Delurey," p. 147; Provincial Register, 1896–1914, p. 252, November 11, 1911.

71. Provincial Register, 1896–1914, p. 250, October 9, 1913; Grimes, "Delurey," p. 147; *Philadelphia Bulletin,* March 10 and 11, 1914.

72. Provincial Register, 1896–1914, June 20, 1912.

73. Grimes, "Delurey," p. 153.

74. For example, Trustee Minutes, 1:121–22, May 2, 1906.

75. Grimes, "Delurey," p. 150.

76. *Villanovan,* December 1917.

77. Ibid., April 1917.

78. Ibid., October 1917.

79. House Chapter Book, 1916–30, p. 58, August 31, 1918; Talbot, *St. Joseph's,* pp. 121–22.

80. Varga, *Baltimore's Loyola,* p. 208; Cheyney, *University of Pennsylvania,* p. 380.

81. *Villanovan,* October 1918.

82. Ibid.

83. Ibid.; Middleton Journal, 2:195.

84. Talbot, *St. Joseph's,* p. 121.

85. *Villanovan,* December 1918.

86. Ibid., February 1919; *Belle Air 1922,* p. 26.

87. Sermon of Reverend James Dean, O.S.A., at Diamond Jubilee Mass of Villanova College—1918, Villanova University, Miscellaneous, APA.

# Chapter 4: Catholic Gentlemen

1. *Catalogue 1922–23,* p. 17.

2. Dolan, *American Catholic Experience,* p. 242.

3. Ibid., pp. 268–71.

4. Ibid., pp. 271–72.

5. Cardinal Dennis J. Dougherty, quoted in Thomas J. Donaghy, F.S.C., *Philadelphia's Finest: A History of Education in the Catholic Archdiocese, 1692–1970* (Philadelphia, 1972), p. 175.

6. Ibid.

7. On Cardinal Dougherty, see Hugh J. Nolan, "The Native Son," in James F. Connelly, ed., *The History of the Archdiocese of Philadelphia* (Philadelphia, 1976), pp. 339–418; and Nolan, "Cardinal Dougherty and the Present Aggiornamento," *RACHSP,* September 1965, pp. 188–90.

8. *Catalogue 1902–3* and *1906–7; Villanova College Bulletin 1939–40* (hereafter *Villanova Bulletin*).

9. For more on this phenomenon, see William P. Leahy, S.J., "The Rise of the Laity in American Catholic Higher Education," *RACHSP,* Fall 1990, pp. 17–32.

10. *Villanova Bulletin, 1936–37* and *1940–41.*

11. *Villanovan,* February 12, 1929; October 8, 1929; January 17, 1933; October 3, 1933; October 2, 1934; January 21, 1936; *Belle Air 1934,* p. 263; *1936,* p. 54; *Student Handbook 1931,* p. 7.

12. *Villanovan,* October 22, 1929; October 18, 1932; November 6, 1934.

13. Philip Gleason, *Keeping the Faith: American Catholicism Past and Present* (Notre Dame, Ind., 1987), pp. 166–72. For the complete English text of *Aeterni Patris,* see *The Papal Encyclicals, 1878–1903* (Raleigh, N.C., 1981), 2:17–21.

14. Philip Gleason, "In Search of Unity: American Catholic Thought, 1920–1960," *CHR,* April 1979, p. 195.

15. *Villanovan,* Spring 1937 (this was a special spring edition and does not carry a specific date). See also issue of May 2, 1939.

16. Ibid., December 1, 1936; see also November 13, 1934.

17. *Belle Air 1940,* n.p.

18. *Villanovan,* February 20, 1934.

19. "Life Has Many Sides," admissions brochure, 1934, VUA.

20. *Villanova Bulletin 1940–41,* p. 26.

21. Ibid., p. 22.

22. Despite its importance as a collection of suburban communities, there is no satisfactory history of the Philadelphia Main Line. There is a fascinating section on the upper-class families of the Main Line in Baltzell's *Philadelphia Gentlemen,* pp. 201–5. Beyond this there are a number of amateur histories. The best of these are *Lower Merion: A History* (Ardmore, Pa., 1992), which deals with several of the more important communities on the Main Line; and Barbara Alyce Farrow, *The History of Bryn Mawr* (Bryn Mawr, Pa., 1962). There is also the greatly outdated work by J. W. Townsend, *The Old "Main Line"* (Philadelphia, 1922). On "Androssan," see *Philadelphia Inquirer Magazine,* April 28, 1994.

23. Baltzell, *Philadelphia Gentlemen,* pp. 292–334. See also Baltzell, *The Protestant Establishment: Aristocracy and Caste in America* (New York, 1964), pp. 209–12.

24. On the 1920s and its youth culture, there are Frederick Lewis Allen, *Only Yesterday* (New York, 1931); Beth L. Bailey, *Front Porch to Back Seat: Courtship in Twentieth-Century America* (Baltimore, 1988); Paula S. Fass, *The Damned and the Beautiful: American Youth in the 1920s* (New York, 1977); Paul Goodman and Frank O. Gatell, *America in the Twenties* (New York, 1972); Paul Carter, *The Twenties in America* (Arlington Heights, Ill., 1975); Robert Sklar, ed., *The Plastic Age* (New York, 1970).

25. Gleason, "In Search of Unity," p. 193.

26. *Villanovan,* October 22, 1929; *Philadelphia Inquirer,* November 10, 1929. Enrollment, Villanova University, Miscellaneous History, APA.

27. Brubacher and Rudy, *Higher Education,* pp. 330–53.

28. Horowitz, *Campus Life,* pp. 11–16.

29. *Belle Air 1922,* p. 27.

30. Ibid., *1924,* p. 33.

31. Ibid., *1922,* p. 67.

32. *Villanovan,* March 1924, June 1925, and February 26, 1929; *Belle Air 1934,* p. 263; *1937,* p. 44.

33. *Villanovan,* October 8, 1929, October 14, 1930.

34. "Life Has Many Sides."

35. The changing numbers and names of these clubs appear in issues of the *Belle Air* during the 1920s and 1930s.

36. *Villanova Bulletin 1940–41,* pp. 26–27; *Belle Air 1924,* pp. 101–10.

37. *Villanovan,* October 18, 1932.

38. On the evolution of college fraternities, see Brubacher and Rudy, *Higher Education,* pp. 120–39; Rudolph, *American College and University,* pp. 144–49, 369–70, 464; Power, *Catholic Higher Education,* p. 139; Veysey, *The American University,* pp. 292–93.

39. *Villanovan,* December 1918.

40. This information was drawn from a number of issues of the *Belle Air* and the *Villanovan* during the 1920s and 1930s. Also of interest is the invitation to the Fifth Annual Belle Air Ball, January 7, 1927, VUA.

41. Horowitz, *Campus Life,* pp. 123–28.

42. This quotation, as well as a brief history of Junior Week, appeared in the Junior Week Program for 1962, VUA.

43. Accounts of these events again may be found in the *Belle Air* and the *Villanovan* during this period.

44. *Villanovan,* March 26, 1929; November 28, 1933; December 4, 1934.

45. Ibid., November 1927.

46. *Villanovan,* November 5, 1929; October 25, 1932; October 30, 1934.

47. Trustee Minutes, 1:185, July 2, 1927; 2:5, June 22, 1929; Definitory Meetings, 1924–34, p. 117, May 29, 1929; House Chapter Book, 1916–30, p. 275, May 21, 1929.

48. House Chapter Book, December 6, 1938.

49. Wallace, *Notre Dame,* pp. 144–49. Stuhldreher left Villanova in 1935 to become a coach at the University of Wisconsin. He died in 1964 or 1965. See *Villanova Alumnus,* February 1965, p. 1.

50. Trustee Minutes, 2:16; House Chapter Book, 1916–30, June 6, 1927.

51. House Chapter Book, 1930–64, p. 121, October 23, 1939.

52. *Villanova Alumnus,* May 1938, p. 1.

53. *Villanovan,* April 21, 1931; *Villanova Alumnus,* February 1965, p. 1; *Philadelphia Bulletin,* December 20, 1928.

54. Donaghy, *La Salle,* p. 113; David H. Burton and Frank Gerrity, *St. Joseph's College: A Family Portrait* (Philadelphia, 1977), p. 39; Jones, *Haverford College,* p. x.

55. By the spring of 1950, the college had gone through three live wildcats and had acquired a fourth from the Florida Everglades who was known as Count Villan IV. See *Villanovan,* April 4, 1950, and *Philadelphia Bulletin,* April 5, 1950; December 13, 1971.

56. *Villanovan,* March 1926, p. 47; April 8, 1930. *Inquirer,* January 22, 1994.

57. See also *Villanovan,* October 29, 1935.

58. Ibid., November 21, 1933.

59. Ibid., February 18, 1930.

60. *Philadelphia Bulletin,* May 7, 1930.

61. Ibid., September 24, 1959.

62. On the rise and popularity of college football in general, see Brubacher and Rudy, *Higher Education,* pp. 121–39; Rudolph, *American College and University,* pp. 376–93; Veysey, *The American University,* pp. 275–77.

63. *Villanovan,* February 14, 1933.

64. See *Belle Air 1939.*

65. *Villanovan,* February 7, 1933.

66. Ibid., April 4, 1933.

67. Ibid., October 18, 1932; November 8, 1932; November 15, 1932; October 24, 1933; November 21, 1933.

68. Ibid., May 16, 1933.

69. *Student Handbook 1931*, p. 12.

70. Ibid.

71. *Villanovan*, October 14, 1930; November 8, 1932.

72. Ibid., October 8, 1929; October 15, 1929.

73. Ibid., April 1924, p. 12.

74. Ibid., November 1, 1932.

75. Trustee Minutes, 1:150, June 6, 1919; Definitory Record, 6-1914 to 10-1919, p. 91, June 26, 1918; p. 97, September 12, 1918; p. 138, September 27, 1919; Definitory Record, 11-1919 to 2-1924, p. 1, November 21, 1919; p. 9, January 26, 1920; House Chapter Book, 1916–30, p. 76, June 5, 1919; p. 103, November 24, 1920; *Belle Air 1922*, p. 28; *Villanovan*, April 1919; *Philadelphia Bulletin*, October 28, 1920; January 19, 1921; Treasurer's Report, Villanova Alumni Association, January 30, 1920, Alumni file, VUA.

76. Trustee Minutes, 1:64, June 19, 1922; Definitory Record, 11-1919 to 2-1922, p. 95, June 29, 1922; p. 105, October 27, 1922; p. 106, November 14, 1922; p. 122, May 22, 1923; *Villanovan*, April 1923; January 15, 1929; January 29, 1929; *Catholic Standard and Times*, July 8, 1922.

77. On Eyre and McIlvain, see Tatman and Moss, *Philadelphia Architects*, pp. 252–53, 518.

78. Trustee Minutes, 1:167, August 16, 1923; 1:168, January 14, 1924; Definitory Meetings, 3-1924 to 6-1932, p. 17, May 1, 1924; p. 104, May 16, 1928, and May 30, 1928; p. 109, June 26, 1928; House Chapter Book, 1916–30, p. 137, October 5, 1922; p. 138, November 24, 1922; p. 139, December 19, 1922; p. 150, May 7, 1923; p. 169, April 23, 1924; p. 171, April 25, 1924; p. 187, October 28, 1924; p. 252, May 9, 1928; p. 261, August 9, 1928; *Belle Air 1941*, n.p.; *1984*, p. 135; *Villanovan*, April 1923, p. 4; November 1924, pp. 8–9; *Philadelphia Bulletin*, October 9, 1924, June 1, 1928.

79. Tatman and Moss, *Philadelphia Architects*, pp. 547–48.

80. Donaghy, *La Salle*, p. 89; Burton and Gerrity, *St. Joseph's*, p. 18.

81. A Survey and Plan of Fund Raising for Villanova College, Prepared by the John Price Jones Corporation, 150 Nassau Street, N.Y., N.Y., July 23, 1929, VUA.

82. Ibid. See also the campaign brochure, "Villanova Shall Go Farther," 1930, VUA.

83. *Public Ledger*, April 2, 1932.

84. Trustee Minutes, 2:66, February 25, 1936; *Belle Air 1933*, p. 13; 1930 Fund Drive, Villanova University, Miscellaneous file, APA. For details, see Chapter 6.

85. House Chapter Book, 1916–30, p. 251, April 30, 1928; *Philadelphia Bulletin* January 30, 1928; *New York Post*, January 30, 1928; *New York Evening World*, January 30, 1928; *Boston Transcript*, January 30, 1928; *Villanovan*, January 29, 1929; March 21, 1929; *Belle Air 1928*, pp. 48–63.

86. Trustee Minutes, 2:11, September 10, 1932; 2:28, May 1, 1933; Definitory Record Book, 1932–38, p. 13, November 7, 1932; House Chapter Book, 1930–64, p. 39, September 21, 1932; Rev. Edward V. Stanford, O.S.A., President to Very Reverend Mortimer A. Sullivan, O.S.A., Provincial, August 21, 1932, Stanford Papers, VUA; *Belle Air 1933*, p. 14; *Philadelphia Bulletin*, August 2, 1932.

87. The art historian Lloyd Goodrich, who had earlier visited Villanova in order to examine the Fedigan portrait, was so alarmed upon reading of the fire that he wrote to Villanova's president, Reverend Edward V. Stanford, O.S.A., to inquire about the portrait, which he knew had hung in the monastery. Father Stanford answered Goodrich a few days later to assure him that the painting had survived with just minor damage sustained in the process of rescuing it from the burning building. Goodrich to Stanford, August 10, 1932, and Stanford to Goodrich, August 18, 1932, Stanford Papers.

88. *Philadelphia Bulletin*, October 19, 1933.

# Chapter 5: Villanova and the World

1. *Villanovan*, May 14, 1935; November 5, 1935; March 9, 1937; February 8, 1938; January 6, 1940; February 18, 1944; July 18, 1944; *Villanova Alumnus*, February 1940, p. 6; Fall 1944, p. 4; March 1966, pp. 1, 4.

2. *Villanovan*, May 23, 1933; Trustee Minutes, 2:29, May 16, 1933.

3. Donaghy, *La Salle*, pp. 111–12; Burton and Gerrity, *St. Joseph's*, p. 23.

4. *Villanovan*, October 18, 1932; October 13, 1936; Trustee Minutes 2:43, October 16, 1934; 2:55, October 29, 1935; 2:85, November 17, 1936; Annual Report of the Registrar, 1940–41, p. 15, VUA.

5. See Thomas Ferguson, "From Normalcy to New Deal: Industrial Structure, Party Composition, and American Public Policy in the Great Depression," in *International Organization* (1984), pp. 41–94; Paul Kleppner, ed., *The Evolution of American Electoral Systems* (Westport, Conn., 1981).

6. *Villanovan*, October 25, 1932; November 1, 1932; October 20, 1936.

7. Ibid., March 13, 1934; April 10, 1934; October 2, 1934; Trustee Minutes, 2:44, October 16, 1934.

8. *Villanovan*, March 21, 1933; October 23, 1934; October 30, 1934; December 4, 1934; January 15, 1935; January 14, 1936; May 5, 1936; November 13, 1936; April 27, 1937; October 24, 1939

9. Ibid., November 27, 1934.

10. Ibid., November 1, 1938.

11. For the English text of *Rerum Novarum*, see *Papal Encyclicals, 1878–1903*, 2:241–61; for *Quadragesimo Anno*, see ibid., *1903–1939*, 3:415–43.

12. James Terence Fisher, *The Catholic Counterculture in America, 1933–1962* (Chapel Hill, N.C., 1989), p. 75.

13. Ibid., p. 93; David O'Brien, "American Catholics and Organized Labor in the 1930s," *CHR*, October 1966, pp. 323–49.

14. For brief biographical information on Deverall, see *The American Catholic Who's Who, 1954–1955* (Grosse Pointe, Mich., 1954), p. 105.

15. Stanford to Reverend Philip S. Moore, C.S.C., May 29, 1939, Stanford Papers.

16. Memorandum from Stanford to Bursar, Villanova College, October 8, 1935, Stanford Papers.

17. Stanford to William E. Howe, September 20, 1937, Stanford Papers.

18. Flier for *The Christian Front*, Stanford Papers.

19. Richard Deverall, "Religion and Economics," Social Justice Leaflet No. 2, VUA.

20. On this phenomenon, see Gleason, *Keeping the Faith*, pp. 26–28, 112–14, 166–68.

21. Deverall to "Reverend Father" (a circular letter to pastors), n.d., VUA.

22. Norman McKenna, "The Social Encyclicals," *The Christian Front*, Social Justice Leaflet No. 1, VUA.

23. Press release from the Christian Front, February 5, 1937, VUA.

24. Deverall to "Dear Friend" (a circular letter to supporters of the Christian Front movement), April 28, 1937, VUA.

25. Ibid.

26. *Villanovan*, January 12, 1937.

27. Ibid., November 1, 1938.

28. Ibid., December 1, 1936.

29. Ibid., November 24, 1936.

30. This decision to devote the 1939 *Belle Air* to combating Communism was applauded by the *Villanovan* in the issue of March 14, 1939.

31. *Belle Air 1939*, n.p.

32. *Villanovan*, March 8, 1938.

33. For an overview of this issue, see Robert H. Vinca, "The American Catholic Reaction to the Persecution of the Church in Mexico," *RACHSP*, March 1968, pp. 3–37.

34. *Villanovan*, February 5, 1935.

35. Ibid., April 16, 1935; *Philadelphia Bulletin*, April 16 and 18, 1935.

36. James R. O'Connell, "The Spanish Republic: Further Reflections on Its Anticlerical Policies," *CHR*, July 1971, pp. 275–89; Gabriel Jackson, *The Spanish Republic and the Civil War, 1931–1939* (Princeton, 1965).

37. *Villanovan*, October 6, 1936.

38. Ibid., February 14, 1939.

39. Richard J. Walton, *Swarthmore College: An Informal History* (Swarthmore, Pa., 1986), p. 46.

40. *Villanovan*, February 28, 1939.

41. Ibid., March 10, 1936.

42. Ibid., March 20, 1935; March 27, 1935.

43. Ibid., November 22, 1938.

44. Ibid., April 6, 1937.

45. Ibid., October 22, 1935; April 28, 1936.

46. On so-called American isolationism during this period, see Selig Adler, *The Isolationist Impulse: Its Twentieth Century Reaction* (New York, 1961), pp. 219–90; Robert A. Divine, *The Reluctant Belligerent: American Entry into World War II* (New York, 1979); John E. Wiltz, *From Isolation to War, 1931–1941* (New York, 1968).

47. Walton, *Swarthmore*, pp. 50–51; interview with Ray Cummings, September 8, 1994.

48. *Villanovan*, November 6, 1934.

49. Ibid., January 15, 1935.

50. Ibid., October 8, 1935; November 5, 1935; November 12, 1935; March 16, 1937.

51. Ibid., April 7, 1936.

52. Ibid., December 9, 1936.

53. Ibid., October 11, 1938. See also Raymond J. Sontag, "Appeasement, 1937," *CHR*, January 1953, pp. 385–96.

54. Sister Marie Veronica Tardey, *The Role of Joseph McGarrity in the Struggle for Irish Independence* (New York, 1976), pp. 231, 344.

55. *Villanovan*, November 1, 1938; January 10, 1939.

56. Ibid., October 17, 1939.

57. Aloysius L. Fitzpatrick, *Villanova Alumnus*, February 1939, pp. 13, 15.

58. Stanford, Address at the Formal Opening of Villanova College for the Scholastic Year, 1939–40, September 22, 1939, Stanford Papers.

59. Stanford, "Alumni Talk," *Alumnus*, Fall 1940, p. 2.

60. *Villanovan*, October 31, 1939; October 15, 1940.

61. Ibid., October 14, 1941.

62. Ibid., April 29, 1941.

63. Ibid., March 18, 1941; April 27, 1941; October 7, 1941; November 18, 1941; November 25, 1941.

64. Ibid., March 16, 1946.

65. Ibid., August 25, 1942.

66. Ibid., March 28, 1944. In an editorial on March 10, 1944, the student newspaper upheld the decision of Eire (the independent Irish Republic) to remain neutral in the war.

67. Ibid., June 5, 1945.

68. Ibid., December 9, 1941.

69. House Chapter Book, 1930–64, p. 127, June 28, 1940.

70. *Villanovan*, February 4, 1941; February 11, 1941; February 18, 1941; February 17, 1942; July 14, 1942; Trustee Minutes, 2:150, March 18, 1941.

71. *Villanovan*, January 13, 1942; January 20, 1942; October 27, 1942; October 3, 1944. "Wartime Changes at Villanova," admissions brochure, 1942, VUA.

72. *Villanovan*, December 16, 1941; March 14, 1942; *Belle Air 1943*, n.p.

73. Stanford, *Villanova Alumnus*, December 1941, p. 2; February 1942, p. 2.

74. *Villanovan*, July 28, 1942; November 3, 1942; *Belle Air 1943*, n.p.; interview with Ray Cummings, September 8, 1994.

75. Stanford to Chief of the Bureau of Navigation, Navy Department, July 31, 1940; September 3, 1940; December 10, 1941; Rear Admiral Chester W. Nimitz, U.S.N. to Stanford, August 9, 1940; Frank Knox, Secretary of the Navy, to Stanford, May 20, 1941; Stanford to Knox, May 27, 1941; Captain A. T. Bidwell, Assistant Chief of the Bureau of Navigation, Navy Department to Stanford, June 3, 1941, Stanford Papers; *Villanovan*, March 3, 1942; March 10, 1942; Trustee Minutes, 2:171, June 1, 1943.

76. *Villanova Alumnus*, October 1943, p. 3; *Belle Air 1943*, n.p.

77. *Villanova Alumnus*, October 1943, p. 3.

78. *Belle Air 1944*, n.p.; *Villanovan*, November 10, 1942.

79. Ibid., July 21, 1942; August 11, 1942; August 18, 1942; February 8, 1944; April 25, 1944; June 6, 1944; September 26, 1944; *Belle Air 1942, 1943, 1944*, passim.

80. Ibid.

81. Trustee Minutes, 2:167, October 20, 1942; 2:169, November 25, 1942; 2:174, November 16, 1943; 2:176, March 21, 1944; 2:178, June 20, 1944; 2:184, December 5, 1944; 2:186, January 13, 1945; 2:191, July 17, 1945; 2:197, November 20, 1945.

82. See Trustee Minutes listed in note 81.

83. Donaghy, *La Salle*, pp. 116–20; Burton and Gerrity, *St. Joseph's*, pp. 25–26; Wallace, *Notre Dame*, pp. 176–77.

84. Wallace, *Notre Dame*, p. 176.

85. Trustee Minutes, 2:42, May 15, 1934; 2:89, January 18, 1937; 2:124, January 16, 1939; 2:137, November 14, 1939; "Centennial News-Letter," April 1941, VUA.

86. Trustee Minutes, 2:89, January 18, 1937; Minutes of the Meeting of the Executive Committee of the Centennial of Villanova College, December 17, 1939, VUA.

87. *Belle Air 1940, 1941, 1942, 1943*.

88. House Chapter Book, 1930–64, September 10, 1942; *Belle Air 1943*, n.p.; *Villanovan*, September 14, 1942; *Philadelphia Inquirer*, September 18 and 21, 1942; *Record*, September 19, 1942; *Philadelphia Bulletin*, March 27, 1943.

89. Stanford, "Address of Welcome," in *One Hundred Anniversary Convocation Address*, VUA.

90. *Villanovan*, August 21, 1943.

## Chapter 6: College to University

1. That Villanova's President John M. Driscoll saw these earlier programs as antecedents to university status is clear from the report that he wrote in 1977. See Triennial Report, Villanova University, 1975–77, VUA. See also Richard D. Breslin, *Villanova: Yesterday and Today* (Villanova, Pa., 1972), pp. 7–8.

2. Breslin, *Villanova*, p. 35.

3. A Report of the President to the Chairmen and Members of the Board of Trustees and to the Members of the Faculty of Villanova College, May 8, 1940, pp. 9–19, Stanford Papers.

4. Ibid., p. 1.

5. Ibid., p. 2.

6. Ibid., pp. 5–7.

7. Ibid., pp. 15–20.

8. Ibid., p. 17.

9. Ibid.

10. Ibid., pp. 20–21.

11. Trustee Minutes, 2:82, May 9, 1936; 2:90, March 23, 1937; 2:144–45, May 29, 1941; Memorandum as to Faculty Reaction to President's Report of May 8, 1940, Stanford Papers; *Villanova Alumnus,* May 1940, p. 3; Record of Actions Taken at Joint Conference of Representatives of Association of American Colleges and American Association of University Professors on Academic Freedom and Tenure, Stanford Papers; memorandum of Professor James M. Bergquist to author, February 28, 1994; *Philadelphia Bulletin,* December 5, 1936.

12. Survey and Plan, 1929, p. 42.

13. Ibid., p. 71; "An Inside Story," p. 5 (promotional brochure, 1930, circulated among Catholic parishes), VUA.

14. Survey and Plan, pp. 68, 80, 87.

15. This assertion was later confirmed by the social historian E. Digby Baltzell, in *Philadelphia Gentlemen,* pp. 223–61, 292–334, and in *The Protestant Establishment,* pp. 206–14.

16. Survey and Plan, p. 91.

17. Trustee Minutes, 2:66, February 25, 1936; *Philadelphia Bulletin,* April 19 and 23, 1930, June 1, 1930.

18. House Chapter Book, 1930–64, p. 33, July 6, 1932; *Villanovan,* March 21, 1933; *Villanova Alumnus,* February 1940, p. 6.

19. *Villanovan,* February 21, 1933; Trustee Minutes, 2:91, March 23, 1937; *Villanova Alumnus,* May 1938, p. 8; September 1938, p. 5; May 1939, pp. 3, 15; December 1940, p. 2.

20. House Chapter Book, 1930–64, p. 34, July 6, 1932.

21. Scholarship poster, 1935, APA.

22. Trustee Minutes, 2:12, October 19, 1932; Rev. E. V. Stanford, O.S.A., Pres., to Pastors of Augustinian Churches, June 12, 1933, Correspondence 1930s, APA.

23. Rev. E. V. Stanford, Pres., O.S.A., to Rev. John H. Crawford, O.S.A., Faculty Director of Athletics, September 6, 1932; November 21, 1932; Rev. John H. Crawford, O.S.A., to Harry H. Stuhldreher, July 28, 1932, Correspondence 1930s, APA; Trustee Minutes, 2:13–14, November 21, 1932; *Philadelphia Bulletin,* November 22, 1932.

24. "Perpetuate Your Class at Villanova," 1935, brochure issued by the Alumni Association, VUA.

25. Trustee Minutes, 2:67–68, February 25, 1936.

26. Villanova University, Finances, Bequests, and Scholarships—Miscellaneous, APA; Trustee Minutes, 2:88, January 18, 1937; 2:96, October 19, 1937.

27. *Villanovan,* December 10, 1935; Trustee Minutes, 2:91, March 23, 1937; *Villanova Alumnus,* October 1939, p. 3.

28. *Villanova Alumnus,* October 1940, p. 7; February 1941, p. 1; October 1941, p. 4; Summer 1944, p. 21. Also indicative of the disappointing results of the campaign is a mailing put out by the Alumni Centennial Fund entitled "You'd be blue too!" (1941), VUA.

29. Memorandum from E. V. Stanford, May 14, 1944, Stanford Papers.

30. *Villanovan*, July 18, 1944.

31. Bergquist to author, February 28, 1994.

32. *Philadelphia Inquirer*, July 1, 1944; *Villanovan*, July 18, 1944; *Curriculum Vitae*, Reverend Francis X. N. McGuire, VUA.

33. McGuire, *Villanova Alumnus*, Winter 1946, p. 2.

34. Reverend Edward J. McCarthy, O.S.A., to "Dear Confrere," May 25, 1973, McCarthy Papers, VUA.

35. *Villanova Alumnus*, October 1946, p. 3.

36. Trustee Minutes, 2:209, October 15, 1946; *Belle Air 1947*, pp. 16–17; *Villanova Alumnus*, Summer 1946, p. 2.

37. Trustee Minutes, 2:210, November 15, 1946; 2:226, October 19, 1948; *Belle Air 1952*, p. 17; *Villanova Alumnus*, Autumn 1945, p. 3; October 1946, p. 3; *Philadelphia Bulletin*, September 26, 1946; *Inquirer*, August 31, 1946; December 7, 1946.

38. Trustee Minutes, 2:240, October 11, 1949; 3:30, September 24, 1956; *Villanovan*, October 4, 1949; October 7, 1952; October 12, 1954; September 18, 1956; September 30, 1964.

39. *Villanova Alumnus*, October 23, 1957.

40. *Villanova Bulletin 1944–45*, pp. 10–16; *1963–64*, pp. 9–33.

41. On the phenomenon of increasing numbers of lay faculty and administrators in Catholic colleges and universities, see Leahy, "Rise of the Laity," *RACHSP*, Fall 1990, pp. 17–32.

42. Trustee Minutes, 2:82, May 19, 1936; 2:91, March 23, 1937; 2:149, February 18, 1941; House Chapter Book, 1930–64, p. 123, January 27, 1940; *Belle Air 1937*, p. 47; *1940*, p. 246; *Villanovan*, April 30, 1940; Charles E. Dagit of Henry D. Dagit and Sons to The Very Reverend Mortimer A. Sullivan, O.S.A., Provincial, February 8, 1946, APA; *Villanova Alumnus*, February 1941, pp. 1–2; May 1941, p. 3; October 1941, p. 4.

43. Trustee Minutes, 2:209, October 15, 1946; 2:211, December 17, 1946; 2:212, January 22, 1947; Provincial Definitory, 1938–53, pp. 149–50, January 9, 1947; *Philadelphia Bulletin*, January 22, 1947.

44. *Main Line Times*, May 2, 1963; *Villanova Alumnus*, May 1966, p. 5; *Villanovan*, March 8, 1967; September 18, 1968.

45. Trustee Minutes, 2:191, July 17, 1945; 2:207, September 23, 1946; *Villanovan*, August 14, 1945; May 24, 1949.

46. Definitory Minutes, 1938–53, May 2, 1950; Trustee Minutes, 3:19, October 25, 1955; *Villanovan*, August 2, 1956; October 31, 1956; *Belle Air 1957*, p. 5; *Philadelphia Bulletin*, October 20, 1963.

47. Trustee Minutes, 2:279, March 2, 1954; House Chapter Book, 1930–64, p. 249, December 11, 1953; *Belle Air 1956*, pp. 98–99.

48. *Philadelphia Bulletin*, May 18, 1960; *Philadelphia Inquirer, Today Magazine*, March 18, 1962; *Main Line Times*, August 27, 1959; *Catholic Standard and Times*, May 20, 1960.

49. Trustee Minutes, 3:36, April 29, 1957; 3:45, March 6, 1958; House Chapter Book, 1930–64, p. 293, November 10, 1958; *Villanovan*, September 24, 1959; March 21, 1962.

50. Address Delivered by Father Donnellon on the Occasion of the Laying of the Cornerstone for the New Science Building, Donnellon Papers, VUA.

51. *Philadelphia Bulletin*, May 24, 1946; August 9, 1964; *Suburban and Wayne Times*, May 21, 1964; *Catholic Standard and Times*, November 3, 1961; August 7, 1964; *Villanovan*, October 2, 1963.

52. Trustee Minutes, 3:12, April 19, 1955; House Chapter Book, 1930–64, p. 258;

*Villanovan*, November 16, 1955; March 14, 1956; *Philadelphia Bulletin*, December 10, 1954.

53. *Philadelphia Bulletin*, January 19, 1968; March 19, 1971.

54. *Villanova Alumnus*, March 1968, p. 1; *Villanovan*, November 17, 1978.

55. *Villanova Alumnus*, Autumn 1945, p. 2.

56. Ibid., Summer 1946, p. 2; November 1948, p. 2; January 1949, p. 7; January 1951, p. 2.

57. Evaluation Survey and Case Book, by American City Bureau, August 10, 1953. p. 127, VUA.

58. Ibid., p. 39.

59. Ibid., p. 87.

60. Ibid., pp. 127–28.

61. Ibid., pp. 20, 37.

62. Ibid., p. 68.

63. Ibid., p. 31.

64. Ibid., pp. 98–99; *Villanova Alumnus*, December 1953, p. 6.

65. *Philadelphia Inquirer*, April 7 and 8, 1954; *Philadelphia Bulletin*, December 3, 1954; June 26, 1955; *Daily News*, April 7, 1954.

66. *Villanova Alumnus*, December 1953, p. 5; March 1954, p. 2; *Inquirer*, December 3, 1954; Address by Honorable James A. Farley to the Graduating Class of Villanova College . . . , May 19, 1942, Commencement Addresses, VUA.

67. Perspective, 1958–60, Development Foundation brochure, 1960, n.p., VUA.

68. Definitory Minutes, 1938–53, pp. 149–50, January 9, 1947; House Chapter Book, 1930–64, p. 310, December 9, 1960; Trustee Minutes, 2:261, March 29, 1952; 2:283, May 4, 1954; 3:39, September 17, 1957; Annual Report of the President, 1969–70, pp. 3–4, VUA; *Philadelphia Bulletin*, March 19, 1953.

69. Harold G. Reuschlein, *Villanova University School of Law* (Prospect, Ky., 1991), pp. 9, 10; interview with Harold G. Reuschlein, December 8, 1994. House Chapter Book, 1916–30, p. 272, April 15, 1929; Inspection Report, Villanova University Law School, April 13–16, 1980, by the American Bar Association, VUA.

70. City Bureau Survey, 1953, p. 99.

71. Breslin, *Villanova*, p. 15.

72. An Act to Incorporate the Augustinian College of Villanova . . . , section 3.

73. Breslin, *Villanova*, pp. 14–16; *Villanovan*, November 24, 1953; An Act to Incorporate Villanova University in the State of Pennsylvania, Section 1, VUA; Trustee Minutes, 2:260, February 19, 1952; *Philadelphia Bulletin*, November 17, 1953.

74. On the administration of American colleges and universities, see Brubacher and Rudy, *Higher Education*, pp. 354–95; James A. Perkins, ed., *The University as an Organization* (New York, 1973).

75. City Bureau Survey, 1953, p. 28.

76. Ibid., p. 15.

77. Ibid., p. 51.

78. Ibid., pp. 199–220.

79. Ibid., p. 16.

80. Ibid., p. 139.

81. Ibid., pp. 57–58, 114–15.

82. Ibid., pp. 77, 125.

83. Ibid., pp. 40, 43.

84. Ibid., p. 42.

85. Ibid., pp. 41–43, 100.

86. Report of the Inspection of Villanova University by an Evaluating Committee of the Middle States Association of Colleges and Secondary Schools, February 7–10, 1960, p. 6, VUA.

87. Andrew M. Greeley, *The Changing Catholic College* (Chicago, 1967), p. 5. Also critical of Catholic colleges and universities during the postwar period was John T. Ellis, "American Catholics and the Intellectual Life," *Thought,* Autumn 1955, pp. 351–88; and Philip Gleason, "The Crisis in Catholic Universities: A Historical Perspective," *Catholic Mind,* September 1966, pp. 43–55.

88. Greeley, *The Changing Catholic College,* p. 86.

89. *Villanova Alumnus,* October 1951, p. 11; December 1951, p. 2.

90. Breslin, *Villanova,* pp. 29–40.

91. Brubacher and Rudy, *Higher Education,* pp. 369–76.

92. *Horace Mann League of the United States v. the Board of Public Works of Maryland et al. No. 356.*

93. The Preamble of the By-Laws of the Board of Trustees of Villanova University in the State of Pennsylvania (1968), VUA.

94. Ibid., section 1.

95. Ibid., sections 2 and 8.

96. *Daily News,* July 14, 1969.

97. Varga, *Baltimore's Loyola,* p. 466; Wallace, *Notre Dame,* pp. 226–27; Theodore M. Hesburgh, C.S.C., *God, Country, and Notre Dame: The Autobiography of Theodore M. Hesburgh* (New York, 1990), pp. 174–78; Burton and Gerrity, *St. Joseph's,* pp. 60–61.

98. Breslin, *Villanova,* pp. 79–88; *Villanovan,* February 17, 1960; December 21, 1966; February 15, 1967; Annual Report of the President, 1965–66, p. 4; 1967–68, p. 3, VUA.

99. Faculty Handbook, 1957, p. 22; A Declaration by the Villanova Chapter, AAUP, 1960, AAUP Papers: President's file, VUA; Report to the Faculty Council from the ad hoc study committee on the Villanova University Senate and the appropriate role of faculty service and leadership in governance, pp. 21–22, VUA. This last document is undated, but internal evidence suggests that it was drawn up about 1987.

100. Report to Faculty Council (see note 99), p. 23.

101. Record of Actions Taken at Joint Conference of Representatives of Association of American Colleges and American Association of University Professors on Academic Freedom and Tenure, November 8, 1940; William C. A. Henry to Ralph E. Hinstead, General Secretary, AAUP, May 26, 1941, AAUP Papers: President's file, VUA.

102. James L. Miller, Chairman, Villanova AAUP to Rev. Francis X. N. McGuire, O.S.A., February 14, 1950; Miles B. Potter, Chapter Secretary to Very Rev. Joseph M. Dougherty, Chairman, Board of Athletic Control, February 21, 1950, AAUP Papers: President's file, VUA.

103. Minutes, AAUP, January 13, 1950; April 20, 1950; March 20, 1952; October 26, 1955; October 15, 1956, AAUP Papers: Minutes file, VUA; Report of the Chapter President, 1960–61, AAUP Papers: President's file, VUA; *Villanovan,* February 8, 1967; February 5, 1969.

104. See Dr. Albert H. Buford, Dean of Graduate Studies, to Bernard F. Reilly, April 13, 1967, AAUP Papers: President's file, VUA.

105. Faculty Handbook, 4th rev. ed., 1969, pp. 10–11, VUA.

106. Ibid., p. 13.

107. Driscoll to Rev. Patrick J. Rice, Vice President for Administration, November 4, 1968, Driscoll Papers.

108. History of Tenure Policy, 1960–72, Retrenchment file, VUA.

109. Faculty Handbook, 5th rev. ed., 1975, pp. 36–37, VUA; History of Tenure Policy, 1960–72.

110. Faculty Handbook, 5th rev. ed., 1975, pp. 33–35.

111. Minutes, College [of Liberal Arts and Sciences] Curriculum Committee, March 21, 1968, Arts and Sciences file, VUA; *Villanova Bulletin 1970–71,* p. 23.

# Chapter 7: Tradition and Change

1. For background on the postwar period in America, see James Gilbert, *Another Chance: Postwar America, 1945–1960* (New York, 1981); Eric Goldman, *The Crucial Decade and After* (New York, 1960); David Halberstam, *The Fifties* (New York, 1993); William L. O'Neill, *American High* (New York, 1986).

2. On the theme of containment and self-restraint in American life during the postwar period, see Elaine Tyler May, *Homeward Bound: American Families in the Cold War Era* (New York, 1988).

3. *Villanovan,* October 22, 1946.

4. Ibid., January 22, 1946.

5. *Belle Air 1947,* pp. 148–49; *1948,* pp. 204–5; *1952,* p. 176; *Villanovan,* May 21, 1946; May 8, 1951; December 13, 1949; January 12, 1954; March 6, 1957; April 3, 1957; January 16, 1959; February 25, 1959; February 17, 1960.

6. For example, see *Villanovan,* February 29, 1956. Also helpful are the Shamokinaki dance programs, VUA.

7. *Belle Air 1948,* p. 142; *1950,* n.p.; *1957,* p. 217; *Villanovan,* May 3, 1949; May 1, 1950; Junior Week program, 1962, VUA.

8. *Villanovan,* November 8, 1949.

9. Ibid., October 2, 1957.

10. Ibid.

11. Ibid., October 10, 1962.

12. Ibid., July 17, 1945; November 13, 1945.

13. *Belle Air 1963,* p. 3.

14. Ibid., *1953,* pp. 68–69; *1955,* p. 33; *1956,* p. 87; *Villanovan,* February 14, 1950; January 16, 1951; *Villanova Alumnus,* May 1952, p. 9.

15. See May, *Homeward Bound.*

16. *Villanova Alumnus,* October 1953, p. 2.

17. Ibid., December 1951, p. 1.

18. Ibid., October 1952, p. 2.

19. Ibid., May 1952, p. 14.

20. Ibid., October 1946, p. 2.

21. *Villanovan,* March 14, 1950; *Villanova Alumnus,* December 1951, p. 8.

22. *Villanova Alumnus,* October 1954, p. 5.

23. Bergquist to author, February 28, 1994.

24. *Villanova Alumnus,* March 1953, p. 2.

25. Ibid., December 1954, p. 6.

26. Ibid., p. 8; *Villanovan,* February 21, 1962.

27. *Villanovan,* December 14, 1954.

28. *Philadelphia Bulletin,* November 8, 1956.

29. Vincent P. De Santis, "American Catholics and McCarthyism," *CHR,* April 1965, pp. 1–30.

30. *Villanovan*, October 27, 1953.

31. Ibid., March 23, 1960.

32. Ibid., April 12, 1961.

33. Ibid., April 21, 1953.

34. Ibid., May 13, 1964.

35. Ibid., January 12, 1959. See also October 3, 1950.

36. Ibid., October 10, 1950.

37. Ibid., December 5, 1956.

38. *Philadelphia Bulletin*, February 3, 1959; February 17, 1961; May 2, 1961; May 20, 1961; *Inquirer*, May 3, 1961; *Times Herald* (Norristown, Pa.), September 28, 1961; *Catholic Standard and Times*, February 17, 1961.

39. *Villanovan*, April 22, 1964.

40. Ibid., November 4, 1952; October 31, 1956.

41. Ibid., September 25, 1957.

42. Ibid., October 27, 1960; November 10, 1960.

43. Ibid., February 12, 1946.

44. Ibid., March 22, 1949.

45. Ibid., October 31, 1949; April 4, 1950.

46. Report on the Inspection of Villanova University, 1959, p. 13.

47. Ibid.

48. *Belle Air 1956,* p. 87.

49. Ibid., *1959,* p. 29.

50. *Villanova Alumnus,* January 1949, p. 5; *Philadelphia Bulletin*, December 4, 1954; December 13, 1954; December 14, 1954.

51. *Philadelphia Bulletin*, May 6, 1964; *Daily News*, May 7, 1964.

52. Bergquist to author, February 28, 1994.

53. *Villanovan*, March 18, 1964; May 3, 1965; November 3, 1965; April 18, 1966; April 14, 1969; *The Spires,* April 1982, p. 1.

54. *Inquirer*, February 2, 1963; *Main Line Times*, March 1, 1962; February 13, 1964; *Villanovan*, January 16, 1958; February 13, 1963; March 17, 1965.

55. *Villanovan,* September 26, 1973; December 9, 1983.

56. Annual Report of the President, 1965–66, pp. 5–6, VUA; *Villanova Bulletin 1965–66,* p. 4; *Belle Air 1971,* pp. 126–27.

57. *Inquirer*, October 21, 1963; *Main Line Times*, October 10, 1963; *Villanovan*, February 9, 1966; March 2, 1966; August 4, 1967; September 27, 1967; February 19, 1969; April 8, 1970.

58. *Villanovan,* May 14, 1958; September 20, 1964; November 12, 1964; February 1, 1967; February 23, 1967; April 5, 1967; October 8, 1969.

59. Ibid., September 20, 1967.

60. Memorandum of Patricia A. Winner to Robert J. Capone, Alumni Director, February 9, 1987, VUA; *Philadelphia Bulletin*, August 5, 1939.

61. *Villanovan*, October 1917; October 9, 1934; March 12, 1940; July 14, 1942; November 14, 1944; July 17, 1956; *Belle Air 1942,* p. 154; *1943,* n.p.; *Main Line Times*, November 1, 1930.

62. *Villanovan*, February 28, 1950. See also the articles "Let's Make Villanova Non Co-Educational," *Villanovan*, October 26, 1954; "Girl's Letter Assails View Opposing VU Coeducation," *Villanovan*, November 23, 1954; "Villanova's Ideal Girl," February 20, 1957; and "Perspective: Pro and Con Coeducation," *Villanovan*, October 23, 1957.

63. *Main Line Times*, September 11, 1958; *Catholic Standard and Times*, September 12, 1958.

64. House Chapter Book, 1930–64, February 1953, n.p.; *Villanovan*, October 9, 1951; February 25, 1959.

65. Winner to Capone, February 9, 1987; Report of Villanova University submitted to Middle States Association of Colleges and Secondary Schools, January 1960, p. A48.

66. *Philadelphia Bulletin*, December 3, 1963; *Daily News*, December 11, 1963; January 1, 1965; January 10, 1965; *Villanovan*, October 8, 1954; October 19, 1954; November 23, 1954; December 7, 1954; October 19, 1955; January 18, 1956; February 29, 1956; December 9, 1964; December 16, 1964.

67. Bergquist to author, February 28, 1994.

68. Program for "Piper-heidsieck '98," 1950; program for "The Man in the Gray Flannel Toga," 1962, VUA; *Philadelphia Bulletin*, April 24, 1956. Whelan died in 1972. For an obituary, see *Villanova Alumnus*, February 1972, p. 1.

69. *Philadelphia Inquirer*, May 5, 1957.

70. *Villanova Alumnus*, April 1950, pp. 1–12; May 1950, p. 1; April 1951, p. 10; December 1951, pp. 4–5; May 1952, p. 9; *Main Line Times*, April 27, 1950; April 16, 1959.

71. Turf and Tinsel programs, 1949, 1955, 1956, 1960, VUA.

72. *Belle Air 1966*, p. 13.

73. *Philadelphia Bulletin*, October 15, 1967.

74. *Villanovan*, October 11, 1967; Annual Report of the President, 1967–68, n.p., VUA.

75. Burton and Gerrity, *St. Joseph's*, p. 68.

# Chapter 8: Villanova Counterculture

1. For an overview of the counterculture, see Landon Y. Jones, *Great Expectations: America and the Baby Boom Generation* (New York, 1980); Edward P. Morgan, *The 60s Experience: Hard Lessons about Modern America* (Philadelphia, 1991); William L. O'Neill, *Coming Apart: An Informal History of America in the 1960s* (New York, 1971); Edward Quinn and Paul J. Dolan, eds., *The Sense of the 60s* (New York, 1986).

2. Horowitz, *Campus Life*, pp. 220–44.

3. For example, see *Philadelphia Daily News*, June 24, 1974; *Philadelphia Bulletin*, May 12, 1971; *Villanovan*, October 2, 1981.

4. *Villanovan*, February 15, 1967; March 8, 1967; January 28, 1970; February 4, 1970.

5. Ibid., March 18, 1959; November 6, 1963; January 10, 1964; April 27, 1966; February 12, 1968.

6. *Suburban and Wayne Times*, November 3, 1968; *Villanovan*, February 21, 1968; October 7, 1970; memorandum of Dr. Fred J. Carrier to author, March 9, 1994.

7. *Villanovan*, February 1, 1967.

8. As defined by the *American Heritage Dictionary* (Boston, 1985), p. 902.

9. *Villanovan*, October 8, 1969.

10. *Villanovan*, October 8, 1969; April 8, 1970; November 4, 1970; November 11, 1970; April 2, 1971; February 23, 1972; March 11, 1972; October 10, 1974; *Philadelphia Bulletin*, April 23, 1971; April 10, 1974; *Inquirer*, April 23, 1971; *Daily News*, April 1, 1971; *Main Line Times*, April 8, 1971; *Suburban and Wayne Times*, April 29, 1971.

11. Edward Doherty, O.S.A., Reflections on Parietals, December 7, 1970, VUA.

12. *Inquirer*, March 12, 1972. See also the interview of Sherman in the *Villanova Alumnus,* June 1972, pp. 7–9.

13. Reverend Robert J. Welsh, O.S.A., President, to Joseph J. Hicks, Chairman, University Senate, April 16, 1971. This and other communications between the University Senate and the administration and board of trustees may be found in Interaction Between Senate Office and President's Office, 1971–90, VUA.

14. Welsh to Hicks, March 7, 1973.

15. See Gleason, *Keeping the Faith*, pp. 82–96. See also Gleason, "Mass and the Maypole Revisited: American Catholics in the Middle Ages," *CHR*, July 1971, pp. 249–74.

16. *Villanovan*, July 25, 1962; March 20, 1963; September 28, 1968.

17. *Belle Air 1967*, p. 130. See also *Villanovan*, October 16, 1963; November 16, 1966.

18. *Villanovan,* January 31, 1968.

19. Ibid., March 5, 1969; September 22, 1971; October 20, 1971.

20. Ibid., November 15, 1972.

21. Quoted in *Belle Air 1973*, p. 106.

22. Ibid. The dates 1927–72 were incorrect. Although the *Villanovan* had started weekly publication in 1927, it had begun as a monthly magazine in 1916.

23. *Villanovan,* February 14, 1973; *Philadelphia Bulletin*, November 21, 1972; *Inquirer*, November 12, 1972; *New York Times*, December 13, 1972.

24. *Villanovan*, October 7, 1970; December 6, 1972.

25. Ibid., February 1, 1967; October 11, 1967.

26. Ibid., September 17, 1969. The issue for March 8, 1967, included a similar criticism of fraternity hazing.

27. Ibid., January 26, 1972.

28. Ibid., September 17, 1969.

29. Ibid.

30. *Belle Air 1973*, p. 130.

31. *Villanovan*, November 17, 1960.

32. Ibid., April 5, 1967.

33. Ibid., December 7, 1966.

34. Villanova Blue Key Society: An Undergraduate Viewpoint, 1968, p. 21, VUA.

35. The full text of the Student Bill of Rights appeared in the *Villanovan* on November 27, 1968.

36. *Villanova Alumnus,* January 1969, p. 1.

37. *Villanovan*, October 30, 1968.

38. Ibid., October 4, 1972.

39. *Main Line Times*, September 28, 1972; *Today's Post*, September 26, 1972; *Villanovan*, October 30, 1968; February 20, 1974.

40. For a comparison, see the *Philadelphia Bulletin*, May 10, 1970.

41. *Inquirer*, April 22, 1969; April 23, 1969; *Daily News*, April 22, 1969; *Main Line Times*, April 24, 1969. Report of the Tri-Partite Commission to Examine Student Demands, April 26, 1969, VUA.

42. *Inquirer*, February 26, 1970; *Catholic Standard and Times*, March 5, 1970; Harold E. Kohn to Very Reverend Edward L. Daley, O.S.A., Chairman, Board of Trustees, Villanova University, March 10, 1970, VUA.

43. A body called a University Senate had been proposed during the late 1950s, but it is unclear just what it was intended to do. See Minutes, Villanova Chapter, AAUP, February 28, 1958.

44. Ibid., February 12, 1968; interview with Dr. Donald B. Kelley, July 11, 1994.

45. *Main Line Times*, April 24, 1969; *Philadelphia Bulletin*, January 5, 1971.

46. Breslin, *Villanova*, pp. 41–46; *Villanovan*, October 26, 1968; November 20, 1968; January 29, 1970; February 18, 1970; Fred J. Carrier to Villanova Chapter, AAUP, October 30, 1968, AAUP Papers: President's file, VUA.

47. *Villanovan,* November 19, 1969; Breslin, *Villanova*, pp. 46–47; *Villanova Alumnus,* May 1970, p. 1.

48. For this veto, see Welsh to Hicks, cited above. Other significant vetoes are contained in Reverend Edward J. McCarthy, O.S.A., President to Robert W. Langran, Chairman, University Senate, February 27, 1973; February 14, 1974; June 28, 1974, in Interaction Between Senate Office and President's Office, 1971–90.

49. Minutes, AAUP, March 25, 1942; November 2, 1950.

50. A Statement on Faculty Compensation at Villanova University and the Future of the University, AAUP Papers: President's file. See also *Villanovan*, September 21, 1966.

51. Reverend Edward J. McCarthy, O.S.A., to "Dear Faculty Member," November 8, 1973, McCarthy Papers.

52. *Inquirer*, February 25, 1980; February 29, 1980; *Philadelphia Bulletin*, February 28, 1980; *New York Times*, February 24, 1980; Minutes, AAUP, March 17, 1980; October 6, 1980; February 12, 1981; Bergquist to author, February 28, 1994.

53. Report to the Faculty Council, 1986, pp. 25–26.

54. See Joseph Scimecca and Roland Damianano, *Crisis at St. John's: Strike and Revolution on the Catholic Campus* (New York, 1967).

55. *Villanovan*, January 30, 1974; February 6, 1974; March 27, 1974; *Philadelphia Bulletin*, February 3, 1974; University Senate Resolution, January 25, 1974, VUA.

56. *Inquirer*, February 15, 1974; *Catholic Standard and Times*, February 14, 1974; *Villanovan*, February 20, 1974.

57. *Philadelphia Bulletin*, July 11, 1974; August 22, 1974; *Inquirer*, April 10, 1974; September 1, 1974; *Main Line Times*, July 10, 1974; July 11, 1974; February 27, 1975; November 14, 1974; *Catholic Standard and Times*, August 8, 1974; *Villanovan*, July 29, 1974; September 11, 1974; September 25, 1974; November 20, 1974; *The Spires,* April 1975.

58. *Philadelphia Bulletin*, October 20, 1966; *Inquirer*, November 21, 1970; *Main Line Times*, March 26, 1970; *Villanovan*, October 19, 1966; November 16, 1966.

59. *Philadelphia Bulletin*, April 20, 1970; *Villanovan*, April 8, 1970; April 22, 1970; September 24, 1970.

60. *Main Line Times*, April 8, 1971; April 22, 1971; *Suburban and Wayne Times*, April 1, 1971.

61. *Villanovan*, October 1, 1958.

62. Ibid., October 11, 1961.

63. *Catholic Standard and Times*, March 10, 1961.

64. *Villanovan*, January 8, 1965; April 10, 1968; *Philadelphia Bulletin*, January 21, 1965.

65. *Main Line Times*, March 20, 1969; *Suburban and Wayne Times*, March 19, 1970; *Philadelphia Tribune*, March 14, 1971.

66. On the Vietnam War and its effects on American life, including the student protest movement, see Morgan, *The 60s Experience*, pp. 127–68; Alexander Kendrick, *The Wound Within: America and the Vietnam Years, 1945–1974* (Boston, 1974).

67. *Villanovan*, September 28, 1966.

68. Ibid., April 19, 1967.

69. Ibid., October 11, 1967; November 15, 1967; *Philadelphia Bulletin*, November 13, 1967.

70. *Villanovan*, September 17, 1969; October 15, 1969; October 22, 1969; February 25, 1970; September 16, 1970; September 23, 1970; October 21, 1970.

71. *Inquirer*, October 19, 1969.

72. *Villanovan*, October 15, 1969.

73. Ibid., December 10, 1969; memorandum of Carrier to author, March 9, 1994.

74. *Villanovan*, April 8, 1970.

75. Ibid., October 14, 1970.

76. *Philadelphia Bulletin*, October 5, 1969.

77. Carrier to author, March 9, 1994.

78. *Inquirer*, October 19, 1965; December 3, 1970; *San Francisco Chronicle*, October 21, 1965; *Philadelphia Bulletin*, September 5, 1969; December 2, 1970.

79. *Philadelphia Bulletin,* May 6, 1970.

80. *Philadelphia Daily News*, May 7, 1970.

81. *New York Times*, May 13, 1970; *Suburban and Wayne Times*, May 28, 1970; *Times Herald*, May 13, 1970; *Belle Air 1971,* pp. 9, 70; *Villanovan*, July 27, 1970; *Villanova Alumnus,* May 1970, p. 3.

82. *Times Herald*, March 9, 1973.

83. *Inquirer*, May 17, 1971; *Suburban and Wayne Times*, May 25, 1972.

84. The term "Catholic Counterculture" is used in the study by Fisher, *Catholic Counterculture in America*, to refer to Catholic criticisms of certain aspects of American life during the middle decades of the twentieth century.

85. *Villanovan*, September 20, 1967.

86. Quoted in *Philadelphia Bulletin*, August 27, 1969.

87. *Suburban and Wayne Times*, November 3, 1968; *Villanovan*, November 13, 1968. See also *Inquirer*, August 27, 1969.

88. Bergquist to author, February 28, 1994.

89. *Villanovan*, May 5, 1971; *Inquirer*, July 13, 1971; *Philadelphia Bulletin*, April 28, 1971; July 13, 1971; *Daily News*, July 13, 1971.

90. *Villanova Alumnus,* September 1971, p. 1; Memorandum of Bergquist to author, February 28, 1994.

91. *Villanova Alumnus,* September 1971, p. 1.

92. *Villanovan*, September 15, 1971; January 22, 1975.

93. *Today's Post*, September 3, 1971.

94. Ibid.

95. Quoted in *Today's Post*, April 20, 1972.

96. Ibid., January 27, 1975.

97. *Villanovan*, January 22, 1975.

98. *Villanova Alumnus,* November 1971, p. 5.

99. *Inquirer*, September 1, 1971.

100. *Philadelphia Bulletin*, June 30, 1971.

101. *Villanovan*, March 22, 1972.

102. Ibid., October 3, 1973.

103. *Inquirer*, January 27, 1975.

104. *Villanova Alumnus,* June 1974, p. 1.

105. Quoted in *Inquirer*, October 1, 1961.

106. *Villanovan*, January 22, 1975.

107. Ibid., September 10, 1975.

108. *Today's Post*, July 3, 1975.

109. *Main Line Times*, July 10, 1975.

110. *Catholic Standard and Times*, July 10, 1975; *Today's Post*, July 3, 1975.

111. Ibid.

112. *Villanovan*, February 4, 1976.

113. Ibid., September 15, 1976.

114. Ibid., October 6, 1976.

115. Ibid., September 22, 1976.

116. Ibid., September 22, 1976; September 7, 1979.

117. Ibid., November 18, 1977.

118. Ibid., October 7, 1977; April 16, 1982; Summary Minutes, Board of Trustees, December 12, 1973, VUA (hereafter Trustee Summary Minutes).

119. *Villanovan,* September 23, 1977.

# Chapter 9: Attaining Excellence

1. *Villanova Bulletin 1993–94,* pp. 6–7.

2. 125th Anniversary Convocation folder, April 6, 1968, VUA; Invitation to Pontifical Mass, September 13, 1967, VUA; *Villanovan*, April 10, 1968; *Philadelphia Bulletin*, September 13, 1967; April 7, 1968; *Inquirer*, September 14, 1967; April 17, 1968; *Daily News*, September 14, 1967; *Catholic Standard and Times*, March 27, 1968.

3. *Inquirer*, November 25, 1976; *Suburban and Wayne Times*, December 4, 1975; *Villanovan*, January 21, 1976.

4. Report of the Inspection of Villanova University by an Evaluating Committee of the Middle States Association of Colleges and Secondary Schools . . . , 1970, p. 18.

5. *Annual Report of the President*, 1965–66, p. 4. See also *Villanovan*, October 12, 1968; February 15, 1967.

6. Report . . . Middle States Association of Colleges and Secondary Schools . . . , 1980, p. 40.

7. Ibid., p. 5.

8. Institutional Self-Study, Villanova University, Prepared for the Commission on Higher Education, Middle States Association of Colleges and Schools, 1980, pp. 40–44; Self Study, Middle States, 1990, pp. 110–11; *Villanovan*, April 6, 1990.

9. Self Study, Middle States, 1990, p. 33.

10. *Villanovan*, April 6, 1991.

11. Report, Middle States, 1980, p. 5.

12. Ibid., p. 6.

13. Report, Middle States, 1990, pp. 4–5.

14. See, for example, ibid., 1980, p. 6.

15. *Villanovan*, February 18, 1983.

16. Trustee Minutes Summary, November 29, 1976.

17. Self Study, Middle States, 1980, p. 100; *Philadelphia Bulletin*, May 8, 1971.

18. *Villanovan*, November 18, 1977; Prospectus of Villanova University for the Covenant Campaign, January 1977, p. 5.

19. Trustee Minutes Summary, September 12, 1972; September 10, 1974; April 11, 1978.

20. *Villanova Bulletin 1978–80,* p. 19; Self Study, Middle States, 1980, p. 108.

21. Trustee Minutes Summary, April 10, 1973.

22. *Villanovan*, February 12, 1975; January 21, 1976; February 2, 1977; February 9, 1977; February 23, 1977; March 23, 1977.

23. American City Bureau, p. 92; *Villanovan*, November 15, 1961; Harold E. Kohn to

Very Reverend Edward L. Daley, O.S.A., Chairman, Board of Trustees, March 10, 1970, Retrenchment file, VUA. See also Chapters 6 and 7.

24. Minutes, Executive Committee, University Senate, July 5, 1973.

25. Report of the Commission on University Structure and Programs (CUSP), Villanova University, February 4, 1977, p. 66, VUA. See also *Villanovan*, November 26, 1969; November 15, 1972; January 28, 1976.

26. Driscoll to Ad Hoc Committee on the Cost of Athletic Programs at Villanova, September 20, 1976, Driscoll Papers; Self Study, Middle States, 1980, p. 129; *Villanovan*, January 28, 1976; October 6, 1975; November 16, 1979.

27. Trustee Minutes Summary, April 14, 1981.

28. Driscoll, Press Release, "Discontinuance of Varsity Football at Villanova University," April 15, 1981, Driscoll Papers, VUA. Portions of this release appeared in the *Philadelphia Bulletin*, April 16, 1981, and the *Inquirer*, April 16, 1981; *New York Times*, April 17, 1981.

29. *Villanovan*, April 24, 1981; October 2, 1981.

30. David Reisman to Driscoll, May 12, 1982, Driscoll Papers.

31. Robert Kirkwood to Driscoll, May 11, 1981, Driscoll Papers.

32. *Philadelphia Bulletin*, April 19, 1981; *Inquirer*, April 17, 1981; April 28, 1981.

33. The author has based such opinions on the many letters Driscoll received from alumni about the football decision, Driscoll Papers.

34. *Villanovan*, October 2, 1981.

35. Douglas Murray to "Dear Fellow Alumni and Alumnae," n.d., Driscoll Papers, VUA.

36. *Philadelphia Bulletin*, May 8, 1981.

37. Trustee Minutes Summary, July 14, 1981; *Philadelphia Bulletin*, May 20, 1981; *Inquirer*, May 21, 1981; *Villanovan*, September 11, 1981.

38. *Villanovan,* December 4, 1981.

39. Ibid.; *Inquirer*, December 2, 1981; *Philadelphia Bulletin*, December 2, 1981; *Daily News*, December 2, 1981.

40. *Inquirer*, April 16, 1982; *Villanovan*, April 23, 1982.

41. Minutes, Faculty Affairs Committee, April 28, 1982, VUA.

42. *Villanovan*, April 23, 1982.

43. *Daily News*, April 27, 1982.

44. *Villanovan*, September 23, 1983.

45. As early as October 1981 the University Senate had asked the board of trustees to reconsider dropping football. See *Villanovan*, October 9, 1981.

46. Ibid., December 4, 1981; April 23, 1982; October 8, 1982; October 22, 1982; November 5, 1982; November 19, 1982; January 21, 1983; December 16, 1983; December 23, 1983; October 26, 1984; November 2, 1984; March 22, 1985; September 27, 1985; Driscoll to Robert I. Smith, President and Treasurer, The Glenmede Trust Co., January 4, 1984, Driscoll Papers. For a succinct chronology of the football decisions and debate, see the *Villanovan*, December 9, 1983.

47. The board's denial of any overt favoritism toward basketball came in the form of a letter to the *Daily News* by board member Arthur J. Kania, published June 3, 1982.

48. *Sports Illustrated*, April 8, 1985, pp. 31–35; *Inquirer*, April 1, 1985; *Daily News*, April 4, 1985.

49. *Villanovan*, March 29, 1985; April 12, 1985; *Inquirer*, April 3, 1985; April 4, 1985; April 5, 1985; *Daily News*, April 2, 1985; *New York Times*, April 3, 1985; April 4, 1985; *Main Line Times*, April 4, 1985.

50. *USA Today*, November 17, 1989; *Villanova Magazine,* Summer 1988, pp. 2–5; Summer 1990, pp. 19–21; *Villanovan*, March 16, 1979; October 3, 1980; March 27,

1981; December 2, 1988; September 22, 1989; December 1, 1989; December 6, 1991; December 4, 1992.

51. *Sports Illustrated*, January 22, 1962, pp. 30–35; *New York Times*, April 23, 1979; *Philadelphia Bulletin*, May 18, 1979; *Inquirer*, December 10, 1985; *Villanovan*, March 2, 1960; March 8, 1967; January 26, 1977; October 3, 1980; March 27, 1981; November 6, 1981; January 24, 1986.

52. *Villanovan*, April 11, 1986; February 22, 1991.

53. Ibid., September 7, 1990.

54. Ibid., April 10, 1987.

55. *Belle Air 1984*, p. 11; *Villanovan*, October 20, 1971; February 9, 1972; April 7, 1976; December 8, 1976; January 26, 1977; October 7, 1977; September 15, 1978; October 6, 1978; March 14, 1980; September 5, 1980; September 19, 1980.

56. Driscoll to John E. duPont, March 13, 1984, and December 22, 1986, Driscoll Papers; *Main Line Times*, January 23, 1986; *King of Prussia Courier*, June 18, 1986; *Villanovan*, April 16, 1969; March 24, 1970; November 21, 1973; January 30, 1974; November 9, 1979; August 31, 1984; January 24, 1985; September 27, 1985; February 7, 1986.

57. Covenant brochure, VUA.

58. A Prospectus of Villanova University for the Covenant Campaign, January 1977, VUA.

59. Ibid., p. 21; "The Covenant II Reporter," no. 1, Fall 1983; no. 5, Spring 1987, VUA; Driscoll to Dr. Bernard F. Reilly, February 9, 1981, Driscoll Papers; Comprehensive Long Range Financial Development . . . by Marts and Lundy, February 15, 1987, VUA; *Villanovan*, December 10, 1982; April 4, 1986; October 30, 1987.

60. Prospectus, Covenant Campaign, p. 19; Interview with Reverend John M. Driscoll, O.S.A., December 13, 1993.

61. Driscoll to Very Rev. Joseph A. Duffy, O.S.A., Prior Provincial, February 2, 1984, Driscoll Papers.

62. Self Study, Middle States, 1990, p. 85; Annual Report, 1983–84, p. 5; *Villanovan*, September 11, 1981; October 1, 1982; September 9, 1983; March 23, 1984; September 21, 1984; November 1, 1985; September 26, 1986; April 3, 1987; September 16, 1988.

63. *Villanovan*, September 11, 1981.

64. These enrollment figures are taken from the registrar's reports, VUA.

65. *Inquirer*, November 6, 1986; *Blue Prints*, October 15, 1993.

66. *The Spires*, September 1993, p. 3.

67. Self Study, Middle States, 1990, pp. A-105–6; *Statistical Abstract of the United States, 1991*, pp. 456, 457.

68. *The Spires*, December 1975, p. 3.

69. *Villanovan*, October 21, 1964.

70. Ibid., October 13, 1976.

71. Ibid., October 31, 1980.

72. Ibid., November 4, 1988.

73. Ibid.

74. Ibid., October 2, 1992.

75. Driscoll to The President (Gerald R. Ford), September 17, 1976, and Driscoll to The Honorable Jimmy Carter, September 17, 1976, Driscoll Papers; *Villanovan*, September 15, 1976; September 22, 1976; September 29, 1976; October 27, 1976; April 18, 1980; April 25, 1980; November 18, 1983; *Inquirer*, October 28, 1976; November 18, 1983; *Main Line Times*, June 19, 1986.

76. Driscoll to The President (Ronald Reagan), August 13, 1986, Driscoll Papers. The two student letters asking Reagan not to come to Villanova were published in the *Villa-*

*novan*, February 13, 1987. Anger over these student letters was expressed in the *Villa-novan* on February 20, 1987.

77. *Inquirer* ("Main Line Neighbors"), October 27, 1988; March 16, 1989; *Villa-novan*, November 4, 1988; October 28, 1988; March 17, 1989.

78. *Villanovan,* January 25, 1991; February 1, 1991; February 8, 1991; February 15, 1991; March 15, 1991.

79. Ibid., March 22, 1991; April 12, 1991.

80. Ibid., April 5, 1991; April 19, 1991.

81. Horowitz, *Campus Life*, pp. 273–79.

82. *Belle Air 1971,* pp. 36–37; *Villanovan*, April 12, 1985; January 26, 1989; October 27, 1989; February 2, 1990; Michael Okenquist, "A History of the Greek System at Villa-nova," typescript, author's collection.

83. *Villanovan,* January 26, 1989.

84. Horowitz, *Campus Life*, pp. 263–88.

85. Ibid.

86. *Inquirer*, September 16, 1982; *Philadelphia Bulletin*, December 18, 1980; *Main Line Times*, October 1, 1970; February 7, 1980; April 3, 1980; December 11, 1980; September 16, 1982; *Suburban and Wayne Times*, January 17, 1980; January 31, 1980; February 5, 1981; *Villanovan*, October 5, 1979; October 12, 1979; October 19, 1979; November 9, 1979; January 18, 1980; March 28, 1980; November 21, 1980; February 6, 1981; September 18, 1981; June 26, 1981; September 24, 1982; September 23, 1983; April 13, 1984; March 12, 1993; *Blue Prints*, December 1, 1993.

87. *Philadelphia Bulletin*, February 22, 1980; *Suburban and Wayne Times*, February 28, 1980; *Main Line Times*, February 24, 1977.

88. *Villanovan*, February 3, 1984; February 19, 1988; February 26, 1988.

89. Ibid., February 6, 1987. See also the *Villanovan*'s editorial page of September 19, 1986.

90. Ibid., January 27, 1989; February 17, 1989.

91. Ibid., November 14, 1986; March 19, 1993.

92. Self Study, Middle States, 1980, p. 41; Self Study, Middle States, 1990, p. 111; *Villanova Bulletin 1968–69,* pp. 9–37.

93. *Villanovan*, October 20, 1978; *Villanova Alumnus,* November 1973, p. 5; The Villanova Experience, admissions brochure, 1985, n.p., VUA; Undergraduate Admissions Office, Annual Report of Operations, 1989–90, VUA; *Blue Prints*, October 15, 1993. The trend of admitting slightly more women than men has continued into 1994 as more women than men have applied to Villanova, raising the possibility that the once all-male student body will contain slightly more women than men in the years just ahead.

94. *Philadelphia Bulletin*, October 7, 1973; *Villanovan*, September 28, 1984.

95. *Suburban and Wayne Times*, September 11, 1980; *Times Herald*, September 18, 1980; *Villanovan*, September 15, 1989.

96. Self Study, Middle States, 1980, pp. 106–7; *Villanovan*, November 21, 1980; February 20, 1981; October 8, 1982; January 25, 1985.

97. *Villanova Bulletin 1989–90,* p. 21.

98. Self Study, Middle States, 1980, p. 108.

99. Ibid., p. 104.

100. *Villanovan,* January 18, 1980; February 20, 1981; October 8, 1982; February 15, 1985; October 10, 1986; April 7, 1989; March 30, 1990; November 16, 1990; Self Study, Middle States, 1990, p. A-103.

101. Care, a pamphlet from the Office for Social Action, 1969, Affirmative Action file, VUA; *Villanova Bulletin 1993–94,* pp. 11, 342.

102. Self Study, Middle States, 1990, p. 111.

103. Driscoll to Council of Deans and Chairmen, January 29, 1975, Affirmative Action file; *Villanovan*, January 16, 1981; Edward L. Collymore to Administrative Board Members, September 9, 1976, Driscoll Papers.

104. *Villanovan*, November 15, 1991.

105. Ibid., November 22, 1991; see also the editorials in the November 1, 1991, and November 8, 1991, issues.

106. *Philadelphia Bulletin*, December 5, 1955; July 24, 1968; *Inquirer*, December 14, 1953.

107. *Suburban and Wayne Times*, February 19, 1976; July 1, 1976; *Today's Post*, February 20, 1976; *Philadelphia Bulletin*, June 1, 1980; August 10, 1980; August 27, 1980.

108. *Globe Democrat* (St. Louis, Mo.), April 24, 1982; *Suburban and Wayne Times*, May 26, 1983.

109. *Villanovan*, September 21, 1979; September 27, 1985; October 6, 1989; *Suburban and Wayne Times*, October 21, 1982; October 14, 1982; April 4, 1985.

110. *Philadelphia Bulletin*, August 2, 1977; *Suburban and Wayne Times*, August 11, 1977; *Villanovan*, October 10, 1986.

111. *Main Line Times*, April 12, 1977; April 14, 1983; *Villanovan*, April 20, 1977; March 29, 1985; April 26, 1985; *Villanova Magazine,* Fall 1990, p. 12.

112. Rev. Owen Jackson, O.S.A., to Driscoll, November 20, 1978, Driscoll Papers; *Villanovan*, September 21, 1990; September 27, 1991; *Main Line Chronicle*, November 18, 1981.

113. Rev. Michael Glessner, O.S.A., to Rev. Director, Campus Ministry, February 1, 1980, VUA; *Times Herald*, January 31, 1985; *Catholic Standard and Times*, January 31, 1985; *Villanovan*, March 16, 1991; February 8, 1985; March 23, 1990; *Villanova Magazine,* February 1990, p. 14.

114. Trustee Minutes Summary, October 8, 1985; *Villanovan*, March 15, 1985; September 20, 1985; February 21, 1986; April 4, 1986; September 26, 1986; October 7, 1988; Driscoll to Miriam G. Vosburgh, October 21, 1985, in Interaction Between Senate Office and President's Office, 1971–90.

115. *Suburban and Wayne Times*, February 1, 1979; *Villanovan*, September 15, 1989; October 6, 1989.

116. Registrar's reports.

117. Self Study, Middle States, 1990, p. A-104.

118. *Villanova Bulletin 1989–90,* pp. 314–48. These figures do not include the few Augustinians who continued to hold faculty rank while working as full-time administrators.

119. Self Study, Middle States, 1980, p. 49; Villanova University Triennial Report, 1975–77, n.p., VUA; *Villanovan*, September 14, 1984; Driscoll to Rev. Allen D. Fitzgerald, O.S.A., October 25, 1985, Driscoll Papers.

120. *Philadelphia Bulletin*, September 3, 1968; *Daily News*, September 3, 1968; *Villanova Bulletin 1993–94,* p. 341.

121. These figures for the board were supplied by the office of the University president.

122. *Villanovan*, December 9, 1959.

123. Ibid., April 8, 1964.

124. *Philadelphia Bulletin*, March 21, 1968; August 11, 1968; *Delmarva Dialogue* (Wilmington, Del.), March 29, 1968.

125. Quoted in *Villanovan*, September 18, 1968; see also September 28, 1968; October 5, 1968; October 12, 1968; November 20, 1968; *Main Line Times*, August 16, 1968.

126. For some insightful background on this controversy, see Hesburgh, *Autobiography*, pp. 223–45.

127. See, for example, "Abortion: Is It for You?" *Villanovan*, November 18, 1970.

128. *Suburban and Wayne Times*, April 1, 1971.

129. *Villanovan*, January 23, 1974; January 30, 1974; January 22, 1975; December 3, 1982; *Suburban and Wayne Times*, January 26, 1978; February 2, 1978.

130. *Villanovan,* January 29, 1982.

131. Ibid., March 20, 1992.

132. *Philadelphia Bulletin*, May 20, 1977; June 3, 1977; *Main Line Times*, May 24, 1977; May 31, 1977; *Catholic Standard and Times*, May 19, 1977.

133. Driscoll to His Eminence John Cardinal Krol, May 25, 1977; Driscoll to Rev. Richard M. Nahman, O.S.A., Director of the Province Office for Social Justice, June 9, 1977, Driscoll Papers.

134. "Academic Freedom and the Abortion Issue: Four Related Incidents," Report of a Special Committee of the American Association of University Professors, p. 26, VUA.

135. Ibid.

136. For a good account of Maguire and his various activities in the Catholic pro-choice movement, see the entire Special Report of the AAUP, cited directly above.

137. Very Rev. Joseph A. Duffey, O.S.A., Prior Provincial to Driscoll, March 11, 1985, Maguire Case, VUA.

138. *Inquirer*, May 11, 1985; "Academic Freedom and the Abortion Issue: Four Incidents at Catholic Institutions, Report of a Special Committee," *Academe,* July–August 1986, p. 7; Driscoll to Dr. Daniel C. Maguire, May 3, 1985, Maguire Case, VUA.

139. *Inquirer*, May 11, 1985; *Suburban and Wayne Times*, May 16, 1985; Executive Committee, Villanova Chapter, AAUP to Villanova Academic Community, June 17, 1985, AAUP Papers: President's file, VUA.

140. "Academic Freedom and the Abortion Issue," p. 3.

141. Driscoll to His Eminence John Cardinal Krol, September 10, 1986, Driscoll Papers.

142. "Academic Freedom and the Abortion Issue," p. 12.

143. One of Driscoll's severest critics was Robert Kirkwood, Executive Director of the Commission on Higher Education for the Middle States Association of Colleges and Schools. Having praised Driscoll for getting rid of football at Villanova back in 1982, Kirkwood regretted that Driscoll had reversed himself on the football decision and now had compromised on academic freedom. Robert Kirkwood to Driscoll, June 7, 1985, Maguire Case, VUA.

144. *Villanovan*, March 20, 1987; January 29, 1988; *Daily News*, December 9, 1987.

145. *Inquirer*, October 6, 1988; *Main Line Times*, October 6, 1988; *Catholic Standard and Times*, September 29, 1988; *Villanova Magazine,* Fall 1988, pp. 4–7; *Villanovan*, September 9, 1988; September 23, 1988; October 7, 1988.

146. *Catholic Standard and Times*, November 17, 1988; *Villanovan*, November 18, 1988.

147. *Inquirer*, August 21, 1983.

148. *Villanovan*, September 26, 1986.

149. Ibid.

150. *Villanovan,* April 3, 1992.

151. Ibid.

152. *Ex Corde Ecclesiae* (1990), in *Origins: CNS Documentary Service*, October 4, 1990, p. 269. Certain teachings of this document were reiterated and extended in the papal encyclical *Veritatis Splendor* (*The Splendor of Truth*), issued in October 1993.

153. *Ex Corde Ecclesiae*, in *Origins*, p. 269. For a discussion about the possible implications of *Veritatis Splendor*, see *Chronicle of Higher Education*, September 15, 1993.

154. Interview with Reverend Edmund J. Dobbin, June 9, 1994.

155. *Villanovan*, November 8, 1985; November 22, 1985.

156. Self Study, Middle States, 1990, p. 35; *Villanova Bulletin 1993–94*, pp. 57–64; *Main Line Times*, August 12, 1982; May 5, 1983; *Suburban and Wayne Times*, April 9, 1959; September 11, 1980; November 11, 1982; *Delaware County Times*, April 21, 1967; *Catholic Standard and Times*, March 14, 1958; February 25, 1966; *Villanovan*, February 27, 1957; September 15, 1979; February 5, 1988; Driscoll to University Faculty and Staff, September 15, 1982; October 12, 1982, Board of Trustees file, VUA.

157. Self Study, Middle States, 1990, p. 32; *Villanovan*, October 4, 1991; February 14, 1992; September 10, 1992; interview with Dobbin, June 9, 1994.

158. Driscoll to Rev. Lawrence C. Gallen, O.S.A., Vice President for Academic Affairs, February 21, 1984, Driscoll Papers.

159. *Villanovan*, April 22, 1988; Driscoll to Board of Trustees, July 15, 1988, Driscoll Papers; Trustee Minutes Summary, October 13, 1992; interview with Dobbin, June 9, 1994.

160. Trustee Minutes Summary, September 11, 1973; April 12, 1977; September 13, 1977; April 9, 1985; April 10, 1990; *Villanovan*, October 6, 1976; September 29, 1978; September 23, 1977; November 17, 1978; February 23, 1979; March 30, 1984; October 6, 1989; February 16, 1990; April 10, 1992; November 19, 1993; *Villanova Magazine*, Fall 1993, pp. 8–11; *Blue Prints*, November 1, 1993.

161. *Blue Prints*, November 1, 1993. *Villanova Magazine*, Fall 1993, p. 10; Patterson Hall, Project Overview, Villanova University Facilities Management, VUA; Phyllis C. Maier, "Dundale, 1890–1979," typescript, VUA; Elizabeth Biddle Yarnall, *Addison Hutton, Quaker Architect, 1834–1916* (Philadelphia, 1974); David R. Contosta, "Dundale," Historic American Buildings Survey, 1994, VUA.

162. *Villanovan*, February 26, 1988.

163. Ibid., September 9, 1988; October 2, 1992; *Villanova Magazine*, Summer 1990, pp. 15–16; Spring 1991, pp. 19–21; "The Villanova Campaign Briefing (Summer 1993)," pp. 1, 7; interview with Dobbin, June 9, 1994.

164. *Villanovan*, November 22, 1991; October 2, 1992; December 4, 1992; Trustee Minutes Summary, April 11, 1989; February 11, 1991; interview with Dobbin, June 9, 1994.

## Conclusion: Past and Future

1. Driscoll to Louise Fitzpatrick and Eugene Ruane, November 16, 1987, Driscoll Papers; Trustee Minutes Summary, October 13, 1987.

2. *Inquirer* ("Main Line Neighbors"), September 20, 1992; *Delaware County Daily Times*, September 25, 1992; *Villanovan*, October 2, 1992.

3. David R. Contosta and Reverend Dennis J. Gallagher, O.S.A., *Villanova: College to University: 150 Years of Augustinian Tradition and Promise, 1842–1992* (Villanova, Pa., 1992), and *Ever Ancient, Ever New: Villanova University, 1842–1992* (Virginia Beach, Va., 1992).

4. *Villanovan*, September 25, 1992.

5. Ibid., April 23, 1993; *Inquirer*, April 19, 1993; *Villanova Magazine*, Fall 1992, p. 9.

6. For a complete listing of sesquicentennial events, see Villanova University Sesqui-

centennial, 1992–93 Calendar of Events, Sesquicentennial file, VUA. For Opening Weekend, see the official program, "Sesquicentennial," VUA. See also *Villanovan*, September 10, 1992; April 23, 1993; April 30, 1993; September 25, 1992; September 17, 1993; September 24, 1993; *Villanova Magazine,* Fall 1993, pp. 2–7.

7. "Message from the President," in *Ever Ancient, Ever New*, p. 113; "President's Welcome," in *Villanova: College to University, 1842–1992*, p. 2.

# BIBLIOGRAPHIC ESSAY

Essential to any study of Villanova are two archival collections: the Villanova University Archives, located on the Villanova campus, and the Augustinian Provincial Archives, situated several blocks from the university in Villanova, Pennsylvania. These contain a variety of sources, including charters, deeds, mortgages, real-estate transactions, manuscripts, correspondence, memoranda, presidential and other official papers, drawings, photographs, maps, meeting minutes, financial records, student lists, enrollment figures, evaluations, reports, resolutions, memoirs, speeches, sermons, scrapbooks, newspaper clippings, official publications, and a variety of ephemera such as posters, invitations, programs, souvenirs, memorabilia, tickets to campus events, and even articles of clothing. The Villanova University Archives contain the more significant collection of materials relating to the institution, while the Augustinian Archives shed light on Villanova's earlier period. The abbreviations VUA and APA are used, respectively, in the notes and the illustrations to designate the Villanova University Archives and the Augustinian Provincial Archives. (Because both of these archives are in the process of being reorganized, this author decided that citing specific box and file numbers, many of which are being changed, would only confuse future researchers. Thus such numbers do not appear in the notes.)

The minutes of various governing bodies provide valuable information about official decisions, about when they were made, and sometimes the rationale for such decisions. Among these are the minutes of Villanova's board of trustees. Considerations of confidentiality and privacy have led the university to withhold board minutes for the most recent thirty-five-year period, but summaries of board meetings during this time are available to the researcher. Because many decisions affecting Villanova were made by the Augustinian community, the minutes of its various governing bodies are also instructive. These comprise the minutes of meetings held by the Augustinian community on the Villanova campus, as contained in volumes called the House Register—and later the House Chapter Book. College and university matters that affected the entire Augustinian province were taken up by

Augustinian provincial authorities and are recorded in minute books under several titles: Provincial Register, Definitory Record, Definitory Meetings, and Definitory Record Book. As with the board of trustees, minutes generated by Augustinian governing bodies are not available for the most current decades. There exist official minutes from a variety of other organizations and groups within the college/university, including the Alumni Association, the University Senate, Student Government Association, the Faculty Council, the Faculty Affairs Committee, and the local chapter of the American Association of University Professors.

A number of evaluations and reports offer information about conditions at Villanova during various periods, along with suggestions or plans for the future. Among these are the reports of the Middle States Association of Colleges and Secondary Schools and the self-studies prepared for the Middle States examiners. These begin in 1950 and appear at subsequent ten-year intervals. Equally helpful are the fund-raising and planning studies commissioned by Villanova: A Survey and Plan of Fund Raising for Villanova College, by the John Price Jones Corporation (1929); Evaluation Survey and Case Book, by the American City Bureau (1953); Prospectus of Villanova for the Covenant Campaign (1977); Comprehensive Long Range Financial Development, by Marts and Lundy (1987); A Future of Promise: The Villanova Strategic Plan (1991). There was also an evaluation by the Augustinian province in 1959 entitled Report on the Inspection of Villanova University. In addition, there are internal studies commissioned by the university president, the most significant of these being the reports of the Commission on University Structure and Programs (1977) and of the Program Evaluation Committee (1988).

Over the decades, Villanova has generated a number of regular reports (often annually and appearing under various titles) from the president, the treasurer, the registrar, and other institutional offices, which contain helpful statistics and other information. Supplementing these are various brochures, guides, and official publications, including student handbooks, faculty handbooks, and admissions literature. There is also the annual Villanova *Catalogue*, listing courses, degree requirements, faculty, administrative personnel, academic calendars, and other such facts. In more recent years this publication has been known as the *Villanova Bulletin*. The university and its various divisions have also generated dozens of newsletters over the years under numerous and changing titles.

The alumni office published the *Villanova Alumni News* from 1933 to 1936. After a two-year hiatus, a successor called the *Villanova Alumnus* appeared in 1938 and continued under that name until 1974, when it was replaced by *The Spires*. In 1985 *The Spires* became a small alumni newsletter. Meanwhile, the alumni magazine itself was revamped as a more all-encompassing development publication called the *Villanova Magazine*, which first appeared in 1985.

Essential for understanding student life is the student yearbook, *The Belle Air*, which made its debut in 1922. The student newspaper, *The Villanovan* (later simply *Villanovan*), was established in 1916 as a monthly publication and became a weekly newspaper in 1927. Besides reflecting local opinions, this organ is often the only source of news about campus activities.

The Philadelphia metropolitan press has also covered Villanova over the years. Among these are the *Philadelphia Evening Bulletin*, the *Philadelphia North American*, the *Philadelphia Daily News*, the *Philadelphia Inquirer*, the *Philadelphia Press*, the *Philadelphia Record*, and the *Philadelphia Public Ledger*. Newspapers published by Philadelphia's Roman Catholic archdiocese have also carried items and stories about Villanova. The most significant of these is the long-running *Catholic Standard and Times*. Then there are the local newspapers published in the towns and suburban communities around Villanova: the *Main Line Times*, the *Suburban and Wayne Times*, the *Times Herald*, and *Today's Post*. Items about Villanova have appeared in the newspapers of other cities, including the *New York Times*. These newspapers were researched through clipping files and scrapbooks in the Augustinian Provincial Archives and the Villanova University Archives, as well as in the newspaper collections of the Urban Archives of the Samuel Paley Library of Temple University.

Previous histories of Villanova were also consulted. The earliest of these was Thomas Cooke Middleton, O.S.A., *Historical Sketch of the Augustinian Monastery, College, and Mission of St. Thomas of Villanova, Delaware County, Pa.; during the first half century of their existence, 1842–1892* (Villanova, Pa., 1892). Although this is more of a chronology than a genuine critical history, it contains information that is available nowhere else. Because Father Middleton lived at Villanova for the better part of seventy years and occupied positions of considerable power within the college and the Augustinian Province of St. Thomas of Villanova, he was in a position to know almost everything about the institution. In addition to his *Sketch*, Middleton compiled an unpublished journal in two large volumes that contain a wealth of facts and observations, many of them about everyday life at Villanova from 1866 to 1923. Supplementing the journal is a large notebook by Middleton, likewise unpublished, called "Notes on All the Missions in the O.S.A.," as well as a thick scrapbook generated by him. (All three of these works are in the Augustinian Provincial Archives.) Middleton gathered some of the information for the Journal and the Notes through what present scholars would call oral history—that is by interviewing contemporaries about Villanova and its environs. Both the Journal and the Notes, which were private works kept by Middleton himself, contain material their author may have considered too sensitive to include in the published *Sketch*.

An administrative history of the early university years is Richard D. Breslin, *Villanova, Yesterday and Today* (Villanova, Pa., 1972). There is also a pictorial history of Villanova, with text, by David R. Contosta and Dennis J. Gallagher, O.S.A., entitled *Ever Ancient, Ever New: Villanova University, 1842–1992* (Virginia Beach, Va., 1992). The 1943 yearbook, *The Belle Air*, included a centennial history of the college, with numerous illustrations. Although interesting, it contains some factual errors and is quite incomplete. On the Villanova law school there is Harold G. Reuschlein, *Villanova University School of Law* (Prospect, Ky., 1991).

Histories of the Augustinian communities and biographies of various Augustinians of the Province of St. Thomas of Villanova are Arthur J. Ennis, O.S.A., *No Easy Road: The Early Years of the Augustinians in the United States, 1796–1874* (New York, 1993); John J. Gavigan, O.S.A., *The Augustinians from the French Revolution to Modern Times*, vol. 4 of *History of the Order of St. Augustine* (Villanova, Pa., 1989); Joseph George, "Very Rev. Dr. Patrick E. Moriarty, O.S.A., Philadelphia's Fenian Spokesman," *Quarterly Journal of the Pennsylvania Historical Association,* July 1981, pp. 221–33; Thomas F. Roland, O.S.A., *The Order of St. Augustine in the United States of America, 1796–1946* (Villanova, Pa., 1947); Joseph L. Shannon, O.S.A., ed., *Men of Heart*, 2 vols. (Villanova, Pa., 1983, 1986); Francis E. Tourscher, O.S.A., *Old Saint Augustine's in Philadelphia, With Some Records of the Work of the Austin Friars in the United States* (Philadelphia, 1937).

In addition to these written sources about Villanova, the present author has conducted several interviews of administrators, faculty, and alumni. These are listed in the notes.

Among the better histories of American higher education there are John S. Brubacher and Willis Rudy, *Higher Education in Transition: A History of American Colleges and Universities, 1636–1976* (New York, 1976); Lawrence A. Cremin, *American Education: The Metropolitan Experience, 1876–1980* (New York, 1988), which deals with colleges and universities in the context of American education as a whole; Richard G. Hoftstadter and C. DeWitt Hardy, *The Development and Scope of Higher Education in America* (New York, 1952); W. Bruce Leslie, *Gentlemen and Scholars: College and Community in the "Age of the University," 1865–1917* (University Park, Pa., 1992); James A. Perkins, ed., *The University as an Organization* (New York, 1973); Frederick Rudolph, *The American College and University: A History* (New York, 1962); and Laurence R. Veysey, *Emergence of the American University* (Chicago, 1965).

Works helpful in understanding the history of curriculum and curriculum reform are Charles William Eliot, *Educational Reform* (New York, 1898);

Abraham Flexner, *Medical Education in the United States and Canada* (New York, 1910); Hugh Hawkins, *Between Harvard and America: The Educational Leadership of Charles William Eliot* (New York, 1972); and Frederick Rudolph, *Curriculum: A History of the American Undergraduate Course of Studies Since 1636* (San Francisco, 1977). An excellent volume on the history of student life is Helen Lefkowitz Horowitz, *Campus Life: Undergraduate Cultures from the End of the Eighteenth Century to the Present* (New York, 1987).

Studies of Catholic higher education include John Tracy Ellis, "American Catholics and the Intellectual Life," *Thought,* Autumn 1955, pp. 351–88; Philip Gleason, "The Crisis in Catholic Universities: A Historical Perspective," *Catholic Mind,* September 1966, pp. 43–55, and "The Curriculum of the Old-Time Catholic College: A Student's View," *Records of the American Catholic Historical Society of Philadelphia* (*RACHSP*), March–December 1977, pp. 101–22; Andrew M. Greeley, *The Changing Catholic College* (Chicago, 1967); Robert Hassenger, ed., *The Shape of Catholic Higher Education* (Chicago, 1967); William P. Leahy, S.J., "The Rise of the Laity in American Higher Education," *RACHSP,* Fall 1990, pp. 17–32; Neil G. McClusky, ed., *Catholic Education in America: A Documentary History* (New York, 1964), and *Catholic Education Faces Its Future* (Garden City, N.Y., 1969); Edward J. Power, *A History of Catholic Higher Education in the United States* (Milwaukee, 1958).

Several studies of individual colleges and universities were used for comparative purposes: Edward Potts Cheney, *History of the University of Pennsylvania* (Philadelphia, 1940); Robert Emmett Curran, S.J., *The Bicentennial History of Georgetown University, 1789–1889* (Washington, D.C., 1993); Thomas J. Donaghy, F.S.C., *Conceived in Crisis: A History of La Salle College* (Philadelphia, 1966); David Dunigan, S.J., *A History of Boston College* (Milwaukee, 1947); Theodore M. Hesburgh, C.S.C., *God, Country, Notre Dame* (New York, 1990); Rufus M. Jones, *Haverford College: A History and Interpretation* (New York, 1933); David B. Potts, *Wesleyan University, 1831–1910: Collegiate Enterprise in New England* (New Haven, 1992); Francis X. Talbot, S.J., *Jesuit Education in Philadelphia: St. Joseph's College, 1851–1927* (Philadelphia, 1927); Nicholas Varga, *Baltimore's Loyola, Loyola's Baltimore* (Baltimore, 1990); Francis Wallace, *Notre Dame: Its People and Its Legends* (New York, 1969); Richard J. Walton, *Swarthmore College: An Informal History* (Swarthmore, Pa., 1986).

On Catholics, Catholicism, and various aspects of Catholic culture, there are Patrick Allitt, *Catholic Intellectuals and Conservative Politics in America, 1950–1985* (Ithaca, N.Y., 1993); Barry J. Coleman, "Some Roots of American Nativism," *Catholic Historical Review* (*CHR*), July 1958, pp. 137–46; John Cogley, *Catholic America*, expanded and updated by Rodger

Van Allen (Kansas City, Mo., 1986); Robert D. Cross, "The Changing Image of the City Among American Catholics," *CHR,* April 1962, pp. 33–52; Jay P. Dolan, *The American Catholic Experience: A History from Colonial Times to the Present* (Notre Dame, Ind., 1992); John Tracy Ellis, *American Catholicism* (Chicago, 1969); Philip Gleason, "In Search of Unity: American Catholic Thought, 1920–1960," *CHR,* April 1979, pp. 185–205, and *Keeping the Faith: American Catholicism Past and Present* (Notre Dame, Ind., 1987); James Hennesy, *American Catholics: A History of the Roman Catholic Community in the United States* (New York, 1981); John Higham, "Another Look at Nativism," *CHR,* July 1958, pp. 147–58; James Hennesey, S.J., "Square Peg in a Round Hole: On Being Roman Catholic in America," *RACHSP,* December 1973, pp. 167–82; Thomas T. McAvoy, C.S.C., "The Irish Clergyman in the United States," *RACHSP,* March 1964, pp. 6–38; George M. Marsden, *Religion and American Culture* (New York, 1990); Randall M. Miller and Thomas D. Marzik, eds., *Immigrants and Religion in Urban America* (Philadelphia, 1977).

On the Catholic church in Philadelphia, see James F. Connelly, ed., *The History of the Archdiocese of Philadelphia* (Philadelphia, 1976); Thomas J. Donaghy, F.S.C., *Philadelphia's Finest: A History of Education in the Catholic Archdiocese, 1692–1970* (Philadelphia, 1972); Michael Feldberg, *The Philadelphia Riots of 1844: A Study of Ethnic Conflict* (Westport, Conn., 1975); Joseph L. J. Kirlin, *Catholicity in Philadelphia* (Philadelphia, 1909); Hugh J. Nolan, "Cardinal Dougherty and the Present Aggiornamento," *RACHSP,* September 1965, pp. 188–90; Marie Veronica Tarpey, S.C., *The Role of Joseph McGarrity in the Struggle for Irish Independence* (New York, 1976).

Historical context for Villanova's suburban environs may be found in Edwin P. Alexander, *On the Main Line: The Pennsylvania Railroad in the Nineteenth Century* (New York, 1971); Winifred B. Atterbury, ed., *Radnor: A Pictorial History* (Wayne, Pa., 1992); David R. Contosta, "Dundale," Historical American Buildings Survey, 1994; John T. Faris, *Old Roads Out of Philadelphia* (Philadelphia, 1917); Barbara Alyce Farrow, *The History of Bryn Mawr* (Bryn Mawr, Pa., 1962); *Lower Merion: A History* (Ardmore, Pa., 1992); J. W. Townsend, *The "Old Main Line"* (Philadelphia, 1922). On suburbs in general, see Robert Fishman, *Bourgeois Utopias: The Rise and Fall of Suburbia* (New York, 1987); Kenneth Jackson, *Crabgrass Frontier: The Suburbanization of the United States* (New York, 1975); John Stilgoe, *Borderland: Origins of the American Suburb, 1820–1939* (New Haven, 1988) and *Metropolitan Corridor: Railroads and the American Scene* (New Haven, 1983). Biographical information on the architects who designed the Villanova campus is available in Sandra L. Tatman and Roger W. Moss, *Biographical Dictionary of Philadelphia Architects* (Boston, 1985).

Useful works on Philadelphia are E. Digby Baltzell, *Philadelphia Gentle-*

*men: The Making of a National Upper Class* (1958; reprint, Philadelphia, 1979); Nathaniel Burt, *The Perennial Philadelphians: The Anatomy of an American Aristocracy* (Boston, 1963); Dennis Clark, *The Irish in Philadelphia: Ten Generations of Urban Experience* (Philadelphia, 1973); William Cutler III and Howard Gillette, *The Divided Metropolis: Social and Spatial Dimensions of Philadelphia, 1800–1975* (Westport, Conn., 1980); Allen F. Davis and Mark H. Haller, *The Peoples of Philadelphia: A History of Ethnic Groups and Lower-Class Life, 1790–1940* (Philadelphia, 1973); John Lukacs, *Philadelphia: Patricians and Philistines, 1900–1950* (New York, 1981); Sam Bass Warner, *The Private City: Philadelphia in Three Periods of Its Growth* (Philadelphia, 1968); Russell Weigley, ed., *Philadelphia: A 300-Year History* (New York, 1982); *Workshop of the World* (Wallingford, Pa., 1990).

Shedding light on the larger social and cultural context of Villanova's development from its mid-nineteenth-century origins through World War I are Glenn C. Altschuler, *Race, Ethnicity, and Class in American Thought, 1865–1919* (Arlington Heights, Ill., 1982); Jacques Barzun, *Classic, Romantic, Modern* (Chicago, 1961); Michael Feldberg, *The Turbulent Era: Riot and Disorder in Jacksonian America* (New York, 1980); John Higham, *Strangers in the Land: Patterns of American Nativism, 1860–1925* (New York, 1963); Walter E. Houghton, *The Victorian Frame of Mind* (New Haven, 1957); Daniel Walker Howe, ed., *Victorian America* (Philadelphia, 1976); Colleen McDannell, *The Christian Home in Victorian America, 1840–1900* (Bloomington, Ind., 1986); Henry F. May, *The End of American Innocence* (Chicago, 1959); William L. O'Neill, *The Progressive Years: America Comes of Age* (New York, 1975); E. Anthony Rotundo, *American Manhood: Transformations in Masculinity from the Revolution to the Modern Era* (New York, 1993); Robert W. Wiebe, *The Search for Order, 1877–1920* (New York, 1967).

Social context for changes in student life at Villanova between the two world wars, and especially in the 1920s, is provided in Beth L. Bailey, *Front Porch to Back Seat: Courtship in Twentieth-Century America* (Baltimore, 1988); Paul Carter, *The Twenties in America* (Arlington Heights, Ill., 1975); Paula S. Fass, *The Damned and the Beautiful: American Youth in the 1920s* (New York, 1977); Paul Goodman and Frank O. Gatell, *America in the Twenties* (New York, 1972); Robert Sklar, ed., *The Plastic Age* (New York, 1970).

On the background of Villanovans' attitudes toward politics and foreign affairs during the interwar period, see Selig Adler, *The Isolationist Impulse: Its Twentieth Century Reaction* (New York, 1961); Paul Conkin, *The New Deal* (Arlington Heights, Ill., 1975); Robert A. Divine, *The Reluctant Belligerent: American Entry into World War II* (New York, 1979); Thomas Ferguson, "From Normalcy to New Deal: Industrial Structure, Party Composition, and American Public Policy in the Great Depression," in *International Organization* (1984), pp. 41–94; James Terence Fisher, *The Catholic Counterculture in America, 1933–1962* (Chapel Hill, N.C., 1989); John A. Garraty, *The Great Depression* (New York, 1986); William M. Halsey, *The Survival of American Innocence: Catholicism in an Era of Disillusionment, 1920– 1940* (Notre Dame, Ind., 1980); Gabriel Jackson, *The Spanish Republic and the Civil War, 1931–1939* (Princeton, 1955); Paul Kleppner, ed., *American Electoral Systems* (Westport, Conn., 1981); Paul L. Murphy, *Political Parties in American History, 1890–Present* (New York, 1974); David O'Brien, "American Catholics and Organized Labor in the 1930s," *CHR,* October 1966, pp. 323–49; James R. O'Connell, "The Spanish Republic: Further Reflections on Its Anticlerical Policies," *CHR,* July 1971, pp. 275–89; Robert H. Vinca, "The American Catholic Reaction to the Persecution of the Church in Mexico," *RACHSP,* March 1968, pp. 3–37; John E. Wiltz, *From Isolation to War, 1931–1941* (New York, 1968).

Providing context for Villanova during World War II and the postwar period are H. W. Brands, *The Devil We Knew: Americans and the Cold War* (New York, 1993); Vincent P. De Santis, "American Catholics and McCarthyism," *CHR,* April 1965, pp. 1–30; James Gilbert, *Another Chance: Postwar America, 1945–1960* (New York, 1981); Eric Goldman, *The Crucial Decade and After* (New York, 1960); David Halberstam, *The Fifties* (New York, 1993); John Lukacs, *A History of the Cold War* (New York, 1961); Elaine Tyler May, *Homeward Bound: American Families in the Cold War Era* (New York, 1988); Thomas G. Patterson, *On Every Front: The Making of the Cold War* (New York, 1979): Richard Pollenberg, ed., *America At War: The Home Front, 1941–1945* (Englewood Cliffs, N.J., 1968); Ellen Schrecker, ed., *The Age of McCarthyism* (Boston, 1994); Allan M. Winkler, *Home Front U.S.A.: America During World War II* (Arlington Heights, Ill., 1986).

Works relating to the counterculture of the 1960s and early 1970s are John Tracy Ellis, "The Church in Revolt, the Tumultuous Sixties," *The Critic,* January–February 1970, pp. 12–21; Landon Y. Jones, *Great Expectations: America and the Baby Boom Generation* (New York, 1980); Alexander Kendrick, *The Wound Within: America and the Vietnam Years, 1945–1974* (Boston, 1974); Edward P. Morgan, *The 60s Experience: Hard Lessons About Modern America* (Philadelphia, 1991); William L. O'Neill, *Coming Apart: An Informal History of America in the 1960s* (New York, 1971); Edward Quinn and Paul J. Dolan, eds., *The Sense of the 60s* (New York, 1986); Theodore Roszak, *The Making of a Counter Culture* (Garden City, N.Y., 1969).

# INDEX